the spicy food lover's bible

the spicy food lover's bible

The Ultimate Guide to Buying, Growing, Storing, and Using the Key Ingredients That Give Food Spice ✳ With More Than 250 Recipes from Around the World

Dave DeWitt & Nancy Gerlach

Stewart, Tabori & Chang
New York

Published in 2005 by
Stewart, Tabori & Chang
115 West 18th Street
New York, NY 10011
www.abramsbooks.com

Canadian Distribution:
Canadian Manda Group
One Atlantic Avenue, Suite 105
Toronto, Ontario M6K 3E7
Canada

Library of Congress Cataloging-in-Publication Data
DeWitt, Dave.
  The spicy food lover's bible / Dave DeWitt and Nancy Gerlach.
      p. cm.
  Includes bibliographical references and index.
  ISBN 1-58479-411-9
  1. Cookery. 2. Spices. I. Gerlach, Nancy. II. Title.

TX714.D495 2005
641.6'383—dc22

                            2004021540

Edited by Marisa Bulzone
Designed by Anna Christian
Graphic Production by Kim Tyner

The text of this book was composed in Adobe Caslon and Seria.
Printed in the United States of America

10 9 8 7 6 5 4 3 2 1
First Printing

Stewart, Tabori & Chang is a subsidiary of

LA MARTINIÈRE
GROUPE

This book is dedicated to
our traveling and cooking companions in life,
Mary Jane Wilan and Jeff Gerlach

acknowledgments

Thanks to all of our friends who assisted with this project:

Paul and Judy Bosland, Marisa Bulzone, Pat and Dominique Chapman, Melanie Falick, Jim Fergusson, Larry Greenly, Ian Hemphill, Margaret Henderson, Patrick Holian, Sharon Hudgins, Ellie Leavitt, Lois Lyles, Scott Mendel, Marie Permenter, Paul Ross and Judie Fein, Devagi Shanmugan, Wayne and Christy Scheiner, Denice Skrepcinski, Richard Sterling, Molly Wales, Anne-Marie Whittaker, Harald and Renate Zoschke

contents

preface

It is appropriate that our tenth book together should be our largest, both in size and scope. For years we devoted ourselves solely to chile peppers, and we wrote many books and articles on that subject. But the world of spicy foods extends beyond hot pods, and at the suggestion of our agent, Scott Mendel, we investigated roots (ginger, horseradish, and wasabi), seeds (mustard and all kinds of pepper), and powders (rubs and spice blends) in addition to chiles and hot sauces.

After we determined that no one volume contained the food history, culinary usage, and recipes for all this hot stuff, and that the resources existed to assemble it all, this book was born. It has been the most challenging and satisfying project of our long collaboration. The one thing that amazed us the most was the lack of a nontechnical book on black pepper, surely one of the most fascinating and influential spices. Until one is written, our treatment here must suffice.

We would like to note that we like our food in the medium to medium-hot heat range; we are definitely not trying to burn everyone up. For people who are sensitive to pungent spices, it is a simple matter to use fewer of them in these recipes. It is easy to add more hot stuff, nearly impossible to remove it, and problematic to dilute the dish by adding more nonpungent ingredients. We recommend that you taste as you go, adding spicy ingredients in small amounts until you reach a comfortable heat level. The final recipe chapter suggests delicious cool-downs, just in case you overdo it.

So get ready to journey back in time, travel around the world, and create international spicy meals as you become a spicy food lover!

why cooks spice up their foods

There are many theories about why cooks have added the spices in this book to their foods from the dawn of cooking. Among them:

* Spices make foods taste better.
* Eating spicy foods cools us down during hot weather (the "eat-to-sweat" hypothesis).
* Spices disguise the taste of spoiled food.
* Spices add nutritional value to food.
* Spices kill harmful bacteria in food and aid in food preservation (the antimicrobial hypothesis).

Which of these theories is correct?

The First Cornell University Study

In 1998, Jennifer Billing and Paul W. Sherman published the results of a Cornell University study in the *Quarterly Review of Biology* that examined the reasons why humans might use spices. They studied 4,578 recipes from ninety-three cookbooks on the traditional, meat-based cuisines of thirty-six countries; the temperature and precipitation levels of each of these countries; the horticultural ranges of forty-three spice plants; and the antibacterial properties of each spice.

The first thing they discovered was that many spices were incredibly antibacterial. For example, garlic, onion, allspice, and oregano are the best all-around microbe killers, killing almost everything. Next come thyme, cinnamon, tarragon, and cumin, which kill about 80 percent of all bacteria. Chile peppers fall in the next group, with about a 75 percent kill rate. In the lower ranges of 25 percent are black pepper, ginger, and lime juice.

Next, Billings and Sherman found that "countries with hotter climates used spices more frequently than countries with cooler climates. Indeed, in hot countries nearly every meat-based recipe calls for at least one spice, and most include many spices, especially the potent spices, whereas in cooler countries substantial fractions of dishes are prepared without spices, or with just a few." Thus the estimated fraction of food-spoilage bacteria inhibited by the spices in each recipe is greater in hot than in cold climates, which makes sense, since bacteria thrive in warmer areas.

The researchers addressed the various theories. First, obviously spices make food taste better. "But why do spices taste good?" the researchers asked. "Traits that are beneficial are transmitted both culturally and genetically, and that includes taste receptors in our mouths and our taste for certain flavors. People who enjoyed food with antibacterial spices probably were healthier, especially in hot climates. They lived longer and left more offspring."

Billing and Sherman discounted the "eat-to-sweat" theory, noting that not all spices make people sweat and that there are easier ways to cool down, like moving into the shade. Regarding the theory that spices mask the odor of spoiled food, they noted that this idea "ignores the health dangers of ingesting spoiled food." And since spices, except for chiles and citrus, add minimal nutritional value to food, that theory goes nowhere.

That leaves just two theories: that spices make foods taste good, and that they kill harmful bacteria—and those two theories are inseparable. "I believe that recipes are a record of the history of the coevolutionary race between us and our parasites. The microbes are competing with us for the same food," Sherman says. "Everything we do with food—drying, cooking, smoking, salting or adding spices—is an attempt to keep from being poisoned by our microscopic competitors. They're constantly mutating and evolving to stay ahead of us. One way we reduce food-borne illnesses is to add another spice to the recipe. Of course that makes the food taste different, and the people who learn to like the new taste are healthier for it. We believe the ultimate reason for using spices is to kill food-borne bacteria and fungi."

The Second Cornell University Study

In 2001, Paul W. Sherman and Geoffrey A. Hash continued the examination of spices in human diet with a study entitled "Why Vegetable Recipes Are Not Very Spicy," published in *Evolution and Human Behavior*. They compiled information from 2,129 vegetable-only recipes from 107 traditional cookbooks of thirty-six countries. Then they examined the history of the spice trade and discovered that for thousands of years spices have been traded all over the world, resulting in their availability in most world cuisines. The most traded spices are, first, black pepper, and then chile pepper.

Many studies have proven the antibacterial properties of spices, that spices are more prevalent in warm climates than cool climates, and that the concentrations of spices in recipes are sufficient to kill bacteria. It is true that cooking eliminates the antimicrobial properties of some spices, such as cumin, but it has no effect on others, such as chiles.

The researchers compared the vegetable-only recipes to the meat recipes previously studied according to the spices found in the recipes and discovered that vegetable recipes use far fewer spices than meat recipes. They attributed this to the fact that bacteria "do not survive or proliferate as well in vegetables, so adding spices is not as necessary." Interestingly, the four most common spices in both the meat and vegetable recipes were onion, black pepper, garlic, and chile peppers. Onion appeared in more than 60 percent of both types of recipes; black pepper in about 60 percent of the meat recipes and 48 percent of the vegetable recipes; garlic in 35 percent of the meat recipes and 20 percent of the vegetable recipes; and chile peppers in 22 percent of the meat recipes and 18 percent of the vegetable recipes.

Vegetable-based recipes called for fewer spices than meat recipes in all thirty-six countries. The countries using the most spices in both vegetable and meat recipes were, in descending order, India, Vietnam, Kenya, Morocco, Mexico, Korea, and the Philippines. Following were France, Israel, and South Africa.

The researchers concluded, "By every measure, vegetable-based recipes were significantly less spicy than meat-based recipes. Results thus strongly support the antimicrobial hypothesis."

Americans Embrace Pungency

We're in the "spices make food taste better" camp, and we believe that the hotter spices—the ones featured in this book—add another dimension to food and prevent it from being boring and bland. However, we believe that spices should not overwhelm the flavors of the dish but rather enhance them. If a few million harmful bacteria are wiped out during the spicing process, that's fine too. Here in the United States, with refrigerators and freezers in almost every home, the antimicrobial hypothesis simply does not explain the rush to embrace spicy foods over the past two decades. We have some theories about why chile peppers and other spicy ingredients have become so popular here:

* Immigration patterns have changed, leading to increased ethnic diversity. New citizens from Asia, Africa, Latin America, and the Caribbean bring with them the hot and spicy ingredients of their native cuisines. Immigrants open restaurants and markets, making ethnic and spicy foods commonplace.
* Americans are more knowledgeable now; they realize that most chiles and spicy foods won't hurt them.
* The hobbies of cooking, gardening, and traveling are ever more popular.
* A large number—literally hundreds—of ethnic and hot-and-spicy-food cookbooks have been published since 1978.

* The Internet has generated an information explosion.
* Chiles and fiery foods are increasingly available in mainstream locations such as supermarkets and fast-food outlets.
* Constant media attention has generated publicity; trade shows, consumer shows, and festivals as well as newspapers and magazines celebrate chiles and fiery foods.
* The enormous increase in manufacturing has put thousands of fiery food products on the market.
* The "addiction syndrome." Chiles and other spices are not physically addicting —you don't have withdrawal symptoms when you stop eating them. But they *are* psychologically addicting; spicy-food lovers miss the burn if they're deprived of spicy food for a while. We never hear anyone say, "Oh, I used to eat spicy food, but now I'm back to bland." Once someone starts enjoying fiery foods, she is likely to continue consuming them for life.

But perhaps the most fundamental reason for the boom in spicy foods is a major shift in the way many Americans are eating. Our revelation began in Philadelphia while we were dining with Liz Rozin, who hosted an incredibly diverse dinner at Serrano Restaurant during the Book and the Cook Festival. Liz is a food historian with fascinating insights into the origins of spicy cuisines. "When we look at the broad spectrum of human flavoring practices, we see one curious correlation," she writes in *The Primal Cheeseburger*. "The heavier the dependence on plant or vegetable foods, the more pronounced the seasonings; the heavier the consumption of animal foods, the less pronounced the seasonings. Those cuisines that clearly demonstrate a highly spiced or complex seasoning profile—Southeast Asia, India, Africa, Mexico—all have long relied on high-plant, low meat diets." Her theory, interestingly enough, directly contradicts the Cornell University studies above!

Of course, the United States, unlike these cultures of high seasoning, relied on beef, pork, and chicken as well as dairy foods in its early days. Vegetable foods in the United States were eaten primarily in the same regions where the cuisine was also the spiciest: the South and the Southwest.

When Liz turns her attention to chile peppers in high-vegetable, low-meat cultures, she notes that "the pattern of acceptance, the level of enthusiasm with which the pungent chiles were enfolded into certain existing traditions, seems to indicate that the unique stimulation they provide is an important compensation for foods that are somehow less satisfying, less perfect when eaten unseasoned. And on the other hand, the chiles were largely ignored or rejected by cuisines and areas of the world where meat and other animal foods were a significant focus of the diet."

At least three other major food trends have paralleled the move toward spicy foods over the past two decades: natural foods, vegetarian foods, and low-fat foods. Despite the very recent popularity of high-protein diets, overall meat consumption has declined as well. This sets the scene for the modern return of Liz Rozin's theory of why ancient, "less satisfying" foods were highly spiced: we need the heat and flavor of chiles and other spices to make up for the lack of meat and fat flavors in more spartan cuisines. Also, as we eat less fat, such as butter, cream, and heavy sauces that supplied flavor, we have turned to spices to replace them. And with meats like pork being bred leaner and leaner, we're more dependent upon spicy marinades. The new motto of eating in the twenty-first century might be, "The healthier you eat, the more you need to spice up the food."

To sum up, Paul Sherman thinks that we add chiles to meat-based recipes to prevent the growth of bacteria, while Liz Rozin believes we use chiles to spice-up bland vegetables. Perhaps they are both correct. But we do know one thing: spicy foods have conquered America, and they are not going away.

part one:
the hot stuff

1 Roots: Ginger, Horseradish, & Wasabi

ginger

Both of us recall our first experience with ginger during childhood: tasting our mothers' homemade ginger snaps, those spicy cookies with just a hint of a bite. Only quite a few years later did either of us experiment with the freshly peeled root, but now all forms of ginger find their way into our kitchens. We should point out immediately that, technically, ginger is not a root but rather a rhizome, an underground stem that looks like a tuber—or a thick root. It is one of the most fragile of all the spicy ingredients; its heat fades quickly, especially after processing and when cooked.

The word *ginger* originally derives from the Sanskrit *shringavera*, "of horned appearance," an allusion to the shape of the rhizomes. It was transliterated to the Greek *ziggiberis* and then became *zingiber* in Latin, *ginibre* in early French, and *giniber* in Old English, from which we got the word we use today.

Ginger may be the oldest spice of all, dating to about 4,000 B.C. A clue to its extreme age is the fact that it is grown only by dividing its rhizomes, and not from seed, an indication that it has been under human control for so long that it has lost the ability to propagate from seed. It is one of the few spices with this trait. Also, there is no evidence that cultivated ginger appears anywhere in a wild form.

The Plant and Its Pungency

ZINGIBER OFFICINALE

Ginger is part of the genus *Zingiber*, of the family Zingiberaceae. The genus has about a hundred species of perennial plants, many of which are grown as ornamental plants. The different species of *Zingiber* have many culinary uses—for example, the shoots and flowers of *Zingiber mioga*, Japanese ginger, are used fresh or pickled as a flavoring in Japanese cuisine.

The principal cultivated ginger is *Zingiber officinale*, a deciduous perennial native to tropical Asia with thick, branching rhizomes, upright stems, and long, pointed leaves. The flowers, yellow-green with purple and yellow lips, are quite lovely. The plant can grow up to four feet tall.

There are many cultivated varieties, or cultivars, of spice ginger, with rhizomes that vary in color and pungency. In India, the favorites are 'Cochin' and 'Wynad Manantody', while Jamaica boasts yellow ginger, or 'Tambric', and three cultivars of blue ginger: 'Frog', 'Bulbous', and 'Chinese Blue'. In China, a favorite cultivar is 'Canton'. The flavor and heat level varies greatly, as Australian spice expert Ian Hemphill notes: "The flavour will be similarly tangy, sweet, spicy and warm to hot, depending upon when it has been harvested, as to a large degree early harvested ginger is sweet and tender, while later harvested rhizomes are more fibrous and pungent."

The volatile oils causing ginger's pungency are called gingerols and shogaols. The shogaols, which appear when ginger is dried, are much more pungent, so dried ginger is hotter than fresh. It also contains less water, so its pungency is more concentrated. Gingerol is commonly used to treat poor digestion, heartburn, and motion sickness.

Two related plants that are used principally in Asian cuisines (especially Thai) are the galangals: greater and lesser. Both are members of the Zingiberaceae family, but not the genus *Zingiber*. Greater galangal (*Alpinia galanga*) is spicy, but not quite as pungent as ginger; it is usually ground with chiles and herbs to make the seasoning paste that is the basis of red and green curries. Lesser galangal (*Kaempferia galanga*), hotter than greater galangal, is used as a spice in Indonesian cooking. Fresh ginger can be substituted in recipes in equal amounts for lesser galangal, but use twice as much ginger if greater galangal is called for.

Grown commercially in tropical regions, ginger is a worldwide crop. According to the Food and Agriculture Organization (FAO) of the United Nations, world production in 2002 was 988,182 metric tons. The leader was India with 275,000 metric tons, followed by China (236,976), Indonesia (150,000), Nigeria (95,000), Nepal

(87,909), Bangladesh (42,000), and Thailand (32,500). By contrast, Jamaica, a country famous for its ginger, produced only 620 metric tons; production there has fallen off because of the tedious hand labor needed to peel the rhizomes. The United States produced 6,530 metric tons of ginger, grown in Florida and Hawaii. Other countries having significant production are the Philippines, the Fiji Islands, Bhutan, Sri Lanka, Costa Rica, Cameroon, the Republic of Korea, and Malaysia.

Ginger requires rich, well-drained but not sandy soil, neutral to slightly alkaline, in partial shade or full sun, and requires high humidity. The plants need a ten-month growing season to produce the greatest number of rhizomes. The planted rhizomes must have an "eye," or growing node, like a potato. In home gardening, the rhizomes can be planted in pots at least a foot in diameter or, in tropical climates, in rows two feet apart, with the rhizomes a foot apart in the rows. In the north they can be grown in full sun, but they prefer light shade in warmer regions. Ginger is best planted in the warm regions of the Northern Hemisphere between February and May, and large rhizomes take about nine months to mature. By then, the aboveground foliage will have turned brown and died back. With luck, there will be striking flowers, but these are uncommon with *Zingiber officinale*. Use of a 14-28-14 fertilizer is recommended for neutral soils, 18-18-18 for acid soils.

Rhizomes harvested periodically during the growing season will have the less fiber than those left to mature fully. These fresh young rhizomes will keep in a cool, dry place for about three months, so they can be shipped long distances.

Preserving Ginger Rhizomes

Basically, there are two methods of processing ginger. One is to preserve it in brine or syrup, or in crystallized form. The other is to dry it and, optionally, grind it into powder. The first step in preserving it is to brine the peeled young rhizomes in barrels in a series of salt solutions for about a week. To preserve ginger in syrup, the brined rhizomes are washed and soaked in cold water to remove the salt and then boiled, first in water, then several times in a sugar syrup, until the rhizomes have absorbed a large amount of sugar. During the final boiling, most of the water evaporates, leaving a very thick syrup. The rhizomes can be left in the syrup and bottled, or removed, drained, dried, and sprinkled with sugar to make crystallized ginger.

Pickled ginger is made from fresh rhizomes sliced paper-thin, then placed in a vinegar solution. The acetic acid in the vinegar turns the ginger pink.

Dried ginger is made from more mature rhizomes, which are peeled by the farmers. Traditionally left to dry in the sun, ginger is instead increasingly furnace-dried. After drying, the rhizomes are ground into powder and bottled.

Ginger oil pressed from fresh ginger is used in medicine, perfumery, and cordials and ginger wine. The oil, which is pale yellow, amber, or light green, is used both externally to treat bruises and aches, and internally for nausea and motion sickness. A combination of oil and dried, ground ginger is used as a commercial food flavoring, spicing up candies and soft drinks such as ginger beer and ginger ale.

Ginger Throughout History

Cultivated ginger first appeared between northern India and China perhaps six thousand years ago. Its domestication and early history is unknown, but it was one of the first Asian spices to reach Europe. Around 500 B.C., Confucius mentioned the beneficial properties of ginger, and a hundred years later, Persian traders brought back ginger from India. Starting in A.D. 25 through 220, ginger appears in Chinese medical literature as a remedy for diseases thought to be induced by cold weather. Later, the spice was an essential ingredient in what became Cantonese cuisine.

Starting around A.D. 110, caravans from China arriving in central Asia carried large amounts of ginger and silk, to be traded for Roman goods such as gold, silver, glassware, and wine. Thus ginger reached Rome, where it was used primarily as a medicine and an antidote for poisons. By A.D. 200 it was listed as a taxable commodity by the Romans, shipped from Alexandria in Egypt. It was an expensive medicine, costing fifteen times as much as black pepper.

Around A.D. 400, Chinese ships carried live ginger plants growing in ceramic pots, probably because eating the rhizomes eased seasickness—a common remedy in folk medicine today. Ginger became increasing important in Chinese culture, and by 750 the Chinese were flavoring their beloved tea with powdered ginger. By 973, ginger and other Asian spices were available in Spain, provided by Jewish traveling merchants called Radanites. Crusaders returning to England and Europe brought ginger with them, so by 1250 it was commonly available as a medicine. In 1274 Marco Polo, traveling in Sichuan, China, noted that an enormous amount of ginger was grown and exported, bringing vast profits to the locals.

In the West, the culinary use of ginger began in medieval Europe; ginger was expensive but still in great demand. Nearly every sauce recipe contained the spice, including a yellow sauce with ginger and saffron and a green sauce with ginger, cloves, cardamom, and green herbs. Guillaume Tirel, cook to Charles V of France and author of the cookbook *Le Viandier de Taillevent* (1375), created a condiment called cameline sauce. Composed of ginger, cinnamon, cloves, cardamom, mace, and long pepper pounded together and mixed with bread soaked in vinegar and salt, this became the king's favorite sauce for dipping roast game. Around this time, ginger was preserved

The first "soda pop" made in the United States was Vernor's Ginger Ale, created in Detroit, Michigan, in 1866.

in sugar in England; by 1393 a pound of ginger would buy a sheep, and it was the second most commonly used spice after black pepper. Something that valuable was bound to attract attention. In 1561 John Hawkins, an English privateer, hijacked a Portuguese slave ship and traded three hundred slaves at Hispaniola for ginger, pearls, and sugar, giving ginger a role in the start of the English slave trade.

Sometime during the early part of the sixteenth century, Francisco Mendoza, son of the viceroy of New Spain, introduced the cultivation of ginger to the West Indies and tropical America; by 1547, a thousand tons of ginger were exported to Spain from the West Indies. By 1585 the first shipment of Jamaican ginger had reached northern Europe. Ginger was the first Asian spice to be successfully grown in the New World, but not the last, as we shall see later.

Ginger became very well established in the New World. By 1740, it was cultivated heavily in the Parish of St. Ann, Jamaica, and subsequently more than a thousand acres were planted in the area around Christiana, now regarded as the production center of the world's finest ginger. Such cultivation had an impact on America: by 1776, ginger was included in the standard rations of American soldiers during the Revolutionary War. Ginger ale was first sold by New York's Tontine Coffee House around 1796, and in 1866, the first "soda pop" made in the United States was Vernor's Ginger Ale, created in Detroit, Michigan, by James Vernor. Canada Dry Ginger Ale began production in 1890 in Toronto as McLaughlin Belfast Style Ginger Ale. In 1907, the name was changed to Canada Dry, with the slogan "The Champagne of Ginger Ales." (Ginger ale is non-alcoholic, while ginger beer can be either.)

Ginger and Nutrition

Ginger is a good source of vitamin A and calcium and provides iron, phosphorus, riboflavin, and some protein. A quarter cup of sliced fresh ginger has 17 calories, 0.4 grams of protein, 3.6 grams of carbohydrates, 0.2 grams of fat, and 0.5 grams of fiber.

Forms of Ginger

Fresh ginger rhizomes are usually peeled and grated for use in many international recipes; they can also be juiced or preserved in syrup. When selecting fresh ginger, avoid wrinkled skin or dried out, bruised, shriveled, cracked, or moldy rhizomes. Seek out a sharp aroma and a minimum of small protrusions on the rhizomes. Grated ginger mixed with vinegar and bottled can often be substituted for freshly grated ginger. Ginger juice, available in some specialty markets and natural food stores, is considered to be a tonic; it can be used to make ginger tea when added to hot water. To make ginger juice yourself, simply peel the youngest, freshest rhizomes and process them in a juicer.

Typically, Indians pickle ginger with spices, while the Chinese and Japanese use only vinegar, salt, and pepper. In Japan, pickled ginger in thin slices, known as *gari*, is considered a palate refresher, commonly served with sushi and sashimi, while pickled ginger stalks make an edible garnish for grilled fish.

Dried ginger is used to flavor cookies such as ginger snaps, cakes, chutneys, and sauces. There are two grades: cracked, which is usually used in pickling and canning recipes, and powdered. The finest-quality powdered ginger is a light buff color and is free from fiber. To substitute fresh ginger for ground, use 1 tablespoon ground fresh ginger for ⅛ teaspoon dried, ground ginger. Do not substitute dry ginger for fresh in Asian dishes.

Storage

Fresh ginger can be stored unwrapped in the produce drawer of the refrigerator, but it lasts longer when placed in zip-top plastic bags. One interesting way to preserve fresh rhizomes is to peel them, place them in a glass jar, and cover with dry sherry, which will keep them fresh for three or four weeks. Peeled rhizomes can also be frozen whole and stored in a zip-top plastic bag. When you need to use a piece, cut it off while it is still frozen to avoid repeated thawing and refreezing. Commercial grated ginger should be stored in the refrigerator after opening. Ginger preserved in syrup or crystallized will keep in the cupboard for more than a year. Dried ginger slices can be kept indefinitely in glass jars in the cupboard, provided they are not exposed to excessive humidity. Ground ginger should be kept tightly sealed in glass jars in a spice cabinet.

Culinary Uses

Fresh ginger, commonly used in spice and curry pastes, tends to neutralize fishy smells and flavors. It is also used in chutneys and pickles. A topping of freshly grated ginger perks up cooked vegetables such as carrots, yams, or greens. For mild heat, use 2 teaspoons per pound of vegetables; for medium, 1 tablespoon; and 3 tablespoons for hot.

Ground ginger is commonly used for baking in breads, scones, and cookies, as well as in puddings and baked vegetables and apples.

horseradish

Dave's mother, Barbara, was an expert at roasting meats, and she prided herself on not overcooking them, as so many of her neighbors did in the 1950s. Her pork was cooked medium, her leg of lamb medium rare, and her standing prime rib of beef (a Christmas Day tradition) was rare and served with a powerful horseradish sauce. She had no idea she was carrying on a tradition that had originated many hundreds of years before—she just knew that her family loved the pungency of the horseradish with the slices of rare beef.

The English word *horseradish* is thought to originate from "hoarse radish," meaning a radish that is "hoarse," or coarse and strong. The French term for it, *raifort*, means "strong root," certainly an apt description.

The Plant and Its Power

Native to southeastern Europe, horseradish, or *Armoracia rusticana*, belongs to the crucifer family, which also includes radishes and mustard. Botanists believe that it originally grew wild in Russia, Poland, and Finland. It is an upright, stout perennial with a thick taproot and oblong, toothed leaves.

There are two types of horseradish, common and Bohemian. The common types have broad, crinkled leaves and are considered superior, while the Bohemians have narrow, smooth leaves and better disease resistance. There are many cultivars, such as 'Maliner Kren' and 'Improved Bohemian' in the United States and 'Bagamerer Delikat', 'Danvit', 'Pozna', and 'Erlagen' in Hungary.

Horseradish is grown on about three thousand acres in Illinois, Wisconsin, New Jersey, California, and Virginia in the United States, as well as in many European countries.

Both commercial and home cultivation are easy, requiring only well-drained, rich soil with a lot of organic material. Treat the soil with aged manure, and that should be all the fertilizer you will need. Horseradish can be grown in sun or partial shade, but select a garden site apart from your regular vegetable garden because horseradish is invasive and will take over. It is difficult to eradicate once established because portions of roots left in the ground will sprout and grow into new plants, which is the way to

ARMORACIA RUSTICANA

grow them—from root divisions. Horseradish can also be grown from seed, but the plant produces so few seeds that it's easier to use a root clone.

Dig a hole a foot wide and as deep as the shovel. Place the roots at a 45-degree angle in the hole so that the roots can fully develop. The top of the root, where the plant will sprout, should be just protruding from the soil. Water the plant well after planting and irrigate if needed during the hot months of the summer.

In the home garden, young horseradish leaves can be picked and used fresh or cooked like greens. The roots are harvested in the fall—they need frost for peak pungency, flavor, and color. The leaves are cut off about a week before digging up the roots by plowing or using a gardening fork. Wash the roots and remove the lateral roots, saving the taproot for future planting. If you live in a warm climate, remove all the roots from the ground, treating the plant as an annual. Store the main taproot to be replanted the next year in the refrigerator in a zip-top bag. Before processing, the picked roots are packed away from sunlight, which will turn them green. The outer section of the root is the only part used, as the inner core is less pungent, rubbery, and difficult to grate.

When the root is cut, peeled, or scraped, the broken cells release two components, sinigrin and myrosin, that combine to form the volatile oil allyl isothiocyanate (AITC), the same compound found in the oil of black mustard seeds. The result is an intensely pungent aroma and flavor that goes to the back of the throat and attacks the nasal membranes. In fact, AITC is so pungent that it can kill the bacteria *Listeria* and *E. coli*. AITC loses its pungency rapidly when heated, and is not stable in cold water. But adding vinegar or other acidic ingredients like lemon juice greatly retards the hydrolysis of AITC and keeps horseradish pungent. This is how grated horseradish is processed for bottling.

Horseradish History

Unlike that of the chile pepper, black pepper, or even ginger, the history of horseradish is very sketchy. Horseradish played no role in the spice trade, and was mostly confined to central Europe and the midwestern United States in later times. It was first cultivated relatively recently, probably around the beginning of the Christian era, and there is no mention of it in classical literature. Writers who insist that it appears there are probably confusing horseradish with the black radish, which was known to the Greeks and Romans. The origin of cultivated horseradish could be Hungary or the Caspian Sea region, but by the thirteenth century it was established in the wild in central Europe. In 1542 Fuchsius, in his *Historia Stirpium*, gave the first description of the horseradish root used as a condiment. The herbalist William Turner, in 1548, refers to it as "red cole," which is thought to refer not to the color of the root but to its pungency, as being like a "red-hot coal." In 1597 John Gerard wrote in *The Herball, or Generall Historie of Plants*, "The horse radish, stamped with a little vinegar put thereto, is commonly used among the Germans for sauce to eate fish with and such like meates as we do mustarde." Use of the wild and eventually cultivated root spread throughout Europe, and by 1650, cooks in both Britain and France were using horseradish regularly in sauces.

In the United States, horseradish was reported growing wild near Boston, Massachusetts, by 1840, and by 1850, commercial cultivation of it began as European immigrants planted farms in the Midwest. Ten years later, bottled horseradish was being sold; it was one of the first convenience foods. In 1869 the H. J. Heinz Company started packing processed horseradish in clear bottles. By 2000, six million gallons of prepared horseradish was being produced in the United States annually, using twenty-four million pounds of harvested roots.

other ways you can use horseradish:

- Add it, along with hot sauce, to tomato juice—or to a Bloody Mary, if you are so inclined—for a morning bracer.

- Mix it with mustard to up the condiment's bite.

- Add it to scrambled eggs, omelettes, and hash browns.

- Grate it sparingly into potato salad, coleslaw, or dips.

- Add it to soups just before serving.

- Spike prepared barbecue sauces with it.

- Mix it with sour cream to add to mashed or baked potatoes.

- Add it to tartar sauce, seafood cocktail sauces, hollandaise sauce, mayonnaise, and salad dressings.

- Make horseradish butter with mustard and a little yogurt.

Horseradish and Nutrition

A very pungent root that controls bacterial infections and reduces fever, horseradish has a lot of flavor and no fat. One tablespoon of prepared horseradish contains 6 calories, 1.4 grams of carbohydrates, 14 milligrams of sodium, 44 milligrams of potassium, 9 milligrams of calcium, and 5 milligrams of phosphorus.

Forms

When buying fresh horseradish, avoid blemished or sprouting roots. Generally speaking, the whiter the root, the fresher it is. Peel only what you are going to use and grate or shred in a food processor. Make sure your kitchen is well ventilated, as the pungent oils are volatile. Dehydrated granules, flakes, or powder are readily available; just add vinegar to power them up.

Varieties of prepared horseradish include ordinary vinegar-based, cream style, and beet horseradish. Other products flavored with horseradish are mustard, cocktail sauce, other sauces, dips, spreads, relishes, and dressings.

Storage

Smaller roots can be stored in the refrigerator in zip-top plastic bags for up to two weeks, or frozen for a couple of months. Grated or otherwise processed horseradish should be kept in the refrigerator. The dried forms should be stored in sealed glass containers in the spice cabinet.

Culinary Uses

Horseradish preparations are usually served cold, as heat robs them of much of their pungency and flavor. Often horseradish is made into a sauce or paste and served with roast beef or cold meats like ham or corned beef. Sometimes beet juice is added to grated horseradish to brighten the color, and it is also often mixed with vinegar. It is commonly served with fish in Europe; for example, in Norway the grated root is mixed with whipped sweet and sour creams, vinegar, and sugar to make a sauce called *pepperotsaus* that is served with cold, boiled fish such as salmon. The French mix it into cream sauces with lemon juice. Horseradish is one of the ingredients in the imitation wasabi commonly served with sushi (see next page). In Austria, freshly grated horseradish is mixed with grated sour apples and lemon juice to make a relish for fried or roasted meat. Horseradish represents the bitter herbs *marror* or *morror* on the Passover seder plate. It symbolizes the hardships experienced by the Hebrews when they were slaves in Egypt.

wasabi

When you go to your favorite sushi restaurant and are served the green paste called wasabi, 99 percent of the time you are being served imitation wasabi, made from horseradish, Chinese mustard, cornstarch, and blue and yellow food coloring. Real wasabi is a rare and expensive delicacy that is confined mostly to Japan. In 1999, wholesale prices for wasabi in Japan ranged from $25 to $85 per pound, and retail prices soared to more than $100. Even in Japan, a mere 5 percent of sushi shops can afford to use fresh wasabi. Only recently has real wasabi been made available in the United States; growers like Pacific Farms in Oregon charge about $25 for six 43-gram tubes (about half a pound). They also sell wasabi plants for home gardening, but that is a difficult process.

The Plant and a Familiar Fire Source

There is a dispute over the botanical name of wasabi, a perennial herb native to Japan and eastern Siberia; some sources give it as *Eutrema wasabi*, and others *Wasabia japonica*. Wasabi is said to mean "mountain hollyhock." Like horseradish, wasabi is cruciferous, related to mustard and cabbage, and it grows about two feet tall. The plant's most pungent part, as with ginger, is a rhizome. Its pungency comes from allyl isothiocyanate, the same chemical found in horseradish and black mustard. Cultivated varieties of wasabi include 'Daruma', the most popular, and 'Mazuma', which has more heat.

Wasabi has been cultivated in its native Japan since the tenth century, but it is notoriously difficult to grow; its natural environment is in or near cold, shaded mountain streams with just the right mineral balance. Outdoor cultivated wasabi plants require a constant supply of cool, running water, a loose gravel bed, an ambient air temperature between 48° and 64°F, and shade to protect their leaves from the sun. Wasabi can be grown from seed or from rhizome offshoots and requires eighteen months or more to mature.

In Japan, growers traditionally constructed wasabi beds up to three feet deep using graduated sizes of gravel placed alongside cold streams, precisely arranged so water runs through them in a uniform pattern. The last such beds in Japan, however,

> Even in Japan, a mere 5 percent of sushi shops can afford to use fresh wasabi.

EUTREMA WASABI

were reportedly built more than two hundred years ago. The highest-quality wasabi is bed-grown and called *sawa* wasabi; when the plant is grown in fields, it is called *oka* wasabi, which is generally considered to be inferior in appearance and flavor.

It is possible to grow wasabi in pots or in the garden under shade netting, but only if you live in a cool, moist climate, or in an air-conditioned greenhouse, with constant misting. It is grown in semi-aquatic conditions in greenhouses in British Colombia and in straight compost under shade netting in Seattle, where the plants are misted twice daily. On the coast of Oregon, Pacific Farms grows wasabi hydroponically in greenhouses, allowing harvest and replanting every week of the year. In New Zealand wasabi is raised in raised beds in streams.

The wasabi harvest usually occurs in the spring, after the plants have established a new set of bright green leaves. The harvested rhizomes with the roots removed resemble knobby, thin, elongated pineapples.

Wasabi and Nutrition

Wasabi has considerable amounts of potassium, calcium, and vitamin C. Since it is consumed in such small quantities, however, it is not a significant source of such nutrients. More significantly, it contains cancer-fighting isothiocynates; studies in Japan indicate that wasabi is effective against stomach cancer cells. It is thought to be antibacterial, one reason it is eaten with raw fish—to prevent food poisoning. It also has antifungal properties.

Forms

Raw wasabi rhizomes, which can range in size from a couple of inches to nearly a foot in length, are sold in markets in Japan in pans of water. Avoid shriveled rhizomes. Trim off any dark edges before grating and scrub with a brush. Traditionally, a sharkskin grater, or *oroshi*, is used to transform the rhizome into a fine, pale green paste. If an *oroshi* is not available, a ceramic grater with very fine teeth is preferred over a stainless steel grater, but the latter can be used. Once the wasabi rhizome is grated, it is rinsed under cool water, drained, formed into a ball, and allowed to stand at room temperature for at least five minutes for the flavors to fully form. It should be consumed within twenty minutes, before its pungency dissipates.

As is most wasabi paste, "wasabi powder" from Japan is an imitation.

In Asian markets, wasabi is sometimes available in pickled form: the leaves, flowers, stalks, and rhizomes are chopped, brined, and mixed with sake, mirin, and sugar. In Japan, a wasabi wine and a wasabi liqueur are available.

Storage

Keep the wasabi rhizomes wrapped in damp paper towels in the refrigerator, where they will last about a month. Rinse in cold water once a week.

Culinary Uses

Freshly grated wasabi, mixed with soy sauce, is familiar as a condiment with sushi and sashimi. It is also added to soups and noodle dishes in Japan. American growers have used wasabi in drinks, in appetizers like pâté, in dips and sauces, in salad dressings, and in seafood and meat entrées.

2. Pods: Chile Peppers & Hot Sauces

chile peppers

An enormous amount of information is easily available on chile peppers and the hot sauces made from them, unlike some of the other spices detailed in this bible. A mini-industry of hot and spicy publishing has sprung up over the past two decades, including two consumer magazines, more than a hundred books on chiles and spicy foods, hundreds of Web sites, and thousands of technical and popular articles. Your authors confess to having played a major role in the chile information explosion that continues to this day. Obviously, there is far more material on the subject than can be included here, so we have decided to give a broad overview that highlights the most important information on the subject. For more in-depth coverage, we suggest our two books, *The Whole Chile Pepper Book* and *The Chile Pepper Encyclopedia*, as well as two comprehensive Web sites, the Fiery Foods & Barbecue SuperSite (www.fiery-foods.com) and the Chile Pepper Institute's site (www.chilepepperinstitute.org).

Nomenclature

Treatises have been written about the etymology of the various words used to describe the capsicums: *pepper*, *chile*, *chili*, *chilli*, and chile pepper, chili pepper, and chilli pepper. *Pepper*, of course, is derived from the early confusion with the black pepper genus, *Piper*, while *chilli*, *chile*, and *chili* are, in order, the Nahuatl (Aztec), Spanish, and American English spellings. Yes, our preferred term, *chile pepper*, is redundant and uses the Spanish spelling, but at least it cannot be confused with chili con carne or black pepper.

The Plant and Its Power

Chile peppers are perennial subshrubs, native to South America, that are grown as annuals in colder climates. They are a part of the large nightshade family, or Solanaceae, and are closely related to tomatoes, potatoes, tobacco, and eggplants. They are not related to black pepper, *Piper nigrum*.

The chile pepper genus is *Capsicum*, from the Greek *kapto*, appropriately enough, meaning "to bite."

The active principle that causes heat in chile peppers is a crystalline alkaloid generically called capsaicin, produced by glands at the junction of the placenta and the pod wall. The capsaicin spreads unevenly throughout the inside of the pod and is concentrated mostly in the placental tissue that holds the seeds.

Capsaicin is an incredibly powerful and stable alkaloid, seemingly unaffected by cold or heat, thus retaining its original potency despite time, cooking, or freezing. Because it has no flavor, color, or odor, the precise amount of capsaicin present in chiles can only be measured by a specialized laboratory procedure known as high-performance liquid chromatography (HPLC). Capsaicin is one of the most pungent compounds known, detectable to the palate in dilutions of one to several million. It is slightly soluble in water, but very soluble in alcohols, fats, and oils.

Why are some people more sensitive to capsaicin than others? We used to think it was because super tasters have more taste buds in the mouth, but that theory is not true: taste buds can only detect sour, sweet, bitter, salty, and umami flavors. (Umami is the flavor of monosodium glutamate, or MSG.) In 2003, scientists Elizabeth D. Prescott and David Julius of the University of California, San Francisco, identified a lipid molecule called PIP2 that plays a crucial role in controlling the strength of the burning sensation caused by capsaicin. A lipid molecule is a fatty molecule, insoluble in water but soluble in fat solvents and alcohol—just like capsaicin. In the mouth, there is

Chile peppers are a member of the nightshade family, and closely related to tomatoes, potatoes, eggplant, and tobacco.

a capsaicin receptor called TRPV1, and the lipid molecule PIP2 is bound to it. In the presence of capsaicin, the PIP2 molecule separates from the receptor, causing a painful sensation. Here's the scientific description: "In this process, the capsaicin receptor (TRPV1) is sensitized by phosphatidylinositol-4, 5-bisphosphate (PIP2) hydrolysis following phospholipase C activation." That's quite a mouthful.

Now, what governs the degree of pain? The strength of the binding of the molecule to the receptor, say the scientists—the stronger the binding, the more powerful the pain sensation when the capsaicin causes the separation. And what determines the strength of the binding? To quote the researchers: "Thus, modification of this PIP2 regulatory domain by genetic, biochemical, or pharmacological mechanisms may have profound effects on sensitivity of primary afferent nerve fibers to chemical and thermal stimuli under normal or pathological conditions."

In plain language, sensitivity to capsaicin is determined by genetics—some people's lipid molecules have a stronger bond with capsaicin receptors than others.

the five domesticated species of the chile pepper genus capsicum

SPECIES	TRANSLATION	DESCRIPTION
annuum	"annual"	"Annual" is an inaccurate designation, as chile peppers are perennials. This species comprises most of the commonest varieties, such as New Mexican, jalapeño, bell, and wax peppers.
baccatum	"berry-like"	These are the South American peppers commonly known as ajís.
chinense	"from China"	"From China" is also an incorrect designation, since the species originated in the Amazon Basin. These include the extremely hot habaneros.
frutescens	"shrubby" or "brushy"	This is the familiar tabasco.
pubescens	"hairy"	The South American rocotos and the Mexican manzanos.

But the fact that biochemical and pharmacological mechanisms can also play a role could explain why some people become desensitized to capsaicin and can take more and more heat.

Further study will reveal even more information regarding this process, so stay tuned. And by the way, if you are worried about capsaicin destroying your five to ten thousand taste buds, you should know that all of them are replaced every two weeks, anyway. So forget about your taste buds and concentrate on the binding of your lipid molecules!

Growing the Heat

Of all the spice plants covered in this book, chile peppers are the easiest to grow in the home garden. For complete information on home gardening, see *The Pepper Garden* by Dave and Dr. Paul Bosland, and *Too Many Chiles*, by Dave, Nancy, and Jeff Gerlach. For purposes of this book, we are going to briefly summarize the basic techniques.

About two months before the time to transplant seedlings into the garden, we start the seeds in plastic six-pack seedling growers, just like commercial greenhouses do. We use a commercial potting soil rather than garden soil because the seedlings' roots receive more oxygen and thus grow faster in the lighter mixture.

The six-packs are set in trays on top of heating wire or tape to keep soil temperatures above 75°F, since warm soil can radically increase the germination percentage of most chile varieties. After sprouting, the seedlings should be grown in full sun in a greenhouse or window so they do not become "leggy" and topple over. Leggy seedlings may be pinched back to make a bushier plant and to ensure that leaf growth does not overwhelm stem growth. Keep the seedlings moist but not wet; overwatering will cause stem rot. It will also be necessary to fertilize the plants after they have put out their first true leaves. We use an all purpose, water-soluble fertilizer (15-30-15), one-half teaspoon to a gallon of water, every time we water our seedlings. When growing seedlings in the house, remember that cats love to graze on tender young plants—which will not harm the cats but will destroy the chiles.

Chile peppers should not be set out in the garden until after the last frost, and ideally should not be set out until the temperature of the garden soil four inches below the surface reaches 65°F. Before transplanting, the seedlings should be "hardened off" by placing the trays outside for a few hours each day during warm, sunny days. Constant movement of the seedlings from light breezes will strengthen the stems and prepare the plants for the rigors of the garden. Chile pepper gardeners living in particularly chilly regions should wait until the plants blossom before planting them in the garden. Chiles can also be planted in large containers, as long as the soil is well drained.

The garden soil should have plenty of organic material such as aged compost added to it. If the garden plot is to be irrigated, use a shovel to make rows and furrows and then set the chile pepper plants two feet apart. It is possible to set plants closer together; this spacing has worked best for us mainly because it enables us to harvest the pods without stepping on the plants. Some gardeners place the chiles as close as one foot apart so the plants will shade each other and protect the fruit from sunburn. If necessary, protect young chile plants from freak frosts and cutworms by covering them with glass or plastic jars at night.

After you've transplanted the chiles, the garden should be thoroughly mulched. Use several layers of newspaper in hot climates or black plastic film in cool summer climates. In locations where summer temperatures regularly reach the nineties, black plastic in a garden can raise the temperature so high that the plants will stop flowering. Layers of newspaper weighted down with soil reflect sunlight, hold water, and provide additional organic material for the soil after they disintegrate.

Chiles need regular water and plenty of it, but overwatering is the biggest mistake of the home gardener. Well-drained soil is the key here, and the first indication of overwatering is water standing in the garden for any length of time. Some wilting of the plants in the hot summer sun is normal and is not always an indication that the plants need water.

A high-nitrogen fertilizer encourages foliage growth, but it should be discontinued after flowering. Some growers encourage root growth by adding a teaspoon of phosphate two inches below the planting hole during transplanting.

In order to set fruit, the plants require daytime temperatures between 65°F and 80°F and night temperatures above 55°F. Flowering decreases during the hottest months of the summer, and in fact, extremely hot or dry conditions will result in the blossoms dropping off the plant. In the early fall flowering picks up again, but in northern regions fall blooms are unlikely to yield fruit. In most locations the first hard frost will kill the plants, and at that point all the remaining pods should be removed.

Quite a few obnoxious pests and disgusting diseases can attack chile plants, but we have been lucky. The most serious problem we encountered was an aphid attack on the seedlings in the greenhouse. Fortunately, we avoided the most serious pepper diseases, such as mosaic virus, which is spread by aphids and causes leaf mottling. Anthracnose is a fungal disease that causes soft spots in the pods and makes them susceptible to rot; it is spread by spores, so avoid touching the plants and pods when they are wet. Also, do not grow beans close to chiles, as both are susceptible to anthracnose. Chiles are also attacked by wilt disease, which is promoted by overly wet soil. In all cases, remove all diseased plants and destroy them.

The Most Popular Spice—Or Spicy Food?

Of all the spicy ingredients in this book, chile peppers are the most widely cultivated commercially, grown in nearly every tropical and temperate country in the world. There is quite a debate over whether chiles or black pepper are the most traded and popular spice. The argument is difficult to settle, as black pepper is grown only as a spice, but chile peppers are grown as a spice when powdered, as a food when used as a vegetable, and as a major ingredient in prepared foods. Statistics give us the answer: In 2002, worldwide black pepper production was about 321,000 metric tons, while in 1986 in India alone, chile pepper production was about 708,000 tons. Black pepper may be the most widely used *spice* around the world, but there is no question that in production—and use in cuisine—chile peppers outweighs black pepper by a factor of at least eight. India is the largest producer of chile peppers, followed by Mexico, Indonesia, China, Korea, Thailand, Ethiopia, the United States, Taiwan, and Malaysia. Virtually no black pepper is grown by home gardeners, but tons of chile peppers are.

We recommend the technique of staggered harvesting, which means that the chiles in the garden can be used all year long. Usually the first chiles available are the small ones used green in fresh salsas—the serranos, jalapeños, and the young green pods of other varieties such as habanero. Varieties such as poblano, 'Big Jim', and Española can either be eaten or processed as soon as they are about four inches long or allowed to turn red before picking and drying. However, a few varieties, such as cayenne and santaka chiles, are generally used only in their dried state.

It is important to continue harvesting the ripe pods as they mature. If the pods are allowed to remain on the plant, few new ones will form, whereas if the pods are continuously harvested, the plants will produce great numbers of pods. The best time to pick chiles for drying is when they first start to turn red. This timing will stimulate the plant into further production, and the harvested chiles, strung up to dry, will turn bright red. When harvesting, it is best to cut the peppers off the plants with a knife or scissors, as the branches are brittle and will often break before the stem of the chile pod.

Early History and Domestication

The genus *Capsicum* originated in the remote geologic past in an area bordered by the mountains of southern Brazil to the east, by Bolivia to the west, and by Paraguay and northern Argentina to the south. Not only does this location have the greatest concentration of wild species of chiles in the world, but here, and only here, representatives of all the major domesticated species within the genus do grow.

Scientists are not certain about the exact time frame or method for the spread of both wild and domesticated species from the southern Brazil–Bolivia area, but they suspect that birds were primarily responsible. The wild chiles (like their undomesticated cousin of today, the chiltepin) had erect, red fruits that were quite pungent, which discouraged mammals from eating them and digesting them. But they were very

The Diversity of Italian Peppers

In Italy, "peperoncino" simply means pepper, as in chile pepper. That term is very general, but still, people are surprised to learn that the peperoncinos there range in size from half-inch long, piquin-like fruits to pods large enough to be strung up to dry in the sun. There is great variation among the peppers of Italy, and this must be taken into consideration when cooking. Both the variety of peperoncino and its form (fresh or dried) should be known to create the most authentic Italian peperoncino dishes.

In Calabria, all of the peperoncinos are *Capsicum annuum* and their major cultivated varieties have Latin names as if they were separate species, which of course they are not—they are pod types only. We collected the following names from the ingredients lists of Calabrian peperoncino products. The descriptors are *acuminatum* (pointed fruit, like a de arbol); *cerasiferum* (small, round, like a cherry pepper); *abreviatum* (shortened, like a pimiento or cheese); and *fasciculatum* (fasciculated, or pods clustered like mirasol or santaka). There are at least two descriptors missing, one for a piquin-like fruit illustrated here, and one for an elongated chile similar to *piment d'Espelette* that can be dried in ristra form, on strings. However, an Italian—rather than Latin—term is used for the piquin-like fruits: *diavoletti*, or little devils.

attractive to various species of birds, which, unaffected by the pungency, ate the whole pods. The seeds of those pods passed through their digestive tracts intact and were deposited on the ground, encased in a perfect fertilizer. In this manner, chiles spread all over South and Central America long before the first Asian tribes crossed the Bering land bridge and settled the Western Hemisphere.

When humankind arrived in the Americas more than 10,000 years ago, about twenty-five species of the genus *Capsicum* existed in South America. Five of these species were later domesticated; however, some of the other wild species were and still are occasionally utilized by man. Two of the five domesticated species of chiles, *C. baccatum* and *pubescens*, never migrated beyond South America. *Baccatum*, known as "Ají" merely extended its range from southern Brazil west to the Pacific Ocean and became

Additionally, there are many local names for the peperoncinos in Italy:

* Pevium, Peveron (Liguria)
* Peuvroun (Piedmont)
* Peverun (Lombardy)
* Pevrun, piviron (EmiliaRoma)
* Pepe rosso, pepe d'India (Tuscany)
* Peparuolo (Campania)
* Pepedinie (Abruzzo)
* Pipi infemali (Calabria)
* Pipi russi (Sicily)
* Pibiri moriscu (Sardinia)
* Frangistello, diavulicchiu, cerasella pupon, zafarano, mericanill (Lucania)
* Diavolicchio (Basilicata)

According to the Scalise family, owners of the peperoncino company Delizie di Calabria, about 250 acres are planted with peperoncinos on farms owned by families and some large corporations. They are grown as annuals during the typical spring and summer growing seasons. In the fall, some of the pods are dried in furnaces but others are strung together much like ristras. As one observer noted: "One of the most colorful sights encountered throughout the afternoon are the strings of red chile peppers hanging out to dry from windows and balconies, on clothes lines, spread out on the hoods of cars, and nailed to trees in the country. In markets, old women in black sit beside their piles of produce, patiently sewing up strings of chilies with a needle and thread." Other pods are sold fresh, salted down, or made into sauces and jams and jellies.

After drying, the peperoncino pods are often added to flavored vinegars and olive oil. When added to olive oil, it is called *olio santo*, or holy oil. This oil is used in salads, over pasta, and to flavor seafood dishes. But most of the peperoncinos are consumed as crushed pods or powders, because they are so easily dried. They are added to numerous vegetable dishes, pasta sauces, and are used in the manufacture of salami. Particularly famous are Calabrian spicy sausages, or *soppressata*, which are excellent appetizers or sandwich fillers.

a domesticated chile of choice in Bolivia, Ecuador, Peru, and Chile. Likewise, *Capsicum pubescens* left Brazil to be domesticated in the Andes, where it is known as Rocoto.

Three other *Capsicum* species that were later domesticated are *annuum*, *chinense*, and *frutescens*. These closely related species, which share a mutual ancestral gene pool and are known to botanists as the *annuum-chinense-frutescens* complex, later migrated individually to Central America and Amazonia and were all in place when humankind arrived on the scene. Apparently, each type was domesticated independently—*annuum* in Mexico, *chinense* in Amazonia (or possibly Peru), and *frutescens* in southern Central America. These three species have become the most commercially important chiles, and the story of their domestication and further spread is revealed in the archaeological record.

The earliest evidence of chile peppers in the human diet is from Mexico, where archaeologists discovered chile seeds dating from about 7500 B.C. during excavations at Tamaulipas and Tehuacan. These finds and an intact pod from Peru's Guitarrero Cave (dated 6500 B.C.) seem to indicate that chiles were under cultivation approximately 10,000 years ago. However, that date is extremely early for crop domestication, and some experts suggest that these specimens were harvested in the wild rather than cultivated by man.

It was in Mexico that the *annuum* species reached its greatest diversification of pod shapes. By the time the Spanish conquerors arrived in what is now Mexico, chile peppers of all sizes and shapes were available in the marketplaces, as recorded by historians such as Bernardino de Sahagún, who described "hot green chiles, smoked chiles, water chiles, tree chiles, beetle chiles, and sharp-pointed red chiles." Chiles were combined with virtually every meat and vegetable available, and were even used in hot chocolate drinks.

Dispersion Around the World

Shortly after Christopher Columbus brought back the first chile pods with seeds from the West Indies, the word was out about the pungent pods. Peter Martyr, a cleric in the service of the Spanish court at Barcelona, wrote in 1493 that the new hot pepper was called "*caribe*, meaning sharp and strong," and that "when it is used, there is no need of black pepper." From that point on, chiles spread like wildfire across the globe.

From 1493 on, chile seeds from the West Indies were available to the Spanish and Portuguese for transmittal throughout Europe and to ports anywhere along their trade routes. Spanish and Portuguese ships returning home were loaded not only with gold and silver but with packets of the seeds of the New World plants, destined for monastery gardens. Monks and amateur botanists carefully cultivated the capsicums and provided seed to other collectors in Europe.

The Beloved Espelette Pepper of France

A little known chile is acclaimed in—of all places—southwestern France, where it has gained controlled-name status, much like Champagne sparkling wine and Roquefort cheese. That chile is *piment d' Espelette*, or the Espelette pepper, and it has become a cultural and culinary icon in that part of Basque country.

When Columbus brought chile peppers to Europe from the Caribbean after his second voyage in 1493, they were first grown as curiosities in monastery gardens in Spain and Portugal. But soon the word got out that the pungent pods were a bargain substitute for the more expensive black pepper.

Chiles became established in just one region in France: the Nive Valley in the southwest, and especially in the village of Espelette to the south. It is believed that chiles were introduced there by Gonzalo Percaztegi in 1523, the same year that corn made its first appearance. At first thought to be related to black pepper and even called "long black American pepper," it wasn't until the seventeenth century that the Espelette was placed in its own genus.

Much like ristras in the American Southwest, the red pods of the Espelette peppers are threaded on cords and are hung on the sides of buildings and from racks. The strings of peppers, translated variously as "braids" or "tresses," are allowed to dry in the sun and then ground into powder or made into commercial pastes. Interestingly the earliest use of the ground Espelettes is connected to yet another crop unique to the Americas: cacao.

In the seventeenth century, chocolate became very popular in Europe both in candies and in drinks. Chocolatiers in Bayonne, perhaps influenced by tales of Montezuma's favorite drink, combined Espelette powder and chocolate. A century later, hams from the Basque area were covered with Espelette pepper to redden the ham before curing. The powder was also used in the making of Bayonne hams and some pâtés, sausages, blood sausages, rolls, and pies. From this point on, Basque cooks began using the Espelette pepper in place of black pepper in seafood dishes.

By the 1960s, the Espelette pepper became so popular that the village of Espelette, population 1700, established the Celebration of Peppers. The first festival was in 1967, and it is held annually the last Sunday in October. It now attracts more than 10,000 people and features food, music, dance, and games.

As the popularity of the peppers grew in France, the farmers realized that they had a very unique product, one that deserved recognition and protection. They did not want farmers in other regions to grow, for example, paprika and call it Espelette. At first they formed cooperative enterprises to protect their interests, and eventually they applied to the National Institute for Trade Name Origins for an Appellation d'Origine Controlee (AOC). On December 1, 1999, an AOC was granted to Espelette peppers and products.

In 1494, papal bulls of demarcation divided the world into Spanish and Portuguese spheres of influence; Portugal controlled Africa and Brazil, while Spain effectively ruled the remainder of the colonies of the New World. Thus Spanish and Portuguese traders spread chiles from both the Iberian Peninsula and their major colonies throughout the Eastern Hemisphere by way of their extensive trade routes.

Traders carried seeds to Africa and India, and from there they were dispersed to Southeast Asia, the islands of Indonesia, and then to China, Japan, and the Philippines. Eventually, chiles were transported to the islands of the Pacific. Within one hundred years of their discovery in the Western Hemisphere, chiles had circumnavigated the globe, spicing up numerous regional and national cuisines.

Chiles Invade the United States

According to many accounts, chile peppers were introduced into what is now the United States by Juan de Oñate, who in 1598 established the first Spanish settlement in what is now New Mexico. However, they may have been introduced to the Pueblo Indians of New Mexico by the Antonio Espejo expedition of 1582–83. According to one of the members of the expedition, Baltasar Obregón, "They have no chile, but the natives were given some seed to plant." By 1601 chiles were on the list of Indian crops, according to colonist Francisco de Valverde, who also complained that mice were a pest who ate chile pods off the plants in the field.

After the Spanish began settlement, the cultivation of chile peppers exploded, and soon they were grown all over New Mexico. It is likely that many different varieties were cultivated, including early forms of jalapeños, serranos, anchos, and pasillas. But one variety that adapted particularly well to New Mexico was a long green chile that turned red in the fall. Formerly called Anaheim because of its transfer to the more settled California around 1900, the New Mexican chile was cultivated for hundreds of years in the region with such dedication that several distinct varieties developed. These varieties, or "land races," called Chimayó and Española, adapted to particular environments and are still planted today in the same fields they were grown in centuries ago; they constitute a small but distinct part of the tons of pods produced each year in New Mexico.

During the 1700s, peppers were popping up in other parts of the country. In 1768, according to legend, Minorcan settlers in St. Augustine, Florida, introduced the Datil pepper, a land race of the *chinense* species. Supposedly, this pepper was transferred from the Caribbean to Africa and then to Minorca in the Mediterranean, from which it was brought to Florida. However, some historians believe that this story is all bunk and that Datil peppers were introduced into Florida via trade with the Caribbean islands, a simpler explanation that makes a lot more sense.

Other varieties were introduced during the eighteenth century. In 1785, George Washington planted two rows of "bird" peppers and one row of cayenne at Mount Vernon, but it is not known how he acquired the seed. Another influential American, Thomas Jefferson, was also growing peppers from seed imported from Mexico.

By the early 1800s, commercial seed varieties became available to the American public. In 1806 a botanist named McMahon listed four varieties for sale, and in 1826 another botanist named Thornburn listed "Long" (cayenne), "Tomato-Shaped" (squash), "Bell" (oxheart), "Cherry," and "Bird" (West Indian) peppers as available for gardeners. Two years later, squash peppers were cultivated in North American gardens, and that same year, the 'California Wonder' Bell pepper was first named and grown commercially.

Travelers and historians were beginning to notice the influence of chile peppers in the rather primitive American Southwest. "The extravagant use of red pepper among the [New] Mexicans has become truly proverbial. It enters into nearly every dish at every meal, and often so predominates as entirely to conceal the character of the viands," wrote Josiah Gregg in 1844 in his book *The Commerce of the Prairies*.

In 1846 William Emory, chief engineer of the army's Topographic Unit, was surveying the New Mexico landscape and its customs. He described a meal eaten by people in Bernalillo, just north of Albuquerque: "Roast chicken, stuffed with onions; then mutton, boiled with onions; then followed various other dishes, all dressed with the everlasting onion; and the whole terminated by chile, the glory of New Mexico."

Meanwhile, things had been heating up in the West. In 1896 Emilio Ortega, former sheriff of Ventura County, California, brought back New Mexican pepper seeds with him during a visit to New Mexico. He planted them near Anaheim, where they adapted well to the soil and climate. By the time Ortega opened the first pepper-canning operation in Ventura (1898), the pod type that originated in New Mexico was known as Anaheim, a name that would stick long after Anaheim was paved over and turned into Disneyland. (In 1987, the name of the pod type was changed to the more accurate New Mexican, and 'Anaheim' became a cultivar of the New Mexican pod type.)

In 1907 Fabian Garcia, a horticulturist at the Agricultural Experiment Station at the College of Agriculture and Mechanical Arts (now New Mexico State University), began his first experiments in breeding more standardized chile varieties; in 1908 he published *Chile Culture*, the first chile bulletin from the Agricultural Experiment Station. In 1913, Garcia became director of the Experiment Station and expanded his breeding program.

During this time, more European varieties were introduced. In 1911, the first pimientos from Spain arrived in Georgia. S. D. Riegel, a talented farmer, developed a

The Smoked Pimentón of Spain

Everyone knows that Columbus carried chile peppers to Spain from the New World on his second voyage in 1493, but why didn't the cuisine of Spain become fired up like that of India, or even Hungary? No one knows for certain. As in Italy, there are a few hot and spicy dishes in Spain, but chiles did not dominate the cuisine—except in one part of Extremadura in the far west, the same region where they were first introduced. That hotbed of chiles is the valley of La Vera, where the *pimientos* (chiles) are grown and smoked to make the famous spice *pimentón de la Vera*.

Some sources speculate that the *pimentón* tradition in La Vera was started by a group of monks from the Yuste Monastery in Cáceres in the sixteenth century. According to Janet Mendel, author of *Traditional Spanish Cooking*, when the Spanish emperor Charles V abdicated the throne of Spain in 1555 and retired to the Yuste monastery, he loved *pimentón* immensely. He recommended it to his sister, Queen Mary of Hungary, and that is how paprika became popular in that country. (Other sources give credit to the Turks for introducing chiles into Hungary at a later date.)

These days, *pimentón* is the region's main source of income. In early March, farmers germinate the seeds and grow seedlings in greenhouses. They are transplanted to the fields in May. Some of the fields are so remote that they are not accessible to tractors and other farm equipment, so farms use mule labor to prepare the fields, and ride mules to the fields to remove weeds by hand. In all the fields, the crop is picked by hand in

line of pimientos from Spain in Spalding County, eventually released as 'Perfection Pimiento' in 1913. In 1915–16, the South also witnessed the first American production of paprika in South Carolina, but the crop was soon abandoned in favor of cotton.

Finally, in 1917, after ten years of experiments with various strains of pasilla chiles, Garcia released 'New Mexico No. 9', the first attempt to grow a chile with a dependable pod size and heat level. 'No. 9' became the chile standard in New Mexico until 1950, when Roy Harper, another horticulturist, released 'New Mexico No. 6', a variety that matured earlier, produced higher yields, was wilt resistant, and less pungent.

October when all the pods are bright red but still pliable. In eastern Spain, where it is drier, the pods can be dried in the sun. But in Extremadura, fall rains raise the humidity to the level where the pods would rot or mold. So in the La Vera valley, they are placed in burlap sacks and then loaded on flatbed trucks that haul them to the drying buildings.

The *pimientos* are slowly dried over smoldering holm oak logs for ten to fifteen days and are hand-turned twenty-four hours a day before they are ready to be processed into *pimentón*. The smoke-dried pods are then ground into powder (the *pimentón*) and packed in bulk containers. The majority of the *pimentón* goes to the sausage factories, where it is used to spice up, flavor, and brighten up the famous Spanish *chorizo*. But it is also packed in tins for the consumer market. There are three varieties of *pimentón*—sweet (*dulce*), hot (*picante*), and bittersweet (*agridulce*).

Pimentón de la Vera was the first chile pepper product to be granted a *Denominacion de Origen*, or controlled name status. (The second was the *piment d'Espelette*, which was granted a French *Appellation d'Origine Controlee*). Controlled name status means that other varieties of *pimientos* cannot be called *pimentón*, and that consumers are guaranteed that the product is made in the same, time-honored manner. Look for the letters "D.O." on any product labeled as *pimentón*.

Sweet *pimentón* is great for flavoring potatoes, rice, and fish recipes, while the traditional bittersweet, smoky variety is used as a flavoring for smoked meats and in beans, game dishes, and stews. The hot type is used in winter soups, chorizo, and Galician *pulpo*, or octopus. The octopus is boiled and sliced, then sprinkled with olive oil, salt, and hot *pimentón* powder. Interestingly, there are recipes for *chorizo* and potato stews that utilize all three of the types of *pimentón*. Substitutions for *pimentón* include hot paprika and New Mexican ground red chile, but for a better approximation of the smokiness of the *pimentón*, mix in some ground chipotle chile.

Conversely, hot *pimentón* can be substituted for any recipe calling for paprika or ground red chile. Chili con carne enthusiasts should experiment with *pimentón* in their never-ending quest to improve their chili.

'New Mexico No. 6' was by far the biggest breakthrough in the chile breeding program. According to the late Dr. Roy Nakayama, who succeeded Harper as director of the Agricultural Experiment Station, "The 'No. 6' variety changed the image of chile from a ball of fire that sent consumers rushing to the water jug to that of a multi-purpose vegetable with a pleasing flavor. Commercial production and marketing, especially of green chiles and sauces, have been growing steadily since people around the world have discovered the delicious taste of chile without the overpowering pungency."

By 1919, the total U.S. acreage in peppers was 15,290, with a value of $3.1 million. Seven years later, the acreage in seven important states was about the same (15,430), but the value had climbed to $5 million. New Jersey led all states with 7,500 acres. In 1928, 'Calwonder Bell' was released as an official variety after 100 years of cultivation. During the period of 1930 to 1950, chile pepper acreage in New Mexico averaged between 900 and 1,200 acres.

The popularity of chili con carne cook-offs in the 1960s would further increase awareness of chile peppers, especially in Texas and California. The Chili Appreciation Society—International (CASI), founded in 1951, boasted more than two hundred "pods" (chapters) in Texas during the mid-1950s, and a similar organization, the International Chili Society (ICS), was formed in California.

In 1957 at the New Mexico Agricultural Experiment Station, Roy Harper modified 'New Mexico No. 6' to sustain its pods from their early green color until they matured to red; the new, still less pungent variety was called 'New Mexico No. 6-4'. With its moderate size (six to seven inches long), thick flesh, and uniform skin texture, which made it easy to work with and dehydrate, 'No. 6-4' became the chile industry standard in New Mexico; over thirty years later it was still the most popular chile commercially grown in the state, though other chile varieties such as 'Big Jim' and 'New Mexico R-Naky' found favor with home gardeners.

Roy Nakayama took over the chile pepper breeding program at New Mexico State University in 1960. Recognized in the 1970s as "Mr. Chile," Nakayama helped expand New Mexican chile growing, which totaled 1,200 acres between 1949 and 1959, into a thriving industry that reached 15,000 acres in 1979, and 28,700 acres in 1996. Before he retired in 1985, he would develop 'Española Improved', a hot chile designed to mature quickly for farmers in regions with short growing seasons. But perhaps his most far-reaching contribution was 'NuMex R Naky'. Before the introduction of this low-heat chile in 1985, the United States had imported paprika, a spice and a coloring agent, from Hungary and Spain. However, this new variety turned out to be perfect for paprika; New Mexico farmers turned the tables, exporting about one-third of their harvest to worldwide markets, including Africa, Hungary, and Spain.

On the agricultural front, the 1970s began with Ben Villalon founding the Texas pepper breeding program at the Agricultural Experiment Station in Weslaco (1970). That same year, Dr. Walter Greenleaf of Auburn University bred the tobacco-mosaic-virus-resistant variety 'Greenleaf Tabasco'. In 1973 the first National Pepper Conference was held, proof that peppers were finally being regarded as a serious crop plant in this country.

The Chile Institute at New Mexico State University was founded in 1991 to promote chile peppers worldwide.

During 1975, chile pepper acreage in New Mexico climbed to 9,200, and Roy Nakayama released 'NuMex Big Jim', which boasted the longest pods of any chile pepper—up to an astounding seventeen inches. That year also marked the publication of the first cookbook solely devoted to hot and spicy foods, *The Hellfire Cookbook* by John Cranwell. During the next twenty-seven years, twenty-three similar titles would follow as U.S. cooks discovered chile peppers and spicy foods.

In 1991, acreage of tabascos under cultivation in Lousiana dropped to a low of 75, and the plants were used mostly for seed. Also in 1991, bell pepper distribution in the United States reached 219,300 tons (including imports), up from the year before by 23,550 tons. The top bell-producing states were Florida, California, New Jersey, Texas, North Carolina, and Georgia. Top importing countries were Mexico and the Netherlands. That same year, the Chile Institute was founded at New Mexico State University to assemble a permanent archive of capsicum information and to promote chile peppers worldwide. New Mexico is by far the largest commercial producer of chile peppers in the United States, with about 25,000 acres under cultivation.

Today, Dr. Paul Bosland, who took over the New Mexico chile breeding program from Dr. Nakayama, is developing new chiles resistant to chile wilt, a fungal disease that can devastate fields. He has also created varieties to produce brown, orange, and yellow *ristras* for the home decoration market. The breeding and development of new chile varieties—in addition to research into wild species, post-harvest packaging, and genetics—is a major ongoing project at New Mexico State, but modern horticultural techniques have finally produced fairly standardized chiles.

Chiles and Nutrition

Most of the research on the nutritional properties of hot peppers has concerned New Mexican pod types, which are consumed more as a food than a condiment. The long green pods are harvested, roasted and peeled, and stuffed or made into sauces. Some of the green pods are allowed to turn red on the bush; after harvesting, the red chiles are used as the primary ingredient in red chile sauces. Green chiles are quite high in vitamin C, with about twice the amount by weight found in citrus, while dried red chiles contain more vitamin A than carrots. Vitamin C is one of the least stable of all the vitamins; it will break down chemically with heat, exposure to air, solubility in water, and dehydration. Vitamin A, however, is one of the most stable vitamins and is not affected by canning, cooking, or time.

A high percentage of the vitamin C in fresh green chiles is retained in canned and frozen products, but the vitamin C content drops dramatically in dried red pods

New Mexico is by far the largest commercial producer of chile peppers in the United States, with about 25,000 acres under cultivation.

and powder. Each hundred grams of fresh ripe chile pods contains 369 milligrams of vitamin C, which diminishes by more than half to 154 milligrams in dried red pods. Red chile powder contains less than 3 percent of the vitamin C of ripe pods, a low 10 milligrams.

The amount of vitamin A dramatically increases as the pod turns red and dries, from 770 units per 100 grams of green pods to 77,000 in freshly processed dried red pods. This hundredfold rise in vitamin A content is the result of increasing carotene, the chemical that produces the orange and red colors of ripe peppers. The recommended daily allowances for these vitamins are 5000 IU for A and 60 milligrams for C. These allowances can be satisfied daily by eating about a teaspoonful of red chile sauce for A, and about one ounce of fresh green chile for C.

Each hundred grams of green chile contains less than two-tenths of a gram of fat—a very low amount. Since no cholesterol is found in vegetable products, peppers are free of it. The fiber content of fresh hot peppers is fairly high (between 1.3 and

Roasting Chiles

All of the long green chiles must be roasted and peeled before being used in a recipe. Blistering or roasting the chile is the process of heating it to the point when the tough transparent skin is separated from the meat of the chile so it can be removed. The method is quite simple.

While processing chiles, be sure to wear rubber gloves to protect yourself from the capsaicin, which can burn your hands and any other part of your body that you touch. Before roasting, cut a small slit in each chile close to the top, so that the steam can escape. The chiles can then be placed on a baking sheet and put directly under the broiler or on a screen on the top of the stove.

Our favorite method is to place the pods on a charcoal grill about five to six inches from the coals. Blisters will soon indicate that the skin is separating, but be sure that the chiles are blistered all over or they will not peel properly. Immediately wrap the chiles in damp towels or place them in a plastic bag for ten to fifteen minutes—this "steams" them and loosens the skins. For crisper, less-cooked chiles, plunge them into ice water to stop the cooking process.

2.3 grams per hundred grams of chile), and many of the dishes prepared with them utilize starchy ingredients such as beans, pasta, and tortillas. And the sugar in chiles is in the form of healthy complex carbohydrates.

Fresh green chile contains only 3.5 to 5.7 milligrams of sodium per hundred grams—a very low amount.

Forms

Literally hundreds of varieties of peppers are grown in the world, but only a dozen or two are used for cooking in the United States. The following survey is not intended to be exhaustive, but rather a general description of the most popular peppers used in the United States.

Fresh peppers   Available from the garden or the market, fresh peppers are becoming increasingly popular with greater availability. The most ubiquitous peppers are, of course, the familiar bells, which have no heat except for a variety called 'Mexi-Bell', with a mild bite. The poblano, similar in size to a bell, is a Mexican pepper with moderate to mild heat; it is often stuffed with cheese and baked.

The most readily available hot peppers in the produce sections of supermarkets are jalapeños and yellow wax peppers. The latter are usually mild and are stuffed or chopped for use in salsas and salads. Jalapeños and serranos—either green or fresh red—are used in a similar manner, and are often floated whole in soups or stews to provide a little extra bite, then removed before serving. Another variety that sometimes appears fresh is the cherry pepper, though this mild pepper is often pickled.

Several varieties of the long green New Mexican chiles are available fresh in the Southwest and occasionally in other locations. 'No. 6-4', the most commonly grown, is available from August through early November. Its hotter cousin, 'Sandia', is usually not seen in the green, or immature, form. The mildest New Mexican is 'Anaheim', a California variety that is available most of the year. Occasionally, New Mexican chiles are identified by their grower (such as Barker) or by a regional appellation (Chimayó or Hatch or Luna County), which further confuses the issue.

We find that freezing is the most flavorful method of preservation. If the pods are to be frozen whole (rather than chopped), they do not have to be peeled first. In fact, they are easier to peel after they have been frozen. After roasting the chiles, freeze them in the form in which you plan to use them—whole, in strips, or chopped. If you are storing them in strips or chopped, peel the pods first. A handy way to put up chopped or diced chiles is to freeze them in ice-cube trays with sections. When frozen, they can be popped out of the trays and stored in a bag in the freezer. When making a

Other Prepared Chile Products

There are more varieties of manufactured chile products than any other spicy ingredient in this book—proof of chile's incredible diversity. These include:

* Barbecue sauce, using all kinds of chile, including chipotle, habanero, jalapeño, serrano; and from many countries, including Africa, Asia, and the United States
* Cheeses
* Condiments, including chile oil, horseradish, ketchup, and meat sauce (cocktail, poultry, steak)
* Drinks and drink mixes
* Dry mixes (enchilada sauces, etc.)
* Grilling sauces
* Hot sauce, including Caribbean-style, fruit, habanero, Louisiana-style, specialty chile (chipotle, jalapeño, serrano, other), wing sauce, and world beat (African, Asian)
* Meats, including sausages and ribs
* Mustards
* Olives

* Pasta sauces
* Pickled products
* Prepared dips
* Prepared sauces (red chile, green chile, enchilada)
* Relishes
* Salad dressings
* Salsa, including chipotle, fruit, habanero, tomatillo
* Snacks, including chips, crackers, jerky, nuts, pretzels, snack mixes
* Soups and stews, including chili con carne
* Spice blends, including curry powders and meat rubs, jerk seasoning, dry salsa mixes
* Sweet and hot sauces (hot fudge, glazes)
* Sweet heat (candy, cakes/pastries, cookies, jams/jellies)
* Table seasonings
* Vinegars

soup or a stew, just drop in a cube! This eliminates the problems inherent in hacking apart a large slab of frozen chiles when you need just a couple of ounces.

New Mexican chiles are available fresh in season by overnight delivery. They are found canned in most U.S. markets and frozen in some parts of the Southwest.

Other fresh chiles that are sometimes found in markets (especially farmers' markets) are serranos and habaneros. The serranos—smaller, thinner, and hotter than jalapeños—are the classic chiles of the Mexican fresh *pico de gallo* salsas. Habaneros, the world's hottest peppers, are lantern-shaped orange or red devils that have a unique, fruity aroma in addition to their powerful punch. Use them with caution. Generally speaking, any of the small fresh peppers may be substituted for each other; however, they are not a substitute for poblanos or the New Mexican varieties in recipes. The smaller chiles—habaneros, serranos, and jalapeños—can be frozen without processing. Wash the chiles, dry them, place them one layer deep on a cookie sheet, and freeze them. After they are frozen solid, store them in a bag. Frozen chiles will keep for nine months to a year at 0°F. All the small peppers can be frozen whole with no further processing needed, and their texture holds up surprisingly well in the freezer.

Like fresh peppers, with dried chiles, the larger they are, the milder. The large dried peppers, such as ancho (a dried poblano) and the New Mexican varieties, are mild enough to be the principal ingredients of sauces. The smaller varieties, such as piquin, are too hot for this purpose and are generally used as condiments or in stir-frying. All dried peppers can be ground into powders (see pages 66–67).

Four main large peppers are used as the base for sauces: ancho, pasilla, New Mexican, and guajillo. The ancho is a wide, dark pepper with a "raisiny" aroma. It is the only pepper that is commonly stuffed in its dried form (the pod is softened in water first). The pasilla is a long, thin, dark pepper that also has a raisiny or nutty aroma. Along with the ancho, it commonly appears in Mexican mole sauces.

The most common way to use the red New Mexican chiles is to hang them in long strings, or *ristras*, until they are ready to be used in cooking. Then they are commonly rehydrated and combined with onions, garlic, oil, spices, and water to make the classic New Mexican red chile sauce, a common topping for enchiladas in the Southwest. The guajillos, a shortened and hotter version of the New Mexican chiles, are commonly used in sauces in northern Mexico.

There are a bewildering number of small, hot pods, ranging in size from that of a little fingernail (the chiltepin) to the skinny six-inch cayenne. Some varieties include piquin, Thai, santaka, de arbol, mirasol, and tabasco. These chiles appear in stir-fry dishes, are floated in soups or stews, or are used to add heat to sauces that are too mild. A specialized dried chile that has become quite popular is the chipotle, a smoke-dried red jalapeño.

hot sauce

ommercial hot sauces are manufactured from pureed chiles and numerous other ingredients including vegetables, fruits, spices, seasonings, and acidic additions such as vinegar and citrus juices. Salsas are a type of hot sauce of Mexican origin and are considerably thicker and chunkier than the typical bottle cayenne sauce.

The first bottled cayenne sauces appeared in Massachusetts around 1807. These were probably homemade and similar to English sauces that were decorated with silver labels. Sometime between 1840 and 1860, J. McCollick & Company of New York City produced Bird Pepper Sauce in a large cathedral bottle that was nearly eleven inches tall. This sauce is significant because it was probably made with the wild chiles called chiltepins or bird peppers.

In 1849, the first mention of tabasco peppers occurred in the *New Orleans Daily Delta* of December 7: "I must not omit to notice the Colonel's pepper patch, which is two acres in extent, all planted with a new species of red pepper, which Colonel White has introduced into our country, called Tabasco red pepper." The colonel referred to is Maunsel White, one of the earliest growers of tabasco peppers.

These *frutescens* peppers, introduced into Louisiana from Tabasco, Mexico, were soon grown in quantity by Edmund McIlhenny of Avery Island, who transformed them from obscurity into one of the most famous peppers in history. Tabasco peppers were mashed, salted, aged, and then strained and mixed with vinegar to produce McIlhenny's famous Tabasco sauce. In 1868 the first 350 bottles of sauce were shipped to wholesalers, and by 1870 McIlhenny obtained a patent for Tabasco brand hot pepper sauce. The rest is history: Tabasco has become the best-known and best-selling hot sauce in the world.

Around this same time, a cookbook entitled *Mrs. Hill's New Cookbook*, by Annabella Hill of Georgia, contained an interesting recipe for barbecue sauce that contained butter, mustard, vinegar, black pepper, and red pepper—almost certainly cayenne. So it is evident that there was a general tradition of the home cooking of hot sauces in the South. Mrs. Hill also included a recipe for a curry sauce using prepared curry powder.

From an excavated wreck of the good ship *Bertrand*, dated 1874, we know that Western Spice Mills of St. Louis was making hot sauce around that time; 173 of their bottles were uncovered. That same year (some say 1875), Eugene R. Durkee of Brooklyn, New York, applied for a patent on a hexagonal "Chilli Sauce" bottle, but although the patent application survives, no actual bottle has ever been found. E. R. Durkee & Company became a rather large spice and condiment company; the brand name exists to this day. Around this same time, W. K. Lewis & Co. in Boston were producing a pepper sauce in a square cathedral-shaped bottle.

In 1877 Willam H. Railton, a Chicago businessman who owned the Chicago Preserving Works, began using a Maltese cross–shaped label for table sauces "prepared from a Mexican formula." He applied for a trademark in 1883, and by 1884 he was buying large ads for his Chili Colorow Sauce. Interestingly enough, although it was a "chili" sauce, the advertising copy claimed that it was "expressly suitable for family dining, possessing a fine, rich body of exquisite flavor and has neither the fiery nor nauseous taste which characterizes most sauces." With a typical nineteenth-century patent-medicine pitch, the copy went on to claim, "It relieves indigestion and cures dyspepsia. Physicians recommend it highly."

During the 1880s and '90s, several hot sauces sprang up, including C&D Peppersauce, manufactured by Chace and Duncan in New York City in 1883, but we have nothing left but the bottle. Sometime around 1900, the Bergman and Company Pioneer Pickle Factory in Sacramento, California, began selling Bergman's Diablo Pepper Sauce in five-inch tall bottles with narrow necks that resembled the typical hot sauce bottle of today. About the same time, a Detroit company, Horton-Cato, manufactured Royal Pepper Sauce in a bottle with a bulbous bottom. And sometime shortly after 1889, Heinz produced Heinz's Tabasco Pepper Sauce in a elegant bottle; but alas, even Heinz couldn't compete with the "real" Tabasco sauce produced by McIlhenny.

After the death of Edmund McIlhenny in 1890, the family business was turned over to his son John, who immediately inherited trouble in the form of a crop failure. John attempted to locate tabasco chiles in Mexico but could not find any to meet his specifications. Fortunately, his father had stored sufficient reserves of pepper mash, so they weathered the crisis. However, that experience taught the family not to depend solely upon tabasco chiles grown in Louisiana. Today, tabascos are grown under contract in Honduras, Colombia, and other Central and South American countries, and the mash is imported into the United States in barrels.

John McIlhenny was quite a promoter and traveled all over the country publicizing his family's sauce. "I had bill posters prepared," he once said, "and had large wooden

Tabasco has become the best-known and best-selling hot sauce in the world.

signs in the fields near the cities. I had an opera troupe playing a light opera. At different times I had certain cities canvassed by drummers, in a house-to-house canvass. I had exhibits in food expositions, with demonstrators attached. I gave away many thousands of circulars and folders, and miniature bottles of Tabasco pepper sauce."

In 1898, another Louisiana entrepreneur (and former McIlhenny employee) named B. F. Trappey began growing tabasco chiles from Avery Island seed. He founded the company B. F. Trappey and Sons and began producing his own sauce, also called Tabasco. The McIlhenny family eventually responded to this challenge by applying a trademark for their Tabasco brand in 1906. This did not deter other companies from using the name Tabasco in their products, however; in 1911, the Joseph Campbell Company began selling Campbell's Tabasco Ketchup and described it as "the appetizing piquancy of Tabasco Sauce in milder form."

Spurred by the success of McIlhenny's Tabasco Pepper Sauce, other companies sprang up all over the country. Charles E. Erath of New Orleans began manufacturing Extract of Louisiana Pepper, Red Hot Creole Peppersauce, in bottles nearly eight inches tall in 1916. A year later, La Victoria Foods began manufacturing Salsa Brava in Los Angeles, California. In Louisiana in 1923, Baumer Foods began manufacturing of Crystal Hot Sauce, and in 1928 Bruce Foods started making Original Louisiana Hot Sauce—two brands that are still in existence today.

The Louisiana hot sauce boom continued; in 1929, Trappey's expanded to two plants, one in Lafayette and one in New Iberia. That same year, the McIlhenny family won a trademark infringement suit against Trappey's, ending thirty-one years of competition between identically named sauces. Finally, only the McIlhenny sauce could be called Tabasco, and competitors were reduced to merely including tabasco chiles in their list of ingredients.

Other Pepper Sauces and Salsas

In 1941 Henry Tanklage formed La Victoria Sales Company to market a new La Victoria salsa line. He introduced red taco sauce, green taco sauce, and enchilada sauce—the first of their kind in the United States. He took over the entire La Victoria operation in 1946, which today has ten different hot sauces covering the entire salsa spectrum, including Green Chili Salsa and Red Salsa Jalapeña.

During the 1940s and '50s, hot sauces were sold exclusively in small grocery stores, and manufacturers were always searching for new products. In 1952 La Victoria invented and introduced the first commercial taco sauce in the United States. And in 1955, La Preferida began manufacturing a line of salsas. That same year, incidentally, the first McDonald's opened.

A wave of food change swept the country in the 1970s. Sometimes called the "whole foods movement," the trend emphasized cooking with fresh, unadulterated ingredients. Vegetarianism increased in popularity, health food stores sprang up everywhere, and a new concept in selling food was launched—the gourmet retail shop, which specialized in selling exotic, imported foods and products not available in the large supermarkets. The stage was set for yet another boom in hot sauces, and this one was led by the smaller manufacturers who made these specialty products.

In 1975 Patti Swidler of Tucson, Arizona, launched Desert Rose Salsa, a line specifically designed to be sold in specialty food shops. Patti told food journalists bluntly, "People are making salsa that is no longer salsa. I still find people gravitate toward authentic flavors."

Four years later, in Austin, Texas, Dan Jardine would begin production of Jardine's commercial salsa, perhaps jump-starting Austin's reputation (disputed by San Antonio) as the hot sauce capital of America. "Austin is a unique place in the United States," he said. "There seems to be a lot more salsa companies trying to start here." A count by *Austin American-Statesman* food editor Kitty Crider in 1993 totaled forty-eight Austin-made salsas.

Between the years of 1982 and 1987, Mexican sauce sales jumped 16 percent; suddenly these products were at the top of the sauce and gravy category. In 1983, Panola Pepper Company in Lake Providence, Louisiana, began with 2,000 gallons of sauce made by Bubber Brown from his mother's recipe. That same year, Frank's Red Hot Cayenne Pepper Sauce was introduced by Durkee-French in an advertising blitz; Red Hot would eventually challenge Tabasco for U.S. market share.

In 1987 Pace saw a major rival enter the fray as Geo. A. Hormel & Co. licensed a restaurant's name and introduced Chi-Chi's brand; it would eventually capture a large share of the market. The same year Robert Spiegel, Dave DeWitt and Nancy Gerlach (coauthors of this book), founded *Chile Pepper* magazine, the first major national publication to feature hot sauces, their recipes, and advertisements for many manufacturers, large and small.

The following year, Lisa Lammé opened Le Saucier in Boston, believed to be the first retail shop devoted to sauces and specializing in hot sauces. Macayo Foods of Phoenix introduced a line of taco sauces in pourable plastic bottles that same year, and the first National Fiery Foods Show was held in El Paso. That show, which started with a mere thirty exhibitors, would expand to two hundred exhibitors in 1995, showcasing hundreds and hundreds of brands of sauces and salsas along the way.

A wave of food change in the 1970s led to another boom of hot sauces, this one led by smaller manufacturers of specialty products.

3 Seeds: Mustard & All Kinds of Pepper

mustard

It figures that the first contact with mustard for most of us is its use as a condiment for hot dogs—perhaps its most common use. But there's a lot more to mustard than hot dogs, as it's a versatile spice that is combined at some point in cooking with every other spicy ingredient featured in this book.

The word *mustard* comes from the medieval Latin term *mustum ardens*, meaning "burning wine must," because mustard preparations were made by crushing the seeds with unfermented grape must, or juice. That process resulted in releasing the pungent—or burning—qualities of the seeds. That Latin phrase then became the Old French *moustarde*, which became the modern French *moutarde*—in English, *mustard*.

The Plant and Its Potency

As often occurs, scientists do not agree on the botanical names of the various species of mustards. White mustard, or *Brassica alba*, is often known as either *Sinapis alba or Brassica hirta*, while black mustard is known as *Brassica nigra*, and brown mustard is named *Brassica juncea*. Further confusing the issue are the common names given to these species. White mustard is also called yellow mustard because of the pale yellow color of the seeds, which are so tiny they can number 15,000 to an ounce. Brown mustard is sometimes called black mustard, but its seeds are dark red to brown, and black mustard is also known as Indian mustard, Chinese mustard, and mustard greens.

All mustards are annual plants living in temperate climates, which often grow as weeds. White mustard grows to six feet tall in some areas and loves full sun. From sowing in the spring to harvesting takes only about two months, so it's a fast-growing plant. The most commonly cultivated mustards are the white and brown varieties. Black mustard grows too tall (up to fifteen feet), and its seeds drop too easily for mechanical harvesting. Mature mustard plants are harvested much like wheat, stacked in sheaves to dry, and then threshed to remove the seeds. Mustard is not usually cultivated in the home garden.

World production of mustard seed was 468,000 metric tons in 2002. The largest producer was Canada, with 154,000 metric tons; other countries with significant production were Nepal (134,000 metric tons), the United States (56,000), the Czech Republic (32,213), and Burma (Myanmar), with 30,024 metric tons.

Mustard seed contains about 30 percent oil, the source of the spice's pungency. This pungency is released when a liquid such as water, wine, or vinegar is added to the ground seed. The enzyme myrosin then combines with a glycoside, sinigrin, to produce the sulfur compound allyl isothiocyanate (the same compound resposible for the bite of horseradish and wasabi), in a reaction that takes about ten to fifteen minutes. Black mustard is the most pungent of the three species, with brown next and white the least pungent. More important than the type of seed is the liquid used to make the mustard paste, however: water makes the hottest mustard, vinegar tends both to temper the heat and to prevent deterioration of the pungent oil, and wine produces a pungent, spicy flavor.

Mustard in History

White mustard is native to the Mediterranean and the Near East, while black mustard originated in Eurasia, and brown mustard, in Asia. There is evidence of mustard being used as early as 3000 B.C. in Sumeria, and its culinary usage in Asia dates to 1500 B.C.

Mustard is mentioned in the Bible as "the greatest among herbs," yet the Greeks regarded it as primarily a medicinal plant. The Greek scientist Pythagoras, in the sixth century B.C. wrote that mustard was a cure for scorpion stings. In the fifth century B.C., Hippocrates described a number of decoctions using crushed mustard seeds, and Herodotus mentioned mustard as a cultivated plant.

In a famous case of mustard one-upmanship, in 334 B.C. Darius III of Persia sent Alexander the Great a bag of sesame seeds to symbolize the size of his army. Alexander sent back a bag of mustard seeds, symbolizing the power of *his* army. Of course, mustard prevailed over sesame; Alexander defeated Darius in 331 B.C. at Gaugamela.

The Roman scientist Pliny the Elder wrote that lazy women would become ideal housewives if they consumed mustard, thus ushering in its culinary use. The first cookbook, by Apicius, had numerous mustard sauces for birds like ostrich, crane, doves, and duck and also for boar and fish. Beets were boiled and then served in a mustard vinaigrette. Prepared mustard in Roman times was made in much the same way as it is today. Apicius describes it clearly: The seed is soaked in cold water for two hours, then ground in a mortar, then it is mixed with vinegar.

The Romans apparently spread mustard throughout their empire, and some sources indicate that Julius Caesar's troops first brought mustard seeds to Dijon, France. By the ninth century A.D., it was grown on imperial estates and in monastery gardens in France. (The French interest in mustard survives today in a classic condiment of French cuisine, *sauce Robert*.) Dijon, in Burgundy, became the French mustard capital, and in 812 Charlemagne ordered that mustard be grown on all his estates. Around this time, the monks of Saint-Germain-des-Prés, near Paris, were acclaimed for the quality of their mustard. In 1336 in Dijon, France, the duke of Burgundy gave a banquet for France's Philippe de Valois at which guests consumed 300 quarts of mustard, and mustard from Dijon became famous throughout Europe. A little later, Dijon established regulations requiring mustard to be made from "good mustard seed soaked in good vinegar."

In Asia, mustard was first mentioned in Chinese medical texts in 609; by 907 white mustard, originally from the Mediterranean region, was grown for the first time in northern China.

By the twelfth century mustard had arrived in Germany and England, and the thirteenth-century Catalan book *Libre de Sent Sovi* gives a recipe for making mustard with finely ground mustard seed, broth, and honey or sugar, noting that "French style" mustard uses vinegar rather than broth.

The handwritten 1390 manuscript of the first English cookbook, *Forme of Cury* (Art of Cookery), includes a recipe for preparing mustard: "Lombard Mustard: Take mustard seed and wash it and dry it in an oven, grind it dry. Sieve it through a sieve. Clarify honey with wine and vinegar, stir it all well together and make it thick. Thin with more wine if necessary."

The Portuguese explorer Vasco da Gama took a barrel of mustard on his voyage to India in 1497; around this time, the typical English household used eighty-six

Some sources indicate that it was the troups of Julius Caesar who first brought mustard seeds to Dijon, France.

pounds of mustard seed each year, along with five pounds of black pepper and two and a half pounds of ginger. In the sixteenth century, the British mustard industry began in Tewkesbury. Tewkesbury mustard, mixed with horseradish and formed into small condiment balls that kept well until mixed with various liquids, became famous for its pungency.

Mustards began to spice up European cookbooks. In 1529 the Spanish cookbook *Libro de Guisados* contained three mustard recipes, including two for "French Mustard." The Dutch cookbook *Eenen Nyeuwen Coock Boeck* (1560), by Gheeraert Vorselman, contains recipes for two mustards made in the "Roman way."

In 1634 Dijon, France, began to regulate mustard producers, called *moutardiers*; clean clothes were required for workers, and only brown or black mustard seeds could be used. Twenty-three mustard makers were given exclusive rights to manufacture the condiment by the king.

Mustard was not only a condiment; it was a remedy. Nicholas Culpepper, in *The English Physician Enlarged* (1653), recommended mustard as a treatment for weak stomachs, colds, toothaches, joint pains, and skin problems, while John Evelyn, in *Acetaria: A Discourse on Sallets* (1699), described mustard as "exceedingly hot and mordicant, not only in Seed but Leaf also of incomparable effect to quicken and revive the Spirits; strengthening the Memory, expelling heaviness, preventing the Vertiginous Palsie [giddiness]."

Mustard was transferred to America during the 1700s by Spanish priests who traveled up and down the California coast, scattering mustard seeds along what would be called the Mission Trail so that the quick-growing plants would mark the path for the following groups of missionaries.

Around this time, mustard was enormously popular in Europe, and nearly a hundred varieties of prepared mustard were sold. Flavorings included capers, truffles, anchovies, rose petals, vanilla, cloves, nutmeg, and even nasturtiums. In 1720 a Mrs. Clements of Durham, England, sifted the hull from milled mustard and invented the yellow flour, or farina, then known as Durham mustard but now called simply dry mustard. In 1722 Durham mustard became the first commercial dry mustard, and advertisements running in the *London Journal* bragged that "one spoonful of the Mustard made of it will go as far as three sold at chandlers' shops, and is so much wholesomer." A year later, in 1723, a monumental date in French mustard-making, Jean Naigeon, a Dijon *moutardier*, substituted unfermented wine, or "must," for the vinegar in prepared mustard, creating the more flavorful Dijon style that we know and love today.

Imported mustard seed was relatively late to arrive in the United States. In 1735 it arrived in the South; the *South Carolina Gazette* reported, "Just imported from

Colman's
Mustard was
so popular in
the mid-1800s
that four trains
were often
required to
transport
one day's factory
production.

London by John Watson . . . mustard seed." Mustard was even bigger business in Europe; in 1742, Keen & Sons started a mustard business on Garlick Hill in London to supply the city's chop houses and taverns; in 1747 the mustard-making House of Maille was founded in Paris; and in 1777, Grey Poupon mustard began to be manufactured at Dijon, France, by Maurice Grey, with backing from an investor named Poupon, using automatic, steam-driven mustard-making machines. By 1812, Dijon was producing eighty-four different varieties of mustard; four years later Denis Bornier bought the ancient Messigny Mill on the river Suzon in Dijon and began mustard milling and manufacturing. The Bornier brand is still produced today.

The United States started catching up in 1822, when English immigrant William Underwood, later the deviled-ham mogul, opened the first U.S. spice-grinding company, located in Boston, and began producing ground mustard with English-style labels. He undercut the price of imported mustard and began to control some U.S. markets like New Orleans.

The following year, miller Jeremiah Colman established a mustard business near Norwich, England, using a combination of white and brown mustard seeds. In time, grocers across England carried the red tins with the yellow label, and it was supplied to the army and Royal Navy. Of course, his brand is still in existence today.

Apparently fed up with products that "stimulate carnal appetites," in 1829 Massachusetts Presbyterian clergyman Sylvester Graham attacked mustard, ketchup, pepper, and white bread in sermons, but he failed to stop the rush to consume the popular condiments both in the United States and abroad. In 1852 Plochman's Mustard was founded at Premium Mustard Mills, followed by Gulden's Mustard, introduced into England in 1862 by New York entrepreneur Charles Gulden, who had a shop on Elisabeth Street. Continuing to stimulate carnal appetites, in 1866 Colman's Mustard was so popular that it received a royal warrant from Queen Victoria. Four trains were often required to transport one day's production from the Norwich factory, and its advertising campaign boasted, "It purges the body of toxic products, relieving pain, giving a feeling of warmth and well-being, and an increased flow of blood; it stimulates capillary circulation, relieves rheumatism, colds, flu, bronchitis, coughs on the chest, aches in the nape of the neck, neuralgia in the side of the face, and toothache."

Classic mustards still in existence today soon appeared in North America. In 1867, G. S. Dunn & Company, a dry mustard miller, was founded in Hamilton, Ontario, and in 1903 the Raye family built a mill in Eastport, Maine, and began grinding mustard to make sauces for the growing sardine industry. Today, theirs is the last American stone mill still grinding mustard.

New styles of mustard soon followed; in 1904 French's Cream Salad Mustard, milder and designed for use in salad dressings, was produced by George F. French and introduced by the R. T. French Company of Rochester, New York, at the World's Fair in St. Louis. It was so popular that the company claimed that it was the world's best-selling mustard. By 1915, sales of the product exceeded $1 million, a huge sum at that time.

In 1926, Colman's Mustard bought R. T. French's Cream Salad Mustard and became the largest mustard producer in both England and the United States. With the assistance of the London advertising agency S. H. Benson, they began advertising with posters on the sides of buses asking, "Has Father Joined the Mustard Club?"

In 1937 Dijon mustard was granted an *appellation contrôllée d'origine*, "controlled name of origin," meaning that the name could not be used for mustards produced outside the region of Dijon. Today, Dijon mustard can be made outside the region if it uses the traditional process.

During the 1940s, nearly half of all sardines processed in the United States were packed in mustard sauce, and in 1946 Heublein purchased the American rights to Grey Poupon mustard and began manufacturing. Today's Grey Poupon Dijon mustard is made by R.J.R. Nabisco in Oxnard, California.

The popularity of mustard grew rapidly in the United States from the 1950s on. By 1989, mustard sales topped $211 million, and that figure grew to more than $300 million by 2002. In 1992, a museum devoted to the condiment, the Mt. Horeb Mustard Museum, opened in Mt. Horeb, Wisconsin.

Mustard and Nutrition

Mustard contains between 28 and 36 percent protein and supplies calcium, magnesium, potassium, and niacin. A gram of mustard flour (powder) contains 4.3 calories and has only trace amounts of fat and no cholesterol. The heat of mustard does not linger but dissipates quickly and is said to stimulate the appetite. The essential oil retards growth of molds, yeasts, and bacteria.

Mustard is used externally in bandages, plasters, and poultices for respiratory infections, arthritic joints, and skin eruptions. A mustard foot bath is a traditional remedy for colds and headaches. In Chinese medicine, mustard is taken internally for bronchial congestion, coughs, and joint pains. Mustard plasters, made by adding water to mustard powder and spreading the mixture on a bandage, can be quite hot and can irritate the skin, eventually causing blisters, so care should be taken and the plaster removed when it becomes uncomfortable.

Forms

Besides being made into pastes of all kinds, mustard seeds are widely used uncrushed in preserving such foods as sauerkraut, sausages, and pickles. Mustard powder, or flour, is produced by grinding together white and black mustard seeds and then sifting the mixture to remove the hull fragments and adding wheat flour for bulk, turmeric for a bright yellow color, and small amounts of sugar, salt, and spices. Because the hulls have been removed, this powder is quite pungent. Dry mustard is often flavored with hot spices such as chile powder or ground black pepper, or mild herbs such as basil, tarragon, thyme, cumin, or mint. Even fresh ingredients such as ginger or horseradish can be added. The powder can then be mixed with water, vinegar, ale, or cider to make an instant prepared mustard.

Commercially prepared mustards are pastes and are described in several ways. American mustard uses only white mustard seeds; English, a mixture of white and black seeds; German, black or brown seeds; and French, brown mustard seeds. By pungency, there are strong mustards (mostly black, sometimes brown seeds) or mild mustards (white seeds or white and brown seeds). Two additional categories are whole-grain mustards and flavored mustards.

The type of seed used is only one factor in mustard's pungency; milder mustards are made by leaving in a percentage of the less pungent hulls. Of these whole-grain mustards, the most famous are the Dijon mustards. There are three types of French mustard: Bordeaux, which is mild and brown and often contains herbs such as tarragon; Dijon, which is stronger, pale yellow, and usually without extra flavorings; and Meaux, which is mild because it is made with the unmilled, crushed seeds. Ninety percent of all French mustards are the Dijon type. German mustard is of the Bordeaux type and is often flavored with herbs. Chinese mustard is simply mustard flour mixed with water.

Flavored mustards have additional herbs, spices, or other flavorings added—among them horseradish, chiles, lemon, peppercorns, mint, basil, tarragon, chives, ginger, and curry powder. It is theoretically possible to create a mustard using every spicy ingredient in this book. Sweet mustards have sugar or honey added to them, and the bright yellow color of some American-style prepared mustards comes from the addition of turmeric.

Mustard oil, 93 percent allyl isothiocyanate, is a polyunsaturated cooking oil pressed from the seeds of the brown and black varieties. Most mustard oil is manufactured in India. Because of its high smoking point, it is used to stir-fry or deep-fry and is very popular in Indian cooking; it loses its pungency when heated.

> Ninety percent of all French mustards are the Dijon type.

Storage

Store mustard seeds in airtight containers, preferably glass, in a cool, dry cupboard or spice rack. Store dry mustard the same way. Prepared mustards kept in airtight containers in the refrigerator will keep their strength for about a year. Mustard oil should also be kept in the refrigerator, to slow the oxidation process.

Culinary Uses

Whole mustard seeds are commonly used in pickles and sausages or added to coleslaw, potato salad, and cooked cabbage and beets. Crushed, they are added to dips for seafood, and to salad dressings. Other sauces and condiments, such as mayonnaise, vinaigrettes, and dill sauces, use powdered or prepared mustard as an ingredient. Dry mustard is often added to pickles and chutneys, where it serves as a preservative. Prepared mustards are served cold as condiments for cold meats or hot sandwiches like pastrami, or added to hot dishes at the end of the cooking process so that the heat of cooking will not kill the pungency of the mustard. Mustard is often used in glazes for roasted meats, in sauces for ham or corned beef, and in casseroles, salad dressings, and cocktail sauces.

black pepper

The world of black pepper ranges from the mundane—a shaker of bland, finely ground pepper on a Formica tabletop at a truck stop—to the exotic—vines of pungent berries climbing tall poles on faraway tropical islands, a bizarre history, and complex chemistry. Interestingly, a popular history and cookbook devoted solely to black pepper has yet to be written, so until one is published, this treatise will have to suffice.

The word *pepper* originated with the Sanskrit (and later, Hindi) *pippali*, which at first referred to long pepper. It was transliterated as *péperi* in Greek, *piper* in Latin, and finally *pepper* in English, *pfeffer* in German, and *poivre* in French.

The Plant and Its Pungency

The genus *Piper* contains more than a thousand species of shrubs, vines, and small trees. It is part of the Piperaceae family, which also includes the genus of ornamental house-plants *Peperomia*. There are numerous cultivated varieties of *Piper nigrum*—more than seventy-five are grown in India alone, with the most popular being 'Karimunda'. A hardy, somewhat woody perennial evergreen vine that grows in tropical climates, black pepper can climb to thirty feet but is usually restricted to ten to fifteen feet in cultivation. Its oval, dark green leaves can reach seven inches long by four inches wide. The flowers, borne at the nodes, form spikes that have 50 to 150 yellowish florets, are usually hermaphroditic but sometimes unisexual, with staminate and pistillate flowers on the same plant or on different plants. Flowering begins at the base and spreads to the top of the vine in about a week. Pollination occurs mostly during rainfall. The fruit, variously called a corn or berry, is ⅕- to ¼-inch in diameter and is harvested when green or orange just turning to red.

In commercial cultivation, pepper vines are propogated through stem cuttings. The cuttings are planted at the base of poles from six to twenty feet high; trimmed to the height of the pole, the vines can bush to five feet wide. Curiously, in some parts of the world, the vines are shaded from the direct sun by trees or netting, but in other regions they are not.

PIPER NIGRUM

It takes three to five years to establish vines that will flower and fruit, but after they begin producing they will bear fruit from fifteen to thirty years. To stimulate the production of flower spikes, the terminal buds of the vines are pruned off. In India, a typical yield for plants in their peak production, about eight years old, is about a thousand pounds per acre. Interestingly, one of the main diseases of *Piper* plants is a fungus called root rot, or *Phytophthora*, which is also a problem for chile pepper plants.

Pepper vines can be successfully grown by home gardeners in any climate without frosts. Grown in a greenhouse, the plants are dormant in the winter, resuming growth in the spring. Since they are relatively low-light plants, they can be grown in pots indoors, but the space and height needed for the vines makes this difficult. Our friend Paul Bosland, the chile pepper horticulturist at New Mexico State University, has been growing a *Piper* for five years in his greenhouse, and it has yet to flower, probably because of extremely high ultraviolet light levels. In Dave's greenhouse, where the plants receive diffuse light in all seasons, they flowered the first year, but many of the flower spikes dropped off. Here the vines grow up a two-inch-diameter PVC pipe. They are planted in a mixture of commercial potting soil and a little perlite and sand, fertilized with a mild solution of 15-30-15.

In commercial plantations, the plants flower in May and June in the Northern Hemisphere, and the berries are ready for picking from November to March. Ladders are placed against the posts and workers carefully handpick the spikes at the optimum ripeness for whichever type of pepper is being processed, placing them in mesh bags tied around their waists. The berries are stripped from the spikes and either processed into green pepper or dried in the sun on woven mats or concrete slabs.

Pepper contains the alkaloid piperine, which gives it its characteristic aroma, flavor, and pungency. Black pepper contains up to about 5 percent piperine, and long pepper has 6 percent. Piperine is perceived on the lips and the front of the tongue. It is not nearly as pungent as capsaicin; a 100-parts-per-million solution of piperine is roughly equivalent to a 1- or 2-parts-per-million solution of capsaicin.

The major extract of black pepper is called oleoresin black pepper, and it is important in food manufacturing. It is extracted from the pepper by using solvents such as hexane, which are evaporated off, leaving a thick oil. The bouquet comes from the volatile essential oil, and the bite comes from nonvolatile piperine.

Black pepper oil, used in herbal medicine and aromatherapy, is made when the peppercorns are crushed and undergo steam distillation. Up to half a ton of peppercorns must be processed to yield a single quart of black pepper oil, resulting in 2002 retail prices of about $20 for one-third ounce.

Black Pepper in History

Ian Hemphill, the Australian herb and spice expert, has observed, "The history of pepper is almost the history of the world spice trade. No individual spice has had such far-reaching effects on commerce, voyages of discovery, cultures, and cuisines over the centuries, than the history of pepper has." (See our separate chapter on the spice trade.)

Black pepper is mentioned in the Vedas, the ancient sacred literature of the Hindus, which date from approximately 1500 B.C. (some authorities claim an earlier date of about 5000 B.C.). In Epic Period literature, dating from around 2000 B.C., long pepper is referenced in the preparation of young buffaloes for banquets, served "floating in a spicy sauce."

The Malabar Coast of Kerala in southwestern India became renowned for its black pepper, cinnamon, ginger, and cardamom as growers there sold the spices to the Phoenicians and the Arabs. Most of the Malabar's spices were carried to Alexandria for re-export around the Mediterranean. Interestingly enough, the cultivation of the spices was somewhat haphazard, and some authorities believe that they were collected in the wild rather than actually farmed. "Even pepper and cardamom and other spices much demanded by the Arabs and Europeans were not cultivated or produced in a systematic manner," writes Dr. K. K. N. Kurup of Calicut University. "From an early period of history, pepper had become the staple commodity of trade between India and Europe. However,

> No other spice has had a greater affect on world history than pepper.

the efforts of man in its production were very little. The only human effort involved in the production of spices was the gathering of the commodity from the plants."

According to some sources, pepper is a cultigen, a cultivated plant, like a banana, that is not known to have a wild or uncultivated counterpart. Botanist Howard Scott Gentry observes, "It fits so snugly into what is regarded as an incipient agricultural pattern and in a wooded maritime Asian area, it may be very ancient; just how many thousands of years we may never know." So we simply do not know if the pepper trade began with a wild plant or not.

Pepper became enormously popular in Rome. "Sprinkle with pepper and serve" is the last step in a recipe for diced pork and apples from the world's oldest surviving cookbook, *De Re Coquinaria* (On Cookery), attributed to the Roman writer Apicius, who lived during the reign of Tiberius (A.D. 14–37). Nearly all of his 478 recipes contain pepper. These spiced-up dishes, which used exotic animals like ostrich, crane, parrot, and flamingo, were primarily aimed at the rich, who could afford expensive spices, and introduced an entirely new way to eat.

Of course, there was a lot of money to be made in pepper and other spices. When Emperor Domitian had a spice market constructed in Rome in A.D. 92, its main street was Via Piperatica—Pepper Street.

The writer Pliny, who knew of three kinds of pepper—long, black, and white— complained that the use of gold to buy so much pepper would lead to Rome's decline. He estimated that 100 million *sesterces* a year—roughly $25 million in 2002 dollars— were spent by the Empire on spices from India, China, and Arabia, a huge sum for the time. By contrast, the United States currently imports about $500 million worth of pepper each year.

Despite the heavy and frequent use of pepper in Roman dishes, cooking could not account for all the pepper in Rome. Food historian Maguelonne Toussaint-Samat has a theory: "Pepper more than any other spice, being stronger and more abundant than the others, came to be seen as a symbol of power and virility, qualities reflected in its powerful and aggressive flavour. The symbolic factor rated high, since such huge amounts, which could hardly all have been consumed, would have been bound to go stale." Persius the satirist used the word *sacrum*, something a miser would hoard, to refer to pepper.

Duty was levied on imported pepper at the rate of 25 percent of its value, making it wildly expensive, and the only currencies acceptable to the Indians and their Arab intermediaries were wine, gold, and silver.

As the Roman Empire declined, pepper bribes were used to thwart attacks by the Romans' enemies. In fact, Roman officials saved the city from Visigoth attack in A.D. 408 by paying a tribute that included 3,000 pounds of peppercorns, and in A.D. 452,

Pepper is named for the area where it is grown or the port from which it is shipped.

the Romans bought off Attila the Hun with pepper and cinnamon. When Rome eventually fell, the supply of pepper to northern Europe through Italy was interrupted until the Crusades.

Pepper and Nutrition

Generally speaking, pepper is consumed in such small quantities as a spice that it will not do much to fulfill the minimum daily requirements of nutrients needed by the human body. That said, black peppercorns contain about 50 percent carbohydrates, significant amounts of protein, and fiber, but only 3 percent fat. They also supply, in small quantities, calcium, iron, magnesium, phosphorus, potassium, sodium, niacin, vitamin C, and vitamin A.

As can be expected of a pungent spice, pepper has played a long and storied role in folk medicine and herbal treatments. Ayurveda, the healing doctrine of India, holds that pepper is dry, therapeutically healing, and a digestive. It is said to sharpen the appetite and relieve the symptoms of colds and sore throats. Other conditions pepper has been said to treat over the millennia include migraine headache, stomachache, intestinal worms, asthma, indigestion, night blindness, flatulence, diarrhea, impotence, hemorrhoids, amnesia, skin disorders, hair loss, poisoning, gonorrhea, vertigo, cholera, gout, and paralysis of the tongue.

In aromatherapy, pepper oil is used topically for bruises, muscle pain, to increase circulation, and to prepare the muscles for exercise. It is often mixed with other oils, such as lemon, juniper, ginger, and clove. Care should be taken when applying pepper oil; mixing with other oils is advised so that the pungent oil does not cause kidney damage through absorption by the skin.

Piperine is being studied in modern medicine as a possible bioavailability agent. For example, when taken with piperine, the drug Rifampicin is effective in much smaller doses during treatment for tuberculosis—the piperine makes more of the drug available to the human system. Piperine's reputed anticonvulsant, antimicrobial, antiprotozoal, antiinflammatory, and anticarcinogenic activities, as well as its role in enhancing digestion, have also been the subject of studies.

Forms

Black pepper is the generic term for peppercorns that are picked green, just as they are starting to turn red, fermented briefly, then sun-dried until they are wrinkled and black. During the drying process, the piperine in the berries turns the pericarp (the outer skin) black and forms volatile and nonvolatile oils, while the inside remains pale. Solar dryers and wood-burning furnaces are also used.

principal types of pepper in commerce

NAME	COLOR	COUNTRY OF ORIGINATION	CHARACTERISTICS
Malabar	black	India (state of Kerala)	All Indian pepper is generally called Malabar, which is quite pungent with a resinous aroma.
Tellicherry	black	India	Any Malabar pepper that has large berries. It is less pungent than Malabar, and considered to be the most complex in flavor.
Lampong	black	Indonesia (island of Sumatra)	It has uniform berries and is highly pungent.
Sarawak	black	Malaysia	Sarawak black pepper is one of the principal peppercorns of commerce. It has small, light-colored peppercorns.
	white		Sarawak white pepper is exported exclusively to the British Commonwealth, Europe, and Southeast Asia.
Brazilian	black	Brazil	Noted for the smooth surface of berries. Brazilian black peppercorns are one of the main sources of U.S. pepper imports.
	white		Brazilian white pepper is lighter in color and less pungent than the Muntok variety. Most of it is exported to Argentina and Western Europe, with minor quantities to the United States.
Muntok	white	Indonesia	All of the crop of the island of Bangka is used for white pepper production; this pepper is relatively mild.
Chinese	white	China	Light in color and very mild in flavor.

White pepper is made by submerging fresh peppercorns in water for several days to soften the pericarp, which is then rubbed off. The inner core is then dried in the sun. It is also possible to produce a form of white pepper from dried black peppercorns by grinding the black pericarp off, forming "decorticated black pepper," with the color of white pepper but a flavor more like that of black pepper. White pepper's whiteness will increase if the peppercorns are soaked in running water. The white pepper of the port of Muntok, on the island of Bangka off the southwest coast of Sumatra in Indonesia, is considered to be finest.

After drying, both black and white peppercorns are graded based on their weight, size, volatile oil content, and area of origin. "Pinheads," or immature berries, are eliminated, as are empty berries that float when placed in water.

Green peppercorns have a green, "herbal" flavor and a pungency that affects the nose, much like horseradish. The berries are picked green, then pickled in vinegar or brine or freeze-dried, a costly process that results in green peppercorns that closely approach freshly picked berries in color and flavor. Green peppercorns can also be simply dehydrated in the sun after being boiled for twenty minutes to kill the piperine, so that they turn a pale green color. Interestingly, some pepper plantations treat ripened red berries in the same manner, creating red pepper (not to be confused with pink "peppercorns"). More pungent than green pepper, this is a very rare commodity.

Selecting Pepper

When buying pepper, consider the most important characteristic you are looking for. Is it pungency, bouquet, or appearance in the food being prepared? Here is a brief buying guide for the basic forms of pepper.

* **Green pepper** is available freeze-dried, dehydrated, and brined or vinegar-packed. Select containers with medium-sized, whole berries. If packed in a liquid, make sure that the liquid is clear.
* When buying **black pepper**, look for unbroken, uniform, debris-free peppercorns. Go for the largest, freshest, most full-scented peppercorns, although some, like Tellicherry, are so subtle that the aroma is not apparent until the peppercorns are cracked.
* When buying **white pepper**, look for whole, uncracked berries and uniform color.
* **Ground pepper** quickly loses flavor and pungency. It is graded by the size of mesh the particles must pass through: for example, a 10-mesh screen has ten openings per linear inch, and a 30-mesh screen has thirty. Here are the designations and mesh size: "cracked" (10–16 mesh), "coarse grind" (20–30 mesh), "shaker grind" (30–60 mesh), and "fine shaker grind" (60 mesh). The coarser the grind, the longer the pepper will last. Buy only uniformly ground pepper and look for a sell-by date.

Storage

All pepper should be stored in an airtight glass container (never plastic) out of direct light and away from any moisture source. Black peppercorns will last indefinitely when

Other principal black pepper–growing countries are Vietnam, Ceylon, Thailand, Nigeria, and China.

properly stored, but the shelf life of white pepper and coarsely ground black pepper is about a year. Green peppercorns packed in vinegar or brine will last about a month in the refrigerator, while water-packed ones should be used within a week.

Grinding

All experts on the subject say to avoid buying ground pepper and to always grind your own. This makes the most of pepper's volatile oils and pungency.

To grind peppercorns of all kinds, you can use a mortar and pestle, but that method is labor-intensive and will not grind evenly or finely. A ceramic mortar and pestle is preferred over a wooden one because wood absorbs the flavors of what is being ground and can produce off flavors in subsequent grindings. Electric spice mills and coffee grinders can also be used, but there are very specific tools for grinding peppercorns.

During our research, we uncovered an enormous selection of peppermills and pepper grinders. The best ones have a ceramic grinding surface and a grind adjustment. It doesn't seem to matter if a grinder is manual, electric, or electronic. Antique pepper mills, highly prized collectibles in Europe, are catching on in the United States.

Culinary Usage

Pepper is one of the most universally used flavoring agents, appearing in processed meats, fish, vegetables, mayonnaise, fish crackers, vinegar, tea, coffee, liquor, Worcestershire sauce, salad dressings, and many others.

Mix Different Types of Pepper   Grind together black, white, and pink peppercorns with coriander seeds to add a new dimension to smoked meats and fish and vegetables such as corn, winter squash, and sweet potatoes.

Sauces   Green peppercorns are often combined with liquor such as bourbon and meat stock to make a sauce that is served over grilled lamb or veal chops. They are also used in salad dressings and soups.

Baking   Most bakers prefer white pepper, which is more subtle when used in cakes, muffins, and focaccia. Other baked goods that benefit from using white (and in some cases, black) pepper include pastries, tart shells, vegetable breads such as pumpkin or zucchini, carrot cake, biscuits, and cookies.

Desserts   One of the most common modern uses of cracked black pepper is in simple desserts. Today chefs are sprinkling black pepper, long used in gingerbread, over fruits such as berries, mango, pineapple, melon slices of all kinds, and orange sections.

commercial pepper preparations

Numerous manufacturers produce every conceivable blend of various peppercorns, often including pink "peppercorns." Additionally, there are pepper products combined with other ingredients, including:

NAME OF BLEND	INGREDIENTS
Lemon pepper blend	Ground black and white peppercorns and dehydrated ground lemon peel.
Garlic pepper blend	Ground black and white peppercorns and dehydrated ground garlic.
Onion pepper blend	Ground black and white peppercorns and dehydrated ground onion.
Sarawak green pepper sauce	A product of Malaysia, this contains green peppercorns ground to a puree and mixed with vinegar, salt, sugar, and spices.

other piper species

In addition to *Piper nigrum*, two other members of the *Piper* genus are still used in the worldwide spice trade. During a trip to Australia, we were able to purchase both long pepper (*Piper longum*) and cubeb pepper (*Piper cubeba*) at Herbie's Spices in Rozelle, just outside Sydney, so they still can be found. There are two other important *Pipers*: kava, or *Piper methysticum*, whose leaves are used in the South Pacific to make a soporific drink, and betel, *Piper betle*, whose leaves are used in the chewing of betel nut. However, neither of these plants are used to spice foods.

Long Pepper

Long pepper was the first pepper to be traded and was the most favored type of pepper for hundreds, if not thousands, of years before black pepper achieved dominance. It was highly prized—and priced—during the Roman Empire, costing about three times as much as black pepper. Although the leaves are similar to those of black pepper, the berries merge into a single, podlike structure that resembles the catkins (pollen dispersal parts) of trees like willows or mulberries.

Long pepper originated in Southeast Asia and is mostly cultivated in Thailand and Indonesia. Its pungency is greater than that of black pepper, a result of high piperine content. Long pepper has sweet overtones, making it combine well with cheese. In India, its main usage is in pickles (*achars*). Long pepper is also used in the spice mixtures of North Africa, including *ras el hanout* and *berbere*. The "pods" are crushed in a mortar before use.

Cubeb Pepper

Cubeb, or tailed pepper, is native to Indonesia; it is used in medicine and formerly had some importance in the spice trade. It is grown primarily in Java but also in Sierra Leone and the Congo. The pungent part is a berrylike black pepper, except larger with a stem, or "tail." Cubeb pepper is pungent and slightly bitter. The pungency is caused by cubebin, a totally different compound from piperine.

Cubebs were formerly a substitute for black pepper but fell into disfavor because of their bitterness when black pepper became well distributed. Cubeb is still used in some North African spice mixtures, such as *ras el hanout*.

other "peppers"

There are many plants called pepper in various languages, but not all of them have a bite. For example, in Jamaica, allspice is called "pimento," which is the masculine form of the Spanish *pimenta*, meaning pepper. But as tasty as allspice is, it has no pungency at all, so we can eliminate it from this survey. Neither are the pink "peppercorns" from the Brazilian pepper tree, which are often included in peppercorn mixtures, pungent at all, so we have excluded them as well.

There are, however, three unrelated plants from around the world that produce pungent berries or seeds called pepper. At one time or another, all have been used as substitutes for black pepper, and all are still used in various international dishes. They are all available through international spice sellers.

Melegueta Pepper: Grains of Paradise

The origin of the word *melegueta* is obscure, but the Liberian coast was known to the Portuguese as Terra di Malaget. "Grains of paradise" refers to the spice's high value during the Middle Ages. Other names are Guinea pepper, a reference to the African country, and alligator pepper, which seems to be a corruption of *melegueta*.

The botanical name of melegueta is *Aframomum melegueta*, sometimes *Amomum melegueta*, and the plant belongs to the ginger family, Zingiberaceae. It is related to cardamom and yields pods filled with spicy seeds. Do not confuse this pepper with the Brazilian chile of the *Capsicum frutescens* species, malagueta.

The spiciness is found in the seeds, which are similar to cardamom seeds, about ⅛-inch in diameter, and reddish brown in color. The pungency is spicy and comes from gingerols. Melegueta is not as strong as black pepper, so it must be used in greater quantity. The seeds are used in veterinary medicine and also West African herbal medicine.

The melegueta is native to Africa's western coast, or the "Grain Coast" of Ghana, Liberia, Cote d'Ivoire, Togo, and Nigeria. It is grown mainly in Ghana today. The history of the melegueta pepper is rather short; the first known reference in literature is in 1214, when it is mentioned as "melegetae." It reached Holland by 1358. During the fifteenth century, when the sea route to India had not yet been discovered and black pepper was exorbitantly expensive, grains of paradise were a cheaper substitute. They were transported across the Sahara by camel caravan and used in medieval Europe as a flavoring for beer. In England, Queen Elizabeth I was fond of melegueta, using it in food and drink, but its excessive use in beer caused it to be banned.

Originally a flavoring for wine, now melegueta seeds are an ingredient in Van Gogh gin. They have a nutlike oiliness and flavor notes recalling nutmeg, coriander, and cinnamon. Ground in a spice mill, they can be used as a substitute for black pepper, although they have a totally different flavor. Store the seeds as you would black pepper. Their principal use today is in North African spice mixtures such as Tunisia's *qalat dagga*.

Melegueta pepper spices up vegetables such as potatoes, eggplant, and pumpkin. The ground seeds can be used as a crust for baked fish. A tasty spread for toast combines goat cheese, melegueta, thyme, and olive oil.

Sichuan Pepper

Fagara, as it's known in China, is called Sichuan pepper because the plant is native to the Sichuan (formerly Szechwan) province of China. In Sichuan, it is known as *huajiao*, and in English the berries are also called Chinese pepper and anise pepper. Its botanical name is *Xanthoxylum pipertum*, and it is the dried berry of a small tree in the prickly ash family. The berries are rust colored and measure about three-sixteenths of an inch in diameter. It is the husk of the berry that is pungent, not the tiny black seeds inside. The berries are only mildly pungent, but are numbing to the mouth and tongue, a sensation that is called *ma* in Chinese. The slight burning sensation is called *la*, so consuming *fagara* is called a *ma la* experience. The leaves are not pungent, but when ground they become Japanese *sansho* spice.

Sichuan pepper is now difficult to find in Asian markets in the United States. In 1968, the USDA banned the importation of these berries because the prickly ash tree is actually a type of citrus and may carry an infectious canker that could infect orange trees. But the department didn't enforce the ban on *fagara* until 2002, when agents began seizing Sichuan pepper in stores. If travelers attempt to bring Sichuan pepper from another country, they face a $1,000 fine. The ban was lifted in 2004 for Sichuan peppercorns that have been heat-treated.

If you can find them, Sichuan pepper berries should be roasted slightly before being ground. Sichuan pepper is used in Chinese five-spice powder and in the Japanese spice blend *shichimi togarashi*; it is essential for spicy Sichuan cookery, where it is used as a table condiment—salt and Sichuan pepper are toasted together in a skillet and then ground to a coarse powder. Store Sichuan pepper as you would black pepper.

In *sha momo*, the national dish of Tibet, ground yak meat is flavored with Sichuan pepper, garlic, ginger, and onion and then stuffed into noodles, which are served with a fiery chile sauce.

Australian Mountain Pepper

This little-known spice is quickly gaining fans as commercial cultivation begins. Dave investigated Australian mountain pepper on a trip to Sydney, finding the plant in the Botanic Garden and the spice in small bags at Herbie's Spices in Rozelle.

Known botanically as *Tasmannia lanceolata*, a member of the Winteraceae, a small family from Southeast Asia, mountain pepper is native to moist, temperate rainforests in Tasmania, Victoria, and southern New South Wales. A shrub or small tree that grows from six to fifteen feet tall, it is also called mountain pepper, mountain pepper-leaf, pepperberries, Tasmanian pepper, native pepper, and Dorrigo pepper (a separate species in the same genus). Its Aboriginal name is *mourao*.

The peppercorn-like fruits are produced on female plants, ripening in the summer and fall. The berries are mostly harvested from the wild, but trial plantings have been established in south Australia.

The pungency in the leaves, berries, and seeds of Australian mountain pepper is caused by polygodial, which produces two effects: a biting, eye-watering heat greater than that of black pepper but is short-lived, and the numbness of the tongue the Chinese call *ma*. The aroma is often described as turpentine-like.

There is no evidence that this plant was ever used by indigenous people in either food or medicine. The use of the berries seems to date from 1993, when Paul James, a seller of native foods, first experimented with the berries. They have become more and more popular as the "bush food movement," which promotes the consumption of native foods, has swept Australia. The essential oil is now used as a confectionery flavoring.

Mountain pepper leaves are dried in a well-ventilated area and then ground in a spice mill. The berries are dried in the same manner and stored like black pepper-corns, or preserved in brine. Sometimes they are frozen, but this is not recommended because the berries get mushy. Freeze-drying is more effective.

The ground leaf, used just like black or white pepper, is an ingredient in native lemon pepper and barbecue spices, but the berry is not used in spice blends because of its extreme pungency. Australian spice expert Ian Hemphill warns: "With mountain pepperberry however, extreme caution is suggested and my rule of thumb is to use only one tenth of the quantity when compared to conventional pepper. Only the brave, fool-ish, or taste-bud-deficient would entertain putting ground mountain pepperberries di-rectly onto food; they are just so hot and numbing, that when not cooked, the flavour attributes cannot be fully appreciated." He advises putting the berries into slow-cooked dishes like soups, stews, and crock-pot recipes, so that the pungency dissipates and the "unusual" flavor comes out.

The spice is used before grilling to season kangaroo steaks, which Dave tried in Sydney, as well as to spice up emu burgers. It flavors a marinade for grilled meats of all kinds when mixed with vegetable oil, and can be a spice in pestos. Long simmer-ing eventually eases the intense pungency. Ground mountain pepper is also added to Asian curry dishes, salad dressings, and pickles. Whole mountain pepper leaves are used in the same way as bay leaves, and are removed from the dish before serving. Ground mountain pepperleaf is used to make a crust on smoked salmon.

At least two commercial products, Diemen Pepper Tapas Oil—olive oil steeped with mountain pepper—and Diemen Pepper Pepperberry Vinegar, are being produced in Australia.

4 Powders: Spice Blends, Rubs, & Curry

Powders are defined as ground dried chiles, spices, herbs, and various other ingredients (such as nuts, seeds, salt, sugar, and flours) used to flavor meats and vegetables during the cooking process, or added as condiments to the finished dish. Often these powders are mixed with water, oil, or other liquids, or combined with onions and/or garlic, to make pastes.

chile powders

All chiles can be dried and ground into powder—and most are, including the hottest of all, the habanero. Crushed chiles, or those coarsely ground with some of the seeds, are called *quebrado*. Coarse powders are referred to as *caribe*, while the finer powders are termed *molido*. In our homes, we actually have more powders available than whole pods because the powders are concentrated and take up less storage space. We store them in small, airtight bottles. The fresher the powders, the better they taste, so don't grind up too many pods at once.

To grind the smaller chiles, first make certain they are completely dried and are so brittle that you can break them in half. Use an electric spice mill, and be sure to wear a painter's mask to protect your nose and throat from the pungent cloud of powder that you will create. The color of the powders will range from a bright, electric red-orange (chiltepins), to light green (dried jalapeños), to a dark brown that verges on black (ancho). Red pods can be made darker by dry-toasting them in skillet on top of the stove, stirring constantly.

To grind the larger chiles, first place them on a cookie sheet in a medium oven until they are brittle and break when bent. Be sure to turn them often so they don't burn. Break the chiles into small pieces before grinding them. Occasionally, two steps are needed—a coarse grind in the blender and then a fine grind in the spice mill.

Some competition chili cooks grind their own secret blends of chiles that are added at the cook-off. John Thorne, author of *Just Another Bowl of Texas Red*, suggests that "an ideal blend would start with a base of New Mexican chiles, mixed with some dark and wrinkled ancho chiles (for their deep, earthy flavor), and one or two pasillas (for their nuttier piquancy). To this combination, add a controlled amount of one of the truly fiery peppers—de arbol or piquin to give the chili its true heat. The best powdered chile is made at home from a blend of different dried chiles—especially the milder ones. For while the fiery pods give chili myth and heat, the sweeter ones give it a depth of flavor."

Commercial Chili Powders

These chili con carne blends take powdered chiles a step further by adding spices. John Thorne warns about the commercial blends, "Ordinary chili powder is a predetermined mixture of powdered chile and seasoning; its familiar stale flavor and musty odor summons nostalgia and indigestion in equal proportion. Use it only as a last resort."

Commercial chili powders are usually comprised of 80 to 85 percent powdered chiles, but they can contain up to 40 percent salt! Some unexpected spices also crop up, such as ginger, saffron, cinnamon, allspice, and anise. Other unneeded ingredients are maltodextrin, monosodium glutamate, and tricalcium phosphate.

Some chili experts believe that cooks will always use commercial blends. "If you are to have consistency in your attempts to make the perfect bowl of chili," one chili expert advised, "you must take into account that no two chili powders are alike."

Many cooks grind their own blends of chiles and spice to make chili powder. The most common ingredients are chiles, paprika, garlic powder, ground oregano, salt, and cumin. Other occasional ingredients in home blends are turmeric, celery seed, cloves, coriander, sugar, and dried onion flakes.

Some commercial chili powders can contain up to 40 percent salt.

a survey of the world's powders and spice blends

There are probably as many different powders and spice blends found around the world as there are individual spices. And each will have a flavor that is not only unique to its locale, but so intrinsically a part of the indigenous palate that its omission would completely change the character of a dish. Think of *choucroute* without caraway seeds or chicken *paprikash* without the paprika, which is the first and perhaps the most famous of the powders we discuss here.

Europe

The most famous spice powder in Europe is paprika, the name of which derives from the Hungarian *paparka*, a variation on the Bulgarian *piperka*, which in turn was derived from the Latin *piper*, for "pepper." In the United States, the term paprika simply means any nonpungent red chile, mostly New Mexican pod types that have had their pungency genetically removed. In Europe, however, paprika has much greater depth, having not only distinct pod types but also specific grades of the powders made from these pod types.

The most likely theory for the importation of paprika into Hungary hold that the Turks first became aware of chile peppers when they beseiged the Portuguese colony of Diu, near Calicut, India, in 1538. This theory suggests that the Turks learned of chile peppers during that battle and then transported them along the trade routes of their vast empire, which stretched from India to Central Europe. According to Leonhard Fuchs, an early German professor of medicine, chiles were cultivated in Germany by 1542, in England by 1548, and in the Balkans by 1569. Fuchs knew that the European chiles had been imported from India, so he called them "Calicut peppers."

First the Hungarian herdsmen flavored their stews with paprika, then the fishermen of the Danube added it to their fish dishes. From that point on, the landed gentry, the aristocracy, and the royal courts readily adopted the hot spice, and the Danube region developed Europe's first genuine chile cuisine. In the sunny south of

Hungary, the brilliant red pods decorated gardens everywhere, and even today, that part of the country is the heart of paprika country. In 1569, an aristocrat named Margit Szechy listed the foreign seeds she was planting in her garden in Hungary. On the list was "Turkisch rot Pfeffer" (Turkish red pepper) seeds, the first recorded instance of chiles in Hungary. Upon Mrs. Szechy's death and the subsequent division of her estate, her paprika plots were so valuable they were fought over bitterly by her daughters.

The famous "Hungarian flavor," which is unique to the cuisine of that country, is created by the combination of lard, paprika, and spices. Chopped onions are always cooked to translucency in the lard; paprika and sour cream are added to pan drippings after meats have been browned to make a rich sauce, which is then served over meat and peppers. There are many versions of hot and spicy recipes with the generic terms of *gulyas* ("goulash") and *paprikas* ("paprikash").

types of hungarian paprikas

NAME	HUNGARIAN NAME	DESCRIPTION
Special Quality	Különleges	The mildest and brightest red of all Hungarian paprikas, with excellent aroma.
Delicate	Csipmentes Csemege	Ranging from light to dark red, a mild paprika with a rich flavor.
Exquisite Delicate	Csemegepaprika	Similar to Delicate, but more pungent.
Pungent Exquisite Delicate	Csípös Csemege, Pikant	A yet more pungent Delicate.
Rose	Rózsa	Pale Red in color with strong aroma and mild pungency.
Noble Sweet	Édesnemes	The most commonly exported paprika; bright red and slightly pungent.
Half-Sweet	Félédes	A blend of mild and pungent paprikas; medium pungency.
Hot	Erös	Light brown in color, this is the hottest of all the paprikas.

Note: The hottest paprikas are not the bright red ones, but rather the palest red and light brown colored ones.

The great pepper-growing areas around Kalocsa and Szeged have just the right combination of soil characteristics, temperature, rainfall, and sunshine required to cultivate these plants successfully. In March, the pepper seeds are put in water to germinate, then transferred to greenhouse beds. Seven weeks later, in May, the small pepper shrubs are re-planted in the open fields. Harvesting starts at the end of the first week in September and lasts for about a month, depending on weather conditions. By harvest time, the mature plants will have grown to a height of sixteen to twenty-four inches. And the pepper pods—three to five inches long and about one to one and a half inches wide—will have ripened from green or yellow to bright red.

In Kalocsa, the annual harvest is celebrated with a paprika festival in September. Known as the Kalocsa Paprika Days, it features an exhibition of food products and agricultural machinery, a professional conference on the topic of paprika, various sports events, a "Paprika Cup" international chess tournament, and a fish soup cooking contest. But the highlight of all this is the Paprika Harvest Parade, complete with local bands and colorful folk-dancing groups, followed that same night by a Paprika Harvest Ball.

So how do those tons of newly-picked peppers get turned into the condiment known as paprika, in all of its many forms? Before the Industrial Revolution, farmers used to string all their ripe peppers by hand and hang them up in a protected place to dry. After a certain period of time, the drying process was completed in large earthenware ovens. The peppers were then crushed underfoot, and finally pounded into a powder by means of a *kulu*, a huge mortar with a large pestle driven by human power. Water mills later replaced the *kulu* for grinding paprika, and by the late 1800s steam engines were being used for this task.

But until the mid-1800s it was difficult to control the pungency of the paprika produced. The capsaicin that gives paprika its spicy flavor is found in the pod's veins and seeds, which were removed by hand before the crushed dried peppers were ground into a powder. This was a time-consuming and inexact process, which yielded paprikas in taste from rather mild to fairly hot. The results were unpredictable.

In 1859, the Palfy brothers of Szeged invented a machine for removing the veins and seeds, then grinding the dried pods into a quality-controlled powder. The mill-master could now determine exactly how much capsaicin was to be removed and how much should be retained. The Palfys' technique continued to be used in Hungarian factories for almost a century—until the fairly recent introduction of modern automatic machines that wash, dry, crush, sort, and grind the peppers in a continuous process.

The Palfys' invention made possible the large-scale commercial production of very mild ("Noble Sweet") paprika, which had a much bigger export market than the hotter-tasting varieties. As the industry expanded to meet both local and foreign demand for this mild (but still richly flavored) paprika, the growers saw the advantage of cultivating a spice pepper that did not need to have its veins and seeds removed.

Ferenc Horvath of Kalocsa developed the first variety of Hungarian pepper that was "sweet" throughout—meaning that its veins and seeds contained very little capsaicin indeed. This kind of pepper is now favored by growers in the regions of Kalocsa and Szeged. It can be used alone, ground to produce a mild but flavorful paprika powder—or in combination with other, hotter peppers to produce some of the standard varieties of paprika marketed by the Hungarians. But with all this emphasis on the demand-and-supply of *mild* paprika during the past one hundred years, one is tempted to speculate that Hungarian food *before* Horvath and the Palfys must have been much hotter than it is today.

We recommend that cooks use imported Hungarian paprika such as Szeged, and if it is too mild, they should heat it up with ground cayenne.

Other European spice blends include:

* Mixtures for curing fish that combine spices and herbs with salt and sugar. The spices are often black pepper, oregano, and dillweed (not seed). Gravlax, a traditional Swedish dish, is prepared by treating salmon with such a cure.
* Pickling spice, used in pickles of all kinds. This typically contains yellow mustard seed, black peppercorns, dill seed, fennel seed, allspice berries, cloves, bay leaves, cinnamon quills, and small hot chiles, all left whole.
* Quatre épices, used in charcuterie to cure meats such as salami. It contains white pepper, nutmeg, ground ginger, and cloves.

Africa and the Middle East

* *Baharat*, very popular in Turkey and the Middle East, is used much as the Indians use garam masala, to spice up meat (particularly lamb shanks) and vegetables. It contains paprika, black pepper, cumin seeds, coriander, cassia, cloves, cardamom, and nutmeg.
* *Berbere*, from Ethiopia, contains long pepper, chiles, cardamom, cumin, fenugreek, ginger, onions, garlic, paprika, allspice, nutmeg, and cloves. Raw meat flavored with *berbere* is a traditional Ethiopian dish known as *kifto*.
* *Charmoula* is a Moroccan spice paste made with onion, garlic, parsley, red chile, paprika, salt, and ground pepper. It is used to spice up fish and vegetables.
* *Dukkah*, from Egypt, is a mixture of spices and nuts. Bread is dipped in olive oil and then the *dukkah*. It is also used as a coating for chicken and fish. Hazelnuts, pistachios, sesame, coriander, cumin, salt, and black pepper are the main ingredients.

* *Harissa* comes from the Arabic word *harasa*, meaning to break, crush, or grind. This Tunisian spice paste is made from dried red chiles, garlic, cumin, mint, cinnamon, coriander, caraway, salt, and olive oil. It is mixed into salads, soups, stews, and couscous and is sometimes used as a sandwich spread. It can also be thinned with water, olive oil, and lemon juice to make a sauce used over grilled meats.
* *La kama* is a Moroccan spice mix used to flavor soups and stews. It contains black pepper, powdered ginger, turmeric, cinnamon, and nutmeg.
* *Mit'mit'a* is a very hot Ethiopian spice mixture containing chiles, cardamom, cloves, and salt.
* *Niter kebbe* is Ethiopian curried butter, a basic ingredient and a condiment for bread. It is made with fresh ginger, onion, garlic, butter, cayenne, cinnamon, fenugreek, cumin, basil, cardamom, oregano, turmeric, and nutmeg.
* *Qalat dagga*, also known as Tunisian five-spice seasoning, is used in lamb and vegetable dishes. It contains grains of paradise, or melegueta pepper, as well as cloves, black peppercorns, cinnamon, and nutmeg.
* *Ras el hanout* is a Moroccan spice mix containing up to twenty-five spices, herbs, and flowers. The name means "shopkeepers' choice," and there are hundreds of variations. Its most common ingredients are black pepper, chile, mace, fenugreek, cumin, cardamom, rosemary, thyme, and flower petals such as rose, orange, and saffron. It is commonly used to spice up *tajines*.
* *Tabil*, from Tunisia, is a blend of coriander, caraway, garlic, and crushed chile that is sprinkled over grilled meats.
* *Talia*, a Yemeni mix of fried onion and garlic mixed with chiles, is spread on toasted bread.
* *T'iqur qarya awaze* is an Ethiopian green chile paste containing jalapeños, bell peppers, garlic, fresh ginger, vegetable oil, cardamom, cilantro, and holy basil. It is used as a dip for bread and meats.
* *Wot* spices, used in Ethiopia to spice up *wots*, or stews, are a blend of chiles, black peppercorns, cloves, nutmeg, and turmeric.
* *Zahtar*, a North African mixture of sesame seed, sumac seed, thyme, and cayenne, is sprinkled over vegetables.
* *Zhug*, a spice paste from Yemen, contains cilantro, green chiles, garlic, cardamom, black pepper, and olive oil.

India

Curry is a name for a style of cooking, as well as for a spice mixture of nearly infinite variations. Since curry is now used worldwide, it has its own section in this chapter.

Other Indian spice mixtures include:

* *Chat masala*, a potato seasoning made with ground asafetida, mint, ginger, *ajowan*, cayenne, salt, mango powder, cumin, and dried pomegranate seeds.
* Garam masala, a spice mixture similar to curry powder from northern India, used to flavor meats and vegetables. It contains cumin, coriander, cardamom, black peppercorns, cloves, mace, bay leaf, and cinnamon.
* *Panch phoran*, a seed and spice mixture used on fried potatoes that contains brown mustard, nigella, cumin, fenugreek, and fennel seed.
* *Sambhar* powder, used in South Indian soups. It is made of coriander seed, *besan* flour, cumin seed, black peppercorns, salt, fenugreek, brown mustard seed, chile powder, cinnamon, turmeric, curry leaves, and asafetida powder.
* Tea spice, used to flavor tea. It contains ground ginger, black pepper, mint, cardamom, cloves, and nutmeg.

Asia

* *Bumbu* is an Indonesian spice paste containing onions, chile, garlic, lemongrass, galangal, and ginger.
* Chinese five-spice powder is used to season pork and duck and contains star anise, fennel seeds, cassia or cinnamon, Sichuan pepper or black pepper, and cloves. Added to salt and heated, it makes five-spice salt, which is used as a dip or condiment with roasted, grilled, or fried meats.
* *Sambal* is an Indonesian spice paste with chiles, onions, garlic, fish sauce, tamarind, and brown sugar.
* *Shichimi togarashi*, also known as Japanese seven-flavor powder, is a seasoning and condiment for Japanese soups, noodle dishes, and tempura. It contains chile flakes, powdered Sichuan pepper leaves (*sansho*), black and white sesame seeds, tangerine peel, marijuana seeds, white poppy seeds, and brown mustard seed.
* Thai curry pastes, called *kaengs*, contain chiles, cumin, coriander, onions, peppercorns, mint, lemongrass, ginger, and garlic, and sometimes cinnamon, cloves, mace, nutmeg, and shallots.

The Caribbean and Latin America

* Adobo powder, a popular seasoning in the Spanish Caribbean, is combined with fruit juices and fresh garlic to make a marinade. It contains salt, white peppercorns, cumin, and garlic powder.
* Bajan seasoning, from Barbados, is a seasoning paste used as a marinade for meats and chicken and is added to soups and stews. It contains green onions,

lime juice, fresh parsley, thyme, marjoram, chives, garlic, habanero chiles, paprika, cloves, and salt.

* *Chimichurri*, an Argentinian spice paste, contains ají chiles, garlic, peppercorns, oregano, bay leaf, and parsley. It is used on grilled meat and poultry.
* Colombo curry paste, named after the capital of Sri Lanka, is used in Martinique and Guadeloupe. It contains turmeric, coriander, mustard seed, black peppercorns, cumin, garlic, ginger, and habanero chiles.
* Jerk seasoning can be in dry, paste, or sauce form, and is used to marinate smoke-grilled pork and chicken in Jamaica and other Caribbean islands. Based on allspice (pimento), this spice mixture also contains dried thyme, powdered ginger, black pepper, cloves, nutmeg, and cinnamon. Jerk seasoning is often made and stored as a powder, and later added to onion, green onions, habanero chiles, brown sugar, dark rum, and soy sauce to make a cooking paste or sauce.
* Trinidad curry paste contains coriander, anise, cloves, cumin, fenugreek, peppercorns, mustard seed, turmeric, garlic, onion, and habanero chiles.
* Trinidad herb seasoning paste uses Spanish thyme, a succulent plant also called Indian borage, and habanero chiles, green onions, parsley, celery leaves, garlic, vinegar, salt, and ground ginger. It is used as a marinade for meat and chicken.
* West Indian masala is a transplanted version of the Indian masala used to flavor meats and fish. It contains coriander, fenugreek, fennel seed, mustard seed, cumin seed, and chile powder.

North America

Moles Perhaps the most famous spice mixtures in North America are the Mexican *moles*. The word *mole*, from the Náhuatl *molli*, means "mixture," as in *guacamole*, a mixture of vegetables (*guaca*). Some sources say that the word is taken from the Spanish verb *moler*, meaning to grind. Whatever its precise origin, the word used by itself embraces a vast number of sauces utilizing every imaginable combination of meats, vegetables, spices, and flavorings—sometimes up to three dozen different ingredients. Not only are there many ingredients, there are dozens of variations on mole—red moles, green moles, brown moles, fiery moles, and even mild moles.

The earliest moles were simple compared with what was to come after the Spanish invasion. Ana M. de Benítez, who reconstructed pre-Columbian dishes based on de Sahagún's descriptions, used four different chiles (ancho, mulato, pasilla, and chipotle), plus tomatoes, garlic, pumpkins, tomatillos, and chayote as the basis of her moles. The addition of Eastern Hemisphere ingredients such as almonds, raisins, garlic, cinnamon, and cloves would eventually transform the basic mole of the Aztecs into a true delicacy.

Mole poblano, originally called *mole de olores* ("fragrant mole"), is the sauce traditionally served on special occasions such as Christmas that combines chiles and chocolate, a popular and revered food of the Aztecs. Moctezuma's court consumed fifty jugs of chile-laced hot chocolate a day, and warriors drank it to soothe their nerves before going into battle. However, the story of how chocolate was combined with chile sauces does not involve warriors, but rather nuns.

Legend holds that *mole poblano* was invented in the sixteenth century by the nuns of the convent of Santa Rosa in the city of Puebla. It seems that the archbishop was coming to visit, and the nuns were worried because they had no food elegant enough to serve someone of his eminence. So, they prayed for guidance and one of the nuns had a vision. She directed that everyone in the convent should begin chopping and grinding everything edible they could find in the kitchen. Into a pot went chiles, tomatoes, nuts, sugar, tortillas, bananas, raisins, garlic, avocados, and dozens of herbs and spices. The final ingredient was the magic one: chocolate. The chocolate, they reasoned, would smooth the flavor of the sauce by slighly cutting its heat. Then the nuns slaughtered their only turkey and served it with the mole sauce to the archbishop, who declared it the finest dish he had ever tasted.

This is a great legend, but a more likely scenario holds that the basic mole of the Aztecs was gradually transformed by a collision of cuisines. Regarding the use of chocolate, since that delicacy was reserved for Aztec royalty, the military nobility, and religious officials, perhaps Aztec serving girls at the convent gave a royal recipe to the nuns so they could honor their royalty, the archbishop. At any rate, the recipe for *mole poblano* was rescued from oblivion and became a holiday favorite. De Benítez noted: "In the book on Puebla cooking, published in Puebla in 1877, we find recipes for making forty-four kinds of mole; there are also sixteen kinds of *manchamanteles* (tablecloth stainers), which are dishes with different kinds of chiles."

In Mexico today, cooks who specialize in moles are termed *moleros*, and they even have their own competition, the National Mole Fair held every year in October at the town of San Pedro Atocpan, just south of Mexico City. At the fair, thousands of people sample hundreds of different moles created by restaurateurs and mole wholesalers. This fair is the Mexican equivalent of chili con carne cookoffs in the United States; the *moleros* take great pride in their fiery creations and consider each mole a work of art in the same way that chili cookoff chefs regard their chili con carne. Often the preparation of a family mole recipe takes as long as three days. Their recipes are family secrets not to be revealed to others under any circumstances; indeed, they are passed down from generation to generation.

"If one of my children wants to carry on my business as a *molero* and is serious about it," *molero* Villa Suarez told reporter William Stockton, I will tell them all the

The collision of Aztec tradition and Eastern ingredients raised the level of traditional moles to that of a true delicacy.

secrets when the time comes." But he went on to indicate that if his children were not interested in becoming moleros, his secrets would die with him.

In 1963 a group of *moleros* formed a mole cooperative of sixty partners who banded together for the good of their craft. They shared equipment such as pulverizers and mills, and eventually organized a fair exclusively dedicated to mole, so they formed the *Feria Nacional del Mole*, the National Mole Fair, held in conjunction with the fairs of the local pueblos.

By 1982, the fair had grown so large that the committee moved the location and the date to accomodate all the visitors. The mole fair became a national event and was eventually placed on the Secretary of Tourism's calendar of fairs and fiestas. Each year bigger and better events were presented. As a result, restaurants began featuring more mole specials and tourists had more opportunities to experience the various moles. The National Mole Fair has certainly become one of the premier chile pepper events in the world.

The color of a particular mole depends mostly upon the varieties of chiles utilized. A green mole consists mostly of poblano chiles while a red mole could contain three or four different varieties of dried red chiles, such as chiles de árbol, or cascabels. The brown and black moles owe their color to pasillas and anchos, both of which are sometimes called "chile negro" because of their dark hues when dried. The dark color of *mole negro* can also be the result of roasting the chiles until they are almost black, as is the custom in Oaxaca.

Other than chiles, there are literally dozens of other ingredients added to the various moles, including almonds, anise, bananas, chocolate, cinnamon, cilantro, cloves, coconut, garlic, onions, peanuts, peppercorns, piñons, pumpkin seeds, raisins, sesame seeds, toasted bread, tomatillos, tomatoes, tortillas, and walnuts. Undoubtedly, some *moleros* add coriander, cumin, epazote, oregano, thyme, and other spices to their moles.

But Puebla is not the only state in Mexico with a reputation for moles. Oaxaca, in the south, lays claim to seven unique moles—and dozens and dozens of variations. In *Tradiciones Gastronómicas Oaxaqueñas*, the author, Ana Maria Guzmán de Vasquez Colmenares, noted: "There must be something magical in the number seven, for the number of Oaxacan moles coincides with the wonders of the world, the theological virtues, the wise men of Athens—and for their wisdom which elected the number seven to represent justice."

"There may be seven moles," say the locals, "but thousands and thousands of cooks each has their own private version of all of the moles, so how many does that make?" One magazine writer suggested: "Oaxaca should be the land of 200 moles!"

Mole recipes are family secrets, passed down from generation to generation.

For the record, the seven moles are: *mole negro, mole coloradito, mole verde, mole amarillo, mole rojo, manchas manteles*, and *mole chichilo*. They are all descendants of *clemole*, believed to be the original mole of Oaxaca. It was quite simple, being composed of ancho and pasilla chiles, garlic, cloves, cinnamon, and coriander.

The Oaxacan moles are characterized by unusual chiles that are unique to the region. There are sixty chiles grown only in the state of Oaxaca and nowhere else in Mexico. Of those sixty, about ten commonly appear in the Oaxaca city market. Some of these unusal chiles include *chiles de agua*, which grow erect and are pointed at the end. The *chiles chilhuacle*, which are short and fat, come in two varieties, black and red. The red variety is called "the saffron of the poor" because a small amount of ground *chilhuacle rojo* gives similar coloring to foods. Other unique chiles are the red-orange *chiles onzas*, the yellow *costeño*, and the *pasilla Oaxaqueña* (sometimes called *pasilla Mexicana*), a smoked pasilla that adds a chipotle-like flavor to moles.

Instead of tediously grinding all the ingredients on a *metate* these days, many cooks go to the Benito Juárez market, buy all their chiles, nuts, and seeds, and have them custom-ground in the special *molinos*, or mills in another section of the market. The result is a dark paste which is later converted into a mole sauce. The chiles are toasted black, soaked and ground, and blended with fried tomatoes, tomatillos, and roasted garlic and onions. Then come nuts and seeds—some toasted, some fried. The cooks use almonds, peanuts, pecans, chile seeds, and sesame seeds. There are almost always more sesame seeds than any other seed or nut. They have to be fried slowly and carefully, with lots of love and attention. Hence the affectionate Mexican *dicho* (saying): "You are the sesame seed of my mole."

There are other special ingredients which characterize the different Oaxacan moles. Avocado leaves, difficult to find in the United States and Canada, are used in *mole negro*. Fresh green herbs such as epazote and parsley are the source of the green color of *mole verde*. Pineapple and banana are added to *manchas manteles*, while string beans, chayote and *chiles costeños* are ingredients in *mole amarillo*.

Many different meats are added to moles, from chicken to beef to fish, but by far the most common meat served is turkey. In fact, turkey is so important in *mole negro*, that Mexican writer Manuel Toussaint noted that the turkey in the mole was as important as the eagle in the Mexican flag, and another writer suggested that to refuse to eat *mole negro* was a crime of treason against the homeland!

Barbecue Rubs Meat that is to be grilled or smoked is often treated with spice mixtures and marinades of various types before, during, and after the cooking process.

Now, of course, in the contentious world of barbecue, there is a great debate not only about which of these marinades to use, but whether or not to use them in the first place. Many grillers, for example, would never use a rub on their sirloin steak. And you'll hear it time and time again from the smoking purists: good barbecue doesn't need condiments. No rubs, no marinades, no sops, no sauces. If that's so, please tell us why nearly every recipe you can find for Texas barbecued brisket contains at least two of the three following steps:

1. Massage a rub into the meat and let stand for half an hour before smoking.
2. Apply a sop during the smoking process.
3. Serve the sliced meat topped with a barbecue sauce.

In some recipes, the sliced meat is mixed with the barbecue sauce and allowed to sit before serving. In other recipes, the meat sits in the sop, and barbecue sauces are omitted. Some barbecuers claim that brisket and ribs get a better crust when a rub rather than a sop is used. What we are talking about here is personal preference. Cooking is more of an art than an exact science, which is why at any given time, there are tens of thousands of cookbooks to be found, containing millions of recipes!

Rubs are essentially dry spice mixtures. A rub can be as simple as crushed black pepper, or as elaborate as a jerk or curry rub. Its purpose is to add intense flavor to the meat without excessive moisture. A paste is a rub with a little moisture—usually water, beer, or oil—added to bind it. Generally speaking, rubs are used more with meat and poultry and pastes more with seafood. A notable exception to this rule is Jamaican jerk pork, which can be treated with either a jerk rub, a jerk paste, or in some cases (mostly outside Jamaica), a jerk sauce.

The most important thing to remember about making rubs is to use the freshest possible ingredients, not the ground oregano that's been in your cupboard since 1986. Older spices and herbs oxidize, or turn rancid, and either lose flavor or gain a flavor you don't want on your meat. Buy spices such as mustard, black pepper, cumin, and coriander in whole form and grind them yourself. The same goes for chile peppers—buy the pods, not the powder. Spices should preferably be fresh, but we've bought some incredible dried Mexican oregano in bulk. Dry fresh spices in the microwave and then crush them in a mortar.

You can use a spice mill, a coffee grinder, or a mortar and pestle to make the rubs; just remember not to grind the mixture too finely. The object is not to allow the herbs and spices to release too much of their essential oils, as can happen through the friction and heat of the grinder motor.

Rubs—and particularly pastes—do not store all that well. If you must store a rub, put it in a small jar with a tight seal and place it in a cool, dry cupboard, or in the freezer. Oxygen and light are the enemies of a rub. Pastes can be stored for a few days only in the refrigerator.

Dry rubs are massaged into the meat or poultry, lightly covered, and allowed to sit for as little as a half hour, or as long as a day. When using pastes on seafood, completely cover the shrimp or fish or whatever in the paste, then wrap it tightly in plastic wrap to more fully infuse it with flavor. The same technique works with pastes applied to meat or poultry.

Debates continue to rage about the use of rubs in the barbecue process. Some people state that the rub seals the meat, keeping the juices in, but others warn that salt in the rub will draw out the juices, and they will evaporate. (Most rubs have a little salt in them.) At least one home physicist theorizes that the dryness of the rub attracts moisture from the air and actually adds it to the meat, but this is doubtful. Barbecue writer Richard Langer explains, "A rub draws a portion of the juices from a cut of meat to the surface, there to mingle with the seasoning and form a crust encasing the rest of the meat's juices and flavors."

Food chemistry expert Harold McGee disagrees: "Any crust that forms around the surface of the meat is not waterproof." In the end, it seems, if we use food common sense and don't add additional salt before smoking, and we don't worry about moisture loss—smoked meats are *supposed* to lose moisture as they tenderize—rubs simply add flavor and help make a tasty crust, or burned ends, or bark, as barbecuers call the crust on the thin end of the brisket.

Other North American spice mixtures of note are:

* *Recado*, from the Yucatán of Central America, is a seasoning paste made with annatto seeds, oregano, peppercorns, cinnamon, cloves, allspice, cumin, garlic, and sometimes ancho chiles. It is used to season meats and poultry.
* Cajun spices for blackening meats include paprika, basil, garlic powder, onion flakes, salt, black pepper, fennel seeds, parsley, ground cinnamon, thyme, white pepper, and cayenne.
* Shrimp or crab boil spices are available in several commercial mixtures, the most famous of which is Old Bay Seasoning, made by McCormick & Company. It contains, according to the label, celery seed, salt, mustard, red pepper, black pepper, bay leaves, cloves, allspice, ginger, mace, cardamom, cinnamon, and paprika. Other similar blends contain tarragon, coriander, fennel seed, thyme, and lemon zest in addition to the Old Bay ingredients.

When making a rub, use the freshest ingredients possible.

worldwide curry

Curries are by far the most wide-ranging spice mixtures in the world, so we've done quite a bit of research on the subject. People often think all curries are the same, but this is simply not true; in fact, it merely reflects the similarity of dishes cooked with commercial curry powders. During the research for this book, we kept track of every single ingredient that appeared in curries throughout the world, from *ajowan* (bishop's weed) to yogurt. After eliminating the common meats, fruits, and vegetables, we still counted sixty-six separate ingredients, not including the different types of chile peppers and black pepper.

With such a huge number of ingredients, curries are enormously varied. "Contrary to popular belief," notes Sri Lankan food importer Anura Saparamadu, "there are about as many types of curries as there are spices." And given the total number of curry ingredients, the combinations and permutations of those ingredients provide a nearly infinite variety of flavors in curries. "Even the best Indian cooks will argue endlessly over the inclusion and exclusion of particular spices and herbs," adds Santha Rama Rau, author of *The Cooking of India*.

During our travels, we have dined on curries in India, England, Thailand, Singapore, Malaysia, Australia, Jamaica, and Trinidad, in addition to those made in many Indian restaurants in the United States. We can testify that curries made with fresh ingredients are some of the tastiest culinary creations ever cooked up.

Early History

Curry's oldest tradition, of course, is in India. Some of the spices used in curries—namely cumin, saffron, and fennel—were being ground on stones as early as 4000 B.C. in the Indus Valley, but we have no idea if these spices were actually used in curry-like dishes. We also do not know if the spices were cultivated, collected in the wild, or acquired through trade with other peoples.

Although there is no definitive proof, we suspect that curries originated in the south of India, on the Malabar Coast of Kerala. Here black pepper, cinnamon, turmeric, and cardamom first grew wild, and it was centuries before they spread into the other regions. Interestingly enough, cultivation of the spices was somewhat haphazard; some authorities believe that they were collected in the wild rather than actually farmed.

Although curries per se are not described until much later, curry spices such as black pepper and turmeric are mentioned in the Vedas, the ancient sacred literature of the Hindus, which date from approximately 1500 B.C. (some authorities claim an earlier date of about 5000 B.C.). Nutmeg, mace, saffron, and cardamom were ingredients in candies and perfumes used in early Indian nuptial ceremonies. In Epic Period literature dating from around 2000 B.C., curry spices such as black pepper and mustard are mentioned in the preparation of young buffaloes for banquets.

The Malabar Coast became renowned for its black pepper, cinnamon, ginger, and cardamom as growers there sold the spices to the Phoenicians and the Arabs. As legend holds, Saint Thomas visited the region soon after Christ's crucifixion and was to stay only a few days. But after he tasted the shrimp curries and drank the beverages, he decided to stay for quite a while!

Most of the Malabar's spices were carried to Alexandria for reexport around the Mediterranean. According to S. N. Mahindru, author of *Spices in Indian Life*, "After 700 B.C., the Indian spice trade saw a boom never seen before, because the rich clove and cinnamon-growing areas of Ceylon and Moluccas came under the sovereignty of Bengal kings. The principal traders and shippers were the Arabs, the Dravidians, and the Phoenicians, who shipped spices to their respective markets of good profits." Indian traders also imported spices and other goods from the Spice Islands, China, and Cambodia for reexport.

India supplied ginger to Romans via the Arabs, as well as black pepper, cassia, cinnamon, and cardamom. The Arabs cleverly concealed their Indian connection, spreading rumors that the spices were from Ethiopia, but the Romans eventually did discover the "monsoon route" to India and did some trading directly. However they got them, they paid dearly for their spices, and the only currencies acceptable to the Indians and their Arab intermediaries were wine, gold, and silver. The Roman historian and poet Pliny observed, "No year passes in which India does not impoverish us of fifty million sesterces." The huge payments for spices triggered an economic crisis in Rome, which was unable to pay its armies. Without an army, Rome was at the mercy of the "barbarian" invaders. Thus the Roman lust for spices was one of the factors that brought about the fall of the Roman Empire.

One of the first written mentions of curry-style cookery is attributed to Athenaeus, a Greek miscellanist who lived about A.D. 200. In his *Deiponosophistai* (The Gastronomers), a fascinating survey of classical food and dining habits, he quotes Megasthenes, the third-century B.C. author of *Indica*: "Among the Indians at a banquet a table is set before each individual . . . and on the table is placed a golden dish, in which they first throw boiled rice . . . and then they add many sorts of meat dressed after the Indian fashion."

The first specific mention of curry we could find in Indian literature comes from the longest epic poem in any language (88,000 couplets), the *Mahabharata*, written about A.D. 400 (some sources say the first century A.D.). In one section of the poem, Bhima addresses Yudhishthira about how he planned to live in disguise in the kingdom of King Virata: "I shall appear as the ex-cook of King Yudhishthira as I am well-versed in the culinary art. I shall prepare King Virata's curries and shall supercede even those experts who used to make curries for him before."

The spice trade boomed in medieval India (roughly A.D. 600 to 1500). At the center of it all was Calicut, a city eight miles in circumference described by the Italian traveler Nicolo Contai in 1430 as the "spice emporium of the East . . . a notable emporium for the whole of India, abounding in pepper, aloe, ginger, a larger kind of cinnamon, and zedoary." The Arab chronicler Abder-Razzakm described Calicut in 1442: "One of the greatest shipping centers in the world in this period, from where vessels are continually sailing for Mecca which are for the most part laden with pepper." Other spice products available in Calicut were turmeric and cloves.

These were the riches that awaited the Europeans, who, finally realizing that Africa was not the land of spices despite Arab misinformation, had sailed on to India. The Portuguese were the first to arrive, led by Vasco da Gama, who reached Calicut in 1498. Pedro Alvarez Cabral followed soon after, with 1,500 men in thirty-three ships, and began capturing Arab ships laden with spices. But the local Nairs fought back, destroying much of his armada.

Da Gama returned in force to the Malabar Coast in 1501, fought with the costal principalities, and finally made peace with the maharaja of Cochin, Unni Rama Verma. A deal was soon struck. "In my country, there is abundant cinnamon, pepper, cloves, and nutmeg," said the maharaja. "What I need from your country is gold, silver, coral, and scarlett [cloth]."

The Portuguese captain was allowed to load five ships with pepper, cardamom, and other spices; before he left, he demanded Portuguese exclusivity for the spice trade and the right to build factories and garrisons. A treaty was finally approved in 1513, and the people of Calicut agreed to a Portuguese monopoly on the spice trade from the Malabar Coast. But the Portuguese sailors deserted to the better-paying ships of private merchants, and the Portuguese fell behind on their payments for pepper and other spices.

The Portuguese forever changed curries by introducing chile peppers, which became the principal hot spice in curries from then on. After Christopher Columbus brought chile peppers and their seeds back from the New World in 1493, they had been grown mostly by monks in monasteries. Portuguese explorers carried the chiles to their

The first
mention
of curry in
Indian literature
occurs in the
Mahabharata,
written about
A.D. 400.

ports in Africa and Goa, India, shortly thereafter. Although the exact date of chiles' introduction into India is not known, most experts believe that it was in the early 1500s.

Garcia Orta, a Portuguese chronicler, wrote in 1593: "This Capsicum or Indian pepper is diligently cultivated in castles by gardeners and also by women in their kitchens and house gardens." Nowadays, India is the world's largest producer of chiles, with over two million acres under cultivation. Chiles have become an integral part of Indian cooking and religious lore. Believed to ward off the "evil eye," they are hung for that purpose in many houses and offices, or burned in the kitchen.

The Portuguese remained in India for 450 years; although they colonized only a small part of the subcontinent, they created a world market for Indian spices.

The Moghuls and the British Raj

From the eighth through the sixteenth centuries A.D., India was subjected to a series of Muslim invasions. Turkish tribes swept through India from the west, and the Moghuls invaded from the northwest and settled across most of northern India. There were periodic Muslim kingdoms established in northern India, but not until 1526 did Babur, a descendant of Genghis Khan, conquer Punjab and declare himself emperor of India. So began the Moghul rule of India, which lasted until the beginning of the nineteenth century.

During the sixteenth century, land routes across India began to connect the spice-growing south with northern India, Central Asia, Afghanistan, Tibet, and Bhutan. During the rule of Akbar (1556–1605), the greatest of the Moghul emperors, the cultivation of spices was encouraged all over India, especially in Punjab, where mustard, ginger, poppy seed, sesame, turmeric, coriander, cumin, and chile peppers were grown. Interestingly enough, although Portuguese missionaries attended Akbar's court in Delhi, the Moghuls hardly knew of the Europeans' lucrative spice trade along the Malabar Coast.

The Moghuls not only constructed some of the most beautiful buildings in the subcontinent—including the Taj Mahal—but were great patrons of musicians, artists, and cooks. Feasts in the Moghul courts included classical music of the time, great storytelling sessions, and food fit for—well, emperors.

Akbar's prime minister, Abul-Fazl, in his book *Ain-i-Akbari* (1602), compiled a list of numerous dishes and the curry spices used in them; this is the first mention of chile peppers in Indian cookery. One of the favorite dishes of Akbar's court was a Mughlai curry called *do-piyaza*, or "two onions," which combined four pounds of onions with twenty pounds of meat, seasoned with crushed red chiles, cumin, coriander, cardamom, cloves, and black pepper. Abul-Fazl also recorded the market prices of the various spices;

from most to least expensive, they were saffron, cloves, cardamom, cinnamon, chiles, long pepper, turmeric, dried ginger, coriander, anise seed, fresh ginger, and cumin. Saffron, at four hundred *dinars* per *seer* (900 grams), was two hundred times more expensive than cumin. Today, saffron is still the most expensive spice in the world.

Meanwhile, farther south, the British watched with envy as both the Portuguese and the Dutch prospered with the spice trade in India and the Spice Islands. The British East India Company was founded in London in 1599, with Queen Elizabeth of England granting the company the sole British right to trade with India. The first company ship, the *Hector*, arrived in India the following year, landing at Surat, north of Bombay. The captain of the *Hector*, William Hawkins, searched the interior for jewels and spices and was greeted at the Moghul court by the emperor Jahangir, probably the world's most powerful and wealthy ruler. Jahangir promptly made Hawkins a member of his court and presented him with the most beautiful woman in his harem. He also signed a trade agreement with the British East India Company, which allowed the company to establish trading depots near Bombay. The British had finally established a toehold in India, and by 1626 they had trading centers on both coasts of India.

By 1664, the Dutch had driven the Portuguese out of the Malabar Coast and were competing with the British to buy spices and sell them in Europe. Unable to best the British, however, they were forced to abandon their Indian interests by the end of the eighteenth century, when they concentrated on their holdings in the Spice Islands.

The British influence in India grew stronger after the Dutch left. As early as 1694, the British had established their main pepper factory at Tellicherry because of its "proximity to the finest pepper and cardamom lands of the Malabar," as the company stated. Around 1740, the British East India Company began to establish large pepper, coconut, and cinnamon plantations. Despite the company's motto, "Trade, not territory," India's unstable political situation left a vacuum that the company filled, extending its political influence.

The company's ambitions were not unopposed, however; as soon as Siraj-ud-daula took the throne of the Moghul Empire in 1756, he marched his troops to Calcutta and captured the British-controlled Fort William. That victory led to the imprisonment of about a hundred British soldiers in the infamous "Black Hole of Calcutta," in which all but twenty soldiers died. The suffering of the soldiers inspired generations of Englishmen with a desire to "civilize" India.

The British struck back in 1757 under the leadership of Robert Clive. With an army of 3,000 men, Clive regained Calcutta, soundly defeated the Moghuls, and—in effect—became the king of Bengal. So began the British plunder of India. By 1800 the British East India Company had taken the Malabar Coast by force and also controlled

Bengal and Madurai. The British established "spice gardens" in what is now the state of Tamil Nadu in south India to encourage more scientific cultivation of cinnamon and nutmeg, as well as introducing the cultivation of cloves.

During this time, the British government, realizing the enormous potential for wealth in India and disturbed by the abuses of the East India Company, took control. In 1818 India was made part of the British Empire, and by 1833 the East India Company had lost the right to trade in India. The British would control India until its partition in 1947.

English citizens stationed in India in the early days of the Raj had no choice but to eat native foods because of the difficulty of obtaining British imports. As Jennifer Brennan noted in her book *Curries and Bugles*, "The cooks were talented, mostly. Goanese, Nepalese, Madrassi or Bengali, they had served long apprenticeships with a variety of families and were well used to the idiosyncracies of British tastes. [They] all could, naturally, produce a wide range of Indian food, accented by the regional tastes of their home provinces."

The British may have looted India to a great extent, but they also did some good, especially in the field of agriculture, as India became the world's largest producer of spices. After satisfying the spice demand at home, the country now not only leads the world in chile production but also accounts for 20 percent of the world's black pepper, 50 percent of its dried ginger, 90 percent of its cardamom, and copious amounts of turmeric, saffron, cumin, cloves, fenugreek, cinnamon, and fennel.

The Raj Reversed

While England spread curries around the globe through colonization and emigration, it was slowly itself becoming the curry capital of the world—India included. How ironic, for a country infamous for its bland foods! The British were prepared for the word *curry* as early as 1390 with the appearance of the first English cookbook, *Forme of Cury* (The Art of Cookery). The words *cury* and *curry* were linked by black pepper, galangal, cumin, coriander, cinnamon, cloves, and cardamom—the most popular spices in that early cookbook.

In *Forme of Cury*, hot spices were considered, according to culinary historian L. Patrick Coyle, an "essential luxury" for their digestive qualities and their ability to mask the tastes and odors of food spoilage. "Pepper was the most highly prized," wrote Coyle, "followed by ginger and a related root called galingal, then cubeb, a berry whose taste suggests allspice and peppercorn, and clove, cinnamon, cardamom, cumin, and coriander." Given the fact that all of these spices appear in curries, it was inevitable that the English would warmly embrace Indian curries.

Curry spices were in such demand that around the end of the fifteenth century, Portuguese ships were smuggling black pepper and other Indian spices into England. When the ship *La Rose* was seized by the coast guard at Poole Harbor in England in 1486, she had 1,223 pounds of black pepper aboard and nearly that weight in cloves and ginger. Spices were still being smuggled into England as late as 1750.

In his play *Love for Love* (1695), William Congreve mentioned the pocket nutmeg graters that eventually became very popular in the eighteenth century. During the Georgian period, it became fashionable in London for spices to be sprinkled over food from sterling silver cinnamon casters called muffineers.

Spices were not only added to foods and medicines, they were also blended. An early currylike powder recipe from 1682 called for two ounces of ginger and one ounce each of powdered black pepper, cloves, nutmeg, and cinnamon—the whole blend further mixed with another pound of pepper!

Perhaps the first published recipe for "currey" appeared in 1747 in Hannah Glasse's *Art of Cookery*: a stewed chicken spiced with turmeric, ginger, and fine black pepper. In 1780 *Forme of Cury* was finally printed in book form, and around this time recipes in other cookbooks called for premixed curry powder, which was just beginning to appear in the country. And no wonder! As famed British food writer Elizabeth David notes, "In the case of curries, the complexity and the preparation of the correct spices must have been daunting for even the kitchen staffs of eighteenth and nineteen century England, accustomed though they were to pounding and bashing, mashing and sieving. Some curry ingredients such as poppy seeds and fenugreek are so hard that it is impossible to pound them in an ordinary mortar. . . . Given the difficulties, it is not surprising that ready-prepared curry powders found and find such immediate acceptance." Curry mixes were probably brought back to England by army officers and civil servants serving in India; but by all indications, curry powder production on the subcontinent was a small cottage industry at that time.

Indians themselves soon came to England. After African slavery ended in the 1830s, Indians arrived in England, but not as indentured laborers, as they were in the colonies. Rather, they were a relatively inexpensive source of labor and worked as *ayahs* (nannies), servants, and sailors. Some were students or took civil servant exams, but no matter what their function, the Indians began to influence English food. In the 1840s Charles Francatelli, chief cook to Queen Victoria, provided a recipe for "Indian Curry Sauce" in his book *The Modern Cook*. The recipe called for "Cook's or Bruce's curry paste," so it is evident that English curry products were being made by that time.

According to Indian food expert Julie Sahni, the oldest curry powder factory in India, M. M. Ponjiaji & Co., was founded around 1868. Their recipe is still a closely guarded family secret, she writes, which has remained unchanged since the beginning of the company. The company exported curry powders extensively to England, as did other entrepreneurs.

Near the end of the nineteenth century, a single dinner in India was responsible for a surge of interest in curry in England and Europe. As the story goes, an Englishman named Sharwood dined with the maharaja of Madras; during their meal, the maharaja mentioned a master curry maker named Vencatachellum, who sold his powder in his own shop. Sharwood later visited the shop and somehow obtained the secret recipe for what would later be called Madras curry powder: Chittagong saffron, turmeric, cumin, Kerala coriander, and Orissa chiles.

When Sharwood returned to England, he had a license to import Madras curry powder, along with a pickle of fruits, ginger, sugar, vinegar, and chiles—the first imported chutney. As food historian Maguelonne Toussaint-Samat recounts, "Initially sold only in the best English grocers' shops, curry and chutney soon conquered Europe, and in 1889, at the time of the World Exhibition in Paris, the French Colonial Ministry fixed the legal composition of curry powder sold in France." Today, the Sharwood brand owns a significant market share of the sale of Indian foods in the U.K.

During the heyday of the British Raj in India, roughly from 1858 to the end of World War I, Indian food became very popular in England, its popularity reflecting the English love affair with India. Cookbook author Mulk Raj Anand notes the "peculiar gastronomic enjoyment that curry seems to evoke in the English palate, and the warm associations which it brings into the English mind about India." For British Army aficionados of Indian cooking, the "finishing" of a particular dish with just the right mixture of spices became a hobby, and former officers took pride in their special blends of spices to make the perfect curry.

One of the greatest proponents of curries around this time was Robert Christie. He entertained his friends at the Edinburgh Cap and Gown Club by preparing extensive, full-scale banquets from the regional cuisines of India, with a heavy emphasis on curries. More than thirty curries are described in his section of *Banquets of the Nations*, published in England in 1911. Each of the recipes is individually spiced—no prepared curry powders are called for in the book.

One of the English curry favorites was mulligatawny soup. Countess Morphy, in her 1935 book *Recipes of All Nations*, cites an early British cookbook writer, Dr. Kitchener, about this soup: "Mullaga-tawny signifies pepper-water. The progress of inexperienced peripatetic Palaticians has lately been arrested by this outlandish word being pasted on the windows of English coffee-houses." There are literally dozens of different versions of mulligatawny, using chicken, veal, rabbit, and mutton as the basic meat.

The oldest curry powder factory in India was founded around 1868; their recipe remains a closely guarded secret.

At least one restaurant in London was serving curries around 1930. M. F. K. Fisher wrote in *With Bold Knife and Fork* that the greatest curry she ever ate was in an unnamed "famous Indian restaurant" that served curries labeled "mild" and "hot." Fisher, having been raised in southern California, "before Mexican cooking adjusted itself to the timid palates of invaders from Iowa," boldly said, "Oh, hot, of course." Soon after tasting the curry, tears started streaming down her cheeks. A thoughtful but ill-advised waiter placed a bowl of cracked ice by her bowl, "and everytime I ate a bowl of the curried whatever-it-was, I followed it with a mouthful of the temporary balm." And temporary it was, for "the next day," she wrote, "the insides of my lips were finely and thoroughly blistered." The waiter should have served her yogurt, a surefire burn cure.

In the early 1930s, letters about curries began appearing in the *Times of London*, keeping the love of the subject alive. Mulk Raj Anand noted that "references to the files

Making Freshly Ground Curry Powders

Since grinding a spice into a powder exposes more of its surface area to the air, spices oxidize more quickly in powder form, quickly losing volatile oils and flavor components. We advise cooks to make only enough powder to cook one meal and to avoid storing leftover powder. However, we realize that some cooks will make quite a volume of powder and, being frugal, will store it. In this case, we advise using as small a jar as possible and sealing the top tightly.

Curry pastes store better than powders because the moisture in them retards oxidation and traps the spice oils. But the moisture is also a breeding ground for fungi and bacteria, so pastes should always be refrigerated. Some cooks place a thin layer of vegetable oil over the paste to reduce oxidation even more.

The first step in making curry powder is to roast the spices. This is accomplished by placing the raw spices in a dry skillet on top of the stove, in a dry electric frying pan, or on a baking sheet placed under the broiler or in the oven. The goal is to heat the spices with medium heat until they release their distinct aromas.

of that paper disclosed one or two other letters on the subject. . . . These were mainly tested recipes suggested by Englishmen and Englishwomen for the making of curry—some sensible, others totally inconsistent with the method of cooking curries in India." Anand was inspired by the recipes' lack of authenticity to fill the void with the cookbook *Curries and Other Indian Dishes*, published in 1932.

During the 1950s, though there were only six Indian restaurants in all of England, curry still held the interest of English cooks. But Indian immigration picked up considerably in the late 1950s, and by the time the Commonwealth Immigration Act slowed immigration in 1962, more than 100,000 Indians and Pakistanis had entered England—the first large-scale emigration to England from the Indian subcontinent. By 1991, the total population of Indians, Pakistanis, and Bangladeshis in the U.K. had exploded to one and a half million.

Except in the cases of some dark curry blends, such as those from Sri Lanka, the spices should not be blackened. Also, they should not be heated for too long, or the volatile oils will be lost. Practice is the only way to learn how long to roast the spices. Oily and volatile spices such as cloves, cinnamon, cardamom, and mace are usually not roasted—but there are exceptions.

The next step is grinding the spices. Cooks have several options, including the original method of grinding between two stones, which in this day and age is a bit obsolete. A mortar and pestle can be used, but it takes a lot of muscle power to grind the spices finely enough. Blenders, coffee grinders, and food processors may also be used, but by far the best solution is to use an electric spice mill that is dedicated only to spices. Grind the roasted spices in small quantities so as not to burn out the motor. Avoid grinding whole dried ginger or turmeric without first pulverizing the rhizomes manually (with a hammer), because they are very fibrous and

difficult to grind with home equipment. Some cooks find it easier just to use powdered ginger and turmeric.

Freshly ground spices can be stored for later use, but not for long periods. Two or three months is the maximum for most ground spices, and be sure to store them in small bottles that are tightly capped. Store the spices in a dark place, as sunlight can degrade their flavors.

Blending roasted and ground spices is simple. Either use the spice mill, or place the spices in a shallow bowl and blend them thoroughly with a fork.

Use a food processor or blender to make curry pastes, following the individual recipe directions. Often pastes must be made in two or three batches, and then further mixed by hand. Some pastes must be fried in oil before they are added to the recipe. This procedure removes water from onions and other paste ingredients and recooks the spices to remove their raw flavor. Just take care not to burn the paste.

"With this immigration came their infrastructure," explains England's Pat Chapman, founder of the Curry Club. "Their families came over, they brought their foodstuffs, and very shortly they were opening restaurants on the back streets." The appearance of Indian restaurants in the U.K. coincided with the beginning of a dining-out tradition among the middle class, a custom rare in the war years and the austere 1950s.

"We had never experienced anything like this," Chapman adds. "The food was very, very tasty—and exotic." The food was also relatively inexpensive, and dining out at a curry restaurant soon became one of the most popular social activities in the U.K. As the Indian population grew, the number of restaurants increased, which coincided with the trend toward dining out. By 1991 there were 7,000 curry restaurants in the U.K., 1,500 of them in London alone. In fact, England now has, after India, the largest number of Indian restaurants of any country in the world! It should be noted that the word *curry* in the U.K. is used interchangeably with *Indian food*, so a curry restaurant means an Indian restaurant. These restaurants serve a variety of Indian foods, but they are judged by the quality of their curries.

During the 1980s, fancier curry restaurants began to open, and even the upper class was dining on curries. Curries had conquered the U.K. "The British Empire in India lasted the better part of two hundred years," wrote Peter Chapman (no relation to Pat) in *Bon Appetit*, "but it's only in the past quarter century that curry houses have established themselves in the British culinary imagination. In that short time, they have played a huge role in breaking down the Brits' notorious resistance to all but the blandest of foods."

Pat Chapman has played a large role in the immense popularity of curries in the U.K. His grandfather served in the British Army in India, moving back to England when he retired. His passion for India was passed on to Pat, who was "weaned on curries" during the 1950s at those original six Indian restaurants; curries became Pat's passion.

He turned his passion into a business when he founded the Curry Club in 1982. Soon Pat became the King of Curry, ruling over a curry empire that included a membership of 13,000, a quarterly magazine, a mail-order company with dozens of curry products, a guide to the top 1,000 curry restaurants in the U.K., and numerous curry cookbooks in print.

There seems to be no end in sight for the popularity of curry in the U.K. The number of curry restaurants was expected to top 10,000 in the year 2004. In 1990, two and a half million households cooked curry at home at least once every two weeks, a rise of 80 percent since 1983. Indian food accounted for fully half of the ethnic food market in the U.K. Interestingly enough, the surveys that produced the above figures

After India, England has the largest number of Indian restaurants of any country in the world.

also came up with a statistic about the supposedly bland-loving Brits: only about 5 percent of the people surveyed liked their curries mild; the remainder said they liked theirs hot or medium-hot.

Forms of Curry

Many purists abhor commercial curry powders. "They are anathema to Indian cooking," wrote Dharamjit Singh, author of *Indian Cookery*, "prepared for imaginary palates, having neither the delicacy nor the perfume of flowers and sweet-smelling herbs, nor the savour and taste of genuine aromatics." He added, "Curry powders often contain inferior spices which with age become acrid and medicinal in taste. They not only mask the natural taste of foods, but lend a weary sameness to everything with which they are used."

Indeed, there is a sameness to commercial curry powders, especially those made in the United States to the 1977 U.S. Department of Agriculture standards for curry powder, which calls for the following percentages of spices: coriander, 36; turmeric, 28; cumin, 10; fenugreek, 10; white pepper, 5; allspice, 4; mustard, 3; red pepper, 2; and ginger, 2. However, we should point out that many imported curry powders, especially from India, vary in flavor considerably, as they contain a wider variety of spices used in many different percentages.

Commercial curry powders are basically convenience condiments and should be treated that way. John Philips Cranwell suggests three reasons for using commercial curry preparations: they produce a uniform result with a given recipe; the individual spices necessary to make a certain curry may not be available at a given time; and buying commercial curry preparations saves time and work.

We believe that common sense must prevail. It may be true, as Dharamjit Singh suggests, that "once you have tried [separate spices] you will no more use the packaged curry powder than you would accept another person's taste in the choice of your clothes." But, on the other hand, is it considered bad taste to use a packaged Sri Lankan curry paste if the cook has run out of some of the necessary ingredients to prepare a fresh curry paste? Or, if fresh lemongrass is not immediately available for a Thai curry, should the cook substitute powdered lemongrass or use a packaged curry paste containing fresh lemongrass? These are decisions only the cook can make, and there will certainly be times when convenience will triumph over authenticity.

Our recommendation is that, whenever possible, cooks should use freshly ground or mixed ingredients for curries. Prepared powders and other products can be a backup for cooks lacking the time or certain essential ingredients, but they should whenever possible avoid cheap American curry powders.

Generally speaking, commercial curry preparations fall into the following categories. *Masalas* are spice blends that usually lack turmeric. *Curry powders* contain turmeric (the yellower the powder, the more turmeric it contains), and a large percentage of coriander. Imported powders are generally superior to domestic ones. *Curry pastes* are sealed, moist blends of herbs, spices, and other ingredients such as coconut, onions, fresh chiles, and ginger, usually imported from India, Thailand, Indonesia, and Sri Lanka. *Curry sauces* are available in either bottles or mixes, and are used as marinades or to make an "instant" curry gravy for meats. *Curry oils* are vegetable oils infused with curry spices, and they are generally used as a condiment to add a curry flavor to prepared foods.

Cooking and Serving Curries

Some cooks suggest that curry spices actually take a secondary role to the other ingredients. "Although the dish is called curry," observes Julie Sahni, "the most characteristic ingredient in all classic curries is the slowly cooked, caramelized onions not unlike those used in French onion soup." Indeed, in many cuisines, curry spices provide only a portion of the flavor of the dish. Additional tastes are contributed by lemongrass, galangal, coconut, papaya, tamarind, or other exotic ingredients. And finally, the chosen meats, fish, or vegetables in the curry also add their unique flavors.

Most curries are cooked in large skillets or in woks, so the curry cook is advised to have a selection of shallow, nonaluminum cookware with lids. Wooden spoons are the best utensils for stirring curries, since they do not conduct heat very well.

Curries are convenient to cook for parties, since most can easily be prepared ahead of time and reheated just before serving. They also freeze well, which is a great convenience. Cooks should remember that some curries, such as salads, can be served cold and make good outdoor summer food.

And what other dishes should be served with curries? Most curries are served with some form of rice; plain white rice is usually an excellent accompaniment. Basic condiments often served with curries worldwide include fried eggplant, tamarind jam, candied coconut, candied ginger, pickled vegetables (such as onions), mango chutney, grated fresh coconut, grated roasted coconut, chopped peanuts or almonds, grated or sliced hard-boiled eggs, chopped crisp bacon, chopped tomatoes, and salted fish. The condiments are usually either served in bowls, so that guests may sprinkle them over the curry, or placed on the side of the individual dishes.

5 The Spice Trade

The Classical Pepper Trade

The Arab spice trade with India goes back to around 950 B.C., and at the beginning the story of the spice trade is essentially the story of the pepper trade. The Old Testament, Ezekiel 27–22 refers to it: "The traders of Sheba and Raamah traded with you; they exchanged for your wares the best of all kinds of spices, and all precious stones and gold." Arab traders bought spices from Indians and carried them to the spice markets of Nineveh, Babylon, and later, Alexandria. Interestingly, pepper is scarcely mentioned in early Egyptian and Hebrew literature, apart from an ideograph of what looks like a pepper pot on a Linear B tablet. J. Innes Miller, author of *The Spice Trade of the Roman Empire*, speculates that pepper was not as popular as other spices in the Middle East "because its aroma was unsuitable for perfumes or incense, or because it was not used in Egyptian or Hebrew medicine."

But pepper *was* used medicinally when it reached ancient Greece, where it was fairly common as early as 431 B.C., sometimes adulterated with dried juniper berries. Pepper was mentioned as a cure by Hippocrates, Dioscorides, and Theophrastus, and Plato wrote, "Pepper is small in quantity and great in virtue." Hippocrates recommended pepper with honey and vinegar for the treatment of feminine disorders, and Theophrastus said it was good as an antidote for hemlock poisoning.

In 326 B.C., Alexander the Great encountered pepper for the first time when he was given long pepper under the name *pippali*. Some sources say that Alexander introduced pepper in Greece, but this date seems too late. More likely, the introduction came through the port of Alexandria, which by 80 B.C. had become the greatest spice trading port in the Mediterranean; pepper was so important that one of the entrances to Alexandria was known as the Pepper Gate.

At about this same time, Indian immigrants brought pepper from India to what is now Indonesia and Malaysia. Centuries later these two regions would vie with India for the lead in pepper production and trade.

Around A.D. 17, the Greek sea captain Hippalus discovered how to use the summer monsoon winds to sail between Egyptian Red Sea ports and India. This information was soon acquired by the Romans, who controlled Egypt, and regular voyages began between the Indian spice ports on the Malabar Coast to six Roman ports on the Red Sea, two of which were Myos Hormos and Berenike. Modern excavations of the ruins of two of these ports have yielded peppercorns nearly two thousand years old. In fact, the largest cache of ancient peppercorns ever found—sixteen pounds—was unearthed in Berenike. After unloading the spices camel caravans would move the cargo to Alexandria, and it would be transported to Rome across the Mediterranean by cargo ships.

Around A.D. 590, the Prophet Mohammed married a wealthy spice-trading widow. Many of his Islamic missionaries were also spice traders, and nomadic Arab tradesmen sold Indian spices to the Phoenicians, who controlled the spice trade in the Mediterranean after the fall of Rome, trading them as far north as England.

About this time, pepper was introduced to the Indonesian islands of Java and Sumatra from southern India, and soon trade in pepper from Sumatra to China began. (There is some evidence that this may have occurred as early as A.D. 400.) It took a while, but eventually black pepper won over the Chinese. In 907, the use of black pepper replaced that of *fagara* (Sichuan pepper) in wealthy families in China.

The Venetians Provide Europe's Beloved Spices

Back in Europe, the earliest references to the pepper trade in England appear in the laws of Ethelred (978–1016), stipulating that East German traders who bring their ships up the Thames River to Billingsgate must pay a toll at Christmas and Easter of ten pounds of pepper for the privilege of trading with London merchants. Pepper was so valuable that the guards on London docks had their pockets sewn shut to prevent them from stealing peppercorns. Pepper became a major currency, accepted in many eleventh-century towns as payment for taxes.

Venice provided the ships that carried the Crusaders to the Holy Land during the eleventh century, and the vessels returned with pepper and other spices bought in Alexandria. A single large Venetian ship returning from Alexandria could carry in her holds spices worth 200,000 ducats, and the estimated value of the Venetian spice trade was in excess of a million ducats a year.

Venice became the major spice city, and pepper was the number-one spice, with Europeans importing more than six and a half million pounds a year. Although pepper was only one of many spices traded, it accounted for well over half of all spice imports into Italy. And no other spice came within one-tenth the value of pepper. Why was it so beloved? Food historian Henry Hobson notes, "No spice except pepper made edible heavily salted meat, when no other form of preservation except salting was generally employed in Europe. Salt and pepper stood between carnivorous man and starvation, especially at sea, in the hungry months, and if crops failed." He goes on to note that when the Royal Navy ship *Mary Rose* was raised from the bottom of the sea in the early 1980s, every sailor who went down with her in 1545 was found to have a little bag of peppercorns.

In 1179 the Guild of Pepperers was founded in London, and in France the Corporation of Spicers, or *poivriers* was formed. The English Guild of Pepperers became the Guild of Grossers in the fourteenth century—the origin of the word *grocer*. By now not all pepper was coming from India; the East Indies pepper trade out of Java was booming. Arabian merchants carried pepper to the Middle East, where it was distributed around the Mediterranean, and Chinese merchantmen carried pepper in ever greater amounts to various ports of China.

When the king of Scotland visited his counterpart in England, Richard I, in 1194, he received, in addition to other tokens of hospitality, two pounds of pepper and four pounds of cinnamon every day. As historian Wolfgang Schivelbusch notes, "Besides being used in food, spices were presented as gifts, like jewels, and collected like precious objects." He goes on to point out that several factors caused certain spices to be linked to paradise: their strong bite, their exotic origin, and their exorbitant cost. "Pepper, cinnamon, and nutmeg were status symbols for the ruling class, emblems of power which were displayed and then consumed. The more sharply pepper seared their guests' palates, the more respect they felt for their host."

It is often thought that pepper and other hot spices were used to disguise spoiled meat, but medieval scholar Pamela Nightingale observes, "The use of hot spices in quantities which modern Europeans would find intolerable was not, as popularly supposed, the way in which medieval cooks disguised the unpalatable flavours of rotting meat. All the accounts show that the rich households which used most spices had plentiful supplies of meat, game, and fish. They probably appealed most of all to medieval people because they were a symbol of standing, wealth, and sophistication which linked them to the culture of the East and Byzantium." And spice prices in England in thirteenth century were high. Pepper and ginger were 1 shilling per pound, and mace was the most expensive, at more than 4 shillings a pound.

During this time, the art of preparing spiced sauces developed into a new branch of cookery. A separate saucery was built at Nottingham Castle in 1237. The queen had her own saucery built in Windsor Castle in 1264. The king employed his own saucer, Master William, and bought him a silver sauceboat in 1265. The sauce Master William made for the Feast of Saint Edward in 1264 contained twenty pounds of pepper, fifteen pounds of cinnamon, and twelve and a half pounds of cumin. Meals were literally buried under such sauces, and then silver or gold spice trays were passed around so that the guests could help themselves to even more. Medieval wines were fortified with numerous spices; they were boiled with the spices and then decanted.

But it wasn't just the Europeans who were consuming spices. In 1280 Marco Polo noticed cultivation of pepper on Java, and in 1298 he returned to Venice with tales of spices. He described the Kingdom of Dely as a place that "produced large quantities of pepper and ginger, with many other articles of spicery." He observed about China's love of spices: "I assure you that for one shipload of pepper that goes to Alexandria or elsewhere to be taken to Christian lands, there comes a hundred to the port of Canton." His observation was accurate: in 1382, a Javanese ship recorded forty-five tons of pepper carried on a trading mission to China. In Hangchow, Polo noted that the daily amount of it brought into the port was forty-three loads, or about 10,000 pounds of pepper. Despite high duties, freight, and other charges, a merchant could still make "a most respectable profit."

In 1345, the New Guild of Pepperers was established in London. The guild members were some of the wealthiest merchants, as the price of pepper was now 2 shillings a pound. In her book, *The Magic of Herbs*, C.V. Leyel explained: "The grocers were descended from the pepperers of Sopers Lane and the spicers of cheap, who amalgamated in 1345, and in 1370 adopted the more comprehensive title of engrosser or grocer from the Latin *grossarius*. In a grocer's shop at that time was to be found every sort of medicine, root and herb, gums, spices, oils and ointments." And cooks were buying them, according to recipes in early cookbooks of the time. Two untitled English cookery books, known as the *Harleian Ms. 279* (c. 1430) and the *Harleian Ms. 4016* (c. 1450), call for heavy spicing of 90 percent of the meat and fish dishes. The most common spices in those two books were ginger, black pepper, mace, cloves, cinnamon, and galangal. "The medieval ruling classes had a peculiar penchant for strongly seasoned dishes," noted Wolfgang Schivelbusch. "The higher the rank of a household, the greater its use of spices."

Combinations of spices were used in medicine as well. In *A Leechbook or Collection of Medical Recipes of the Fifteenth Century*, twenty-six spices are used in the cures. For curing coughs, a decoction called Wine of Tyre, containing thirteen herbs and spices, including pepper, mace, nutmeg, cinnamon, and ginger, was recommended. A remedy for aching loins called for nine peppercorns—an expensive cure. A headache powder that "cleansed the brain" and also cured flatulence contained pepper, cloves, saffron, and cumin, plus herbs. Pepper, sage, and mustard were recommended cures for colds. The *Leechbook* also had a suggestion for the pepperer: "A good electuary for a spicer to gather for his trade to give and sell: Take honey and baking-flour, ginger, and the powder of pepper, and barley-wort, seethe them together till it be standing, and then sell it forth."

During the late Middle Ages, pepper declined in importance in Europe, supplanted by ginger, but it returned to prominence in the later sixteenth century. Wolfgang Schivelbusch theorized, "In the fifteenth century the combination of these three factors—increased demand, stagnant transportation technology, and spiraling customs duties—led to a thirty-fold rise in the price of pepper coming from India to Venice." The problem was the tortuous route that pepper and other spices took: from India to Egypt and Syria, by land across the Isthmus of Suez to Alexandria, loaded ships to Venice, and then over the Alps to central and northern Europe.

When the prices the Venetians charged became too much, other nations entered the arena. Clearly, a sea route from India to Europe was necessary to eliminate the middlemen.

The Portuguese and Pepper

Since peppercorns were literally worth their weight in gold, explorers such as Columbus, Magellan, and Vasco da Gama searched for them as they would for any treasure. Thus pepper stimulated the Europeans' exploration of the world. Of course, Columbus did not find black pepper, but rather chile peppers, which he misnamed.

In 1499, Vasco da Gama returned to Portugal from Mozambique with pepper, nutmeg, and cinnamon. This encouraged Pedro Cabral and others to begin a regular spice trade around the Cape of Good Hope. In 1501, da Gama won control of the spice trade for Portugal. His fleet of twenty caravels cut off the spice trade through the Red Sea to Alexandria, where Venetian merchants had been buying them. Pedro Cabral and his fleet of thirty-three ships helped keep control of the Indian seas, seizing any Venetian ships carrying spices. By 1503, Portuguese caravels were transporting 1,300 tons of pepper from the East Indies—six times what Egypt had permitted to be shipped in any one year. The merchants earned profits of as much as 6,000 percent. A year later, spice prices in Lisbon were 20 percent of Venetian prices, breaking the Venetian monopoly.

Pepper, cinnamon, and nutmeg were status symbols. The more sharply pepper seared their guests' palates, the more respect they felt for their host.

Portuguese traders could still get a good price on the European wholesale market. The Municipal Council of Nuremberg complained around this time, "The King of Portugal, Lord of Spices, has set prices just as he pleases, for pepper, which, at any cost, no matter how dear, will not long go unsold to the Germans."

In 1509 the combined Muslim fleet from Egypt, Calicut, and Gujerat was destroyed by Francisco de Almeida at the Battle of Diu—one of the most important battles in history. This victory completely established Portuguese control over the Indian Ocean. In 1511, Portuguese forces under the leadership of Alfonzo de Albuquerque seized the city of Malacca on the Malay Peninsula, one of the most important spice trading centers in the East Indies. As food historian Carson Ritchie wrote, "Portugal, which, it must be remembered, was only a tiny nation with less than a million inhabitants, controlled the cloves from Amboyna in the Moluccas, the nutmeg from Banda and the Celebes, the cinnamon from Ceylon, the pepper from the Malabar Coast, and the ginger of China."

The commercial house of Fugger was the government agent for the sale of pepper and other spices to the rest of Europe. The company's newsletter reported in 1580, "The pepper business is profitable indeed; the Lord God grants by his Mercy that none of the ships take damage either in coming or going, then the merchants wax rich." No wonder; merchants were purchasing the pepper in Calicut, India, for three ducats a hundredweight and selling it for eighty!

Interestingly, the Portuguese brought chile peppers to India during this time, and Indian food was forever changed. During the Mughal rule of Akbar, 1556–1605, chile peppers rivaled black pepper for spice supremacy. Abul-Fazl, Akbar's prime minister in Ain, in *Ain-i-Akbari* described the dishes served at the royal court, reporting that three types of pepper were available to the cooks: round, or black, pepper, used only in the preparation of royal dishes; long pepper; and red pepper. This marks the first mention of chiles in Indian cooking. Red pepper was actually more valuable than long pepper, selling for seventeen dinar per *seer* (900 grams), while long pepper brought only sixteen.

The Dutch Prevail

The Portuguese domination of the spice trade would not last all that long. In 1592, Sir Walter Raleigh's fleet captured the Portuguese carrack *Madre de Dios*, loaded with 537 tons of spices worth half a million pounds. About 90 percent of the spice load was pepper. And the Dutch East India Company jumped into the spice trade in 1599, when four Dutch vessels returned from India with pepper, cloves, cinnamon, and nutmeg. This caused the price of pepper in London to rise from three to eight shillings a pound, forcing the English to form their own British East India Company the same year.

On August 24, 1600, the HMS *Hector*, captained by William Hawkins, landed at Surat, north of Bombay; the English had arrived in India. The British were permitted to open up trading depots north of Bombay, and soon two ships a month were carrying pepper and other spices, raw silk, sugar, muslin, and cotton back to London. The stockholders of the British East India Company realized profits as high as 200 percent.

The Dutch countered in 1602 when the United East India Company combined various Dutch companies and effectively tripled European pepper prices, but the English struck back—by fighting not the Dutch, but rather the Portuguese. That same year, the English captain James Lancaster arrived in Anchin in northern Sumatra, engaged a Portuguese galleon, defeated her, and looted the ship of jewels and silver plate, which he used to purchase pepper in Bantam in Java. Having formed a trading agreement with the Acehnese, who controlled the pepper trade in the East Indies, the following year he returned to London with half his original crew to sell his cargo of more than one million pounds of pepper at a good profit. Lancaster was knighted for his efforts.

During the early part of the seventeenth century, the English, Dutch, and Portuguese were all fighting for control of the spice trade in the East Indies. In 1614, Jan Coen of the Dutch East India Company wrote to his superiors in Amsterdam, "Trade in Asia must be maintained under the protection of our own weapons; and they have to be paid for from the profits of trade. We can't trade without war, nor make war without trade." Around this time the sultan of Aceh ordered the destruction of pepper vines near the capital. The emphasis on growing pepper was leading to the neglect of traditional food crops, and cutting down the vines would discourage the Dutch and English from trading in the region.

Over in India, Portuguese losses at sea, plus Dutch and English competition and the lack of financial and ship resources, spelled doom for the Portuguese spice trade. By 1616, with the Portuguese out of the picture, the Dutch and English continued their sporadic skirmishes. Jan Coen seized Jakarta in 1619, renaming it Batavia. The following year the two countries signed a truce, but war broke out again in 1621, and Coen conquered the Banda Islands and committed atrocities such as mass executions. The English gave up, leaving the Dutch totally in control of the region. By 1663 the Dutch had taken over the pepper trade in Malabar as well, driving out the Portuguese, and were buying 2 million pounds of pepper a year. About the only good news for the Portuguese was that around this time they began growing pepper into their colony of Brazil, though on a small scale at first.

England Rules the Waves

In 1669, the Dutch East India Company was at its height of power in the East Indies, with 150 trading ships, 40 warships, and one thousand soldiers. It paid duties of 40 percent to the Dutch government. From 1678 to 1684, despite the Dutch success in supplanting Portugal, the price of pepper fell in Europe, probably because the Dutch were flooding the market. By the end of the seventeenth century, the Dutch controlled virtually all the spice trade at the points of production but the English still managed to find sources of pepper. They would bribe local princes with gifts, and sea captains did a lot of private trade in pepper, amassing large fortunes.

As with that of Portugal, the Dutch domination of the spice trade lasted only about a hundred years. The Dutch decline, which began in the 1770s, had to do with personnel—or rather the lack of it. From 1602 to1795 there were 4,700 Dutch voyages to East Indies; a million people were employed on these ships, and one-third of them did not return. Holland was being stripped of its population, and historians later charged that the East India Company devoured its own personnel. Other factors were inefficiency and corruption—new ships were not built, and the spice trade suffered.

Sensing the Dutch weakness, England struck in 1780 by declaring war and blockading the Dutch East Indian ports. The Dutch East India Company could not control the prices of pepper, cloves, and nutmeg; and by 1784 was facing financial crisis. In 1795, the English took Malacca from the Dutch, and the following year Ambon fell to English forces. The English occupied all of the Dutch territory except Java, cutting off communication between Batavia and Amsterdam. The financial crisis dealt a death blow to the Dutch, and in 1799 the Dutch East India Company was dissolved. By 1800 the British completely controlled the spice trade not only the East Indies but also in India, and soon they had completely conquered the country. Finally, in 1819, the English took over the island of Singapore, which soon became one of the most important pepper trading centers of the world.

Wolfgang Schivelbusch has observed, "Between the eleventh and the seventeenth centuries, that is, from the time of the Crusades to the period of the Dutch and English East India companies, spices dominated European taste. They were part of it and stamped it from the first stirrings of interest in lands beyond Europe to the conclusion of the conquest of the colonial world in the seventeenth century. Once there was nothing more worth mentioning to be discovered and conquered, and knowledge of the earth became more common, spices apparently lost their tremendous attraction." Except, of course, in the New World.

After the British arrived in India, British East India Company shareholders realized profits as high as 200 percent.

Enter the United States

Soon after the introduction of the spice to what is now the United States, the small town of Salem, Massachusetts, became the pepper capital of the New World. About 8 million pounds a year of the spice passed through New England to other countries aboard clipper ships. Hundreds of fast schooners were built exclusively for the pepper trade, greatly boosting the colonial economy.

In 1778, sailing out of Salem, Jonathan Carnes went to Sumatra, bought pepper, and attempted to bring it back. Apparently he went off course, and his ship was wrecked on a reef in the West Indies. But he did not give up. With backing from the Jonathan Peele family of Salem, Carnes left Salem aboard the *Rajah* and sailed again to Sumatra to buy pepper. In 1797 (some sources say 1799), the *Rajah* returned with 158,544 pounds of bulk pepper shoveled into her hold. The cargo sold for 37 cents a pound and yielded a profit of 700 percent. Carnes and the Peeles kept quiet about the origin of their pepper and made two more voyages in 1798 and 1801, each bringing back about the same amount of pepper.

In 1799, Captain Benjamin Crowninshield sailed the *America* to Calcutta and returned with 95,000 pounds of pepper. More voyages followed as the Crowninshields began to compete with the Steeles.

Soon the word leaked out about Sumatra, and Crowninshield sailed there. Enormous amounts of pepper came into Salem in 1803 and 1804, to be resold in Rotterdam, the Netherlands—a great irony, considering the previous Dutch domination of the pepper trade. One shipment aboard the *America* fetched $140,000 in gold. The American entrance into the East Indian spice trade dramatically increased pepper supplies. Between 1797 and 1822, pepper production in Aceh, Sumatra, increased from 2.13 million pounds to 18.6 million pounds a year.

Between 1795 and 1873, clipper ships made nearly a thousand trips, each 24,000 miles, to Sumatra and back. The import duties at Salem at one time paid for 5 percent of the expenses of the U.S. government. Salem—the nation's sixth largest city in 1790, and the richest per capita—had so many ships plying Asian waters that many Asian traders thought it was a sovereign country. The quantity of pepper being brought back from the East Indies steadily increased. The *Concord* returned in 1803 with 261,937 pounds of pepper. The next year the *Belisarius* arrived with 295,824 pounds. The most brought back on one voyage was probably the *America*'s load of 844,918 pounds in 1801. By 1805, annual reexporting topped 7.5 million pounds, the all-time high for the Salem pepper trade.

In the East Indies, the Americans were trading with the smaller ports, where they could buy pepper at the source rather than dealing with middlemen. These charged more, and sometimes they would demand advance payment for pepper and then sell it to an English or Dutch captain, so the Americans never saw their pepper or got their money back. After a few of these transactions, the Americans decided to deal with the rajahs on the spot. Pepper was purchased with Spanish silver dollars or pieces of eight; the pepper would be weighed, paid for, and transported by the rajah's workers to the American ship.

In 1805 the *Putnam* was hijacked by Malays and never seen again, putting the Americans on their guard. Other American ships were attacked in the years that followed, without dampening the pepper trade. President Thomas Jefferson's solution to British and French privateering, however, which had peaked in 1806, was to embargo more than a hundred Salem ships, keeping them in port. Dubbed the "Tyrannical Embargo," Jefferson's action finally cripped the pepper trade, causing devastating losses in revenue. The embargo allowed England to dominate the seas, eventually leading to the War of 1812. After the war, in 1818, U.S. ships made thirty-five voyages to Sumatra for pepper, but many ships were attacked by pirates.

Around this time, in 1820, Frederic Accum published *A Treatise on Adulterations of Food and Culinary Poisons*, revealing that ground pepper for sale in the United States was being adulterated with black mustard husks, pea flour, juniper berries, and sweepings from store floors. Accum was forced to flee to Berlin to avoid public trial after enraging the food industry. The scandal did not stop the importation of pepper; in 1822, Sumatra produced 18,630,000 pounds of pepper, much of it bought by Salem merchants.

In 1831 the ship *Friendship*, while buying pepper from a trusted rajah, Po Adam, was attacked by Malays, who seized the ship and killed five crew members. Ship's captain Charles Endicott, a veteran of the Sumatra pepper trade, was rescued by the *Governor Endicott* (ironically, named for his ancestor), which retook the *Friendship*, though it had been stripped of everything valuable. Captain Endicott theorized that unscrupulous traders had poisoned the well for the honest ones by stealing pepper during the trading process. Charles Corn, author of *The Scents of Eden*, disagrees: "But this speculation on Endicott's part is unconvincing. A more likely explanation is that three centuries of infidel European colonization of the Indies—the successive waves of Portuguese, Spanish, Dutch, and English—had bred a profound distrust of Christian Europeans on the part of the Muslim Malays, in a part of the world where word spread across the waters with the wind."

The United States government responded by sending the frigate *Potomac* to Sumatra with the orders, "Give the rascals a good thrashing." The *Potomac*, disguised as a merchantman, landed near where the *Friendship* was attacked at Quallah Battoo. A force of three hundred American men attacked the forts of the town, long assumed by the rajahs to be impregnable. Four of the forts were destroyed, at the cost of only a few American lives. The following day, ship's cannons destroyed the remaining fort. The town quickly surrendered under a truce negotiated by Po Adam.

The *Potomac* had succeeded in its mission, but the Malays were not long deterred. In 1834 the *Derby* was attacked by Malays but drove them off; in 1839 Captain Wilkie of the *Eclipse* was brutally murdered, and the frigates *Columbia* and *John Adams* bombarded the town of Quallah Battoo again, destroying all but one fort. The Malays sued for peace again. What the Americans needed was a permanent fort in Sumatra to protect American pepper traders, but this would have gone against the anticolonization philosophy prevalent at the time, and the ultimate American failure to protect the traders led to a decline in the pepper trade. By 1843, pepper prices had dropped in the United States to less than three cents a pound. Thirty years later, the United States formally ended the pepper trade with Sumatra.

The World's Most Popular Spice

The exciting history of black pepper was later transformed into just another story of commodity trading, complete with production challenges, price fluctuations, and tariffs. Pepper no longer stimulated world exploration, caused wars, or witnessed dramatic fortunes being made and lost. However, the cultivation and trade in pepper has not diminished—far from it.

During the twentieth century, pepper production increased dramatically as new plantations were founded in Thailand, Vietnam, China, and Sri Lanka. In the New World, Brazil became the only important producer, with pepper plantations there going back to the 1930s. In 2000, worldwide pepper production topped 254,000 metric tons. Vietnam has become the world's largest pepper exporter and the second largest pepper producer after India. Vietnam, by exporting 56,000 tons of pepper in 2001, left all major pepper exporters behind, including Indonesia (50,000 tons), Brazil (34,000 tons), and Malaysia and India (26,000 tons each). Pepper from Vietnam has been exported to forty countries and territories around the world, including Singapore, Holland, Laos, China, and Hong Kong.

In 2002, world production of black pepper, white pepper, and long pepper was 321,728 metric tons. Indonesia (63,400 tons) was the leader, followed by India (60,000 tons), Brazil (58,678 tons), and Vietnam (51,100 tons.). Other significant producers were Malaysia, China, and Sri Lanka. The United States remains the major importer, followed by Europe, Japan, and North Africa.

The import duties paid on pepper at the port of Salem, Massachusetts, at one point paid for 5 percent of U.S. government expenses.

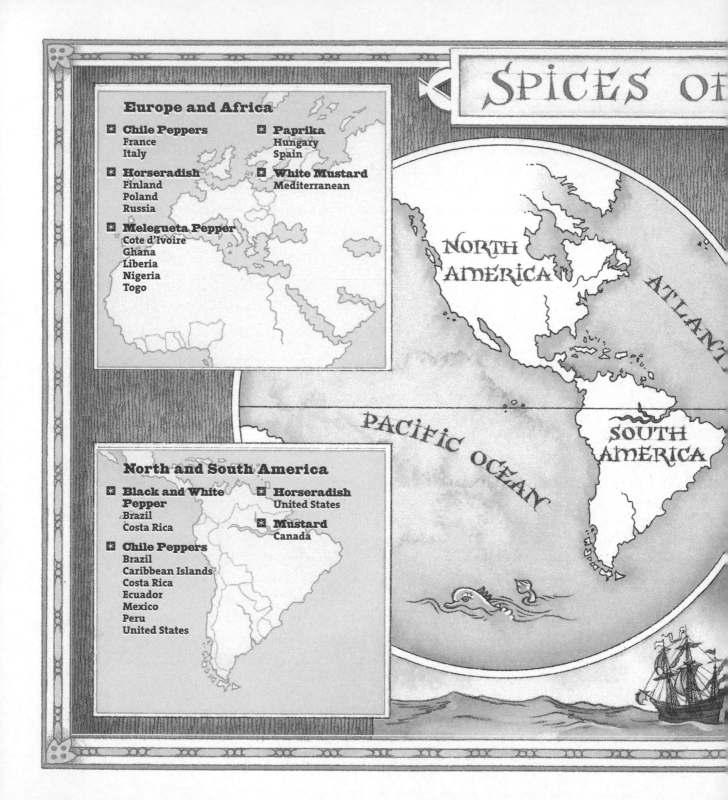

Europe and Africa

- ▣ **Chile Peppers**
  France
  Italy

- ▣ **Horseradish**
  Finland
  Poland
  Russia

- ▣ **Melegueta Pepper**
  Cote d'Ivoire
  Ghana
  Liberia
  Nigeria
  Togo

- ▣ **Paprika**
  Hungary
  Spain

- ▣ **White Mustard**
  Mediterranean

North and South America

- ▣ **Black and White Pepper**
  Brazil
  Costa Rica

- ▣ **Chile Peppers**
  Brazil
  Caribbean Islands
  Costa Rica
  Ecuador
  Mexico
  Peru
  United States

- ▣ **Horseradish**
  United States

- ▣ **Mustard**
  Canada

SPICES OF

NORTH AMERICA

SOUTH AMERICA

ATLANTI

PACIFIC OCEAN

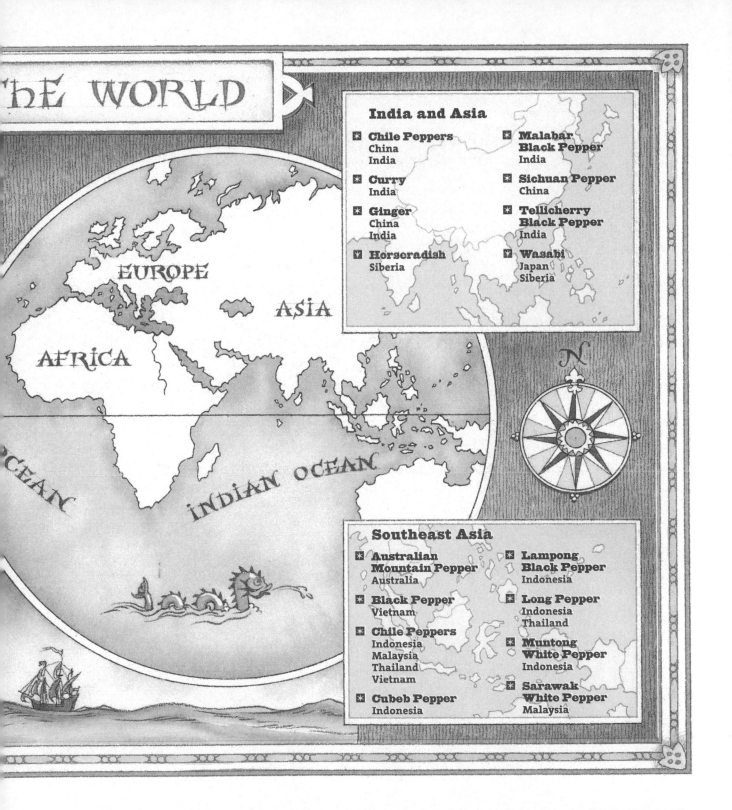

ThE WORLD

India and Asia

- ❇ **Chile Peppers**
  China
  India

- ❇ **Curry**
  India

- ❇ **Ginger**
  China
  India

- ❇ **Horseradish**
  Siberia

- ❇ **Malabar Black Pepper**
  India

- ❇ **Sichuan Pepper**
  China

- ❇ **Tellicherry Black Pepper**
  India

- ❇ **Wasabi**
  Japan
  Siberia

EUROPE

ASIA

AFRICA

INDIAN OCEAN

OCEAN

N

Southeast Asia

- ❇ **Australian Mountain Pepper**
  Australia

- ❇ **Black Pepper**
  Vietnam

- ❇ **Chile Peppers**
  Indonesia
  Malaysia
  Thailand
  Vietnam

- ❇ **Cubeb Pepper**
  Indonesia

- ❇ **Lampong Black Pepper**
  Indonesia

- ❇ **Long Pepper**
  Indonesia
  Thailand

- ❇ **Muntong White Pepper**
  Indonesia

- ❇ **Sarawak White Pepper**
  Malaysia

part two:
the recipes

recipe heat scale

🔥 Mild

🔥🔥 Mild to Medium

🔥🔥🔥 Medium to Hot

🔥🔥🔥🔥 Hot

🔥🔥🔥🔥🔥 Extremely Hot

6 Basics: Seasonings, Sauces, & Condiments

MUSTARD

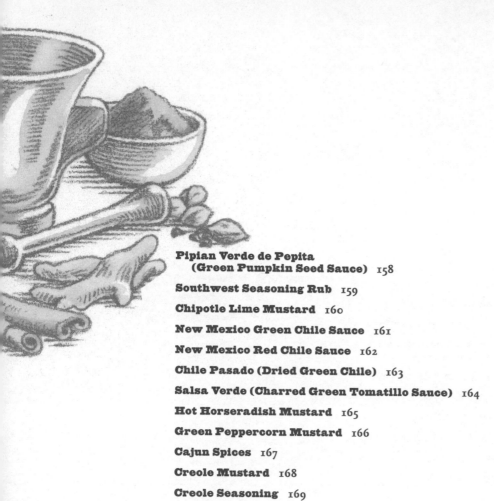

Simple Crystallized Ginger

It is not necessary to buy imported crystallized ginger, especially if you don't mind a little *time in the kitchen. Here is a home preservation technique that produces a delicious treat. Make sure the ginger rhizomes are young and tender, not fibrous.*

1½ cups peeled and sliced ginger
1½ cups sugar

Combine the ginger and sugar, along with ½ cup water, in a saucepan and bring to a simmer over medium heat. Gently simmer the mixture, uncovered, until the ginger is tender, about ½ hour. Remove the ginger slices and place them on a sheet pan.

Return the saucepan to the heat and bring to a boil. Boil the syrup, uncovered, for 15 minutes, until the syrup is very thick.

Pour the syrup over the ginger slices and allow to dry, turning daily, until the sugar crystallizes. Depending on the humidity, this may take several days.

Store the ginger in an airtight container and it will keep indefinitely.

Yield: About ¾ cup

Note: This recipe requires advance preparation.

Prepared Horseradish

This is the basic recipe for grated horseradish; because of the addition of the vinegar, it will retain its heat for about two weeks in the refrigerator. Be sure to work in a well-ventilated kitchen, or the fumes will drive you out the door. Store the horseradish in a tightly sealed glass jar, but don't let the metal lid touch the horseradish, or it will start to corrode the top.

One 4-ounce piece fresh horseradish root,
    peeled and grated
2 tablespoons cider vinegar
1 tablespoon sugar
2 teaspoons salt

Combine all the ingredients in a bowl and stir to blend.

Store the mixture in a glass jar in the refrigerator for up to 2 weeks.

Yield: 1 cup

Creamy Horseradish Sauce

Horseradish sauce is a classic condiment that's served with roast meats—beef in particular—and cooked or raw vegetables. Since horseradish is very volatile and loses its flavor and aroma quickly, this simple sauce should be made close to serving time. For an added hit of heat, we sometimes add ground habanero chile.

⅔ cup sour cream

¼ cup fresh or prepared horseradish,
    store-bought or homemade (opposite page)

2 green onions, finely chopped

1 teaspoon distilled white vinegar

1 teaspoon sugar

¾ teaspoon chopped fresh dill

Combine all the ingredients in a bowl and beat until well mixed. Allow the mixture to sit for 15 to 20 minutes to blend the flavors.

Yield: ⅔ cup

Horseradish Mignonette

Mignonette sauces are a traditional accompaniment to briny oysters or clams on the half shell, and also make great dressings. If fresh horseradish root is not available, bottled commercial products are an acceptable substitute.

½ cup peeled and sliced fresh horseradish; or substitute prepared horseradish, store-bought or homemade (page 112)

¼ cup rice or other mild vinegar

½ teaspoon grated lemon zest

1 tablespoon sugar

½ teaspoon coarsely ground white or black pepper

½ teaspoon salt

¼ teaspoon dried tarragon

½ to ¾ cup olive oil

Place all the ingredients, except the oil, in a blender or food processor. Add ¼ cup of the oil and puree to a paste. With the motor running, slowly add just enough of the oil to form a sauce.

Allow the sauce to sit for 20 to 30 minutes to blend the flavors.

Yield: ¾ cup

Romesco Sauce

Romesco is a classic Spanish sauce that is served with a wide variety of dishes, including the famous tortilla Española *(page 311). From the Tarragona region, this classic Catalan sauce combines almonds with two of the most popular horticultural imports from the New World—chiles and tomatoes. The sauce gets its name from the romesco chile, but these are not readily available outside Spain. A combination of ancho and New Mexican chiles approximates the flavor.*

1 ancho chile, stem and seeds removed

2 dried red New Mexican red chiles, stems and seeds removed

½ cup toasted almonds

5 cloves garlic, unpeeled

2 tomatoes, unpeeled

½ cup red wine vinegar

⅓ cup extra-virgin olive oil, preferably Spanish

Salt and freshly ground black pepper

Preheat the oven to 200°F.

Place the chiles, almonds, garlic, and tomatoes on a baking pan and roast in the oven until the nuts are toasted, the chiles are fragrant, and the skins of the tomatoes and garlic are blistered. The nuts will take about 5 minutes, the tomatoes about 20, and the chiles somewhere in between. Check frequently to be sure nothing burns.

Allow the ingredients to cool. Place the almonds in a spice mill or coffee grinder and process to a powder. Place the chiles in a bowl, cover with hot water, and allow them to steep for 15 minutes to soften. Drain the chiles and discard the water. Remove the skins from the tomatoes and garlic.

Put the almonds, chiles, tomatoes, garlic, and vinegar in a blender or food processor and puree to a smooth paste, adding a little oil if necessary.

Transfer the paste to a bowl and slowly whisk in the oil, 1 teaspoon at a time, until half of the oil is absorbed. Gradually add the remaining oil. Season with the salt and pepper.

Allow the sauce to sit for an hour or two to blend the flavors.

This sauce may be stored, covered, in the refrigerator for 2 to 3 days.

Yield: ⅓ to ½ cup

Cracked Black Peppercorn Mustard

This is a quick, easy-to-prepare mustard with a distinctive peppercorn flavor. Its assertive flavor is excellent on dark breads and with smoked meats, and makes a perfect coating for steaks or burgers before grilling. Add a little of this mustard to beef gravy for an added flavor dimension.

¼ cup whole yellow mustard seeds

¼ cup champagne vinegar

¼ cup hot water

2 tablespoons coarsely cracked
    black peppercorns

1 teaspoon garlic powder

½ teaspoon salt

Place the mustard seeds in a spice mill or coffee grinder and process until finely ground.

Combine the mustard and vinegar in a bowl and stir to mix. Allow the mixture to sit for 15 minutes.

Place all of the ingredients in a blender or food processor and process until smooth.

Spoon the mustard into a sterilized jar, cover, and refrigerate for 1 week before using.

Mustard will keep in the refrigerator, covered, for up to 6 months after opening.

Yield: ½ cup

Dijon-Style Mustard

The term moutarde de Dijon *is strictly controlled by French law. It can only be used on mixtures that contain black and/or brown mustard seeds, and these seeds must be mixed with wine, wine vinegar, or verjuice—the juice of unripe grapes. Any product made with the milder white mustard seeds may be labeled* condiment, *but never* moutarde. *This is a wonderful mustard to use as a base for adding other ingredients, such as fruits and various herbs. The flavor changes from sharp to smooth and mellow, hence the long aging period. The proportions of ingredients used in the French* moutarde *are also a closely guarded secret, but this recipe is the closest we've come to the real McCoy.*

¾ cup mustard powder

1 cup champagne vinegar

1 cup dry white wine

½ cup minced onions

2 tablespoons minced shallots

2 tablespoons minced garlic

2 bay leaves

20 black peppercorns

10 juniper berries

½ teaspoon dried tarragon

¼ teaspoon dried thyme

3 tablespoons lemon juice, preferably fresh

2 teaspoons salt

2 teaspoons sugar

Combine the mustard powder with ¼ cup cold water in a bowl and stir to form a paste.

In a saucepan, combine the vinegar, wine, onion, shallots, garlic, bay leaves, peppercorns, juniper berries, tarragon, and thyme. Bring the mixture to a simmer over moderate heat, and cook until it is reduced by two-thirds. Strain the mixture into a bowl, cover, and chill.

When cooled, stir the vinegar reduction into the mustard paste. Add the lemon juice, salt, and sugar and stir to combine. Let the mixture stand for 30 minutes.

Transfer the mustard to a saucepan and simmer over low heat for 15 minutes. Remove the pan from the heat and allow it to cool.

Spoon the mustard into a sterilized jar and seal. Store the mustard in a dark, cool place for 3 weeks before using.

Mustard will keep in the refrigerator, covered, for up to 6 months after opening.

Yield: 1½ cups

Note: This recipe requires advance preparation.

Quatre Épices

Quatre épices is French for "four spices," and refers to any of several finely ground spice mixtures that have been used in cooking since the fifteenth century. There is no standard recipe for the mixture, but it usually contains black and/or white pepper, nutmeg, cloves, and ginger. Cinnamon sometimes replaces the ginger, allspice the cloves, and mace the nutmeg, but the pepper is never replaced. Quatre épices is traditionally used to flavor charcuteries or pork dishes such as pâtés, and in forcemeats such as sausages and terrines. It also adds an aromatic flavoring to all meats, particularly game, and to dishes that need long simmering such as stews, and it makes a flavorful glaze for baked ham. Not just popular in France, it's also used in the Arab world, particularly in North Africa, where the French have had a presence.

3 tablespoons white peppercorns
1½ teaspoons whole cloves
2½ teaspoons grated nutmeg
1½ teaspoons ground ginger

Place the peppercorns and cloves in a spice mill or coffee grinder and process to a fine powder.

Combine all the ingredients in a bowl and stir to blend.

Store the mixture in an airtight container in a cool, dry place for up to 4 months.

Yield: ¼ cup

Coarse-Grained German-Style Beer Mustard

This full-flavored, coarse-textured mustard is both mild and robustly aromatic with cinnamon and allspice. It's a good accompaniment to sausages, wursts, and ham, as well as an addition to the dressing for German potato salad, or even a coating for roast beef. Other ingredients such as sun-dried tomatoes and chiles can be added to the basic recipe to enhance the mustard.

½ cup yellow mustard seeds
⅓ cup brown mustard seeds
¼ cup mustard powder
1 cup dark beer
1 cup cider vinegar
2 tablespoons brown sugar

4 whole cloves
½ teaspoon garlic powder
½ teaspoon caraway seeds
½ teaspoon ground cinnamon
¼ teaspoon allspice
¼ teaspoon mace

Place the yellow and brown mustard seeds in a spice mill or coffee grinder and pulse to process coarsely.

Combine all the mustards and the beer in a bowl, and allow the mixture to soak overnight.

Heat the vinegar, sugar, cloves, garlic powder, caraway, cinnamon, allspice, and mace together in a nonreactive saucepan over medium heat. Simmer the mixture until it's reduced by half, about 10 minutes. Cool and strain into the mustard mix.

Cook the mustard in the top of a double boiler for 5 to 10 minutes, stirring frequently, until slightly thickened. The mustard will thicken as it cools, so don't cook too long.

Allow the mixture to cool.

Spoon the mustard into a sterilized jar, cover, and refrigerate for 3 days before using.

Mustard will keep in the refrigerator, covered, for up to 6 months after opening.

Yield: 1½ to 2 cups

Note: This recipe requires advance preparation.

Harissa

This fiery chile paste originated in Tunisia, where it is the most important condiment used in cooking. Its popularity has spread all over North Africa, from Libya to Algeria and Morocco, and even to Sicily. Harissa *is derived from the Arabic word for "to break into pieces," referring to the traditional method of preparation, which involves pounding peppers into a coarse paste. Modern methods using a blender or food processor produce a more saucelike* harissa.

There are many variations on this condiment, and although it's available commercially, it's easy to prepare and will keep for many weeks in the refrigerator, so why not prepare it fresh? It's commonly served with couscous, vegetable and meat tagines, and grilled foods, and is also used to flavor soups and egg dishes.

7 dried red New Mexican chiles, stems and seeds removed; or substitute 5 small hot chiles like piquins

1 tablespoon ground paprika

2 tablespoons olive oil

5 cloves garlic

1 teaspoon cumin seeds; or substitute ½ teaspoon ground cumin

1 teaspoon ground coriander

½ teaspoon caraway seeds

2 tablespoons lemon juice, preferably fresh

1 tablespoon chopped fresh mint (optional)

1 teaspoon salt

1 teaspoon freshly ground black pepper

¼ cup olive oil

Place the chiles in a bowl and cover them with very hot water. Allow the chiles to steep for 15 to 20 minutes to soften. Drain the chiles and discard the water.

Place all the ingredients, except the oil, in a blender or food processor and puree until smooth. With the motor running, add the oil in a steady stream to form a thick sauce.

This sauce may be stored, covered, in the refrigerator for up to 3 weeks. Be sure to cover the top with a couple of drops of olive oil to prevent the *harissa* from turning brown.

Yield: ⅓ to ½ cup

Moroccan Charmoula

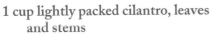

Charmoula *has been referred to as an all-purpose spicy cilantro pesto. Traditionally served with seafood, it can be used as a marinade, or as a fresh sauce on top of baked, grilled, or even poached fish. Don't limit yourself, however, as it's also tasty with chicken or on steamed vegetables.* Charmoula *is used throughout Morocco, and although the blend of spices and herbs may vary, it always contains cilantro, garlic, olive oil, and lemon.*

1 cup lightly packed cilantro, leaves and stems

5 cloves garlic, chopped

3 tablespoons chopped parsley, preferably flat-leaf

3 tablespoon lemon juice, preferably fresh

Zest of 1 lemon

2 teaspoons ground paprika

1 teaspoon ground coriander

1 teaspoon cumin seeds

1 teaspoon ground cayenne

½ teaspoon freshly ground black pepper

2 tablespoons cider vinegar

¼ to ⅓ cup olive oil

Place all the ingredients, except the vinegar and oil, in a blender or food processor and pulse to coarsely chop. With the motor running, slowly add the vinegar and enough of the oil to make a thick paste.

Allow the sauce to sit for 20 to 30 minutes to blend the flavors.

The sauce will keep for up to 1 month in the refrigerator.

Yield: ⅓ to ½ cup

Ras el Hanout

This exotic and complex Moroccan spice blend is prepared with 20 to 30—and sometimes up to 50—different ingredients that range from the common to the downright strange. A typical spice merchant can carry up to 200 different spices and herbs, so it's no wonder that there is a mind-boggling number of variations on ras el hanout, *which means "head of the shop," and refers to the special blend of the shopkeeper. Traditionally, the blends contain dried flowers and also an aphrodisiac such as Spanish fly, monk's pepper, or ash berries. We've included a flower, but not the aphrodisiac. This mixture is best made fresh and is used to flavor tagines, couscous, lamb, and game dishes.*

1 teaspoon caraway seeds
1 teaspoon cumin seeds
¼ teaspoon cardamom seeds
One 2-inch piece cinnamon stick
6 allspice berries
4 whole cloves
¼ teaspoon dried lavender (optional)

1½ teaspoons freshly ground black pepper
1 teaspoon ground ginger
1 teaspoon ground coriander
½ teaspoon ground cayenne
¼ teaspoon ground nutmeg
¼ teaspoon ground turmeric

Heat a heavy skillet over high heat, add the caraway, cumin, cardamom, cinnamon, allspice, and cloves, and dry-roast until the seeds darken and become fragrant, being careful that they don't burn. Allow the mixture to cool completely.

Place the toasted mixture in a spice mill or coffee grinder along with the lavender, and process to a fine powder. Sift the mixture if you want a fine blend.

Combine the toasted mix with the remaining ground spices and stir to blend. Store in an airtight container in a cool, dark, dry place for up to 4 months.

Yield: 2 to 3 tablespoons

La Kama Seasoning

La kama *blend is a typical seasoning in the cuisine of Morocco, and especially in Tangiers, where it originated. A mild spice blend with a gingery undertone, it is used to flavor soups, tagines, and poultry.* Harira, *a popular soup for breaking the fasts of Ramadan, is flavored with this mix.*

1 tablespoon ground ginger
1 tablespoon freshly ground black pepper
1½ teaspoons ground turmeric
1½ teaspoons ground cinnamon
1 teaspoon ground nutmeg

Combine all the ingredients in a bowl and stir to blend.

Store the mixture in an airtight container in a cool, dark, dry place for up to 1 month.

Yield: 1¾ tablespoons

Note: This is a delicate spice blend and doesn't have a long shelf life.

Qalat Dagga
(Tunisian Five-Spices Seasoning)

Qalat Dagga is a very simple North African blend of just five ingredients, the proportions of which vary, depending on the cook. This seasoning, which derives its "tingly" taste from the nutmeg, is traditionally used to flavor lamb and vegetable dishes; since there are only five ingredients, it is very easy to adjust the recipe to suit your tastes.

1 tablespoon black peppercorns

1 tablespoon whole cloves

2 teaspoons melagueta pepper
   (available by mail order; optional)

2 teaspoons grated nutmeg

1 teaspoon ground cinnamon

Place the peppercorns and cloves in a spice mill or coffee grinder and process to a fine powder.

Combine the ground mix with the remaining spices in a bowl and stir to blend.

Store the mixture in an airtight container in a cool, dark, dry place for up to 4 months.

Yield: ¼ cup

North African Tabil

This is another very simple, strong-tasting curry mix that is specific to and very popular in Tunisia. It's made with either fresh ingredients or their dried, ground equivalents. If making it from fresh ingredients, first pound everything into a paste, dry the paste, and then grind the paste to a powder. But it's much easier to start with ground ingredients, as we have here. As well as referring to the mix itself, the word tabil *means coriander, and this mix uses a large amount.* Tabil *is sprinkled over grilled meats and poultry, in stuffings and stews, and on vegetables. It can be made as hot or as mild as you like by adjusting the amount of chile, but the Tunisians like theirs hot.*

¼ cup coriander seeds

1 tablespoon caraway seeds

2 teaspoons dried red chile powder,
    either New Mexican or cayenne

2 teaspoons garlic powder

Place all the ingredients in a spice mill or coffee grinder and process to a fine powder.

Store the mixture in an airtight container in a cool, dark, dry place for up to 4 months.

Yield: ¼ cup

Baharat (Saudi Mixed Spices)

Baharat *means "spice" in Arabic and is derived from the word* bahar, *"pepper." So the definition of this recipe is "mixed spice with black pepper." Used to flavor dishes throughout the Gulf states and in Iraq,* baharat *varies to fit individual tastes, but all the variations use black pepper as a dominant spice. It's traditionally used to flavor kibbeh, a ground lamb and bulgur wheat dish, as well as meat stuffings, tomatoes, and sauces, soups, and stews.*

2 tablespoons freshly ground
   black pepper

2 tablespoons ground coriander

2 tablespoons ground paprika

1½ tablespoons ground nutmeg

1½ tablespoons curry powder, such as
   Cape Curry Powder (page 131)

1½ tablespoons ground dried limes
   (available by mail order; optional)

1½ teaspoons ground cloves

1½ teaspoons ground cumin

¾ teaspoon ground cardamom

Combine all the ingredients in a bowl and stir to blend.

Store the mixture in an airtight container for 1 to 2 months.

Yield: ⅓ to ½ cup

Dukkah (Egyptian Spice Mixture)

Dukkah is a staple in Egyptian households. A blend of spices, seeds, and toasted nuts or chick-peas, it originated in Egypt, but its popularity has spread throughout the Middle East and even "down under" to Australia and New Zealand. It gets its name from the Arabic word for "pound," since the mixture is crushed or pounded to a coarse, rather than fine, powder. The roots of this dish stretch back to the Bedouin tribes that traveled the deserts in the area. When they would gather at night, they'd roast spices, nuts, and seeds over their campfires, pound them into a coarse powder, and make a meal by dipping hunks of bread into olive oil and then the dukkah. Today, Egyptian street vendors sell small paper cones filled with their unique dukkah blend, along with strips of pita bread. Customers then dip the bread into the vendor's bowl of olive oil and then their dukkah. Enjoyed for breakfast and as a snack or appetizer, dukkah is also a very versatile seasoning that can be used as a topping on salads and vegetables, as a coating for poultry and fish, and as a tasty addition to bread.

½ cup hazelnuts

¼ cup coriander seeds

3 tablespoons sesame seeds

2 tablespoons cumin seeds

1 tablespoon black peppercorns

1 teaspoon fennel seeds

1 teaspoon dried mint leaves

1 teaspoon salt

Heat a heavy skillet over high heat, add the hazelnuts, and dry-roast until slightly browned and fragrant, being careful that they don't burn. Remove from the heat and cool completely. Repeat the procedure with each of the seeds and the peppercorns. Allow each of them to cool completely.

Place the nuts and seeds, along with the mint and salt, into a mortar and pound until the mixture is crushed. Or pulse in a food processor to a coarse consistency; do not allow the mixture to become a paste.

Store in an airtight container in a cool place for up to 1 month.

Yield: 1 cup

Zhug (Yemenite Hot Sauce)

Popular with the Yemenite Jews in Israel and in the Middle East, this hot sauce starts with a paste of garlic and peppers plus whatever spices the individual cook chooses, along with cilantro and/or parsley. There are two versions, this green one and a red one that uses red sweet and hot peppers. Tomatoes are sometimes added to tone down the sauce, which can be quite spicy. This quick and easy sauce serves as a table condiment, as a sauce for grilled fish or meat or for eggs, or can be added to soups and stews just before serving. It goes especially well with lamb kabobs.

8 serrano chiles, stems removed; or substitute jalapeño chiles

6 cloves garlic, coarsely chopped

1½ teaspoons caraway seeds

1 teaspoon cumin seeds

1 teaspoon ground cardamom

1 teaspoon freshly ground black pepper

½ teaspoon ground cloves

1 tablespoon lemon juice, preferably fresh

1 cup chopped fresh cilantro

½ cup chopped fresh parsley

½ to ¾ cup olive oil

Salt to taste

Place the chiles, garlic, caraway, cumin, cardamom, pepper, cloves, and lemon juice in a blender or food processor and puree to a smooth paste, adding some of the oil if necessary.

Add the cilantro and parsley, and while the machine is running, slowly add the oil until a "soupy" sauce is formed. Season with salt.

This sauce may be stored, covered, in the refrigerator for up to 2 weeks. Be sure to cover the top with a couple of drops of olive oil to prevent the *Zhug* from turning brown.

Yield: 1½ to 2 cups

Berbere

This flaming hot seasoning, found in virtually every Ethiopian kitchen, is served as a condiment and as an ingredient in the national dish known as w'at *or* w'et. *Ethiopians call berbere hot; we rate it as extremely hot. And as hot as this spice mix is, they have one that is even hotter.* Mit'mit'a, *as they call it, must be nuclear! This version of berbere was given to us by Regina Mueller, who with her husband Phillip was a missionary in Ethiopia for a number of years. Berbere blends are often closely guarded, as the marriageability of Ethiopian women has traditionally been based on the quality of their berbere; Regina was given the recipe by an Ethiopian friend who no longer believed in this custom. She has toned it down from the original, which called for ½ cup of ground cayenne!*

½ teaspoon cumin seeds

½ teaspoon cardamom seeds

¼ teaspoon fenugreek seeds

¼ teaspoon black peppercorns

2 tablespoons onion powder

3 to 4 teaspoons ground cayenne

2 tablespoons onion powder

¾ teaspoon ground ginger

½ teaspoon ground cinnamon

¼ teaspoon ground nutmeg

¼ teaspoon ground allspice

¼ teaspoon ground cloves

¼ teaspoon ground turmeric

¼ teaspoon salt

Heat a heavy skillet over high heat, add the cumin, cardamom, fenugreek, and peppercorns, and dry-roast the seeds until they darken and become fragrant, being careful that they don't burn. Allow the spices to cool completely and then place in a spice mill or coffee grinder and process to a fine powder.

Combine with the remaining ingredients in a bowl and stir to blend.

Store the mixture in an airtight container in a cool, dark, dry place for up to 6 months.

Yield: approximately ¼ cup

Variation: Add water or vegetable oil to create a thick paste and serve as a condiment.

Niter Kebbeh
(Ethiopian Curried Spiced Butter)

An essential ingredient in many traditional Ethiopian dishes, niter kebbeh *is a bright orange clarified butter. It's similar to Indian ghee, but this version has a rich aroma and taste. Clarified butter is good for cooking at higher temperatures than regular butter, because it doesn't contain any of the milk solids that burn. This type of butter is the secret to making a good omelet.* Niter kebbeh *will solidify in the refrigerator but reliquefy at room temperature. Be sure to strain out all of the solids so the butter does not become rancid.*

4 whole cloves

One 1-inch piece cinnamon stick

¾ teaspoon cardamom seeds

½ teaspoon fenugreek seeds

2 pounds (8 sticks) unsalted butter

¼ cup chopped onion

2 tablespoons chopped garlic

1 tablespoon grated ginger

1½ teaspoons ground turmeric

¼ teaspoon freshly grated nutmeg

Heat a heavy skillet over high heat, add the cloves, cinnamon, cardamom, and fenugreek, and dry-roast until the seeds darken and become fragrant, being careful that they don't burn. Allow the mixture to cool.

Melt the butter in a heavy saucepan over low heat; do not let it brown. Increase the heat and bring the butter to a boil, stirring frequently. Skim off the foam that forms.

Add all the remaining ingredients, including the toasted spice mixture, to the pan. Reduce the heat to low and simmer the butter, uncovered, for 45 minutes. Do not stir.

When the milk solids at the bottom of the pan are a golden brown, strain the transparent butter through a linen towel into a bowl. Continue to strain the butter until no solids remain.

Store the butter in the refrigerator or at room temperature for up to 3 months.

Yield: About 2 cups

South African Cape Curry Powder

This curry powder reflects the influence of the Malaysian slaves brought to South Africa by the Dutch and the indentured Indian laborers that worked on the sugar plantations in the 1800s. Some of the curry mixtures contain as few as three ingredients, while others, such as this one, have a more complex mix of spices. Use this powder in any South African dish calling for a curry powder.

2 teaspoons coriander seeds

1 teaspoon black mustard seeds

1 teaspoon black peppercorns

½ teaspoon fenugreek seeds

½ teaspoon fennel seeds

6 whole cloves

3 bird chiles, stems and seeds removed; or substitute piquins or santakas

1 teaspoon ground ginger

1 teaspoon ground turmeric

1 teaspoon ground cardamom

¼ teaspoon ground cumin

Heat a heavy skillet over high heat, add the coriander, mustard, black peppercorns, fenugreek, fennel, and cloves, and dry-roast until the seeds darken and become fragrant, being careful that they don't burn. Allow the ingredients to cool completely and then place in a spice mill or coffee grinder, along with the chiles, and process to a fine powder.

Combine all the ingredients in a bowl and stir to blend.

Store the mixture in an airtight container in a cool, dark, dry place for up to 4 months.

Yield: ¼ cup

Dried Apricot Blatjang
(South African Fruit Chutney)

Blatjangs are South Africa's version of a thick, fruity chutney that has its roots a continent away, in Java. Migrant workers introduced chutneys to the area, and now no Cape Maylay table would be without one. There are many varieties, using ingredients such as peaches, dates, quince, or almonds, but some of the most popular contain dried apricots, as does our version.

1½ cups chopped, dried apricots

¼ cup raisins

1 cup chopped onion

4 dried red chiles, such as cayenne or piquin, stems and seeds removed

½ cup malt or cider vinegar

3 tablespoons sugar

1 tablespoon chopped ginger

2 teaspoons chopped garlic

1½ teaspoons ground coriander

1 teaspoon salt

Put the apricots, raisins, onion, chiles, vinegar, and sugar in a saucepan and add just enough water to cover, about 1 cup. Simmer the mixture over medium-low heat for 10 minutes, until the fruit has softened.

Add the ginger and garlic and continue to simmer until the mixture has softened and the sauce is the consistency of honey, about 15 to 20 minutes.

Remove from the heat, stir in the coriander and salt, and spoon into glass jars. Cool the *blatjang*, cover, and refrigerate.

This chutney will keep for about 2 weeks in the refrigerator.

Yield: 2 to 3 cups

Sambhar Powder

Sambhar curry powder is fundamental to South Indian Brahmin vegetarian cooking. Brahmin curries are known for their crunchy, nutty taste, which they get from the dals (the Hindi word for pulses—dried legumes like lentils, peas, or chickpeas) that are used in curry powders and as a thickener in curries. Because of the desired nutty flavor, don't soak the dals before using. Sambhar powders are widely used to flavor pulses, braised and stewed vegetables, and sauces. If making a large amount of this powder, roast each of the spices separately, but with a small amount we roast all of them at the same time. Asafetida is a very pungent spice that is made from the dried resin of several fennel-like plants. There is no substitute, so omit if it's not available.

1 tablespoon coriander seeds
2 teaspoons cumin seeds
One 2-inch piece cinnamon stick
1 teaspoon brown mustard seeds
½ teaspoon black peppercorns
½ teaspoon fenugreek seeds
1 teaspoon ground turmeric

½ teaspoon asafetida (often found in Asian markets; optional)
6 to 8 small dried red chiles, such as piquins, stems and seeds removed
1 tablespoon *channa dal* (yellow split peas)
2 teaspoons *toor dal* (pigeon peas)

Heat a heavy skillet over high heat, add the coriander, cumin, cinnamon, mustard, peppercorns, and fenugreek, and dry-roast until the seeds darken and become fragrant, being careful that they don't burn. Add the turmeric, and asafetida, if using, and roast for an additional minute. Remove the mixture and cool completely.

Lower the heat to medium, add the chiles, and toast for 2 to 3 minutes. Remove and cool.

Add both the dals to the skillet and roast them until they darken, stirring frequently to prevent them from burning, about 3 to 4 minutes. Allow them to cool completely.

When all the ingredients are cool, place them in a spice mill or coffee grinder and process to a powder.

Store the mixture in an airtight container in a cool, dark, dry place for up to 4 months.

Yield: ¼ cup

Panch Phoran (Bengali Five Spices)

The Bengal region of India is located in the northeastern part of the country, where spices are used whole rather than ground. Panch *means "five" in Hindi, and can sometimes be found in stores; don't, however, confuse it with Chinese five-spice powder, which is a different spice mix altogether.* Kalonji, *or nigella seeds, look like and are sometimes referred to as onion seeds, but they are not. They have a distinct, sharp taste, and are a popular ingredient in both Indian and Iranian cooking. This spice mix is excellent over vegetables, especially eggplant; it is a good frying spice for fish and seafood, meat, and poultry, and is sometimes used in curries.*

2¾ teaspoons fennel seeds

2 teaspoons cumin seeds

1¾ teaspoons black mustard seeds

1 teaspoon fenugreek seeds

1 teaspoon *kalonji* or nigella seeds
    (available in Indian and Asian markets)

Combine all the ingredients in a bowl and stir to blend.

Store the mixture in an airtight container in a cool, dark, dry place for up to 4 months.

Yield: ¼ cup

Garam Masala

In Hindi the word garam *means "hot" or "heating" and* masala *is a mixture of spices; these terms refer to the effects of spices in the body. Garam masala is a mixture of spices that create heat in the body—cinnamon, cloves, black pepper, and cardamom. Toasting the spices before grinding is necessary to release their essential oils. Masalas are prized for their aromatic qualities and are usually formulated for a specific use; they are best added toward the end of the cooking period to get the full effect of their aroma. This masala is a basic blend that is used alone or with other seasonings.*

2 tablespoons cardamom pods
One 3-inch piece cinnamon stick
1 tablespoon black peppercorns
1 tablespoon whole cloves
1 tablespoon coriander seeds
1 teaspoon cumin seeds
¼ teaspoon ground nutmeg

Break open the cardamom pods and remove the seeds. Save the seeds and discard the pods.

Heat a heavy skillet over high heat; add all the ingredients, except the nutmeg, and dry-roast until the seeds darken and become fragrant, being careful that they don't burn. Allow the roasted spices to cool completely and then place them, along with the nutmeg, in a spice mill or coffee grinder and process to a fine powder.

Store the mixture in an airtight container in a cool, dark, dry place for up to 4 months.

Yield: ¼ cup

Bafat (Hurry Curry)

There are scores of curry powders on the market today. Purists may frown on them, but they are indeed useful for making curries in a hurry. Even in India, curry powders have become an integral part of middle-class family life. The following curry powder, called bafat, *is from southwestern India. It can be used in meat, fish, or vegetable dishes. It can even be used the same day for two completely different dishes, each with its own unique flavor!*

⅓ cup coriander seeds

¼ cup cumin seeds

2 tablespoons mustard seeds

2 tablespoons peppercorns

2 tablespoons whole cloves

1 tablespoon fenugreek seeds

2 tablespoons ground cardamom

2 tablespoons ground cinnamon

2 tablespoons powdered turmeric

¼ cup freshly ground, hot red
   chile powder

Dry the whole spices on a cookie sheet in the oven at 200°F for 15 minutes, taking care they do not burn. Remove them from the oven, cool, and grind them in a spice mill in small batches. Combine them with the ground spices in a bowl and mix well.

Store the curry powder in an airtight container in a cool, dark, dry place for up to 4 months.

Yield: About 1½ cups

Tamatar Chatni (Tomato Chutney)

The word chutney *is derived from the East Indian word* chatni, *and the various chutneys serve as condiments to accompany curries. This spicy tomato chutney would traditionally contain jaggery, a dark, unrefined sugar made from palm sap. It's available in Indian markets, but in our version we've substituted brown sugar, which is easier to find. The texture of this chutney can be chunky or smooth, and the flavor complements just about any curry dish. We've been known to puree this chutney and use it in place of ketchup. Although the list of ingredients is rather long, this is a very easy chutney to prepare.*

1 teaspoon ghee (page 238)
   or vegetable oil

2 tablespoons black mustard seeds

¼ teaspoon fenugreek seeds

¼ teaspoon cumin seeds

1 cup chopped onions

1 teaspoon minced garlic

2 tablespoons grated ginger

4 to 6 small tomatoes, peeled and
   coarsely chopped

1 cup malt or cider vinegar

½ cup brown sugar

4 serrano chiles, stems removed, chopped

2 tablespoons seedless raisins

½ teaspoon salt

½ teaspoon ground cinnamon

¼ teaspoon ground turmeric

⅛ teaspoon ground cloves

Heat a heavy saucepan over medium heat, add the ghee, and when it is hot, add the mustard, fenugreek, and cumin seeds and fry until they start to pop and sputter, about 1 minute. Add the onion, garlic, and ginger and sauté for a few more minutes.

Add all the remaining ingredients to the saucepan, raise the heat, and bring the mixture to a boil. Reduce the heat and simmer, stirring frequently, until the chutney starts to thicken, about 30 minutes. Taste and adjust the seasonings.

Spoon the hot chutney into hot sterilized jars, and cover.

Store in the refrigerator, after opening, for up to 2 weeks.

Yield: 2 cups

Nam Prik Gaeng Ped
(Thai Red Curry Paste)

This hot, flavorful paste from Thailand can be added to just about any curry, to add another dimension. All Thai pastes are hot, and they are used as a base in all the country's curries. This one gets its name from the Thai red chiles used, which can be either fresh or dried. If you're using dried chiles, be sure to soak them in hot water to soften before processing. Traditionally a mortar and pestle is used, but we've found it much easier to use a modern blender or food processor. Galangal is a root similar to ginger but not quite as sweet, with a little hint of lemon; ginger is an acceptable substitute. If you decrease the number of chiles to reduce the heat level, you may have to add paprika to maintain the characteristic red color.

1 tablespoon coriander seeds

1 teaspoon cumin seeds

1 teaspoon caraway seeds

1 teaspoon black peppercorns

2 stalks fresh lemongrass

10 to 15 red Thai chiles, stems and seeds removed; or substitute 10 small dried red chiles such as piquins or japones

1 tablespoon chopped garlic

4 small shallots, thinly sliced

1 tablespoon coarsely grated galangal or ginger

Grated zest of 1 small lime

¼ cup chopped fresh cilantro, including the stems

1 teaspoon shrimp paste (available in Asian markets)

1 teaspoon salt

2 to 4 tablespoons vegetable oil, preferably peanut, or more to form a paste

Heat a heavy skillet over high heat, add the coriander, cumin, caraway, and peppercorns, and dry-roast until the seeds darken and become fragrant, being careful that they don't burn. Allow the spices to cool completely, place them in a spice mill or coffee grinder, and process to a fine powder.

Trim the stalks of the lemongrass to about 3 inches in length. Trim away any hard portions, discard the outer leaves, and coarsely chop.

Place all the ingredients, except the oil, in a blender or food processor and, with the motor running, slowly add just enough of the oil to form a paste.

Refrigerate for up to 1 month or freeze for 4 months.

Yield: ½ cup

Nam Prik Krueng Gaeng Kheow Wan (Thai Green Curry Paste)

The green chiles and cilantro in this recipe give this curry paste its name. The krueng *in the name means "engine" in Thai, and the* gaeng *means "curry"; these pastes are used literally to make the dishes "go." Green curry paste is the one used to fire up the hottest of all the Thai curries. Traditionally, the finely chopped rind of the kaffir lime is used to flavor this paste; since it's not readily available, we don't call for it here.*

1 tablespoon coriander seeds

1 teaspoon cumin seeds

5 black peppercorns

3 stalks fresh lemongrass

¼ cup chopped fresh cilantro, including the stems

4 jalapeño chiles, stems and seeds removed, chopped; or substitute serranos or 6 green New Mexican chiles, roasted, peeled, and chopped

10 green Thai chiles, stems removed, chopped

3 tablespoons chopped shallots

2 tablespoons chopped garlic

1 tablespoon coarsely grated ginger or galangal

1 teaspoon shrimp paste (available in Asian markets)

2 to 4 tablespoons vegetable oil, preferably peanut, or more to form a paste

Heat a heavy skillet over high heat, add the coriander, cumin, and peppercorns, and dry-roast until the seeds darken and become fragrant, being careful that they don't burn. Allow the ingredients to cool completely, place them in a spice mill or coffee grinder, and process to a fine powder.

Trim the stalks of the lemongrass to about 3 inches in length. Trim away any hard portions, discard the outer leaves, and coarsely chop.

Place all the ingredients, except the oil, in a blender or food processor and, with the motor running, slowly add just enough of the oil to form a paste.

Refrigerate for up to 1 month or freeze for 4 months.

Yield: ½ cup

Nam Prik Gaeng Mussaman
(Mussaman Curry Paste)

Mussaman curry paste is named for the Muslim spice traders who brought curries to Thailand by way of India a couple hundred years ago and reflects an Indian influence in its spices. Initially the Thais were skeptical about using cinnamon in a hot curry, but one taste changed that. This paste has a rich, warm flavor and is often combined with beef and coconut milk to make a curry served at weddings.

12 dried red chiles, such as piquins, stems and seeds removed

2 tablespoons cumin seeds

1 teaspoon coriander seeds

1 teaspoon whole cloves

1 teaspoon black peppercorns

3 stalks fresh lemongrass

6 shallots

8 cloves garlic

1 teaspoon ground cinnamon

1 teaspoon ground mace

1 teaspoon ground nutmeg

1 teaspoon ground cardamom

1 teaspoon salt

1 tablespoon shrimp paste (available in Asian markets)

2 to 4 tablespoons vegetable oil, preferably peanut, or more to form a paste

Place the chiles in a bowl and cover with very hot water. Allow the chiles to steep for 15 to 20 minutes to soften. Drain the chiles and discard the water.

Heat a heavy skillet over high heat, add the cumin, coriander, cloves, and peppercorns, and dry-roast until the seeds darken and become fragrant, being careful that they don't burn. Allow the ingredients to cool completely, place them in a spice mill or coffee grinder, and process to a fine powder.

Trim the stalks of the lemongrass to about 3 inches in length. Trim away any hard portions, discard the outer leaves, and coarsely chop.

Place all the ingredients, except the oil, in a blender or food processor and, with the motor running, slowly add just enough of the oil to form a paste.

Refrigerate the paste for up to 1 month, or freeze for 4 months.

Yield: ½ cup

Sambal Oelek
(Hot Chile and Lime Condiment)

Sambals *are multipurpose condiments that are popular throughout Indonesia, Malaysia, and India, with a multitude of variations. This basic, hot sambal, which has been called the mother of all Indonesian* sambals, *is also spelled* olek *or* ulek. *Since* oelek *means "hot peppers," we'll go with that spelling. This* sambal *goes well with meats and poultry as well as being a perfect condiment just to add heat to your meal. It can also be used as a base for creating other* sambals *or as a substitute for fresh chile peppers in recipes.*

1 cup dried red chiles, such as piquins or cayennes,
    stems removed
6 cloves garlic
3 tablespoons lime juice, preferably fresh
1 tablespoon vegetable oil, preferably peanut

Place the chiles in a bowl, cover with hot water, and allow them to steep for 15 minutes to soften. Remove the chiles, drain, and discard the water.

Combine all the ingredients in a blender or food processor and puree until smooth. Thin the sambal with more lime juice if desired.

Store in the refrigerator, covered, for up to 2 weeks.

Yield: ⅓ to ½ cup

Sambal Tomat (Tomato Condiment)

Don't let this tomato-based sambal *fool you into thinking it's a dip for chips—it can be extremely hot! The shrimp paste, or* trassi, *isn't toasted in this recipe, as it is in other* sambal *recipes, because it's cooked in the sauce. This* sambal *is good with fish dishes; any extra can be frozen for future use.*

3 tablespoons vegetable oil, preferably peanut

10 shallots, chopped

7 cloves garlic, chopped

10 fresh, large red chiles, such as New Mexican, stems and seeds removed, chopped

2 medium tomatoes, cut in wedges

2 teaspoons shrimp paste (available in Asian markets)

2 teaspoons lime juice, preferably fresh

Salt to taste

Heat a heavy skillet over medium-high heat, add the oil, and when hot, add the shallots and garlic and sauté for 5 minutes, being careful they don't brown. Add the chiles and sauté for another 3 to 5 minutes.

Add the tomatoes and shrimp paste, reduce the heat, and simmer for 10 minutes.

Place the tomato mixture along with the lime juice in a blender or food processor and pulse to form a coarse paste. This *sambal* should not be smooth.

Season with salt and allow to cool before using.

Store in the refrigerator, covered, for 1 week, or freeze for up to 4 months.

Yield: ½ to 1 cup

Sambal Kacang (Spicy Peanut Sauce)

This hot and spicy peanut sauce is probably the one most associated with Indonesian cuisine. Widely popular, there are many variations of this sambal *and a variety of uses. It's used as a dip for* satays, *as a basis for unusual curries, as a dressing for* gado gado, *as an elaborate mixed vegetable salad, and as a sauce for cooked vegetables.* Sambal kacang *also makes a great dipping sauce for an appetizer of crisp garden vegetables. It's traditionally prepared by pounding the peanuts into a paste before using, but we've simplified the recipe by substituting commercial peanut butter.*

1 tablespoon vegetable oil, preferably peanut

3 shallots, minced

1 tablespoon minced garlic

1 teaspoon minced ginger

1 cup chicken broth

½ cup peanut butter, either crunchy or smooth

3 tablespoons lime juice, preferably fresh

1 tablespoon crushed dried piquin chiles; or substitute *Sambal Oelek* (page 141)

1 tablespoon soy sauce

1 tablespoon brown sugar

2 teaspoons Asian fish sauce

Heat a heavy skillet over medium-high heat, add the oil, and when hot, add the shallots, garlic, and ginger and sauté until the shallots are soft and transparent but not browned, about 5 minutes.

Add the chicken broth, raise the heat, and bring to a boil. Reduce the heat and stir in the remaining ingredients. Simmer the sauce, uncovered, for 10 to 15 minutes until thickened.

Serve the *sambal* warm or at room temperature. Do not refrigerate, or the peanut butter will congeal and the flavors will not blend.

Yield: 1 cup

Chinese Five-Spice Powder

This is a traditional Chinese spice mix; sometimes referred to as five-fragrance powder, it was introduced to Europe by English sailors in the late 1500s. It has a powerful anise flavor and is used to flavor dishes throughout southern China, Vietnam, Malaysia, and Indonesia. It's used in stir-fries, marinades, and "red-cooked" dishes (in which the food is braised in soy sauce), and is an important ingredient of Sichuan cooking. Chinese five-spice powder is often only part of the seasoning of a particular dish, used in small amounts. The five spices can vary in their proportions, so adjust the mix to suit your tastes.

6 whole star anise

2 teaspoons Sichuan peppercorns (available by mail order);
   or substitute equal portions of anise and allspice

2 teaspoons whole cloves

1½ teaspoons whole fennel seeds

One 2-inch piece cinnamon stick

Place all the ingredients in a spice mill or coffee grinder and process to a fine powder.

Store the mixture in an airtight container in a cool, dark, dry place for up to 4 months.

Yield: 3 to 4 tablespoons

Ginger Plum Sauce Mustard

This mustard is both sweet and hot, with a crisp, sharp, distinctive flavor. The sweetness comes from the ginger, the plum sauce, and even the vinegar, if Chinese black vinegar is used. This vinegar, which can be found in Asian markets, has a very distinctive fruity, salty, complex, nonacidic taste. This is a very easy mustard to prepare and makes a great dipping sauce for Asian appetizers as well as a glaze on ham or duck.

¼ cup brown mustard seeds, finely ground

½ cup yellow mustard powder

2 tablespoons Chinese black vinegar
(available in Asian markets); or
substitute rice or distilled white vinegar

3 tablespoons Chinese plum sauce
(available in Asian markets)

⅓ cup grated ginger

1 tablespoon brown sugar

1 teaspoon finely minced garlic

Place the mustard seeds in a spice mill or coffee grinder and process to a powder.

Combine the mustards and add the vinegar, plum sauce, and ¼ cup water in a bowl; stir to form a paste. Add the ginger, sugar, and garlic and mix well.

Spoon the mustard into a sterilized jar and refrigerate for 1 week before using.

This mustard will keep in the refrigerator, covered, for up to 1 month after opening.

Yield: 1 cup

Note: This recipe requires advance preparation.

Shichimi Togarashi

This favorite Japanese seasoning sometimes goes by the name of seven-flavor spice, or just togarashi. Named for the togarashi chile, it's a mixture of seven spices, with the chile being the most important ingredient. Sometimes more than seven spices are used, but even then it's called by the same name. This is very hot seasoning with a definite citrus flavor, commonly used to spice udon noodles, soups, and yakitoris. It's used both as a seasoning and as a condiment, added to finished dishes.

3 to 4 tablespoons crushed togarashi chile; or substitute takanotsume, santaka, or piquin chiles

1 tablespoon dried orange or tangerine peel

2 teaspoons white sesame seeds

2 teaspoons black sesame seeds

1 teaspoon Sichuan (*sansho* or *fagara*) pepper (available by mail order); or substitute equal amounts of anise and allspice

1 teaspoon shredded *nori* (available in Asian markets)

½ teaspoon ground ginger

Place all the ingredients in a spice mill or coffee grinder and process to a coarse powder.

Store the mixture in an airtight container in a cool, dark, dry place for up to 4 months.

Yield: ¼ to ⅓ cup

Wasabi Sauce for Beef or Fish

This recipe is a remake of a classic early English horseradish sauce, using Japanese wasabi. It is perfect for rare roast beef or steak, smoked salmon, and any fried or baked fish dish. Make it just before you are ready to serve the meal to retain the wasabi's full potency.

1 tablespoon white wine vinegar

1 teaspoon dry mustard

½ teaspoon lemon juice, preferably fresh

¼ teaspoon sugar

¼ teaspoon salt

Freshly ground black pepper

½ cup plus 2 tablespoons heavy cream, chilled

2 tablespoons wasabi paste

Combine the vinegar, mustard, lemon juice, sugar, salt, and black pepper in a small bowl and whisk to form a smooth paste.

In another chilled bowl, whip the cream until it forms peaks. Add the whipped cream and wasabi to the mustard paste, stirring gently to blend.

Serve immediately.

Yield: ¾ cup

The Earliest Mole Sauce

Why wouldn't the cooks of the prehistoric, ash-covered village of Cerén have developed sauces to serve over meats and vegetables? After all, there is evidence that curry mixtures were in existence thousands of years ago in what is now India, and we have to assume that Native Americans experimented with all available ingredients. Perhaps this mole sauce was served over stewed duck meat, as ducks were one of the domesticated meat sources of the Cerén villagers.

3 tablespoons pumpkin or
    squash seeds (*pepitas*)

4 tomatillos, husks removed

1 tomato, roasted and peeled

½ teaspoon chile seeds,
    from dried chile pods

2 tablespoons red chile powder,
    such as New Mexican, guajillo,
    or Chimayó

1 corn tortilla, torn into pieces

1 teaspoon annatto seeds; or
    substitute achiote paste

3 tablespoons vegetable oil

2½ cups chicken broth

1 ounce Mexican chocolate; or
    substitute bittersweet chocolate

Heat a heavy skillet over high heat; add the pumpkin seeds, and dry-roast until the seeds start to pop. Shake the skillet once they start to pop, continuing until they turn golden, about 3 to 5 minutes. Be sure that they don't darken, and remove from the pan to cool completely. Place the seeds in a spice mill or coffee grinder and process to a fine powder.

Put the pumpkin seeds, tomatillos, tomato, chile seeds, chile powder, tortilla, and annatto or achiote in a blender or food processor and process, using just enough broth to form a paste.

Reheat the skillet over medium heat, add the oil, and when hot, add the paste. Fry the paste, stirring constantly, until fragrant, about 4 minutes.

Whisk in the remaining chicken broth and the chocolate, and cook, stirring constantly, until thickened to desired consistency. If the sauce becomes too thick, thin with either broth or water.

This sauce may be stored in the refrigerator, covered, for up to 4 or 5 days.

Yield: 2 cups

Bajan Seasoning

Found on almost every table in Barbados, this seasoning is the secret to the success of many mouthwatering Bajan dishes, according to our friend Anne-Marie Whittaker, who lives in Barbados. There are an amazing number of variations of this paste in Trinidad as well as Barbados, but they all have a couple of things in common. First, they contain a variety of herbs; and second, they always contain chiles. Bajan seasoning can be added to soups and stews for added flavor, or serve as a marinade and basting sauce for grilled meats, chicken, or fish. One of the most popular uses for Bajan seasoning is to place it under the skin of chicken pieces before grilling, baking, or frying.

2½ cups coarsely chopped onions

½ cup coarsely chopped green onions

5 cloves garlic, chopped

2 bonney peppers, stems and seeds removed; or substitute Scotch bonnet peppers or habaneros

¾ cup cider vinegar

3 tablespoons lime juice, preferably fresh

2 tablespoons vegetable oil

2 tablespoons chopped fresh parsley

1 tablespoon chopped fresh chives

1 tablespoon chopped fresh thyme; or substitute 1 teaspoon dried

1 tablespoon chopped fresh marjoram; or substitute 1 teaspoon dried

1 teaspoon salt

½ teaspoon ground cloves

½ teaspoon freshly ground black pepper

Place the onions, green onions, garlic, peppers, ¼ cup of the vinegar, and the lime juice in a blender or food processor and puree to a coarse paste.

Add the remaining ½ cup of vinegar, the oil, and the herbs and puree the mixture to a smooth paste, adding more oil if necessary.

Place the seasoning paste in a nonreactive bowl, cover, and refrigerate for at least 24 hours before using.

The seasoning will keep in the refrigerator for up to 2 months.

Yield: 1 to 1½ cups

Note: This recipe requires advance preparation.

Trinidad Curry Paste

Many Trinidad curry mixes lack hot chiles; however, Dave found this recipe that does call for them in a nineteenth-century cookbook. This mix of ground spices was brought to Trinidad by migrant Hindu workers. It's called a curry powder when the mix is dry, but the addition of chiles or a liquid turns it into a paste. In Trinidad the Congo chile would be used, but since it is hard to find, use a habanero. This paste can be substituted in recipes calling for a masala or curry powder.

6 tablespoons coriander seeds

1 teaspoon anise seeds

1 teaspoon whole cloves

1 teaspoon cumin seeds

1 teaspoon fenugreek seeds

1 teaspoon yellow or
    brown mustard seeds

1 teaspoon black peppercorns

1 teaspoon ground turmeric

1 large onion, chopped

3 cloves garlic

½ Congo or habanero chile,
    stem and seeds removed

Heat a heavy skillet over high heat, add the coriander, anise, cloves, cumin, fenugreek, mustard seeds, and peppercorns, and dry-roast until the seeds darken and become fragrant, being careful that they don't burn. Allow the mixture to cool completely and then place in a spice mill or coffee grinder and process to a fine powder.

Place the mixture, along with the turmeric, onion, garlic, and chile, in a blender or food processor; with the motor running, slowly add just enough water to form a paste.

Store the paste in the refrigerator, covered, for up to 2 days.

Yield: 1½ to 2 cups

West Indian Masala

Although there are commercial masalas available, we like to make our curry mixes fresh for each dish. They are not difficult to prepare, and when the spices are freshly roasted and ground, they don't have a chance to oxidize and lose flavor. Generally speaking, in the West Indies, when turmeric is added to a masala, the mixture is considered curry powder.

6 tablespoons coriander seeds

2 teaspoons fennel seeds

1½ teaspoons cumin seeds

1 teaspoon fenugreek seeds

1 teaspoon mustard seeds

2 teaspoons ground turmeric (optional)

1 teaspoon ground allspice, preferably Jamaican

Heat a heavy skillet over high heat, add the coriander, fennel, cumin, fenugreek, and mustard seeds, and dry-roast until the seeds darken and become fragrant, being careful that they don't burn. Allow the mixture to cool completely and then place in a spice mill or coffee grinder and process to a fine powder.

Combine the spice mixture, turmeric, if using, and allspice in a bowl and stir to blend.

Store the mixture in an airtight container in a cool, dark, dry place for up to 4 months.

Yield: ½ cup

Mango Kuchela

Relishes, like Indian chutneys, are commonly served with curried dishes. Kuchela, which is also spelled kucheela *and* kuchila, *is just such a hot and spicy East Indian mango relish. Very popular throughout the lower Caribbean islands, it's always made with green mangos, which are green-fleshed, firm, and bitter. Look for green mangoes in Asian markets, but do* not *substitute unripened yellow mangoes.*

2 pounds green mangoes

2 teaspoons coriander seeds

1 teaspoon fennel seeds

½ teaspoon fenugreek seeds

½ teaspoon yellow mustard seeds

¼ teaspoon cumin seeds

¼ teaspoon black peppercorns

4 allspice berries

4 cloves garlic, minced

2 Congo peppers, stems and seeds removed, minced; or substitute habaneros

¼ teaspoon ground turmeric

Salt to taste

⅓ to ½ cup mustard oil (available in Indian and Asian markets)

Note: This recipe requires advance preparation.

Peel and grate the mangoes into a bowl, and using your hands, squeeze as much of the liquid as possible from the fruit. Spread the mangoes out on a sheet pan, cover with a towel, to let them dry for a day, or place the pan in a 250°F oven for 2 hours, or until meat has dried out.

Heat a heavy skillet over high heat, add the coriander, fennel, fenugreek, mustard, cumin, peppercorns, and allspice, and dry-roast until the seeds have darkened and are fragrant, being careful that they don't burn. Allow the mixture to cool completely and then place in a spice mill or coffee grinder and process to a fine powder.

Combine all the ingredients, except the oil, in a bowl and stir to blend. Slowly add just enough of the oil to make a slightly soupy relish.

Store in the refrigerator, covered, for up to 2 weeks.

Yield: 1 cup

Adobo Seasoning

Adobos can be found throughout the areas where the Spanish had an influence. The definition of an adobo can be confusing, as it can refer to three distinct recipes. Adobo, the national dish of the Philippines, is braised chicken, pork, or fish cooked in coconut milk with garlic, vinegar, and soy sauce. In Mexico, adobo *refers to a sauce or seasoning paste made with vinegar, chiles, and herbs, such as chipotle chiles* en adobo. *Here we are referring to the third type of adobo, the Puerto Rican seasoning composed of dry ingredients, which is often mixed with fruit juice and used as a marinade.*

1 tablespoon dried oregano
1 tablespoon garlic powder
1 teaspoon freshly ground black pepper
½ teaspoon ground cumin
¼ teaspoon salt

Combine all the ingredients in a bowl and stir to blend.

Store the mixture in an airtight container in a cool, dark, dry place for up to 4 months.

Yield: 2 to 3 tablespoons

Salsa de Chile de Arbol (Chile de Arbol Salsa)

This simple, earthy salsa is based on those from the Michoacan area of Mexico. It's an un-cooked table salsa used to add tasty heat to dishes; it is never used as an ingredient in a recipe. Charring the tomatoes and chiles gives the salsa a smoky taste. The de arbol chile is a long, slender chile that looks mild enough—but be cautious; it can take the top of your head off, and the heat hangs in there for a long time.

8 to 12 dried chiles de arbol, stems removed
2 Roma tomatoes
3 cloves garlic, unpeeled
1 teaspoon white vinegar
Salt to taste

Heat a heavy skillet over medium heat, add the chiles, tomatoes, and garlic, and dry-roast, shaking the pan occasionally, until the skins start to blacken and the vegetables are soft. This can also be done under a broiler. Cool the vegetables. Remove the skins from the garlic.

Put all the ingredients in a blender or food processor and pulse to coarsely blend, adding just enough water to form a sauce. Season to taste with salt.

This sauce may be stored in the refrigerator, covered, for up to 4 days.

Yield: ½ cup

Salsa Borracha (Drunken Salsa)

Pulque, the fermented milky sap from the maguey or century plant, is the traditional ingredient that provides the borracha *in this salsa. If it's not available, substitute tequila or dark Mexican beer. The pasilla chiles used in this dish are not California pasillas, which are actually ancho chiles, but the dried form of the chilaca, a thin, mild, black chile. Their rich, smoky taste with a hint of chocolate makes this a wonderful sauce to serve with grilled meats and chicken, and no Mexican* barbacoa *would be complete without a bowl of* salsa borracha.

8 pasilla chiles

2 cloves garlic

½ cup orange juice, preferably
    fresh-squeezed

1 cup pulque; or substitute tequila or
    dark Mexican beer

¼ cup chopped white onion

⅓ cup grated *queso anejo*; or
    substitute Parmesan cheese

Salt to taste

Heat a heavy skillet over medium heat, add the chiles and garlic, and dry-roast, shaking the pan occasionally, until the chiles become fragrant and the garlic is soft. Allow the vegetables to cool.

Remove the stems and seeds from the chiles and place in a bowl. Cover the chiles with very hot water and allow them to steep for 15 minutes to soften. Drain and discard the water.

Put the chiles, garlic, and orange juice in a blender or food processor and process to a smooth paste. With the motor running, slowly add the pulque until it's incorporated into the salsa. Season to taste with the salt.

Pour the salsa into a serving bowl, stir in the onion, and garnish with the cheese.

Yield: 2 cups

Mole Coloradito

Oaxaca is known as the "Land of the Seven Moles," mostly because of the various colors of the chiles used. Ancho and pasilla chiles are easy to find and make this an easy mole to duplicate. Lard will yield an authentic taste, but vegetable oil can be substituted. Use this red mole for enchiladas and other dishes calling for a basic Mexican red sauce.

10 ancho chiles, stems and seeds removed

1 pasilla chile, stems and seeds removed

2 medium tomatoes

4 cloves garlic, unpeeled

3 tablespoons lard or vegetable oil

2 slices day-old bread, torn in small pieces

15 blanched almonds

½ cup sesame seeds

One 2-inch piece cinnamon stick

10 whole cloves

5 black peppercorns

1 tablespoon dried oregano, preferably Mexican

2 tablespoons sugar

3 cups chicken broth

Heat a heavy skillet over medium heat and toast the chiles until they slightly puff, turning them frequently to prevent them from burning. Cover the chiles with hot water and allow them to steep for 10 minutes to soften. Drain, discarding the water.

Reheat the skillet, add the tomatoes and garlic, and dry-roast until the skins blacken. Remove and place them in a bowl covered with a damp towel, or in a plastic bag, to "sweat" the skins off the vegetables.

Add 1 tablespoon of the lard or oil to the skillet, add the bread, and fry until it turns a pale gold. Add the blanched almonds, sesame seeds, cinnamon, cloves, peppercorns, and oregano and roast for a couple of minutes. Allow the mixture to cool completely.

Place the chiles in a blender or food processor with enough water to puree until smooth, remove, and strain. Add the bread, the roasted seed and spice mixture, and the tomatoes and garlic and process until smooth. Process the mixture in stages if necessary.

Heat a large saucepan or stockpot over medium heat, add the remaining lard or oil and when hot, add the chile puree and fry for 5 minutes, stirring frequently. Add the sugar, then some of the broth if the mixture gets too thick. Add the seed mixture to the chile puree and simmer for 5 minutes. Stir in the remaining broth, bring to a boil, reduce the heat and simmer for 30 minutes or until the mole has thickened.

Store in the refrigerator, covered, for up to 5 days.

Yield: 2 cups

Mole Poblano

An 1870s cookbook from Puebla gives recipes for different moles but only one, mole poblano en guajolote, or turkey in mole sauce, is called the national dish of Mexico. This mole has descended from an Aztec chile molli dish, and although it's called poblano, it doesn't contain any poblano chiles. In this case "poblano" refers to the people of Puebla, birthplace of this mole. Mexican chocolate can also be used, but if so, be sure to eliminate the cinnamon.

4 dried pasilla chiles, stems and seeds removed; or substitute 2 ancho chiles

4 dried red New Mexican chiles, preferably Sandia, Chimayó, or another hot variety, stems and seeds removed

2 chipotle chiles *en adobo*

1 cup chopped onion

2 cloves garlic, minced

2 medium tomatoes, peeled and chopped

2 tablespoons sesame seeds

½ cup toasted almonds, chopped

½ corn tortilla, torn into pieces

¼ cup raisins

¼ teaspoon ground cloves

¼ teaspoon ground cinnamon

¼ teaspoon ground coriander

2 to 3 cups turkey or chicken broth

3 tablespoons lard; or substitute vegetable oil

1 ounce bitter chocolate, or more to taste

¼ teaspoon freshly ground black pepper

Salt to taste

Heat a heavy skillet over medium heat, add the pasilla and New Mexican chiles, and dry-roast until they puff slightly, turning them frequently to prevent them from burning. Cover the chiles with hot water and allow them to steep for 10 minutes to soften. Drain the chiles and discard the water.

Put all the chiles, onion, garlic, tomatoes, 1 tablespoon of the sesame seeds, almonds, tortilla, raisins, cloves, cinnamon, and coriander in a blender or food processor. Puree this mixture, and with the motor running, add enough of the broth to form a smooth sauce.

Heat a large saucepan over medium heat, add the lard or oil, and when hot, add the chile puree and simmer for 10 minutes, stirring frequently. Add more broth to the sauce to keep it smooth, and to thin if it gets too thick. Reduce the heat, stir in the chocolate, and cook over very low heat for 30 minutes, or until the sauce has thickened. Add the black pepper and season to taste with salt. Garnish with remaining tablespoon of sesame seeds.

Store in the refrigerator, covered, for up to 5 days.

Yield: 2 cups

Pipian Verde de Pepita (Green Pumpkin Seed Sauce)

Pipians are sauces containing ground nuts or seeds. Some are red, and some are green, like this one. Thickening sauces with seeds is a very old practice; it has been common in Mexico since pre-Columbian times. There are many variations of this sauce, using sesame seeds, peanuts, almonds, or as in this recipe, pumpkin seeds. Pumpkin seeds need to be toasted for them to grind well; just be sure to remove them when they turn golden. If they are left longer, they will darken and become bitter. Originally, pipians were served with turkey or duck, but when the Spanish brought chickens to Mexico, they replaced the wild turkeys. This sauce is also good with grilled fish and shrimp. Our version of green pipian sauce adds a little cream for an even smoother texture, but purists can omit it.

1 cup pumpkin seeds, hulls removed

4 serrano chiles, roasted, peeled, stems and seeds removed

2 poblano chiles, roasted, peeled, stems and seeds removed

1 cup chopped onion

2 cloves garlic, chopped

½ cup coarsely chopped fresh cilantro

2 romaine lettuce leaves

1 teaspoon dried oregano, preferably Mexican

¼ teaspoon ground thyme

2 cups broth, vegetable or chicken

2 tablespoons vegetable oil

Salt to taste

¼ cup heavy cream (optional)

Heat a heavy skillet over high heat, add the pumpkin seeds, and dry-roast until the seeds start to pop. Shake the skillet once they start to pop, and continue to roast until they turn golden, about 3 to 5 minutes, being sure they don't darken. Remove from the pan to cool completely. Place in a spice mill or coffee grinder and process to a fine powder.

Put the seeds, chiles, onion, garlic, cilantro, lettuce, oregano, and thyme in a blender or food processor, add 1½ cups of the broth, and process to a smooth sauce.

Heat the oil in the skillet, add the sauce, and cook over medium heat for 5 minutes, stirring constantly until the sauce has thickened. Reduce the heat, add the remaining broth, and simmer for 10 minutes. Season to taste with salt.

Return the sauce to the blender or food processor and puree again until very smooth. Don't tightly cover the container, or the hot sauce will blow the lid off.

Return the sauce to the skillet or a saucepan and reheat if necessary. Remove the pan and stir in the cream, if desired.

Yield: 2 to 3 cups

Southwest Seasoning Rub

This all-purpose rub adds a taste of the Southwest to whatever you use it on. It's a great grill rub for chicken, beef, and pork. It adds another chile dimension to salsas, and the chipotle's hint of smoke complements a pot of pinto beans.

2 tablespoons ground red New Mexico chile,
    such as Chimayó

2 teaspoons ground chile de arbol

1 teaspoon ground chipotle chile

2 teaspoons ground cumin

1 teaspoon freshly ground black pepper

1 teaspoon garlic salt

1 teaspoon salt

Combine all the ingredients in a bowl and stir to blend.

Store the mixture in an airtight container in a cool, dark, dry place for up to 4 months.

Yield: ⅓ cup

Chipotle Lime Mustard

This is a Southwest-inspired mustard that is slightly grainy, with a definite taste of cumin; it's milder than many mustards that don't use chiles. It's good with just about anything: as a marinade for poultry, pork, or beef; mixed with sour cream or mayonnaise for a tasty dip; or as a topping for vegetables.

½ cup yellow mustard seeds
½ cup mustard powder
¼ cup chopped onion
2 teaspoons chopped garlic
⅓ cup cider vinegar
2 chipotle chiles *en adobo*

2 tablespoons lime juice, preferably fresh
2 to 4 tablespoons water
2 teaspoons cumin seeds
1 teaspoon salt

Note: This recipe requires advance preparation.

Place the mustard seeds in a spice mill or coffee grinder and coarsely grind.

Combine the ground mustard seeds, powder, and ½ cup cold water in a bowl and stir to mix. Let sit for 3 hours.

Place the remaining ingredients in a blender or food processor and process until smooth. Stir the mixture into the mustard.

Place the mixture in a saucepan and bring to a boil over medium-high heat. Lower the heat and simmer for 5 minutes or until the mixture thickens slightly, stirring occasionally and adding water to thin. Remember, the mustard will thicken as it cools, so don't cook it too long.

Spoon the mustard into a sterilized jar and refrigerate for 1 week before using.

Mustard will keep in the refrigerator, covered, for up to 6 months after opening.

Yield: 1 to 1½ cups

New Mexico Green Chile Sauce

Green chile sauce is a classic, all-purpose sauce that is basic to New Mexican cuisine. It's at its best made with fresh green chile, although canned chile can be substituted. Finely diced pork can be added, but cook the sauce for an additional half hour if you do. This is a lightly flavored sauce, with a pungency that ranges from medium to wild, depending on the heat of the chiles. Traditionally this sauce is used over enchiladas, burritos, eggs for breakfast, or chiles rellenos, but it's also a tasty addition to nontraditional recipes.

2 tablespoons vegetable oil

½ cup finely chopped onions

1 clove garlic, minced

1 tablespoon all-purpose flour

2 to 3 cups chicken broth

1 cup chopped green New Mexican chiles,
    roasted, peeled, stems removed

1 small tomato, peeled and chopped

¼ teaspoon ground cumin

Salt to taste

Heat a heavy skillet over medium heat, add the oil, and when hot, add the onion and garlic and sauté until they are soft. Stir in the flour and blend well. Simmer for a couple of minutes to cook the flour, being careful it does not brown. Slowly add the broth and stir until smooth.

Add the remaining ingredients, bring to a boil, reduce the heat, and simmer until the sauce has thickened, about 15 minutes. Taste and adjust the seasonings.

Store the sauce in the refrigerator for up to 5 days, or freeze for up to 6 months.

Yield: 2 to 3 cups

New Mexico Red Chile Sauce

The chiles traditionally used for this basic sauce are the kind pulled off ristras, *or strings of chiles. These strings, which originally served to make it easier to sun-dry and preserve the fall red chile crop for use throughout the year, have become a popular southwestern decoration. Use this sauce as a topping for enchiladas and tacos, as a basis for stew, or in any recipe that calls for a red sauce.*

12 dried red New Mexican chiles
2 tablespoons vegetable oil
1 cup chopped onions
2 cloves garlic, chopped
2 to 3 cups beef or vegetable broth
1 teaspoon oregano, preferably Mexican
Salt to taste

Preheat the oven to 250°F.

Arrange the chile pods on a baking pan and roast in the oven for 10 to 15 minutes, or until the chiles become very aromatic, being careful not to let them burn. Remove the stems and seeds and crumble the pods into a bowl. Cover the chiles with very hot water and allow them to steep for 15 minutes to soften. Drain the chiles and discard the water.

Heat a heavy saucepan over medium-high heat, add the oil, and when hot, add the onion and garlic and sauté until they are soft. Add the chiles along with a couple cups of the broth and simmer the sauce for 10 minutes.

Place all the ingredients in a blender or food processor and puree until smooth. Strain the mixture for a smoother sauce.

If the sauce is too thin, place it back on the stove and simmer until it is reduced to the desired consistency; if it is too thick, add more broth. Taste and adjust the seasonings.

Store the sauce in the refrigerator for up to 5 days, or freeze for up to 6 months.

Yield: 2½ to 3 cups

Chile Pasado (Dried Green Chile)

This blackish green, rather nasty-looking dried green chile becomes plump, soft, tasty, and almost green when rehydrated. It keeps forever or longer; this was the method of preserving fresh green chiles before refrigeration. You can dry these chiles in a variety of ways.

2 pounds (approximately 20 pods) of green New Mexican chiles

Before you dry the green chiles, you must first roast and peel them. This can be done by placing them under a broiler, which is time-consuming with 20 pods; on the top of the stove, using a stovetop grill—again time-consuming; or by roasting the pods on a charcoal or gas grill until they blister and start to turn black, turning them often. After roasting, place the chiles in a large bowl covered with a damp towel, or in a plastic bag with a wet paper towel, for ½ hour to steam. Remove and carefully peel the chiles, leaving the stem and seeds intact as much as possible.

To dry the chiles, use any of the following methods. Drying times will vary, but dry them until they are very dark and brittle. Tie four pods together by wrapping string around the stems and place over a line outside in the sun. Do not let the chiles get rained on, and protect them from flies and other insects with by wrapping them lightly in cheesecloth. Lay the chiles on screening in a single layer, place in the sun, and protect them by covering with cheesecloth. With this method, you don't have to worry about leaving the stems intact. Dry them in a dehydrator until they darken and become brittle. Place them on a rack in the oven set at the lowest heat possible. Monitor them closely so they don't burn.

To store the chiles, place in a plastic bag and keep in a cool, dark place, or seal the bag and keep in the freezer.

To reconstitute the pods, break off the stems, place the chiles in a bowl, and cover with very hot water. Allow them to steep for 15 minutes, or until soft. Drain the chiles and discard the water.

Use reconstituted *chile pasado* in any recipe calling for green chile in any form except whole pods.

Yield: About 3 ounces

Salsa Verde
(Charred Green Tomatillo Sauce)

Tomatillos are also called Mexican husk tomatoes or green tomatoes, but they aren't tomatoes and don't even taste like them. They have a tangy, citrusy taste that can at times be very tart, and are used in salsas raw or as in this salsa, cooked. We like to roast the vegetables before using, and include some of the blackened skins to add another dimension to the sauce. But it can also be prepared without roasting the vegetables. Just place all the ingredients in a saucepan and simmer them until soft. This is another all-purpose Mexican/southwestern sauce that can be used with and on other foods, or served as a salsa with chips. In Mexico a molca-jete *would be used to process the salsa, but for ease a blender or food processor can be used.*

1 pound tomatillos, husks left on
1 small white onion, unpeeled
4 to 5 serrano chiles, stems removed
2 cloves garlic, unpeeled
¼ cup chopped fresh cilantro
Sugar to taste
Salt to taste

Heat a heavy skillet over medium-high heat, add the tomatillos, onion, chiles, and garlic, and dry-roast, shaking the pan occasionally, until the skins start to blacken and the vegetables are soft. This can also be done under a broiler. Cool the vegetables. Remove the skins, leaving some of the charred pieces for flavor.

Put the charred vegetables in a blender or food processor and pulse to coarsely chop.

Put the salsa in a serving bowl, stir in the cilantro, and season to taste with sugar and salt.

Yield: 2 cups

Hot Horseradish Mustard

This mustard has a bold, hot, and hearty flavor with a lingering sweet aftertaste from the honey. The heat and flavor build the longer it's allowed to age. It has a slightly grainy texture because the seeds are left whole, but if a smoother mustard is desired, they can be processed after being soaked. This mustard is an excellent spread on corned beef or ham sandwiches.

½ cup dry mustard

¼ cup yellow mustard seeds

⅓ cup cider vinegar

2 tablespoons prepared horseradish, drained

1 clove garlic, minced

3 tablespoons honey

1 teaspoon brown sugar

¼ teaspoon ground white pepper

½ cup white wine vinegar

Combine the dry mustard, mustard seeds, and cider vinegar in a bowl and stir to mix. Allow the mixture to sit to for 15 minutes.

Note: This recipe requires advance preparation.

Place 1 tablespoon of the horseradish and the garlic in a blender or food processor and puree until smooth, adding a little water if necessary. Strain the mixture through a fine sieve into the mustards.

Combine the mustard mixture, honey, brown sugar, and pepper, along with ½ cup hot water, in a saucepan. Bring to a simmer over low heat, stirring constantly, until slightly thickened. Remember that the mustard will thicken as it cools, so don't cook it too long.

Cool the mustard, add the remaining horseradish, and add the white wine vinegar to thin. Spoon the mustard into a sterilized jar and refrigerate for 1 week before using.

Mustard will keep in the refrigerator, covered, for up to 6 months after opening.

Yield: 1 cup

Green Peppercorn Mustard

This robust mustard has a crisp, tart, complex flavor with a definite salty, herbal green pepper-corn flavor. It combines well with strongly flavored meats like beef and fish like salmon. Add to sauces and even gravies, or use as a base for marinades to brush on meats before grilling, or on roasts as a coating crust.

¼ cup yellow mustard seeds

¼ cup dry mustard

½ cup white wine vinegar

½ cup dry white wine

2 teaspoons coarse salt
   (kosher or canning)

½ teaspoon dried tarragon, crumbled

½ teaspoon dill seeds

1 shallot, coarsely chopped

1 teaspoon honey

1 tablespoon green peppercorns,
   drained

Note: This recipe requires advance preparation.

Combine the mustard seeds, dry mustard, vinegar, and ½ cup hot water in a bowl and stir to make a paste. Allow the mixture to sit for 3 hours.

Combine the wine, salt, tarragon, dill seeds, and shallot in a saucepan and bring to a boil. Remove the pan from the heat and allow to steep for 5 minutes. Strain the mixture through a fine sieve into the mustard mixture and stir to combine. Discard the spices in the strainer. Stir in the honey and green peppercorns.

Place the mixture in a blender or food processor and puree until smooth.

Cook the mustard in the top of a double boiler for 5 minutes, stirring frequently. Remember, the mustard will thicken as it cools, so don't cook it too long.

Spoon the mustard into a sterilized jar. Allow the mustard to cool, then tightly cap and refrigerate for a couple of days before using.

Mustard will keep in the refrigerator, covered, for up to 6 months after opening.

Yield: 1 cup

Cajun Spices

Cajun spice mixes are some of most popular seasonings in the United States, and not just in Louisiana. The Caucasian French-speaking residents, or Cajuns, of the Acadiana parishes in southern Louisiana are known for robust, spicy dishes, like jambalaya and étouffée, that use seasonings such as this. Use this mix as a rub on fish, shrimp, poultry, or meat before roasting or grilling, as a seasoning in gumbos, or as a lagniappe, *a Cajun-French word meaning "a little something extra," on salads or vegetables.*

3 tablespoons garlic salt

3 tablespoons freshly ground black pepper

2 tablespoons ground cayenne

2 tablespoons ground white pepper

2 tablespoons onion powder

1 tablespoon ground paprika

1 tablespoon dried parsley leaves

2 teaspoons dried oregano

2 teaspoons ground thyme

½ teaspoon mace

Combine all the ingredients in a bowl and stir to blend.

Store the mixture in an airtight container in a cool, dark, dry place for up to 4 months.

Yield: Approximately 1 cup

Creole Mustard

This mustard, a specialty of Louisiana's German Creoles, is a traditional flavoring in the cuisine of New Orleans, and a must in the preparation of Remoulade Sauce (page 170). A sharp and slightly sweet mustard with a complex flavor, this will definitely clean out the sinuses. Quick and easy to prepare, it's a good accompaniment to shrimp, ham, fish, and poultry, as well as an important flavor ingredient in many Cajun and Creole dishes.

¼ cup yellow mustard powder

1 tablespoon all-purpose flour

1 tablespoon Dijon-style mustard, store-bought or homemade (page 117)

3 tablespoons white wine vinegar

2 teaspoons grated horseradish

1 clove garlic, minced

1 teaspoon sugar

½ teaspoon dried thyme

½ teaspoon ground paprika

½ teaspoon ground white pepper

¼ teaspoon salt

Note: This recipe requires advance preparation.

Combine all the ingredients along with ½ cup water in a saucepan and mix well. Heat to a simmer over medium heat and cook for 2 minutes. Add more water if the mustard gets too thick. Remove the pan from the heat and allow the mustard to cool.

Spoon the mustard into a sterilized jar and refrigerate for 1 week before using.

Mustard will keep in the refrigerator, covered, for up to 6 months after opening.

Yield: ½ cup

Creole Seasoning

Louisiana cooking always starts with a mixture of spices and herbs that almost every cook develops to suit his or her own tastes. The name Creole came from the Spanish word criollo, *which was what they called all the residents of New Orleans of European heritage during the 1700s. Over the years it came to be associated with people of cultured backgrounds. Creole cooking combines Spanish, French, and African influences and is the more refined of the two Louisiana cooking styles. This rub works very well with fish, and especially shrimp. Sprinkle it on seafood and allow it to marinate at room temperature for about an hour before cooking.*

1 tablespoon ground paprika

2 teaspoons garlic powder

1 teaspoon ground cayenne

1 teaspoon freshly ground black pepper

1 teaspoon onion powder

1 teaspoon dried thyme

1 teaspoon dried oregano

1 teaspoon salt

1 bay leaf, stemmed and crushed

½ teaspoon ground allspice

Place all the ingredients in a spice mill or coffee grinder and process to a fine powder.

Store the mixture in an airtight container in a cool, dark, dry place for up to 4 months.

Yield: 3 to 3½ tablespoons

Remoulade Sauce

This is a classic Louisiana recipe with French roots. It's traditionally made with mayonnaise, but ours is a more heart–healthy version. This sauce is great with shrimp, over sliced tomatoes, with pasta, over vegetables and cold meats, in chicken or potato salad, or as an ingredient in deviled eggs.

½ cup Creole mustard, store-bought or homemade (page 168)

¼ cup ketchup

¼ cup cider vinegar

2 tablespoons grated horseradish; or substitute prepared horseradish, store-bought or homemade (page 112)

1 teaspoon Worcestershire sauce

1 teaspoon garlic powder

¾ teaspoon ground paprika

1 teaspoon Louisiana-style hot sauce; or substitute ¼ teaspoon ground cayenne

⅔ cup olive oil

¼ cup chopped green onions

2 tablespoons chopped celery

1 tablespoon minced capers

1 tablespoon chopped fresh parsley

¼ teaspoon ground white pepper

Salt to taste

Combine the mustard, ketchup, vinegar, horseradish, Worcestershire, garlic, paprika, and hot sauce in a bowl and whisk to combine.

Slowly add the oil while continuing to whisk to emulsify the sauce.

Fold in the remaining ingredients, taste, and adjust the seasonings.

Allow the sauce to sit for an hour to blend the flavors. It also can be made a day or two before serving; the flavor improves with time, but it will only keep for 4 to 5 days in the refrigerator.

Yield: 1 cup

Crab-Boil Spices

Crab-boil mixtures contain herbs and spices and are used to season the water in which shrimp, crawfish, and crabs are boiled. There are commercial mixes available, such as Old Bay or Zatarain's, but it's so easy to prepare, why not make your own signature blend?

¼ cup pickling spices, commercial
2 tablespoons yellow mustard seeds
2 tablespoons whole black peppercorns
1 tablespoon salt
1 tablespoon celery seeds
1 tablespoon onion flakes
6 piquin chiles
2 teaspoons ground ginger
4 bay leaves
2 teaspoons dried oregano
1 teaspoon dry mustard

Place all the ingredients in a blender or food processor and pulse to a coarse powder.

Store the mixture in an airtight container in a cool, dark, dry place for up to 4 months.

Yield: ½ cup

7 Appetizers & Snacks

Cracked Black Pepper Sugar Almonds

Caution: these sweet and spicy nuts are addictive! The more you eat, the spicier they get, and you need to eat more than one to get the full flavor. They are a tasty, crunchy addition to accompany a buffet table or party.

2 teaspoons cracked black pepper

½ teaspoon garlic salt

1 tablespoon butter

¼ cup brown sugar

1 cup raw almonds

Preheat the oven to 350°F.

Line an 8-by-8-inch baking pan with aluminum foil, and lightly butter.

Combine the pepper and garlic salt in a bowl and stir to mix.

Heat a nonstick skillet over medium heat, add the butter, and when melted, add the sugar and stir in 2 teaspoons water. Simmer the mixture until the sugar melts. Add the nuts and continue to cook until the sugar bubbles, becomes thick and syrupy, and coats the nuts, about 5 minutes.

Sprinkle the pepper mixture over the top of the nuts and quickly toss to coat. Pour the mixture into the prepared pan.

Put the pan in the oven and roast until the nuts are golden brown, about 10 minutes.

Remove the foil with the nuts and place on a wire rack to cool.

When the nuts are cool, break them apart and serve.

Store the nuts in an airtight container.

Yield: 1 cup

Red Pepper Spiced Pecans and Dried Cranberries

This recipe was provided by our friend Chef Jim Heywood, an associate professor at the Culinary Institute of America, in Hyde Park, New York. He says it's a great cocktail snack. The nuts are both salty and mildly spicy, and when you bite into a cranberry, the sweetness is a pleasant surprise. Jim likes to use Spanish paprika rather than the Hungarian type (which is darker), and table salt rather than sea salt, as it sticks to the nuts better. He also says it is very important to add the butter to the nuts, not the other way around, as the butter will continue to cook if you leave it in the pan, and eventually burn.

1 pound shelled pecan halves
½ pound dried cranberries
1 tablespoon brown sugar
1 tablespoon Spanish paprika

1 teaspoon ground cayenne
2 teaspoons salt
¼ cup (½ stick) butter

Place the pecans and cranberries in a bowl.

Combine the sugar, paprika, cayenne, and salt in a bowl and stir to mix.

Heat a sauté pan over medium heat and add the butter. Cook the butter until it gets foamy and develops a nutty aroma, being careful that it doesn't burn.

Pour the brown butter, as it's called, over the nuts and toss well to coat.

Add the sugar mixture to the nuts, and again toss well to coat.

Serve at room temperature. Store in an airtight container for 2 to 3 weeks.

Yield: 10 to 12 servings

Champiñones al Ajillo (Garlic Mushrooms)

Tapas are Spain's answer to hors d'oeuvres, and the Spanish have turned these small dishes into an art form and a way of life. Mushrooms are a popular tapa ingredient all over Spain, where they are fried, grilled, marinated, or stuffed. Another popular ingredient is Spanish garlic. Prized around the world for its flavor, it's used abundantly in Spanish cooking. There are many variations of the mushroom and garlic combination, but the following one with chile is one of our favorites. White button mushrooms are traditionally used, but any mushroom, such as a sliced portobello or cremini, is a good substitute. If you have access to wild mushrooms, they are wonderful in this recipe.

1½ tablespoons extra-virgin olive oil, preferably Spanish

1 tablespoon chopped garlic

3 tablespoons finely chopped red bell pepper

½ pound mushroom caps, rinsed and drained

3 tablespoons dry sherry, preferably Spanish

2 teaspoons lemon juice

½ teaspoon crushed red chile, such as piquin

1 tablespoon chopped fresh flat-leaf parsley

Salt and pepper to taste

Heat the oil in a heavy skillet over high heat, add the garlic, and sauté until it's soft, about 2 minutes. Add the bell pepper and continue to sauté for an additional minute.

Add the mushrooms, sherry, lemon juice, and chile and simmer, stirring occasionally, until most of the liquid is evaporated and the mushrooms are browned, about 5 to 7 minutes.

Remove from the heat, stir in the parsley, and season with salt and pepper. Serve the mushrooms either hot or at room temperature.

Yield: 4 servings

Aceitunas a la Sevillana
(Olives a la Seville)

Olives, whether black or green, and either whole or in the form of an oil, are a very important part of Spanish cuisine and appetizers, as witness the fact that the Spanish grow over 250 varieties and are the world's largest producer of olive oil. Spain was occupied by the Moors for 800 years, and their influence on the architecture, culture, and food of the Iberian peninsula is very evident. This dish typically uses Andalusian olives, and the variety of herbs with which they are seasoned leaves little doubt of their Arab origins. Serve these olives with a glass of dry Spanish sherry.

Two 7-ounce jars green Spanish olives, preferably Manzanilla, drained

¼ cup dry sherry, preferably Spanish; or substitute white wine

¼ cup cider vinegar

2 piquin chiles, crushed

2 bay leaves

1 teaspoon chopped garlic

½ teaspoon dried oregano

3 sprigs fresh thyme; or substitute ½ teaspoon dried

1 anchovy fillet (optional)

Extra-virgin olive oil, preferably Spanish

Note: This recipe requires advance preparation.

Lightly crush the olives and put them in a glass jar.

Combine all the remaining ingredients, except the oil, in a bowl and stir to mix. Pour the mixture over the olives. Add just enough of the oil to cover, stir well, and refrigerate.

Occasionally open the jar and stir the ingredients. The olives will take at least a week to marinate, but left longer, they will get hotter. The olives will keep for about a month in the refrigerator.

To serve, drain the olives and allow to warm to room temperature before serving.

Yield: 8 servings

Sesame Chicken Yakitori with Wasabi Ginger Glaze

Yakitori got its name from the Japanese words yaki, *"grilled," and* tori, *"poultry" or "chicken," and refers to small pieces of marinated, grilled chicken. But since we've already taken some liberties with the traditional recipe in making this version, you can also make this with pork. Yakitoris are probably the most popular snack food in Japan and make a great appetizer hot off the grill. The glaze can be prepared 3 to 4 hours in advance, be refrigerated, and then warmed to room temperature before using.*

3 boneless, skinless chicken breasts

8 green onions, cut in 2-inch pieces

2 tablespoons toasted sesame seeds

15 bamboo skewers

Glaze

1 cup rice wine or dry sherry

⅔ cup mirin (sweet sake, available in Asian markets)

3 tablespoons sugar

2 tablespoons minced ginger

2 tablespoons minced green onion, including some of the greens

1 tablespoon Asian chile oil (available in Asian markets)

2 teaspoons wasabi paste

1 teaspoon soy sauce

1 teaspoon *shichimi togarashi*, store-bought or homemade (page 146)

¼ teaspoon sesame oil

Cut the chicken either into 1-inch cubes or crosswise into pieces 2 inches long and ½ inch thick and wide. Thread the chicken strips crosswise in an S shape on the skewers, alternating with the onion.

Combine all the glaze ingredients in a saucepan and, over medium-high heat, bring just to boiling. Reduce the heat and simmer, uncovered, until the sauce is reduced by half and forms a glaze, about 5 minutes.

Grill the yakitori over medium heat 2 minutes per side, or until slightly browned. Brush liberally with the glaze and continue cooking for a couple more minutes per side until the chicken is done.

Brush the yakitori a final time with the glaze, sprinkle with the sesame seeds, and serve.

Yield: 4 to 6 servings

Marinated Guero Chiles

Nancy has been served variations of this appetizer all over Baja California, from Puerto Penasco to La Paz. She's sampled these soy-marinated chiles made with fresh chiles de arbol and jalapeños, but the best were made with guero chiles. Many Japanese fishermen work the waters along the coast there; perhaps the use of soy sauce is an indication of the Japanese influence on the cuisine of the Baja.

2 tablespoons vegetable oil

2 dozen fresh guero chiles; or substitute
    fresh jalapeños or hot yellow wax peppers

2 thin slices of onion, separated into rings

¼ teaspoon garlic salt

Freshly ground black pepper to taste

3 tablespoons soy sauce

1 tablespoon lime juice, preferably fresh

Note: This recipe requires advance preparation.

Heat a heavy skillet over medium-high heat, add 2 teaspoons of the oil, and when hot, add the chiles and onion. Sauté until the chiles start to blister and the onions are soft. Remove the pan from the heat and season the mixture with the garlic salt and pepper.

Combine the remaining oil, soy sauce, and lime juice in a nonreactive bowl and mix well. Add the chiles and onions and toss to coat well. Cover the bowl and marinate for 24 hours before serving.

Yield: 24 chiles

Olive and Artichoke Tapenade

Tapenade is a thick paste of olives, anchovies, garlic, and a combination of herbs and seasonings. It originated in the Provence region of France, but its popularity has spread throughout southern Europe, and it is now made everywhere that olives are grown. The paste can be smooth or chunky, but we prefer a mixture with some texture. Processing the topping in a blender or food processor in place of the traditional mortar and pestle makes for a quick and easy tapenade. Serve with a basket of crostini, small slices of toasted bread that have been brushed with olive oil, to top with the tapenade.

3 cloves garlic

1 anchovy fillet

2 tablespoons extra-virgin olive oil

½ cup green olives, pitted

One 6-ounce jar artichoke hearts, drained and chopped

4 to 5 sun-dried tomatoes, packed in oil, drained, chopped

3 tablespoons toasted walnut pieces, chopped

1 tablespoon green peppercorns packed in brine, drained

1 tablespoon lemon juice, preferably fresh

1 teaspoon minced lemon zest

¼ teaspoon coarsely ground black pepper

2 tablespoons grated Parmesan cheese

1 tablespoon chopped flat-leaf parsley

6 slices day-old Italian or country-style bread, sliced ¾ inch thick, toasted and brushed with olive oil

Place the garlic and anchovy in a bowl and mash with the back of a spoon to make a paste, adding a little of the oil if necessary.

Place the garlic paste, remainder of the oil, olives, artichokes, tomatoes, walnuts, green peppercorns, lemon juice, and zest in a blender or food processor and pulse to make a chunky paste.

Combine the paste with the black pepper and cheese in a bowl and stir to mix. Allow the tapenade to sit at room temperature for 30 minutes to blend the flavors. Taste and adjust the seasonings.

Add the parsley, put in a bowl, and serve with the crostini on the side.

Yield: 1 cup

Lemon Tabouleh with Baharat Seasoning

Whether it's called tabouleh, tabbouleh, or tabouli, this dish is popular across the Middle East. The main ingredient in tabouleh is bulgur, which is precooked, cracked, and dried wheat. Originally considered a peasant meal consisting largely of bulgur accompanied by mixed herbs, the dish now is commonly served with mostly herbs and vegetables and minimal bulgur. Adjust the proportions to suit your taste. Most recipes call for soaking the bulgur in water, but we like to use lemon or tomato juice. Adjust the texture by adjusting the soaking time. The only rule is that tabouleh must be freshly prepared; if it sits longer than 4 to 5 hours, the flavors will become overpowering.

½ cup fine-grain bulgur

⅓ cup lemon juice, preferably fresh

¼ cup finely chopped flat-leaf parsley

¼ cup finely chopped green onions, including some of the greens

2 tablespoons finely slivered fresh mint

2 tomatoes, seeds removed, finely chopped

Romaine or other leaf lettuce leaves

Dressing

¼ cup extra-virgin olive oil

2 tablespoons lemon juice, preferably fresh

2 teaspoons *baharat* seasoning, store-bought or homemade (page 126)

¼ teaspoon freshly ground black pepper

Salt to taste

Place the bulgur in a fine sieve and rinse well under cold running water. Drain and squeeze until dry. Put in a bowl, pour the lemon juice over the top and toss to mix well. Allow the bulgur to marinate for 30 minutes. Drain and squeeze out any moisture.

Place the bulgur in a bowl and fluff with a fork to separate the grains. Add the parsley, onion, and mint and toss to mix.

Whisk together the olive oil, lemon juice, *baharat* seasoning, and black pepper. Pour the dressing over the bulgur and allow the flavors to marinate for 30 to 40 minutes. Taste and adjust, adding more lemon juice if desired. Toss with the tomatoes and refrigerate until ready to serve.

To serve, encircle a bowl with the lettuce leaves and mound the tabouleh in the center. Traditionally the lettuce is used as a spoon to scoop up the bulgur mix.

Yield: 4 servings

Turkish Ajvar
with Toasted Pita Wedges

Pronounced "EYE-var," this is a name of Turkish origin given to a popular appetizer made with roasted peppers and eggplant. This recipe is based on one that was collected by our friend Sharon Hudgins on one of her many journeys to research southern Slavic cuisines. Ripe red mild or medium-hot peppers are most often used, although green peppers, unripe tomatoes, and even string beans can be used in an ajvar. Fresh ajvar is always made during the late summer and early autumn, just after the pepper harvest—when many households also can or bottle their own ajvar for use throughout the year. Serve this dish as an appetizer or as a side dish to accompany grilled or roasted meats.

8 to 12 green New Mexican chiles, roasted, peeled, stems and seeds removed

4 medium-sized eggplants, roasted and peeled

⅓ to ½ cup extra-virgin olive oil

1 cup finely chopped onion

4 large cloves garlic, minced

2 teaspoons chopped fresh thyme, or substitute ½ teaspoon dried

1 teaspoon caraway seeds

1 teaspoon ground hot paprika

2 tablespoons red wine vinegar

Salt and freshly ground black pepper

4 rounds pita bread, cut in wedges

Chopped fresh parsley for garnish

Place the chiles and eggplants in a blender or food processor and pulse to coarsely chop.

Heat a heavy skillet over medium heat, add 2 to 3 tablespoons of the oil, and when hot, add the onion and garlic and sauté until softened. Add the thyme, caraway, and paprika and sauté for an additional couple of minutes.

Remove from the heat, add the chiles and eggplants, and stir to mix. Slowly drizzle the remaining oil into the mixture, stirring constantly to incorporate the oil. Add the vinegar, and season to taste with salt and pepper.

Place the pita triangles under the broiler and toast until crisp.

To serve, arrange the pita wedges around the outside of a platter. Put the *ajvar* in a bowl, garnish with the parsley, place the bowl in the center of a platter, and serve.

Yield: 6 to 8 servings

Gravlax with Spicy Mustard Sauce

This Swedish dish takes two days to make, but according to Dave it's well worth the effort. The Vikings in the eighth century are credited with developing gravlax as a way of preserving fish when they were out marauding, pillaging, and raiding. The name comes from the words grav, *"grave," and* laxs, *"salmon," since the fish was often buried in the cold ground to preserve it. The traditional way to serve gravlax is to slice it as thinly as possible, place on black bread or toasted rye bread, and serve with a little mustard sauce spread over the top.*

¼ cup sugar

⅓ cup kosher salt

1 tablespoon coarsely ground black pepper

2 small bunches dill, coarsely chopped

½ bunch chervil, chopped

1 bunch flat-leaf parsley, chopped

1 bunch lemon balm, chopped

2 salmon fillets, about 1½ pounds each

Mustard Sauce

3 tablespoons vegetable oil

2 tablespoons cracked black pepper mustard, store-bought or homemade (page 116)

2 tablespoons sugar

2 tablespoons distilled white vinegar

2 tablespoons finely chopped fresh dill

1 tablespoon mustard powder

1 tablespoon gin or aquavit (optional)

Note: This recipe requires advance preparation.

Combine the sugar, salt, and pepper in a bowl to make the sugar mixture.

In another bowl, combine the dill, chervil, parsley, and lemon balm to make the herb mixture.

In a third bowl combine all the ingredients for the mustard sauce and stir to mix. Cover the bowl and refrigerate.

Place 1 salmon fillet skin side down in a shallow bowl. Sprinkle half of the sugar mixture over the fillet, then half of the herb mixture, the rest of the sugar mixture, and the rest of the herb mixture. Place the second fillet on top of the first, flesh to flesh, and wrap with plastic wrap.

Place the wrapped fillets in a shallow pan and weigh them down with something heavy, like a cast iron skillet filled with a couple of bricks. Refrigerate for 24 hours, then flip the fillets, weigh them down, and refrigerate for another 24 hours.

Thinly slice the salmon; serve with rye or black bread and the mustard sauce.

Yield: 12 or more servings

Grilled Lemon Pepper Shrimp

These tasty shrimp have a definite Asian flavor. Combining sweet and hot is classic, and in this dish, the sweetness of the ginger and citrus zest is paired with the heat of the chiles and black pepper. Great as an appetizer, they can also be served as a main course with sticky rice.

2 pounds medium or large shrimp, shelled and deveined, tails left on

12 bamboo skewers

Marinade

½ cup vegetable oil, preferably peanut

1 tablespoon sesame oil

2 tablespoons grated ginger

4 green onions, coarsely chopped

2 tablespoons finely chopped lemon zest; or substitute orange zest, divided

1 tablespoon coarsely ground black pepper

1 tablespoon light soy sauce

1 teaspoon crushed red chile, such as piquin or santaka

2 star anise, crushed

To make the marinade, heat the oils over moderate heat in a wok or heavy skillet, until a piece of ginger will foam when dropped into the oil. Remove the pan from the heat.

Add the ginger and green onion, half of the zest, the black pepper, soy sauce, chile, and star anise to the oils. Let the marinade sit at room temperature for 2 to 3 hours to allow the oil to flavor. Strain the oil and press on the solids to extract as much flavor as possible.

Put the flavored oil in a resealable plastic bag, add the shrimp, and toss to coat. Refrigerate the shrimp for 4 to 8 hours, turning the bag a couple of times to make sure all the shrimp are marinated.

Soak the skewers in water for 15 minutes before using. Remove the shrimp and reserve the marinade. Thread the shrimp on the skewers using 2 skewers spaced about ½ inch apart. This will hold the shrimp in place and make turning them easy.

Heat the grill to medium hot and grill the shrimp, turning and basting occasionally with the reserved marinade, for about 5 minutes or until they are pink and opaque.

Garnish the shrimp with the remaining zest and serve warm or hot.

Yield: 6 to 8 servings as an appetizer or 4 as a main course

Note: This recipe requires advance preparation.

Satay Daging with Sambal Kacang (Beef Satay with Spicy Peanut Sauce)

 Satays *are popular throughout Malaysia and the 13,000-odd islands that comprise the country of Indonesia, where they are eaten as a snack, an appetizer, or part of the meal itself. They can be made of beef, chicken, pork or lamb, depending on local custom and individual tastes. They never contain vegetables, and are served with a spicy sauce, such as* sambal kacang *(page 143), on the side for dipping.*

1½ pounds sirloin beef, cut in 1-inch cubes

12 bamboo skewers

Vegetable oil, preferably peanut

Sambal kacang, store-bought or homemade (page 143)

Marinade

4 green onions, chopped, including some of the greens

4 to 5 Thai chiles, stems removed; or substitute serrano chiles

1 tablespoon chopped ginger

3 cloves garlic

2 tablespoons peanut oil

1 tablespoon lime juice, preferably fresh

2 tablespoons tamarind juice

2 teaspoons ground coriander

1 teaspoon freshly ground black pepper

¼ teaspoon ground cumin

1 teaspoon sugar

½ cup coconut milk

Note: This recipe requires advance preparation.

To make the marinade, place the onion, chiles, ginger, and garlic in a blender or food processor and puree until smooth, adding some peanut oil, if necessary, to form a paste.

Heat a heavy saucepan over medium-high heat, add the oil and when hot, add the spice paste and sauté the mixture for a couple of minutes. Add the remaining marinade ingredients and simmer until the sauce starts to thicken, about 15 minutes. If the marinade becomes too thick, thin with hot water. Allow the mixture to cool.

Place the beef cubes in a nonreactive bowl or heavy plastic resealable bag, add the marinade, and toss to coat. Marinate the beef overnight in the refrigerator, turning occasionally. Soak the skewers in water 15 minutes before using. Remove the beef and thread on skewers.

Preheat a gas gill to high; if you are using charcoal, the coals should be glowing. Grill the *satays* until done, about 2 to 3 minutes per side. Brush them constantly with the oil and turn frequently to prevent burning. Cut one cube to check for doneness; they should be slightly charred on the outside and just done on the inside.

To serve, place the *satays* on a platter, with *Sambal Kacang* on the side for dipping.

Yield: 4 to 6 servings

Tortilla Roll-Ups

These are popular appetizers in New Mexico. Here are a few of our favorite fillings that are colorful as well as tasty. It's important to tightly roll and refrigerate them, or they won't stay together.

Habanero Pumpkin filling

½ cup canned pumpkin puree

¼ cup sour cream

½ teaspoon dried oregano, preferably Mexican

¼ teaspoon ground habanero chile

1 tablespoon chopped scallions

Green Chile Salmon filling

½ cup sour cream

4 green New Mexican chiles, roasted, peeled, and cut in strips

2 teaspoons dill weed

4 ounces smoked salmon fillets, thinly sliced

Smoked Turkey with Chipotle Cream filling

½ cup sour cream

2 chipotle chiles en adobo, pureed

2 teaspoons lime juice

4 ounces smoked turkey, thinly sliced

1 tablespoon chopped fresh cilantro

Black Bean and Tomatillo filling

½ cup black beans, cooked and mashed

2 teaspoons dried epazote

¼ teaspoon ground chile de arbol

¼ teaspoon garlic powder

4 fresh tomatillos, husks removed, thinly sliced

1 dozen fresh flour tortillas

For the habanero pumpkin roll-ups, combine all the ingredients in a bowl and spread over a tortilla. Roll the tortilla in a jelly-roll fashion and tightly wrap in plastic wrap. Repeat with 2 more tortillas.

To make the salmon tortillas, spread a layer of sour cream over a tortilla. Lay ⅓ of the chile strips on top, sprinkle with the dill, and arrange the salmon over the mixture. Roll up the tortilla and tightly wrap in plastic wrap. Repeat with 2 more tortillas.

Combine the sour cream, chipotle puree, and lime juice in a bowl to make the chipotle cream filling. Spread the mixture on a tortilla and lay the turkey over the top. Sprinkle with the cilantro, roll up, and tightly wrap with plastic wrap. Repeat with 2 more tortillas.

For the final tortillas, combine the beans, epazote, chile de arbol, and garlic powder in a bowl and spread over a tortilla. Top with the tomatillos, roll up, and tightly wrap with plastic wrap. Repeat with 2 more tortillas.

Place the tortillas in the refrigerator for 2 to 3 hours. Just before serving, unwrap the tortilla rolls and slice into 6 to 8 pieces.

Yield: 6 to 8 dozen

Note: This recipe requires advance preparation.

Argentine Empanadas

If you traveled the world, you would be hard pressed to find a cuisine or culture that didn't include some variation of a turnover! The Polish have pierogi, the Russians piroshki; calzones are a favorite in Italy; English Cornish pasties traveled to the British West Indies, where they became Jamaican patties; in India and Pakistan they love samosas; and in Latin countries, you will find empanadas. The Spanish word empanada *means "in dough" or "that which is covered with bread." This is a version of an empanada from Argentina, where they are a very popular appetizer, snack, and/or picnic fare. If you're short on time, a ready-made pie crust can be used for the pastry—just don't roll out the pastry before cutting. Because empanadas are baked, they can be prepared in advance.*

Filling

½ pound ground beef

¼ cup chopped onion

½ cup chopped red bell pepper

3 aji chiles, stems and seeds removed, chopped; or substitute 3 jalapeños

1 small potato, cooked and finely diced

1 tablespoon capers, rinsed, drained, and chopped

12 green olives, chopped

2 tablespoons raisins

2 tablespoons dry sherry (optional)

1 tablespoon ground paprika

1 tablespoon chopped fresh parsley

2 hard-cooked eggs, chopped

Salt and freshly ground black pepper

Pastry

2 cups all-purpose flour

1 teaspoon salt

⅔ cup vegetable shortening, lard, or a combination of the two

4 to 5 tablespoons cold water

1 large egg, beaten lightly with ¼ teaspoon water (for glaze)

To prepare the filling, heat a heavy skillet over medium-high heat, add the beef, and sauté until almost browned. Add the onion, bell pepper, and chiles and continue to sauté until the onions are soft. Add the potato and continue to cook for an additional minute. Pour off the accumulated fat.

Combine all the remaining filling ingredients in a large bowl, add the meat mixture, and stir to mix.

Preheat the oven to 400°F.

To prepare the pastry, combine the flour and salt in a large bowl and stir to mix. Cut the shortening into the dry ingredients using a pastry cutter or two forks. The mixture should resemble coarse cornmeal.

Add the water to the flour mixture, one tablespoon at a time, and lightly toss with a fork to incorporate it. Add only enough water to hold the dough together, so it can be gathered into a ball. Wrap the dough in plastic and chill in the refrigerator for an hour. Bring the dough back to room temperature before rolling.

To make the crust, gently roll out the dough on a lightly floured surface to a thickness of ¼ inch; use a cutter to cut circles to the desired diameter. Place a couple of spoonfuls of the filling off-center on each circle. Brush the edges with water, fold in half, and seal securely using either your finger or a fork.

Brush the empanadas with the egg glaze, place on a lightly oiled baking pan, and bake for 15 to 20 minutes, or until golden.

Remove from the pan and cool on a rack before serving.

Empanadas can be frozen up to 3 months. Bake, then cool completely, and freeze in an airtight container. Reheat without thawing in a preheated 350°F. oven for about 30 minutes.

Yield: 2 dozen appetizer-size empanadas

Ceviche Mexicana

This is a basic Mexican version of ceviche that is easily varied with the addition of seasonal fruits and vegetables. Nancy likes to use diced avocado, jicama, or even cucumbers to contribute not only different flavors but also textures to the ceviche. Adding tomato juice and pulp to the recipe and serving it in a large parfait glass will transform the ceviche into the very popular seafood "cockteles" found all over Mexico.

1 pound any firm white fish, such as snapper, pompano, flounder, or bass, cut into ¾- to 1-inch cubes

2 jalapeño chiles, stems and seeds removed, finely chopped; or substitute serrano chiles

Juice of 8 Mexican limes, or Key limes

1 medium tomato, chopped

½ medium onion, finely chopped

2 tablespoons chopped fresh cilantro

Salt and freshly ground black pepper

Lime wedges for garnish

Note: This recipe requires advance preparation.

Combine the fish and chiles in a nonreactive bowl, add the lime juice, and toss to coat the fish. Cover the bowl and refrigerate for 1 to 4 hours, turning occasionally, until the fish loses its translucency and turns opaque.

Just before serving, add the tomato, onion, and half the cilantro and gently toss to mix. Season with salt and pepper.

Put the ceviche in tall parfait glasses, garnish with the remaining cilantro, place a lime wedge on the rim of the glass, and serve.

Yield: 4 to 6 servings

Calabrian Peppers

The Calabrian region is in the toe of the "boot" of Italy, where the warm climate makes it possible to grow a wide variety of chiles, is known for its spicy cuisine. This simple-to-prepare popular appetizer can be prepared with any peperoncino (hot chile) of a decent size, such as Corno de Toro, Italian frying peppers, chile guero, yellow wax peppers, or banana chiles. Even bell peppers can be used, but be sure to add some crushed chiles to obtain that classic Calabrian heat level.

3 tablespoons extra-virgin olive oil

4 medium to large red and yellow peperoncino peppers, stems and seeds removed, cut in quarters and sliced in strips

⅓ cup fresh bread crumbs

2 tablespoons grated pecorino Romano cheese

1 tablespoon capers, drained and rinsed

1 teaspoon chopped fresh oregano or basil

Crushed red chile to taste

Salt to taste

Chopped fresh flat leaf-parsley for garnish

Heat the oil in a heavy skillet over high heat, reduce the heat, and add the chiles. Sauté the chiles until soft but still with some texture, about 3 minutes. Remove the chiles and pour off half the oil.

Add the bread crumbs, cheese, capers, oregano or basil, and crushed chile, if using, to the skillet and stir to mix. Return the pepper strips to the pan and sauté for an additional 2 minutes. Season with salt to taste.

Remove the skillet from the heat and let it sit for about 10 minutes to blend the flavors.

Place the chiles on a serving dish, garnish with the parsley, and serve.

Yield: 4 servings

Acadiana Deviled Oysters

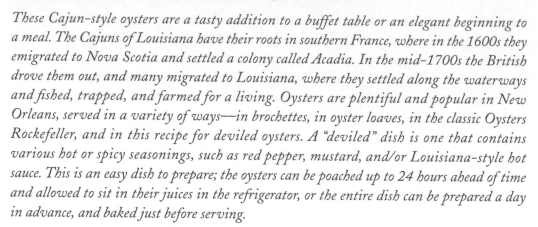

These Cajun-style oysters are a tasty addition to a buffet table or an elegant beginning to a meal. The Cajuns of Louisiana have their roots in southern France, where in the 1600s they emigrated to Nova Scotia and settled a colony called Acadia. In the mid-1700s the British drove them out, and many migrated to Louisiana, where they settled along the waterways and fished, trapped, and farmed for a living. Oysters are plentiful and popular in New Orleans, served in a variety of ways—in brochettes, in oyster loaves, in the classic Oysters Rockefeller, and in this recipe for deviled oysters. A "deviled" dish is one that contains various hot or spicy seasonings, such as red pepper, mustard, and/or Louisiana-style hot sauce. This is an easy dish to prepare; the oysters can be poached up to 24 hours ahead of time and allowed to sit in their juices in the refrigerator, or the entire dish can be prepared a day in advance, and baked just before serving.

24 shucked fresh oysters with their liquor

1½ cups milk

6 tablespoons (¾ stick) butter

½ cup all-purpose flour

1 teaspoon dry mustard

½ teaspoon salt

¼ teaspoon ground cayenne

2 teaspoons lemon juice, preferably fresh

4 drops Louisiana-style hot sauce

2 egg yolks, beaten

¼ cup chopped green onions, including some of the greens

1 teaspoon prepared horseradish, store-bought or homemade (page 112)

1 cup seasoned bread crumbs

8 baking scallop shells

Lemon slices for garnish

Seasoned Bread Crumbs

¾ cup dry bread crumbs

3 tablespoons grated Parmesan cheese

1 tablespoon ground paprika

¼ teaspoon ground white pepper

3 to 4 tablespoons (½ stick) butter or margarine

1 tablespoon dry sherry (optional)

To prepare the bread crumbs, combine the bread with the cheese, paprika, and pepper in a bowl and stir to mix. In a saucepan, melt the butter over medium heat. Pour the sherry, if using, over the bread-crumb mixture and toss to coat. Slowly add just enough of the butter to moisten the bread crumbs. Set aside.

Heat a heavy skillet over medium heat, add the oysters and their liquor, and gently simmer, uncovered, for 3 minutes or until the edges of the oysters begin to curl. Drain the oysters and reserve the pan juices. Coarsely chop the oysters and set aside. Add enough milk to the pan juices to make 2 cups total liquid; set aside.

In a saucepan over medium heat, melt the butter. Whisk in the flour, mustard, salt, and cayenne and cook, stirring, until the butter and flour mixture is bubbling and foamy. Remove the pan from the heat and gradually whisk in the 2 cups of oyster liquid. Return to the heat and cook, stirring constantly, until the sauce is smooth, thick, and boiling. Stir in the lemon juice and hot sauce.

Put the egg yolks in a bowl, and to make sure they don't curdle, slowly add ½ cup of hot oyster sauce, stirring well. Pour the tempered egg yolk mixture into the remaining sauce and blend well. Cook, stirring constantly, over low heat for 2 minutes. Remove the pan from the heat, stir in the green onions and horseradish, and allow the sauce to cool.

Divide the oysters among the scallop shells and spoon about ¼ cup sauce over each portion of the oysters. Top each portion with 2 tablespoons of the seasoned bread crumbs. Cover the shells and refrigerate until you are ready to bake them.

Preheat the oven to 400°F.

Uncover the shells and bake until the sauce is bubbly and the top is lightly browned, about 12 to 15 minutes.

Garnish each serving with a lemon slice before serving.

Yield: 8 servings

Fried Wontons with Feta Cheese and Ginger Plum Sauce Mustard

Wontons don't have to be filled with bean sprouts and other bland ingredients. This is an unusual combination of ingredients, but the sweetness of the ginger and the pungency of the feta cheese blend well, and the sweet sharpness of the mustard complements the wonton. It is definitely a wonton that will have your guests trying to guess the ingredients, especially since the pickled ginger turns the cheese pink! Wontons reheat very well, so they can be prepared ahead of time. If you're making them ahead, fry the wontons until lightly browned. Reheat them in a preheated 300°F oven for about 8 minutes until crisp.

1 cup feta cheese
2 tablespoons heavy cream
1 tablespoon chopped chives
1 tablespoon chopped pickled ginger
1 package wonton skins
Vegetable oil for frying

Ginger Plum Sauce Mustard

¼ cup ginger plum sauce mustard (page 145)
¼ cup rice wine

Put the cheese in a bowl and, using two forks, thoroughly mash it. Add the cream, chives, and ginger and stir to mix. Cover the bowl and chill for a couple of hours.

To assemble the wontons, place one of the skins in your hand or on a flat surface, with the point toward you. Put a teaspoon of the mixture in the far corner. Dot the corner with water and fold over the mixture, tucking the point under the mixture. Moisten the remaining corners, bring together and overlap, pinching firmly to seal. Keep the prepared wontons covered with a damp cloth until you are ready to fry them.

Pour the oil in a deep fryer or saucepan to a depth of 2 inches and heat to 375°F.

Drop the wontons, a few at a time, into the oil; fry for 1 to 2 minutes on one side, turn, and continue to fry about 1 minute on the second side until crispy and browned. Don't crowd the fryer. Remove and drain on paper towels. Repeat with remaining wontons.

Combine the mustard and rice wine in a bowl and serve with the wontons.

Yield: 3 to 4 dozen

Habanero Salmon Cakes with Orange, Pineapple, and Ginger Sauce

This is our more affordable version of crab cakes. These are light, fresh, and tasty; they are both hot and sweet, but the flavors don't clash. The initial taste is that of the salmon, followed by the fruity flavor of the sauce. Small cakes can be served as an appetizer and larger ones as an entrée. We've been known to form them into large patties and use in place of beef on a burger bun.

One 7½-ounce can flaked salmon, drained

1 egg, lightly beaten

⅓ to ½ cup fresh bread crumbs

2 tablespoons finely chopped green onions, including some of the greens

2 tablespoons chopped fresh cilantro

1 tablespoon lime juice, preferably fresh

1 tablespoon mayonnaise

1 habanero chile, stem and seeds removed, minced

½ teaspoon dry mustard

⅛ teaspoon ground allspice

Freshly ground black pepper

All-purpose flour

Vegetable oil for frying

Chopped fresh parsley for garnish

Orange, Pineapple, and Ginger Sauce

⅓ cup chopped pineapple, fresh or canned, drained

1½ teaspoons grated ginger

½ cup white wine; or substitute chicken broth

1 tablespoon cornstarch mixed with 2 tablespoons water

15 mandarin orange segments, fresh or canned, drained

Combine all the ingredients for the salmon cakes, except the flour and oil, in a bowl and stir to mix. Chill the mixture for 30 minutes. Form the mixture into small cakes.

Put some flour on a plate and dust the cakes on both sides with the flour.

Heat a heavy skillet over medium heat and add the oil to a depth of 1 inch. Pan-fry the cakes a few at a time until slightly browned and cooked through. Remove, drain on paper towels, and keep warm.

To make the sauce, combine the pineapple, ginger, and wine in a small saucepan and bring to a boil. Slowly add the cornstarch mixture, and cook until thickened. Stir in the orange pieces and simmer for an additional 2 minutes.

To serve, drizzle some of the sauce on small plates, add the cakes, and top with more of the sauce. Sprinkle the parsley around the plate and serve.

Yield: 12 small cakes

Vietnamese Pork and Shrimp Balls with Spicy Sauce

 These are a variation on the more traditional Vietnamese lettuce rolls. Found in Asian markets, tree ears are a variety of mushroom also known as cloud ear, wood ear, or silver ear.

Sesame oil

2 tablespoons tree ear mushrooms

¾ pound ground pork

½ pound shrimp, peeled and deveined, finely chopped

½ cup finely chopped green onions

1 tablespoon grated fresh ginger

1 tablespoon chopped fresh basil, preferably Thai

2 Thai chiles, stems removed, minced; or substitute serrano chiles

1 clove garlic, finely chopped

1 egg, beaten

1 tablespoon cornstarch

1 tablespoon rice wine or dry sherry

2 teaspoons soy sauce

¼ teaspoon sugar

Boston or red-leaf lettuce leaves for garnish

Dipping Sauce

¼ cup lime juice, preferably fresh

3 tablespoons Asian fish sauce (*nam pla*)

3 tablespoons sugar

4 Thai chiles, stems removed, minced; or substitute serrano chiles

2 cloves garlic, minced

1 tablespoon grated ginger

1 tablespoon chopped fresh cilantro

1 tablespoon finely chopped fresh ginger

¼ cup water

Preheat the oven to 350°F, and liberally oil a baking pan with sesame oil.

Put the tree ears in a bowl, cover with warm water, and allow them to steep for 30 minutes to soften. Drain the mushrooms and finely chop.

In another bowl combine all the ingredients for the sauce and stir to mix. Allow the sauce to sit at room temperature to blend the flavors.

In yet another bowl, combine all the remaining ingredients for the meatballs, except the lettuce, using your hands to mix. Form the mixture into small meatballs about 1½ inches in diameter and place them on the baking pan. Bake the meatballs 30 minutes, or until lightly browned, turning them a couple of times during cooking.

Before serving, place them under the broiler to brown, and then cool until warm.

To serve: Arrange the lettuce leaves on a platter like scoops and top with the meatballs. Sprinkle some of the sauce over the top and serve the remaining sauce for dipping.

Yield: 6 to 8 servings

Spicy Calamari Rings
with Pineapple Plum Dipping Sauce

We consider ourselves lucky in a city the size of Albuquerque to have two Asian markets that sell very, very fresh seafood, some still swimming. Because of this, we are able to buy fresh calamari or squid whenever we wish, although frozen will also work well in this recipe. Many people have a "fear of frying," but the trick to successful frying is to have the oil hot enough (use a thermometer to check), use fresh oil, and allow the oil to heat up between batches. Do it right, and the food doesn't absorb much, if any, oil. The cornstarch coating allows more of the delicate flavor of the squid to come through, and the fruit dipping sauce is a lighter accompaniment to fried calamari than a traditional marinara-type sauce. Be careful not to overcook the calamari, as it has a tendency to turn into rubber bands if cooked too long.

1 cup cornstarch

1 teaspoon ground habanero chile

1 pound, or about 9, squid,
    sliced in rings ½ inch wide

Vegetable oil for frying,
    preferably canola oil

Dipping Sauce

3 slices canned pineapple

2 medium red plums, peeled
    and pits removed

2 canned tomatoes

3 green New Mexican chiles,
    roasted, peeled, stems
    and seeds removed

¼ cup chopped onion

1 tablespoon lime juice,
    preferably fresh

1 tablespoon white wine vinegar

2 teaspoons sugar

1 teaspoon minced garlic

¼ teaspoon dried oregano,
    preferably Mexican

Salt to taste

To make the sauce, put the pineapple, plums, and tomatoes in a blender or food processor and process to a puree. Combine with all the remaining salsa ingredients in a bowl and stir to mix. Allow the mixture to sit for 1 hour to blend the flavors.

Combine the cornstarch and chile in a bowl and stir to mix. Dredge the calamari in the cornstarch mixture so that they are well coated. Shake off the excess coating.

Heat a heavy saucepan over high heat, add the oil to a depth of 2 to 3 inches and heat to 370°F. Fry the squid, a few at a time so as to not crowd the pan, until golden, about 1 minute. Remove and drain on paper towels.

Mound the calamari rings on a platter and serve accompanied by bowls of the dipping sauce.

Yield: 6 servings

8 Starters: Soups & Salads

Molaga-tanni (Mulligatawny Soup)

This classic soup was created in southern India and is a combination of British and Indian influences. It gets its odd-sounding name from the native language, Tamil, in which molaga-tanni means "pepper water." Incidentally, the state of Tamil Nadu is home to Piper nigrum, or black pepper. This flavorful soup is still a favorite in India among the westernized middle class, who enjoy it in their private clubs. There are countless variations on this soup; all are curried, and most are made with coconut milk or cream. In our version, we use a potato to add a creamy texture without the added fat from the coconut milk; the apple gives the dish a hint of sweetness. This is a good way to utilize leftover chicken.

2 tablespoons vegetable oil

¼ cup chopped onion

1 teaspoon minced ginger

1 teaspoon crushed garlic

1½ tablespoons store-bought curry powder or homemade *bafat* (page 136)

1¼ teaspoons ground turmeric

¼ teaspoon ground cumin

3 cups chicken broth

1 potato, peeled and diced

1 green apple, peeled and diced

2 medium tomatoes, peeled and chopped; or substitute one 14-ounce can peeled tomatoes, drained and chopped

2 dried cayenne chiles, stems removed

1 bay leaf

Salt and freshly ground black pepper to taste

1 cup cooked rice

3 to 4 ounces cooked chicken, diced or shredded

Chopped fresh cilantro for garnish

In a stockpot or large saucepan, heat the oil, add the onion, ginger, and garlic and sauté until the onion is soft and transparent. Add the curry, turmeric, and cumin and sauté for an additional couple of minutes.

Add the broth, potato, apple, tomatoes, chiles, bay leaf, and salt and black pepper. Bring the soup to a boil, cover, reduce the heat, and simmer for 45 minutes, until the potatoes are very soft.

Remove the bay leaf, place the soup in a blender or food processor, and puree until smooth. Strain the soup back into the stockpot, add the rice and chicken, and reheat. Taste and adjust the seasonings.

To serve, ladle the soup into individual bowls and garnish with cilantro.

Yield: 4 servings

Ginger Curry Pumpkin Bisque with Peppered Croutons

We don't always end a Thanksgiving meal with pumpkin pie—sometimes we begin the feast with this spicy soup, and its Caribbean island flavor. If you don't want to use pumpkin, any winter squash, such as butternut, acorn, or Hubbard, will do. This is an easy recipe to prepare, but if you want an even quicker version, use canned pumpkin puree or a 12-ounce package of frozen cooked winter squash as a base.

1 quart vegetable broth, preferably homemade

4 cups diced fresh squash or one 15-ounce can pumpkin puree

2 tablespoons butter or margarine

1 tablespoon chopped ginger

1 cup chopped onions

¼ teaspoon ground habanero chile

2 teaspoons curry powder, store-bought or homemade (page 131)

¼ teaspoon ground coriander

¼ teaspoon ground white pepper

Pinch of ground cloves

3 tablespoons orange juice, preferably fresh

¼ teaspoon orange zest

2 tablespoons rum (optional)

Chopped green onions and peppered croutons for garnish

Peppered Croutons

3 slices of bread, crusts removed and cut in squares or 4 to 6 slices of a thin baguette cut in rounds

2 tablespoons butter or margarine

2 tablespoons extra-virgin olive oil

1 garlic clove, thinly sliced

1 teaspoon coarsely ground black pepper

¼ teaspoon dried thyme, crumbled

¼ teaspoon dried sage, crumbled

1½ tablespoons freshly grated Parmesan cheese

Preheat the oven to 325°F.

If using fresh squash, bring the broth to a rapid boil in a large saucepan over high heat. Add the squash, cover, and boil for about 10 minutes or until soft. Remove the squash and reserve some of the broth. Place the squash in a blender or food processor and puree until smooth, adding some of the broth if needed.

Otherwise, place the canned pumpkin puree, along with 3 cups of the broth, in a large stockpot.

Heat a small skillet over medium heat and add the butter or margarine; when it's melted, add the ginger and onion and sauté until the onions are soft. Add the ginger-onion mixture, chile, curry, coriander, pepper, and cloves to the pumpkin puree. Simmer the bisque for 15 minutes.

Meanwhile, make the croutons. Place the bread on a sheet pan and bake in the oven until toasted, turning once, about 10 minutes.

Heat a small saucepan over low heat, add the butter, and when the butter has melted, add the oil, garlic, pepper, thyme, and sage. Simmer the mixture for 5 minutes to blend flavors, being careful that the butter does not brown.

Combine the butter mixture and the croutons in a bowl and toss to coat. Return them to the sheet pan, sprinkle the cheese over the croutons, and return them to the oven. Bake until the cheese browns, about 10 minutes.

Strain the soup, return to the stove, and heat through. Remove the soup from the heat; stir in the orange juice, zest, and rum, if using.

To serve, pour the bisque into a large soup tureen or ladle into individual bowls, and garnish with the onions and peppered croutons.

Yield: 4 to 6 servings

Gulaschsuppe (Goulash Soup)

Variations of this recipe were popular with the roving Magyar tribes of Central Europe who cooked their meat and vegetables over campfires in large kettles. Nothing keeps you warmer on a cold winter night than a bowl of paprika-flavored soup or stew, which heats you from the inside out. Since truly "hot" paprika can be hard to find, we bring up the heat by adding small dried red chiles, rather than additional paprika, which can make the soup excessively sweet. Traditionally, a Central or Eastern European would not serve sour cream with this dish, but I think its creaminess makes a nice finishing touch.

2 slices bacon, diced

1½ pounds boneless chuck or sirloin beef, trimmed and cut in ½- to 1-inch cubes

1 to 2 tablespoons vegetable oil

1½ cups chopped onion

1 tablespoon minced garlic

3 to 4 tablespoons all-purpose flour

1 to 2 tablespoons paprika, preferably hot Hungarian

One 12-ounce can beef broth (2 cans if not using the beer)

One 12-ounce bottle dark beer (optional)

4 to 6 dried red chiles, such as piquins, chiltepins, tepins, or japones

1½ teaspoons crushed caraway seeds

½ teaspoon dried marjoram

½ teaspoon celery seeds

¼ cup red wine vinegar

2 tomatoes, peeled and chopped, or substitute 3 tablespoons tomato paste

1 teaspoon freshly ground black pepper

1 medium potato, peeled and diced

1 cup diced carrots (optional)

½ cup chopped green bell pepper (optional)

Salt to taste

Sour cream for garnish

Variation: Increase the flour to ⅓ cup to thicken the broth and make a stew.

Heat a heavy skillet over medium-high heat, and slowly sauté the bacon to render the fat. Remove the bacon and drain on a paper towel.

Add the beef, in batches, to the skillet and quickly brown. Remove the beef cubes as they become browned and put them in a heavy stockpot. Repeat with the remaining beef, adding oil if necessary.

Add the onion and garlic to the skillet and sauté until they are soft. Add the flour and continue to cook, stirring constantly, until the flour browns, being careful that it doesn't burn. Stir in the paprika, continue to cook for an additional couple of minutes, and add the mixture to the stockpot.

Deglaze the skillet by whisking in a cup of the broth, raising the heat, bringing it to a boil, and scraping the sides and bottom of the skillet to remove all the browned bits and pieces in the pan. Pour the mixture in with the beef.

Add the remaining broth, the beer, if using, and the chiles, caraway seeds, marjoram, celery seeds, vinegar, and tomato. Also stir in the remaining paprika, black pepper, reserved bacon, potato, and, if using, the carrots and bell pepper. Bring to a boil, reduce the heat, and simmer until the vegetables are done and the meat is very tender, about 45 to 50 minutes. Add more broth if necessary to thin to the desired consistency, and salt to taste.

To serve, ladle the soup into individual soup bowls and garnish with a dollop of sour cream.

Yield: 4 to 6 servings

Hot and Sour Soup

We would venture that there isn't a restaurant in the Sichuan Province of China that doesn't have a variation of this wildly popular soup on their menu. They may use chicken, pork, shrimp, or a combination of meats, and there are vegetarian versions with no meat at all. The heat in this dish comes from white pepper, not chiles, as you might suspect. Unfortunately, authentic hot and sour soup cannot be duplicated in this country. Although the world has shrunk and most exotic ingredients are available to anyone anywhere, coagulated duck's blood, essential in the "real deal," is impossible to find. In our version we use Chinese black vinegar, which has a slightly sweet, earthy, salty, complex flavor, in place of rice vinegar or the more acidic distilled white vinegar, which is commonly used in restaurants. Be sure to have all the ingredients prepared and organized before beginning to assemble the soup.

Broth

Reserved chicken bones

1 quart chicken broth

1 teaspoon black peppercorns

1½-inch piece ginger, sliced

Salt to taste

Marinating Sauce

2 teaspoons cornstarch

1 teaspoon salt

½ teaspoon sugar

2 chicken thighs, skin removed, meat cut in 2-by-⅛-inch pieces, bones reserved; or substitute 1 chicken breast

¼ cup dried wood ear mushrooms

½ cup diced tofu

1 teaspoon soy sauce

1 teaspoon sesame oil

¼ cup bamboo shoots

¼ cup green peas

2 to 3 teaspoons ground white pepper

Salt to taste

3 tablespoons cornstarch mixed with ¼ cup water

1 tablespoon sliced green onion

1 egg, beaten

¼ cup Chinese black vinegar (available in Asian markets); or substitute rice vinegar or distilled white vinegar

To make the broth, combine the chicken bones, chicken broth, and the other broth ingredients in a stockpot. Bring the mixture to a boil over high heat, reduce the heat, and simmer for 20 minutes. Remove from the heat and then strain. Remove any meat from the bones or strained solids, and add back to the broth.

Combine all the marinating sauce ingredients with 4 teaspoons water in a bowl and stir to mix. Add the chicken pieces and marinate for 30 minutes.

In another bowl, cover the dried wood ears in warm water. Allow the wood ears to steep for 30 minutes to soften. Drain the wood ears and discard the water.

Bring the broth in the stockpot to a boil, reduce the heat to a simmer, and add the wood ears, the tofu, and the chicken. Simmer for 1 to 2 minutes while stirring continuously so that the chicken pieces don't stick together.

Add the soy sauce, sesame oil, bamboo shoots, peas, and pepper, and season to taste with salt.

Raise the heat and slowly add the cornstarch while stirring until thickened. Add the green onion.

While stirring the soup, add the egg in a steady, slow stream so it will cook in threads.

Remove from the heat and add the vinegar.

Ladle the soup in a large tureen and serve with additional vinegar at the table.

Yield: 4 servings

Broccoli and Mustard Soup

Do you ever wonder what to do with all those broccoli stems you wind up with when you buy it fresh? Well, they can be made into a base for a great-tasting soup that is quick and easy to prepare. The mustard gives the soup a creamy texture without the addition of any cream, so this "cream" soup is low in fat! For a vegetarian version, just substitute vegetable broth for the chicken.

1 pound fresh broccoli, stems chopped and florets reserved

1 medium onion, coarsely chopped

2 chicken bouillon cubes

4 chiltepin chiles, or substitute piquin

2 teaspoons chopped fresh rosemary leaves

1 teaspoon chopped flat-leaf parsley

½ teaspoon ground thyme

½ teaspoon ground marjoram

Salt to taste

½ to ¾ teaspoon ground white pepper

3 to 4 tablespoons Dijon-style mustard, store-bought or homemade (page 117)

Chopped fresh chives for garnish

In a large stockpot place the broccoli stems, onion, bouillon cubes, chiles, rosemary, parsley, thyme, marjoram, and 2 quarts of water. Bring the mixture to a boil, reduce the heat, and simmer for 30 minutes. Allow the mixture to cool slightly.

Place the soup in a blender or food processor and puree until smooth. Strain the soup back into the stockpot. Add the salt, and adjust the seasonings to taste.

Add the broccoli florets and the white pepper, and bring the soup to a simmer over medium-low heat. Simmer until the florets are just done, slightly crisp and still bright green.

Remove the soup from the heat and stir in the mustard. Ladle the soup into a tureen or individual bowls, garnish with the chives, and serve.

Yield: 4 to 6 servings

Red Lentil Soup

This vegetarian soup from India is so full-flavored that you won't miss the meat. We like to cook with lentils because, unlike with many other dried beans, you don't have to plan ahead to soak them overnight, and they cook quickly. This soup makes a great entrée if you reduce the amount of liquid used to 2 cups, don't puree the soup, and serve it over rice.

2 to 3 teaspoons vegetable oil

½ cup chopped onion

1 teaspoon black mustard seeds

3 cloves garlic, minced

4 teaspoons grated ginger

4 small dried red chiles, such as piquin, chiltepin, or de arbol

1 teaspoon ground coriander

½ teaspoon ground cumin

½ teaspoon ground turmeric

3 cups vegetable broth

½ cup red lentils, picked over

1 medium potato, peeled and diced

Chopped fresh cilantro or parsley for garnish

Heat a heavy stockpot or saucepan over medium-high heat, add the oil, and when hot, add the onion and mustard seeds and sauté for 3 to 4 minutes. Add the garlic, ginger, and chiles and continue to sauté for an additional 2 minutes. Stir in the coriander, cumin, and turmeric and heat for an additional minute.

Add the broth, lentils, and potato to the stockpot and heat to just below boiling. Simmer the soup for 30 to 40 minutes, or until the lentils and potatoes are very soft. Put the soup in a blender or food processor and puree until smooth. Strain the soup back into the pot and reheat.

Ladle the soup into individual bowls, garnish with cilantro or parsley, and serve.

Yield: 4 servings

Southwest Salsa Soup with Lime Cream

Using a commercial salsa as a base for this soup makes it quick and easy to prepare, as well as allowing you to choose your spice level, from mild to wild. The heat of the salsa will intensify, so we don't recommend you use a habanero-based salsa or any other that is too hot. This simple soup can also be made more hearty with the addition of cooked pinto or black beans, chicken or turkey, or even whole-kernel corn. Add these to the soup after it has been pureed. For the taste of green chile and chicken enchiladas in soup form, just use green chile salsa and add chicken.

2 to 3 teaspoons vegetable oil

1 cup chopped onion

2 teaspoons chopped garlic

1½ cups tomato-based commercial salsa

3 cups chicken broth, preferably homemade

2 corn tortillas, torn into pieces

¼ teaspoon ground cumin

Salt and freshly ground black pepper to taste

¼ cup chopped fresh cilantro

Lime Cream for garnish (recipe below)

Lime Cream

2 tablespoons lime juice, preferably fresh

½ cup sour cream

¼ cup heavy cream

The cream can be prepared ahead of time and refrigerated until you are ready to serve.

Heat a heavy saucepan or stockpot over medium-high heat, add the oil, and when hot, add the onions and sauté until they are soft. Add the garlic and continue to sauté for an additional minute.

Stir in the salsa, broth, tortillas, cumin, and salt and pepper and bring to a boil. Reduce the heat and simmer until the tortillas are soft. Remove from the heat and cool slightly.

Put the mixture into a blender or food processor and puree until smooth. Taste and adjust the seasonings and stir in the cilantro.

To make the Lime Cream: Combine all the ingredients in a bowl and stir to mix. You will have ¾ cup of cream; refrigerate any that is not used for soup. It will keep for 1 to 2 weeks.

To serve, ladle the soup into individual bowls and garnish with a dollop of lime cream.

Yield: 4 to 6 servings

Grilled Corn and Chipotle Soup

This recipe from the Blue Corn Cafe & Brewery in Albuquerque and Santa Fe was provided by chef Russell Thornton, who says, "Without a doubt it's the single most requested recipe in our restaurants." This simple soup's main components are corn, chipotles, and cream. The chipotles can be either canned chipotles en adobo *or dried; just reconstitute the dried ones in hot water before adding.*

6 medium ears of corn

2 to 3 chipotle chiles *en adobo*; or substitute dried chipotles

¼ cup diced red onions

¼ teaspoon ground white pepper

¼ teaspoon ground cumin

2 cups heavy cream

Vegetable oil for frying

2 corn tortillas, cut in wedges

Corn Relish Garnish

Reserved grilled corn

1 tablespoon diced green bell pepper

1 tablespoon diced red bell pepper

¼ teaspoon minced jalapeño chile

3 tablespoons white wine vinegar

1 teaspoon honey

Salt to taste

To grill the corn, shuck the ears, rub the corn with vegetable oil and salt, and grill over an open flame. Allow some of the kernels to pop and blacken, which will add flavor and character to the soup. Using a sharp knife, scrape off all the kernels, being sure to get every part. Put aside one-quarter of the corn for the garnish.

Combine all the ingredients for the corn relish in a bowl, stir to mix, and season with salt. Allow the mixture to sit for at least an hour at room temperature to blend the flavors.

Put half of the corn along with the chiles, onions, pepper, and cumin and about 1 cup of water in a blender or food processor and pulse briefly until a coarse paste is achieved. Add more water as needed, but don't overblend, as you want to retain some texture.

In a large saucepan over high heat combine all of the ingredients, except the oil and tortillas, along with another cup of water, and bring to a boil. Reduce the heat and simmer for 15 to 20 minutes. The soup needs to cook down by about half.

Heat a heavy skillet over high heat, pour in the oil to a depth of an inch, and heat until hot. Add the tortilla wedges and fry until crisp. Remove and drain on a paper towel.

To serve, ladle the soup into individual bowls; garnish with a dollop of corn relish and a couple of tortilla wedges.

Yield: 4 to 6 servings

Chicken and Andouille Gumbo

Gumbo evolved in the Bayou State and represents a true melting-pot dish that reflects the varied population of Louisiana. French, Acadian, Native American, and African residents all contributed to the culture and cuisine of the area. The title of this Cajun classic is a French patois word that comes from the Bantu word for okra—guingombo. Okra is used in gumbos to provide taste and texture, and to thicken the soup. Gumbos can be made with duck, chicken, ham, shrimp, crab, or oysters. Nancy has even sampled some made from alligator at a "gator" festival outside New Orleans. And yes, it does taste like chicken. The real secret of a good-tasting gumbo is in the dark roux, which provides a toasty, nutty flavor. Gumbos are always served over rice.

2 boneless, skinless chicken breasts, about 5 ounces each, cut in ¾-inch cubes

1 tablespoon Cajun seasoning, store-bought or homemade (page 167)

1 pound andouille sausage, cut in ¼-inch slices

2 tablespoons vegetable oil

1½ cups chopped onion

1 cup diced bell pepper

1 cup chopped celery

3 jalapeño chiles, stems and seeds removed, chopped

1½ teaspoons minced garlic

½ teaspoon dried oregano

½ teaspoon dried basil

2 bay leaves

¼ teaspoon freshly ground black pepper

¼ teaspoon ground white pepper

6 cups chicken broth

1 cup dark roux (see recipe below)

One 10-ounce package frozen okra, thawed

2 to 3 cups cooked white rice

1 cup sliced green onions, including the greens

Salt to taste

½ cup minced flat-leaf parsley for garnish

Roux

1 cup vegetable shortening

1½ cup flour, bread flour preferred

Combine the chicken with the Cajun seasoning in a bowl and toss to coat. Let the chicken sit at room temperature 30 minutes to marinate.

Heat a heavy stockpot over high heat, add the oil, and when hot, reduce the heat to medium. Add the andouille and brown. Add the chicken and onion and sauté for an additional 4 minutes, stirring occasionally.

Add the bell pepper, celery, chiles, and garlic, and sauté for 2 minutes, stirring occasionally. Add the oregano, basil, bay leaves, and peppers and cook for an additional 2 minutes.

Stir in the broth and bring to a boil. Whisk in the roux a little at a time and stir continuously for 5 minutes. Simmer the gumbo for an additional 25 minutes, stirring often.

Add the okra and cook for 20 minutes. Taste and adjust the seasonings, adding more Cajun seasoning if desired. Remove from the heat and stir in the green onions.

To serve, divide the rice between individual shallow soup bowls, ladle the gumbo over the rice, and garnish with the parsley. Serve the gumbo with a bottle of Louisiana-style hot sauce to adjust the heat.

Yield: 4 to 6 servings

Roux

In order to make a dark roux, you need to start with a solid shortening, although some people do use vegetable oil. This can be vegetable shortening, bacon fat, pork or beef drippings, or the traditional lard. Cooked to a deep, mahogany brown color, roux imparts a rich, nutty flavor to dishes such as gumbos.

Heat a heavy skillet over high heat, add the shortening, and when it has melted and starts to bubble, carefully whisk in the flour a little at a time until all the flour is incorporated. Reduce the heat to medium, and stir continually until the roux is a dark brown, about 20 to 25 minutes.

Remove the pan from the heat. To prevent the roux from cooking further and burning, pour into a heatproof container and cool.

Pimentón Garlic Soup
(Spanish Garlic Soup)

The classic garlic soup of Madrid is transformed into a smoky-hot masterpiece with the addition of pimentón, *a powder made from oak-smoked chiles. In Spain,* pimiento *is a generic term for chiles; the one used in* pimentón *is either a long chile that produces a sweet powder, a round cascabel-like chile that is the hot variety, or a third one that is used for* agridulce, *or bittersweet* pimentón. *The trick to a good garlic soup is to cook the garlic very slowly so that it's soft and creamy, not browned. The amount of garlic can be adjusted to suit your tastes. If you can't locate* pimentón, *mix equal portions of red New Mexican chile powder and chipotle powder.*

2 tablespoons extra-virgin olive oil, preferably Spanish

2 to 3 strips bacon, diced

6 to 8 cloves garlic, thinly sliced

1½ tablespoons hot *pimentón*

¼ teaspoon ground cumin

6 cups chicken broth

10 baguette bread slices, crusts removed, sliced ½ inch thick and toasted

Salt to taste

4 eggs

Chopped fresh flat-leaf parsley and 4 lime wedges for garnish

Heat a saucepan or stockpot over medium heat, add the oil and bacon, and when hot, add the garlic, reduce the heat, and slowly sauté until the garlic is soft, being careful that it doesn't brown.

Add the *pimentón* and cumin and stir to mix. Whisk in the broth, bring to a boil, reduce the heat, add the bread, and simmer for 5 minutes. Taste and season with salt.

Carefully break each egg into the soup so that it rests on top of the soup. Cover the pot and simmer until the whites of the eggs are set and yolks are soft, about 4 minutes.

To serve, carefully ladle the soup and an egg into individual bowls, being careful that the yolks don't break. Garnish with the chopped parsley and serve with a lime wedge for sprinkling over the soup.

Yield: 4 servings

Posole (Pork and Posole Corn)

Similar to, yet different from the "pozole" served in Mexico, this popular dish is served as a soup, a main course, or a vegetable side dish. Posole, the processed corn, is the main ingredient of this dish of the same name. It's traditionally served during the Christmas season in New Mexico, when a pot simmering at the back of the stove provides a welcoming fare for holiday well-wishers.

¾ cup dried posole corn

1 to 2 tablespoons vegetable oil

1 pound lean pork,
    cut in 1½-inch cubes

1 cup finely chopped onion

2 garlic cloves, minced

2 cups pork broth

2 to 3 tablespoons ground
    red New Mexican chile

1 teaspoon dried oregano,
    preferably Mexican

Salt to taste

Chopped fresh cilantro, chopped
    onions, and New Mexico
    red chile sauce (page 162)
    for garnish

Flour tortillas

In a large saucepan or stockpot, cover the posole with water and soak overnight. Bring the water and posole to a boil, reduce the heat, and simmer for a half an hour. Add more water if necessary.

This recipe requires advance preparation.

Heat a heavy skillet over high heat, add the oil, and when hot, reduce the heat to medium, add the pork, and brown. Remove the pork when browned, and add it to the posole. Add the onions to the skillet, and if needed, additional oil. Sauté the onions until they turn a golden brown, 5 to 10 minutes. Add the garlic and cook for an additional minute. Transfer the mixture to the pot with the posole.

Add the broth to the pan, raise the heat, and deglaze the pan, being sure to scrape all the bits and pieces from the sides and bottom. Pour the broth into the posole pot.

Add the remaining ingredients to the stockpot, bring to just below boiling, reduce the heat, and simmer for 45 minutes to an hour, or until the posole is tender and the meat is starting to fall apart. Add more broth or water if necessary.

Place the chopped onions for the garnish in a sieve and rinse under cold water to remove the sharpness.

Place the garnishes in small serving bowls, ladle the stew into individual soup bowls, and serve accompanied by warm flour tortillas.

Yield: 4 to 6 servings

Horseradish Soup with Toasted Pumpernickel Croutons

 In many of the Slavic countries, variations of horseradish soup are served as traditional Easter fare. Many of these soups are prepared with root vegetables such as beets, turnips, or, like this one, potatoes, along with a heavy dose of horseradish. This simple, hearty soup is easy to prepare and warms from the inside out. You can substitute smoked turkey for the sausage.

2 tablespoons butter or margarine; or substitute vegetable oil

¼ cup fresh bread crumbs

3 tablespoons chopped shallots

1 quart vegetable or chicken broth

2 cups russet potatoes, peeled and cubed

1 cup grated horseradish; or substitute prepared horseradish, store-bought or homemade (page 112)

1 cup cubed Polish sausage

Salt and freshly ground black pepper to taste

Croutons

4 pumpernickel bread slices, crusts removed, cut into cubes

2 tablespoons olive oil

2 teaspoons ground paprika

To make the croutons, preheat the oven to 325°F. Place the bread on a sheet pan and bake in the oven until toasted, turning once, about 10 minutes. Heat a small saucepan over low heat; add the oil and paprika. Simmer for 5 minutes to blend. Combine the oil mixture with the bread in a bowl and toss to coat. Spread the croutons back on the baking sheet, return to the oven, and bake for 10 minutes or until crisp.

Heat a heavy saucepan or stockpot over medium heat, add the butter, and when melted, add the bread crumbs and shallots. Sauté for one minute to soften the shallots, but don't brown the bread crumbs. Add the broth, potatoes, and horseradish and bring to a boil. Reduce the heat, cover, and simmer until the potatoes and horseradish are very tender, about 45 minutes.

Place the soup in a blender or food processor and process until smooth. Return the soup to the stockpot and season to taste with salt and pepper.

Heat a heavy skillet over medium-high heat, add the sausage, and sauté until the sausage is browned, about 5 minutes. Bring the soup to a simmer, thinning with more broth if necessary.

To serve, ladle the soup into individual bowls and garnish with the croutons.

Yield: 4 to 6 servings

Hearts of Romaine with Dijon Lemon Dressing, Spicy Chile Croutons, and Pecorino Shavings

This salad is a low-fat alternative to Caesar salad. Mustard acts as an emulsifier in a dressing, but in this recipe it is solely a flavoring, as there isn't an oil to bind with a liquid. You can also serve this dressing with other strongly flavored greens such as arugula, oakleaf, mâche, radicchio, mustard, and even fresh spinach.

8 romaine lettuce leaves, torn in pieces

Dijon Lemon Dressing

4 slices red onion, separated into rings

Spicy Croutons

Pecorino Romano cheese for garnish

Dijon Lemon Dressing

3 tablespoons plus 1 teaspoon Dijon-style mustard, store-bought or homemade (page 117)

3 tablespoons lemon juice, preferably fresh

2 cloves garlic, minced

¼ teaspoon salt

¼ teaspoon freshly ground black pepper

Spicy Croutons

2 slices of bread, crusts removed, cut into cubes

3 to 4 tablespoons olive oil

1 teaspoon garlic salt

½ teaspoon ground cayenne

¼ teaspoon freshly ground black pepper

Combine all the dressing ingredients in a bowl and whisk to blend. Allow dressing to sit for 20 to 30 minutes at room temperature to blend the flavors.

To make the croutons, preheat the oven to 300°F. Place the bread on a sheet pan. Either air-dry or place in the oven to dry out the bread. Heat the oil in a small saucepan, add the garlic, cayenne, and black pepper, and simmer for 3 to 4 minutes to blend the flavors. Place the bread cubes in a bowl, drizzle the oil mixture over them, and toss to coat. Spread the bread on the sheet pan again and bake in the oven until toasted. Allow to cool before using.

Place the lettuce in a large salad bowl and toss with enough dressing to coat the leaves. Garnish with the sliced onion, spicy croutons, and, using a vegetable peeler, shavings of pecorino cheese.

Yield: 4 servings

Cracked Peppercorn and Feta Cheese Dressing

This creamy dressing has replaced blue cheese as our "guilty pleasure" dressing. The double hit of black pepper does have a purpose: the finely ground pepper distributes the flavor throughout the dressing, and the cracked peppercorns add a pepper explosion when bitten into. This dressing is better if allowed to sit for half an hour to blend the flavors. For a lighter version, plain low-fat yogurt can be substituted for the mayo. The taste will be different, but still good.

½ cup mayonnaise

¼ cup sour cream

3 to 4 tablespoons crumbled feta cheese

2 teaspoons lemon juice, preferably fresh

2 teaspoons finely chopped shallots

2 teaspoons cracked black pepper

¼ teaspoon finely ground black pepper

¼ teaspoon garlic powder

Salt to taste

Combine all the ingredients in a bowl and stir to combine. Allow the dressing to sit for 30 minutes at room temperature to blend the flavors. Taste and adjust the seasonings.

Yield: ¾ cup

Roasted Red Beet Endive Salad with Toasted Walnuts and Horseradish Cream

People who don't like beets probably haven't had any fresh from the garden. The taste of canned or frozen beets just doesn't compare with fresh, and roasting them brings out their natural sweetness. Beet greens are also tasty and can be sautéed until just wilted and substituted in this recipe. The assertive sharpness of the horseradish is a wonderful contrast to the sweetness of the beets.

1 pound fresh beets

Olive oil

Salt and freshly ground black pepper

½ cup chopped walnuts

3 tablespoons grated horseradish; or substitute prepared horseradish, store-bought or homemade (page 112)

⅔ cup sour cream

1 teaspoon sugar

½ teaspoon freshly grated lemon zest

Chopped endive

1 small red onion, thinly sliced and separated into rings

Preheat the oven to 425°F.

Trim the greens from the beets, leaving about 1 inch of stem. Do not peel them. Rub the beets with the olive oil, and season with salt and pepper. Put the beets in a pan and roast them in the oven for 40 minutes, or until they are tender. Allow the beets to cool until they can be handled. Peel and cut them into ¼-inch slices.

Put the walnuts on a baking sheet and toast them in the oven for 5 minutes, being careful that they don't burn.

Combine the horseradish, sour cream, sugar, and zest in a bowl. Season with salt and pepper and set aside.

To assemble, place some of the chopped endive on chilled salad plates, add the beet slices, and top with the onion rings. Drizzle the horseradish dressing over the top, garnish with the walnuts, and serve.

Yield: 4 to 6 servings

Crispy Asian Garden Salad

Green salads are not traditional fare in most countries of Asia, but we like to add many Asian ingredients to our salads, so we've come up with our own version of how a salad would be served if they did serve salads. This colorful salad is mainly comprised of crispy cabbage, but the surprise crunch comes from the fried noodles. Add some shrimp or grilled chicken and turn this side salad into an entrée.

1 cup rice stick noodles (available in Asian markets)

Vegetable oil for frying, peanut preferred

1 cup thinly sliced Chinese or napa cabbage

¾ cup shredded red cabbage

3 leaves leaf lettuce, torn in small pieces

½ cucumber, diced

3 tablespoons sliced green onions, including some of the greens

2 to 3 tablespoons chopped cilantro

Chopped peanuts for garnish

Dressing

¼ cup peanut oil

1 tablespoon cider vinegar

2 tablespoons lime juice, preferably fresh

1 tablespoon dark sesame oil

1 to 2 teaspoons *sambal oelek*, store-bought or homemade (page 141)

1 teaspoon oyster sauce (available in Asian markets)

2 cloves garlic, crushed

Combine all the dressing ingredients in a bowl and whisk to mix. Allow the dressing to sit for an hour at room temperature to blend the flavors. Taste and adjust the seasonings.

Heat a wok over high heat, add the oil to a depth of 2 inches and when hot, add the noodles. When the noodles puff up, which will be almost immediately, remove them and drain on paper towels.

Combine all the salad ingredients, including the noodles, in a large bowl and gently toss to mix.

To serve, pour the dressing over the salad, gently toss, and garnish with the peanuts.

Yield: 4 servings

Hearts of Palm Salad with Caribbean Kuchela Vinaigrette

This recipe, which combines the sweet taste of melons with the delicate hearts of palm, came to us from the folks at the Pick-A-Dilly restaurant in Nassau, the Bahamas. When they served this salad to us a few years back, the ingredients were arranged in the shape of a palm tree. It was a great presentation, but a little time-consuming, so we've served them mixed together instead. Hearts of palm are the inner portion of the stem of the palmetto (cabbage) palm and taste rather like artichoke hearts. This state tree of Florida is plentiful throughout the tropical areas of the Caribbean. Fresh hearts of palm are almost impossible to find, but they are readily available canned as an acceptable substitute. We use Mango Kuchela (page 152) in the dressing, but you may substitute your favorite fruit chutney.

One 14-ounce can hearts of palm, drained and chopped

1 cup cubed honeydew melon

1 cup cubed cantaloupe, sliced into thin wedges

Chopped lettuce

Star anise fruit, thinly sliced, and fresh mint leaves for garnish

Dressing

2 teaspoons dry mustard

2 teaspoons honey

2 tablespoons mango *kuchela*, store-bought or homemade (page 152)

6 tablespoons lime juice, preferably fresh

3 tablespoons orange juice, preferably fresh

2 tablespoons extra-virgin olive oil

Salt and freshly ground black pepper to taste

To make the dressing, combine the mustard, honey, *kuchela*, and lime and orange juices in a bowl and whisk to blend well. Slowly whisk in the olive oil. Season to taste with salt and pepper. Strain the dressing through a sieve to remove any large chunks of mango.

Combine the hearts of palm, honeydew, and cantaloupe in a bowl, add some of the dressing, and gently toss to coat.

Line individual salad plates with the lettuce. Divide the fruit between the plates, garnish with the star anise and mint, and serve.

Yield: 4 servings

Fattoush (Arab Bread Salad)

Fattoush, *the dish that ends each day of fasting during the month of Ramadan, is popular in all Middle Eastern countries. The word* fattoush *literally means either "wet bread" or "breaking up and crumbling," and both describe this rustic bread salad. This dish originated as a way of using stale bread, and it varies from country to country, depending on tastes and availability of ingredients. We asked our friend Yusuf what an authentic, traditional* fattoush *served at Ramadan is composed of, and he said there isn't one recipe: "People get creative when they don't eat all day; fasting gives you plenty of time to think about food!" In our version, we've used an herb dressing popular in all Arab countries and added hot chiles, just as the Saudis would.*

2 tomatoes, chopped

1 cup peeled and chopped cucumber

½ cup diced green bell pepper

4 green onions, thinly sliced, including some of the greens

2 jalapeño chiles, stems and seeds removed, chopped

1 cup thinly sliced and chopped romaine lettuce leaves

2 pieces pita bread

Herb Dressing

8 ounces plain yogurt

1½ tablespoons chopped fresh mint

1 tablespoon chopped fresh flat-leaf parsley

1 tablespoon chopped fresh chives

1 tablespoon lemon juice, preferably fresh

1 tablespoon prepared horseradish, store-bought or homemade (page 112)

½ teaspoon crushed garlic

¼ teaspoon ground cayenne

Combine all the dressing ingredients in a bowl and stir to mix. Allow the dressing to sit for an hour at room temperature to blend the flavors.

Separate the two layers of the bread and toast them under the broiler until they are crisp. Break the bread into small pieces and set aside.

Combine all the salad ingredients in a bowl and gently toss to mix. Pour the dressing over the salad and toss to coat.

Just before serving, add the bread and toss to mix.

Yield: 4 to 6 servings

Salad Greens with Honey Chipotle Lime Mustard Dressing

Strongly flavored lettuce greens such as arugula, mustard greens, radicchio, curly endive, and spinach are needed in this salad to balance the assertive sweet heat and mustardy bite of the dressing. The avocado provides a creamy contrast to the bold flavors. A number of sharp cheeses can complement this salad, such as Mexican cotija or añejo, Parmesan, pecorino Romano, or goat cheese.

4 to 6 cups chopped mixed salad greens, such as radicchio, curly endive, romaine, and spinach

1 avocado, peeled and sliced

½ red onion, thinly sliced and separated into rings

Cotija or goat cheese, crumbled, for garnish

Dressing

¼ cup honey

3 tablespoons chipotle lime mustard (page 160)

3 tablespoons extra-virgin olive oil

2 tablespoons cider vinegar

1 tablespoon chopped fresh cilantro

1 tablespoon minced shallot

1 chipotle chile *en adobo*, chopped

¼ teaspoon chopped garlic

Salt and freshly ground black pepper

Combine all the ingredients for the dressing in a bowl and whisk to combine. Allow the dressing to sit for an hour at room temperature to blend the flavors.

Place all the salad ingredients, except the cheese, in a salad bowl and toss to mix. Pour the dressing over the salad and gently toss to coat.

Garnish the salad with the cheese and serve.

Yield: 4 servings

Gurkensalat mit Senfsauce (Cucumber Salad with Mustard Dressing)

Cool cucumber salads are often paired with all the wonderful German "wursts" or sausages. This version, with the bite of mustard, also makes a good accompaniment to almost any fish, and is particularly good with poached salmon, trout, pike, or cod. You don't need to salt this salad, as the cucumbers will absorb some of the "brining" salt even though they are thoroughly rinsed. Adjust the mustard to suit your taste, and vary the salad by adding sliced tomatoes just before serving.

2 cucumbers, peeled and thinly sliced

¼ cup thinly sliced red onion

Chopped fresh parsley for garnish

Dressing

¼ cup sour cream or low-fat plain yogurt

2 tablespoons cream or half-and-half

1 tablespoon cider vinegar

1 tablespoon German-style mustard, store-bought or homemade (page 119)

1 teaspoon minced fresh dill; or substitute dry dill weed

¼ teaspoon ground white pepper

Note: This recipe requires advance preparation.

Place the cucumbers and onion in a colander, liberally salt, and let sit for 20 minutes. Rinse the mixture, drain, and pat dry with paper towels.

Combine the dressing ingredients in a bowl and whisk until combined and creamy. Taste the dressing for mustard and add more if needed; there should be a distinct mustard flavor, but not enough to overpower the flavor of the cucumbers.

Add the cucumbers and onions to the bowl and toss well to mix.

Cover with plastic wrap and refrigerate at least 4 hours before serving, or better yet, chill overnight.

Yield: 4 to 6 servings

Nopalitos y Espinacas Ensalada (Spinach Salad with Prickly Pear Cactus)

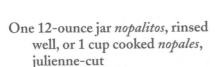

The Spanish word for cactus is nopal, *and* nopales *is the term for the leaves or pads of the opuntia or prickly pear cactus. It's a common sight in Mexico to see a nopales salesman on the street or in a market, scraping the spines off the cactus pads, peeling them, and then cutting them into thin strips. The fresh cactus needs to be processed before eating to reduce the* babas, *or slimy liquid that is released during cooking. This can be done either by boiling and then rinsing the pads, or by grilling the pad for about 4 minutes or until limp. Once the pads are prepared for eating, they are referred to as* nopalitos. Nopalitos *have a tart taste with a texture rather like string beans and are used to flavor stews, soups, salads, and egg dishes. They may be difficult to find fresh outside of the Southwest or Latin markets, but jars of* nopalitos *are more available and can be substituted in recipes.*

One 12-ounce jar *nopalitos*, rinsed well, or 1 cup cooked *nopales*, julienne-cut

3 cups fresh spinach, torn into bite-size pieces

1 small red onion, sliced in thin rings and separated

10 radishes, thinly sliced

6 cherry tomatoes, cut in half

2 tablespoons chopped fresh cilantro; or substitute flat-leaf parsley

½ cup grated *asadero* or mozzarella cheese

Diced avocado for garnish

Dressing

3 tablespoons extra-virgin olive oil

2 tablespoons cider vinegar

2 teaspoons crushed red chile, such as de arbol or piquin

1 teaspoon dried oregano, preferably Mexican

1 teaspoon dried marjoram

¼ teaspoon dried sage

1 clove garlic, minced

Combine all the ingredients for the dressing in a bowl and whisk to mix. Allow the dressing to sit at room temperature for an hour to blend the flavors.

Combine the *nopalitos*, spinach, onion, radishes, tomatoes, and cilantro in a chilled salad bowl and gently toss to mix. Drizzle the dressing over the top and again toss to mix.

Sprinkle the cheese over the top of the salad, garnish with the avocado, and serve.

Yield: 4 to 6 servings

Ensalada con Quinoa de Bolivia (Bolivian Quinoa Salad)

Quinoa, prounced KEEN-wah, is a grain that's native to the Andes, where it was grown on the terraces of Machu Picchu. It was a staple of the Incas, who called it "the mother grain" and considered it sacred. Today, it's still an important food in Peru, Bolivia, and Ecuador. Called a miracle grain because it contains all eight essential amino acids and is therefore a complete protein, its popularity is increasing due to its versatility and flavor as well as its nutritional value. When cooked it becomes almost transparent, and has a delicate yet sweet nutty flavor similar to that of wild rice. Since quinoa is a member of the spinach family, we like to serve it on a bed of spinach, and we've added a touch of citrus to counterbalance the sweetness of the grain.

1 cup quinoa

⅓ cup chopped red bell pepper

¼ cup chopped green onions

2 ají chiles, stems and seeds removed, finely chopped; or substitute yellow wax or jalapeño chiles

1 small orange, divided into segments and chopped

⅓ cup chopped walnuts

¼ teaspoon salt

¼ teaspoon freshly ground black pepper

Chopped fresh spinach, chopped fresh Italian parsley, and orange zest for garnish

Dressing

⅓ cup olive oil

2 tablespoons lime juice, preferably fresh

1 tablespoon white wine vinegar

Place the quinoa in a strainer and rinse until the water runs clear.

Heat a saucepan over high heat; add the quinoa and twice the volume of water. The water should be 1 inch above the surface of the grain. Bring to a boil, reduce the heat, and simmer 15 to 20 minutes, or until the quinoa is tender. The quinoa should absorb all the water, but if some remains, drain. Transfer the quinoa to a large bowl and chill.

Combine all the ingredients for the dressing in a bowl and whisk to blend.

Add the bell pepper, green onion, chiles, orange, and walnuts to the quinoa and season with the salt and pepper. Pour the dressing over the salad and gently toss to mix.

To serve, line a chilled platter with the spinach, mound the quinoa on top, and garnish with the chopped parsley and orange zest.

Yield: 4 servings

Komkomer Slaai
(South African Cucumber Salad)

This is a healthy, quick, and simple-to-prepare South African salad. These salads are eaten after the meal to cleanse the palate and refresh taste buds after a meal of spicy, slightly sweet South African curries. Even though they also contain chiles, they refresh because the salad dressings never use oil, just vinegar. If you grate the cucumber, it becomes a sambal *condiment considered cooling because the cucumber is a cool vegetable.*

3 medium cucumbers, peeled and thinly sliced

Salt

2 jalapeño chiles, stems and seeds removed,
    minced; or substitute serrano chiles

1 tablespoon cider vinegar

1 clove garlic, finely minced

Place the cucumbers in a colander, liberally salt, and let sit for 20 minutes. Rinse the cucumbers, drain, and gently press out all the liquid.

Combine all the ingredients in a bowl and gently toss to mix. Cover and refrigerate for an hour before serving.

This salad should be served chilled.

Yield: 4 to 6 servings

Crab and Alligator Pear Salad with Remoulade Dressing

 Alligator pear *was the term used for avocados years ago, because of the texture of the skin of the Haas variety, and the name pops up every now and then. We'd also guess that if you live near the swamps and bayous of the South, alligators are on your mind a lot of the time. The avocado tree is native to the subtropics and tropics of the Americas and made its way into Florida about the 1820s to 1830s. Remoulade is routinely served with shrimp, but it's also a tasty accompaniment to crab. The components for the salad can be prepared ahead of time, but leave the assembly until the last moment, as the avocado will begin to blacken after it's cut.*

1 pound cooked lump crabmeat

¼ cup finely chopped green onion, including some of the greens

¼ cup finely diced red or green bell pepper

2 tablespoons minced celery

1 tablespoon lemon juice, preferably fresh

1 tablespoon capers, drained and rinsed

1 teaspoon chopped fresh marjoram

Salt to taste

2 avocados

Chopped fresh parsley for garnish

Dressing

½ cup remoulade sauce, store-bought or homemade (page 170)

1 teaspoon Cajun spice seasoning, store-bought or homemade (page 167)

2 tablespoons mayonnaise

1 tablespoon sour cream

Combine the crab, onion, bell pepper, celery, lemon juice, capers, and marjoram in a bowl and gently toss to mix. Season to taste with salt. Cover and refrigerate until time to serve.

Combine all the ingredients for the dressing in a bowl and stir to mix well. Cover and refrigerate until time to serve.

To serve the salads, cut the avocados in half lengthwise, remove the pits, and carefully peel. Slice the avocados and arrange the slices on chilled salad plates. Mound the crab mixture on the avocado slices, top with a dollop of dressing, and garnish the plate with the parsley. Serve additional dressing on the side.

Yield: 4 to 6 servings

Black Bean Mango Salad with Adobo Dressing

This bean salad is a great accompaniment to barbecues as well as to any Caribbean or Latin meal. Turtle beans, as black beans are sometimes referred to, blend well with the sweet taste of the mangoes. We've added a habanero because we like the extra heat, but it can be omitted to reduce the heat level, and other fruits can be substituted for the mangoes. Canned black beans and ready-prepared adobo seasoning make this salad a snap to throw together.

One 15-ounce can black beans, drained and rinsed

2 cups diced mango; or substitute pineapple or peaches

2 tablespoons diced pimentos

2 tablespoons chopped fresh cilantro

1 small habanero chile, stem and seeds removed, minced

Dressing

¼ cup extra-virgin olive oil

¼ cup lime or orange juice, preferably fresh

1 tablespoon adobo seasoning, store-bought or homemade (page 153)

Combine all the dressing ingredients in a bowl and whisk to combine.

Combine all the salad ingredients in another bowl, pour the dressing over the top, and gently toss to mix.

Yield: 4 servings

Horseradish Potato Salad

Here is a hearty potato salad that just begs to accompany a grilled steak. Years ago we figured out what made the kartoffelsalat *in Germany so tangy and tasty; the secret is to douse the hot potatoes with vinegar before they cool. We like the taste of apple cider vinegar, but white vinegar works well also. Vary the amount of horseradish to suit your tastes.*

3 to 4 medium russet potatoes, peeled and cut in ¾-inch cubes

2 to 3 tablespoons cider vinegar

½ cup mayonnaise

¼ cup sour cream

2 to 3 tablespoons prepared horseradish sauce, store-bought or homemade (page 112)

¼ cup minced fresh dill, or 2 to 3 teaspoons dry dill weed

¼ cup finely chopped celery

2 tablespoons finely chopped green or red onion

2 tablespoons finely chopped fresh flat-leaf parsley

1 tablespoon finely chopped chives (optional)

Salt and ground white pepper to taste

In a saucepan or pressure cooker, cook the potatoes until done. Remove from the heat, drain, and place in a bowl. Sprinkle the vinegar over the potatoes and gently toss to mix. Allow the potatoes to cool at room temperature.

Combine the mayonnaise, sour cream, horseradish, and dill. Taste and adjust the seasonings. Cover and chill in the refrigerator.

To serve, add the celery, onion, parsley, and chives to the potatoes and gently toss to mix. Pour the dressing over the top and again gently toss to mix. Season with salt and pepper and serve.

Yield: 4 servings

9 Meat Dishes

Asian Black Pepper-Braised Short Ribs

These slightly sweet, peppery ribs combine many of the intense flavors of Chinese cuisine. Although the list of ingredients is long, don't let it scare you off—this is not a difficult recipe to prepare. The long, slow cooking produces very tender ribs with a very complex sauce. Because they are so strongly flavored, serve these ribs with plain rice and vegetables.

2 pounds beef short ribs, cut in 2- to 3-inch lengths, fat trimmed

2 tablespoons vegetable oil, preferably peanut

1 tablespoon thinly sliced garlic

1 tablespoon thinly sliced ginger

2 tablespoons coarsely ground Sichuan pepper (*fagara*, available by mail order; or substitute equal portions of anise and allspice)

2 tablespoons coarsely ground black pepper

3 star anise

1½ cups unsalted beef broth

1 cup dry red wine

3 tablespoons Chinese black vinegar; or substitute rice vinegar

2 tablespoons dry mustard

2 tablespoons oyster sauce (available at Asian markets)

1 tablespoon brown sugar

1 teaspoon black bean sauce (available at Asian markets)

½ teaspoon Chinese five-spice powder, store-bought or homemade (page 144)

¼ cup chopped green onions

Toasted sesame seeds for garnish

Heat a heavy saucepan over high heat, add the oil and when hot, add the ribs and cook until they are browned on all sides. Remove the ribs and keep warm. Pour off the accumulated fat.

Add the garlic, ginger, peppercorns, and anise to the pan and sauté for a couple of minutes. Add the wine, vinegar, mustard, oyster sauce, sugar, black bean sauce, and five-spice powder, and bring to a boil.

Reduce the heat, return the beef to the pan, cover, and simmer for an hour, or until the meat is very tender and the sauce has thickened. Skim any fat that accumulates off the sauce. Stir in half of the onions and cook for a couple of minutes longer.

To serve, place the ribs on a serving platter, pour sauce over the top, and garnish with the remaining onions and the sesame seeds.

Yield: 4 servings

Medallions of Pork with Flamed Cognac and Green Peppercorn Sauce

This dish is prepared from a pork tenderloin, which is a very tender, generally pricey cut of meat. If you cut your own medallions from a tenderloin, you can pocket significant savings. Because this cut is very lean, it needs to be quickly pan-fried so it doesn't dry out. For a gourmet presentation, serve with a triangle of puff pastry on top of the medallions and sauce. To make the triangles, use frozen puff pastry, cut into triangles, and then bake according to the directions on the package. These triangles can be made ahead and frozen. This sauce also complements beef, lamb, and even chicken, so you can substitute chicken breasts for the pork.

1 tablespoon butter, preferably unsalted

1 tablespoon extra-virgin olive oil

1 small pork tenderloin, 1½ to 2 pounds, trimmed and cut into ½-inch slices

¼ cup finely chopped shallots

⅓ cup cognac

1 cup heavy cream

1 tablespoon water-packed green peppercorns, drained

8 triangles puff pastry (optional) for garnish

Heat a large, heavy skillet over medium-high heat, add the butter and the olive oil, and when hot, add the medallions. Brown the pork, about 2 minutes on each side, and when the meat is done, remove the medallions to a heated platter and keep warm.

Add the shallots to the skillet and sauté until they are transparent. Add the cognac, stand back, and light it with a match. Continue to heat until the flame dies down and then stir to release any bits and pieces from the pan. Reduce the heat to medium and slowly whisk in the cream. Simmer the sauce for 5 minutes to thicken. With the side of a cleaver, crush the peppercorns and stir into the sauce.

To serve, place 3 of the medallions on each plate. Spoon the sauce over the meat, top with the pastry triangles, and serve.

Yield: 6 to 8 servings

Kurdish Shish Kebabs

 Shish kebabs can be made from both ground and cubed meats, and are very popular throughout the Middle and Near East as well as Central Asia. This recipe is based on kebabs from southern Turkey, where chiles are more widely used, but since authentic Turkish chiles are hard to find, we use either cayenne or piquin as a substitute. Serve with a rice pilaf or in a pita bread pocket for a Middle Eastern–style sandwich. Using flat skewers rather than round to mold the meat onto will make cooking a whole lot easier. We separate the vegetables and meat on different skewers because they cook for different lengths of time.

1½ pounds finely ground lamb

¼ cup minced onion

2 cloves garlic, minced

1 egg, beaten

2 tablespoons finely chopped walnuts

1 tablespoon finely chopped fresh mint

2 teaspoons all-purpose flour

2 teaspoons *baharat* seasoning, store-bought or homemade (page 126)

1 teaspoon ground cayenne or piquin chile

½ teaspoon ground cinnamon

¼ teaspoon ground allspice

1 teaspoon salt

½ teaspoon freshly ground black pepper

1 small onion, cut in wedges and separated

1 bell pepper, stem and seeds removed, cut in wedges

4 Italian frying chiles, cut in half, stems and seeds removed

Extra-virgin olive oil

2 to 3 pieces of pita bread, cut in half (optional)

Note: This recipe requires advance preparation.

Combine the lamb, onion, garlic, egg, walnuts, mint, flour, and seasonings in a bowl, and knead with your hands until smooth like dough. Break off pieces of the meat, form on the skewers into ovals, cover, and refrigerate for a couple of hours, or overnight.

Alternately thread the onion wedges, bell pepper, and chiles on separate skewers, beginning and ending with a pepper. Brush the vegetables with the oil.

Preheat a grill to medium-high and grill the skewers until the meat is browned, about 4 minutes on each side, and until the vegetables are tender but still crisp.

To serve, arrange the kebabs on a serving platter along with the warmed pita bread, if using.

Yield: 4 servings

Rendang Daging (Curried Coconut Beef)

This dish from Malaysia and Indonesia features beef simmered in coconut and fresh curry spices and can be served in two different ways, depending on how long it's cooked. When cooked for a shorter period of time and the sauce is soupy, it's referred to as kalio. *When cooked for a longer period, so that the coconut milk and spices form a very thick, dry sauce, it's called* rendang. *Serve with rice pilaf, Mint* Raita *(page 373) to help cool you down, and* Sambal Oelek *(page 141) on the side.*

½ cup grated fresh coconut, or substitute sweetened flaked or shredded coconut

1 tablespoon tamarind paste

1 teaspoon salt

1½ pounds boneless beef, such as chuck or bottom round, cut into 1½-inch cubes

2 stalks lemongrass

2 tablespoons chopped ginger

4 shallots, chopped

3 to 4 fresh chiles, such as serranos or jalapeños, stems and seeds removed

2 cloves garlic

2 teaspoon ground coriander

1 teaspoon freshly ground black pepper

½ teaspoon ground turmeric

2 tablespoons vegetable oil, preferably peanut

2 cups unsweetened coconut milk

2 kaffir lime leaves (optional)

Heat a heavy skillet over high heat and dry-roast the coconut until it turns golden brown, tossing often to avoid burning. Remove the coconut and cool.

Combine the coconut, tamarind, and salt in a nonreactive bowl and mix well. Add the beef and toss well to coat. Cover and marinate in the refrigerator for at least four hours.

Trim the stalks of the lemongrass to about 3 inches in length. Trim away any hard portions, discard the outer leaves, and chop. Combine the lemongrass, ginger, shallots, chiles, garlic, coriander, black pepper, and turmeric in a blender or food processor and puree until smooth, adding a little coconut milk if necessary to form a smooth paste.

Heat a large saucepan over medium heat, add the oil, and when hot, add the spice paste. Cook the paste for 2 minutes, stirring constantly. Add the marinated beef and any juices that have accumulated, and continue to cook for 5 minutes. Stir in the coconut milk and lime leaves, reduce the heat, and simmer, uncovered, until the beef is fork tender and starts to fall apart and the sauce is very thick and dry, about 45 minutes to an hour.

Serve the curry on a large platter, with rice pilaf, mint *raita*, and *sambal oelek*.

Yield: 4 to 6 servings

Note: This recipe requires advance preparation.

Filet Mignon with Balsamic-Dijon Sauce

Incredibly easy and very elegant, this is the perfect dish to serve for company or for a special family celebration. Balsamic vinegar is strongly flavored and can vary greatly in quality, so we recommend that you splurge on a good-quality balsamic vinegar for the richest flavored sauce. This recipe also makes an incredibly rich and tasty gravy for roast beef. To finish this meal, just prepare a crisp garden salad and pop some potatoes in the oven.

1 tablespoon butter,
  preferably unsalted
4 filet mignon steaks
2 shallots, minced
1 cup beef broth
¼ cup balsamic vinegar

¼ cup Dijon-style mustard, store-bought
  or homemade (page 117)
¼ teaspoon minced fresh thyme
¼ teaspoon freshly ground
  black pepper
Chopped fresh thyme for garnish

Preheat the oven to 450°F.

Heat an ovenproof skillet over medium-high heat and add the butter. Season the filets with salt and pepper, and brown the steaks in the skillet on both sides. Place the skillet in the oven and bake for 5 minutes for rare, 7 minutes for medium-rare, or longer if desired. Remove the steaks to a warmed platter and cover loosely with aluminum foil to keep warm.

Return the skillet to the top of the stove, add the shallots, and sauté until they are soft. Add the broth, vinegar, mustard, and thyme, and raise the heat to medium-high. Bring the mixture to a boil, stirring constantly and scraping the pan, until the browned bits and pieces from the pan are dissolved and the mixture reduces slightly.

To serve, drizzle a small amount of the sauce on individual plates, top with a steak, and garnish with some chopped thyme. Serve the steaks with additional sauce on the side.

Yield: 4 servings

Sautéed Lamb Chops
with Black Olive Rosemary Sauce

Rosemary and mustard, both complementary flavors to the distinct taste of lamb, are blended in this sauce with a gentle heat. The loin and rib chops are the most tender cuts, but they are also the most expensive. Chops cut from the leg are less fatty and not as tender, but they have a great flavor. For those who don't care for lamb, a boneless sirloin beef steak is a good substitute. Serve this meal with a dry red wine, baked potato, and a garden salad such as Hearts of Romaine with Dijon Lemon Dressing (page 213) or Crispy Asian Garden Salad (page 216).

2 tablespoons olive oil, divided

4 lamb chops, about ¾ inch thick

Salt and freshly ground black pepper

Sauce

1 shallot, finely chopped

1 clove garlic, minced

8 black olives, finely chopped

1 tablespoon chopped fresh rosemary

½ teaspoon crushed piquin chile

¼ teaspoon cracked black pepper

⅓ cup dry red wine

⅓ cup beef broth

2 tablespoons heavy cream

1 tablespoon horseradish mustard, store-bought or homemade (page 165)

Chopped fresh parsley for garnish

Heat a heavy skillet over medium-high heat and add half of the oil. Season the chops with salt and pepper and sauté them for 4½ to 5 minutes on each side for medium-rare. Remove the lamb chops from the skillet and keep warm.

To make the sauce, add the remaining oil to the skillet Add the shallot and garlic, and sauté until softened. Add the olives, rosemary, chile, and black pepper, and sauté for an additional minute. Stir in the wine and broth, raise the heat to high and bring to a boil. Reduce the heat to medium-high and simmer until the sauce is reduced by half. Slowly add the cream, whisking constantly until the sauce is creamy and heated through. Remove the sauce from the heat and whisk in the mustard. Taste and adjust the seasonings.

To serve, place a little of the sauce on individual plates, top with a lamb chop, and garnish the plate with the chopped parsley

Yield: 4 servings

Chipotle-Barbecued Ribs
with Chile-Grilled Potato Wedges

 There's something magic about chipotle chiles and grilling—maybe it's the fact that these chiles were created with smoke. Serve with a spicy black bean and corn salad and buttermilk biscuits.

Chipotle Barbecue Sauce

4 dried chipotle chiles,
    stems removed

3 dried red New Mexican chiles,
    seeds and stems removed

2 teaspoons vegetable oil

1 medium onion, chopped

4 cloves garlic, chopped

One 12-ounce can beer

3 cups ketchup

½ cup strongly brewed coffee

1½ tablespoons cider vinegar

¼ cup molasses

3 tablespoons Dijon-style
    mustard, store-bought or
    homemade (page 117)

2 teaspoons Worcestershire sauce

½ teaspoon freshly ground
    black pepper

Ribs and Chile-Grilled
Potato Wedges

2 cloves garlic, minced

1 teaspoon ground red
    New Mexican chile

2 tablespoons olive oil

4 pounds pork ribs

Salt and freshly ground
    black pepper

2 medium potatoes, cut in wedges

2 green onions, finely chopped

To make the sauce, cover the dried chiles with hot water and let sit for 30 minutes to soften. Drain the chiles and discard the water. Heat the oil in a saucepan, add the onions and sauté until softened. Add the garlic and sauté for an additional 2 to 3 minutes. Add the remaining sauce ingredients, including the chiles, and bring the mixture to a boil. Reduce the heat and simmer for 20 to 30 minutes. Remove from the heat, place in a blender or food processor, and puree until smooth. Strain if desired.

Combine the garlic, chile, and olive oil for the potatoes and set aside.

Liberally salt and pepper the ribs. Grill over a medium-hot grill for 10 minutes. Move the ribs away from the direct flame and continue to grill for an hour. Brush with the sauce during the last 10 minutes of grilling.

While the ribs are cooking, toss the potatoes in the seasoned oil until well coated. Place in a grill basket and grill for 15 minutes over direct flame until browned, shaking the basket often.

Cut the ribs apart, serve with additional sauce, toss the potatoes with the green onions, and serve.

Yield: 4 servings

Yum Neua (Thai Grilled Beef Salad)

The word yum *refers to a hearty entrée salad of meat or seafood with a chile- and lime-based dressing.* Yum neua—*literally, "tossed beef"—is the name for Thai beef salad. This is a great, simple, easy, and impressive dish for summer patio parties. Have the salad prepared, chilled and plated, and top with the beef hot off the barbecue grill.*

12 ounces top sirloin, tenderloin, or flank steak, trimmed

½ head romaine lettuce, chopped

1 small onion, thinly sliced

1 small cucumber, thinly sliced

8 cherry tomatoes, cut in half

12 fresh mint leaves (optional)

Chopped green onion, including some of the green, chopped fresh cilantro, and chopped roasted peanuts for garnish

Marinade

1 stalk lemongrass

3 tablespoons soy sauce, preferably dark

1 tablespoon Thai fish sauce (available in Asian markets)

3 cloves garlic, minced

2 teaspoons sugar

1 teaspoon sesame seed oil

Dressing

3 tablespoons Thai fish sauce (available in Asian markets)

3 tablespoons lime juice, preferably fresh

3 tablespoons chopped fresh cilantro

2 tablespoons chopped green onions, including some of the green

1 tablespoon grated ginger

1 tablespoon chopped shallots

4 to 5 Thai chiles, stems removed, chopped

To make the marinade, trim the stalk of lemongrass to about 3 inches in length. Trim away any hard portions, discard the outer leaves, and chop. Combine all the marinade ingredients in a bowl and stir to mix. Lightly score the beef (omit this step if using flank steak). Place the beef and marinade in a nonreactive bowl or heavy, resealable plastic bag, toss to coat, and marinate in the refrigerator 2 to 4 hours, or overnight, turning occasionally.

Note: This recipe requires advance preparation.

Combine all the dressing ingredients in a bowl and whisk to mix. Allow the dressing to sit at room temperature for an hour to blend the flavors.

Preheat the grill to high, drain the steak, and discard the marinade. Grill the meat to the desired doneness—4 to 6 minutes each side for medium-rare—remove, and thinly slice. Be sure to cut across the grain for flank steak, or it will be tough.

To serve, divide the lettuce between 4 chilled plates. Top with the onion rings, cucumber, tomatoes, and mint. Top each salad with some of the dressing. Lay the beef on top, add more dressing, and garnish with the green onions, cilantro, and peanuts.

Yield: 4 servings

Goan Pork Vindaloo

Vindaloo is a classic pork curry dish from the state of Goa, an area of India that was populated by Portuguese sailors who carried this dish on their long sea voyages. A layer of fat was placed on top to seal out the air and help in the preservation of the meat on these journeys. The word vindaloo *is a combination of* vin, *which means vinegar, and the Portuguese word for garlic,* albo, *and this dish combines both of these in large amounts. According to Hindu philosophy, the spice combinations in the vindaloo are believed to purify, heal, and cool. Traditionally vindaloos are very pungent and hot, the hottest of all the Indian curries.*

4 dried red New Mexican chiles, stems and seeds removed

4 dried piquin chiles, stems and seeds removed; or substitute cayenne chiles

One 2-inch piece cinnamon stick, crushed

2 tablespoons coriander seeds

2 teaspoons cumin seeds

1 teaspoon fenugreek seeds

1 teaspoon black mustard seeds

1 teaspoon fennel seeds

10 black peppercorns

6 whole cloves

6 cloves garlic

2 tablespoons grated ginger

2 tablespoons vegetable oil

2 pounds boneless pork, trimmed and cut in 1-inch cubes

½ cup coconut vinegar (available in Indian markets); or substitute distilled white vinegar

1 cup chopped onion

2 cups cooked rice

Grated coconut for garnish

Put the chiles in a bowl, cover them with very hot water, and allow them to steep 15 minutes to soften. Drain the chiles, and discard the water.

Heat a heavy skillet over high heat, add the cinnamon, coriander, cumin, fenugreek, mustard, fennel, peppercorns, and cloves, and dry-roast until the spices darken and become fragrant, being careful that they don't burn. Allow the spices to cool completely and then place them in a spice mill or coffee grinder, and process to a fine powder.

Place the chiles, spices, garlic, and ginger in a blender or food processor and puree to a smooth paste, thinning with some of the vinegar if necessary.

Combine the pork, a little of the spice paste, and the vinegar in a bowl and toss to coat. Allow the meat to marinate at room temperature for 30 minutes.

Heat a heavy saucepan over medium-high heat, add the oil and when hot, add the onions and sauté until they are browned. Add the spice paste and sauté for a couple of minutes, adding a little water if the paste becomes too thick.

Add the meat to the saucepan and brown, being careful that the spices don't burn. Add 2 to 3 cups of water, bring to just below boiling, reduce the heat, cover, and simmer until the meat is fork tender, about 1 hour. Remove the lid and turn up the heat to cook off any excess liquid.

To serve, mound cooked rice on a serving platter, top with the vindaloo, and garnish with the coconut.

Yield: 4 to 6 servings

Jungli Mans (Lamb with Chiles)

In the Mewari language of Rajasthan in India, jungli mans *refers to a dish that would be prepared by a stranded hunter who only had the basics with him. It's amazingly tasty, considering the limited ingredients. It is also quite hot, so serve it with some plain basmati rice to help quench some of the fire. Dave collected this recipe on his trip to India.*

2 cups ghee (recipe below),
    or substitute vegetable oil

2 pounds lamb, cut into 1-inch cubes

10 lal mirch chiles; or substitute
    dried cayenne or mirasol chiles,
    stems removed, left whole

2 teaspoons salt

2 cups cooked basmati rice

Ghee

2½ cups (5 sticks) unsalted butter

Heat a heavy saucepan over medium heat, add the ghee, and when hot, add the lamb. Sauté the lamb for 10 minutes, stirring constantly. Add the chiles and salt and continue cooking, adding water as necessary to make sure that the meat neither fries nor boils, but is essentially braised. Continue cooking until the meat is tender, about an hour more, stirring occasionally.

Remove the chiles, and serve with plain basmati rice.

Yield: 4 to 6 servings

Ghee

Ghee is clarified butter and can be made by heating butter until it starts to foam, then simmering until all the solids collect at the bottom of the pan. Pour off the clear liquid on the top and reserve, being careful that none of the solids get into the liquid. Discard the solids. Ghee will keep for months in the refrigerator, and is good for cooking, since it doesn't burn as butter will.

Yield: 2 cups

Jamaican Jerk Pork

The jerk in jerk pork is a spice mixture that was used to preserve meat before refrigeration. These days, the spices are used to season meats for barbecue and to tenderize rather than to preserve. An inexpensive smoker or a covered grill can be substituted for the traditional jerk pit, and is a lot easier than digging a hole in your backyard. Serve with cornbread, Peas 'n' Rice (page 336), a tropical fruit salad, and a cold Red Stripe beer.

One 3- to 4-pound pork butt or loin roast

Jerk Paste

3 to 4 Scotch bonnet chiles, stems and seeds removed, chopped, or substitute habanero chiles

¼ cup chopped green onions, including some of the greens

¼ cup crushed allspice berries; or substitute 2 teaspoons ground allspice

3 tablespoons fresh thyme

3 cloves garlic

2 tablespoons grated ginger

2 tablespoons lime juice, preferably fresh

2 tablespoons red wine vinegar

2 bay leaves

3 teaspoons freshly ground black pepper

2 teaspoons ground cardamom

1 teaspoon ground cinnamon

1 teaspoon ground nutmeg

1 teaspoon salt

3 to 4 tablespoons vegetable oil

To make the jerk paste, either pound the ingredients together using a mortar and pestle or place in a blender or food processor and process. With the motor running, slowly add enough of the oil to make a paste.

Place the roast, fat side down, in a nonreactive pan. Make slashes in the pork about 1½ to 2 inches apart and almost through the roast. Rub the jerk paste over the meat, making sure to get it thoroughly into the slashes. Cover with plastic wrap and marinate in the refrigerator overnight.

Remove the roast and bring to room temperature.

Prepare either the grill or smoker. If using a grill, be sure to use a pan under the pork to catch the drippings so that they don't flare up and burn the meat. Smoke the pork for about 2 to 3 hours, turning the roast every 30 minutes to ensure even browning. Cook until a meat thermometer inserted into the thickest part registers 150°F. Allow the meat to sit for 10 minutes to reabsorb all the juices and for the temperature to rise to 160°F. Then carve the meat and mound on a platter to serve.

Yield: 4 servings

Note: This recipe requires advance preparation.

Variations: Substitute lamb chops, chicken, or turkey for the pork.

Cincinnati Five-Way Chili

The basic recipe for Cincinnati chili is much like others in that it contains beef, onions, and chili powder, but that's where the similarity ends. Cinnamon and a variety of spices such as cloves, ginger, and allspice also contribute to this unique chili. You order the chili by which "way" you like it—two-way is chili over spaghetti, three-way has cheese added, four-way adds onions, and five-way is the works: chili with cheese, onions, and beans, over spaghetti. No matter what "way" you order the chile, it's always served over spaghetti and with oyster crackers.

2 pounds coarse ground beef chuck

1 cup chopped onions

2 cloves garlic, minced

One 6-ounce can tomato paste

1 tablespoon Worcestershire sauce

1 tablespoon red wine vinegar

1 tablespoon commercial chili powder mix

1 teaspoon ground paprika

1 teaspoon ground cinnamon

1 teaspoon ground black pepper

½ teaspoon ground cayenne

1 teaspoon ground cumin

½ teaspoon ground allspice

¼ teaspoon ground cloves

1 bay leaf

2 to 3 cups beef broth

Salt to taste

3 cups cooked spaghetti

Grated cheddar cheese, chopped onions, cooked kidney beans, and oyster crackers as accompaniments

Heat a large saucepan or stockpot over medium heat, add the beef, onions, and garlic, and sauté the mixture until the meat is no longer pink. Break up any large clumps of meat with a spoon.

Add the remaining ingredients, except the spaghetti, raise the heat, and bring to a boil. Reduce the heat and simmer the chili for an hour.

Taste and adjust the seasonings and continue to simmer for 30 minutes, adding more broth if necessary. The chili should be thick, but still thin enough to be ladled over the spaghetti. Discard the bay leaf before serving.

To serve, put the accompaniments into serving bowls, place the spaghetti into individual bowls, and ladle the chili over the top. Have your guests garnish the two-way chili with whatever accompaniments they choose. Serve the oyster crackers on the side.

Yield: 4 to 6 servings

Texas "Chili Queen" Chili

There must be as many recipes for chili as there are cooks in Texas, New Mexico, and Arizona—and every one will declare that theirs is the best. Most chili aficionados will agree, however, that the "chili queens" of San Antonio, Texas, were responsible for making the dish popular. In the 1880s these women cooked up chili in big clay pots during the day and sold their wares from rickety chili stands on street corners all night long. This recipe is our version of the classic San Antonio chili. Health-conscious cooks should prepare it the day before, chill it, and skim off any fat that rises.

6 dried red New Mexican chiles, stems and seeds removed

3 ancho chiles, stems and seeds removed

2 pounds coarse ground beef or sirloin, cut into 1-inch cubes

1 pound coarse ground pork or pork shoulder, cut into 1-inch cubes

1 large onion, chopped

3 cloves garlic, minced

6 chiltepin or piquin chiles

1 tablespoon dried oregano, preferably Mexican

2 teaspoons cumin seeds

1 teaspoon sugar

1 quart beef broth

1 cup tomato sauce

Salt and freshly ground black pepper

2 cups cooked pinto beans (optional)

Place the New Mexican and ancho chiles in a bowl and cover them with very hot water. Allow them to steep for 15 minutes to soften. Drain the chiles and discard the water. Place the chiles in a blender or food processor along with some water, and puree them until smooth. Strain the mixture to remove any remaining pieces of chile skins.

Heat a heavy skillet over medium-high heat, add the meat, and sauté until browned. Drain off any excess fat. If using the cubed meat, add a little vegetable oil to the skillet and then brown the meat. Add the onions and garlic to the skillet and continue cooking until the onions are soft, about 10 minutes. Transfer the mixture to a large saucepan or stockpot.

Heat the pan over medium heat, crumble the chiles over the mixture, and add the oregano, cumin, sugar, broth, and tomato sauce. Simmer the chili for 45 minutes.

Stir in the chile puree, season with salt and pepper, and continue to simmer for an additional 30 minutes. Taste and adjust the seasonings.

To serve, ladle the chili into bowls and serve the beans on the side.

Yield: 6 to 8 servings

Beef Barbacoa-Style

The word barbecue *comes from the Spanish* barbacoa, *but the two words no longer mean the same thing; traditional Mexican* barbacoa *is cooked in a rock-lined pit, not on a grill. Typically, a large stockpot filled with water, carrots, onion, potatoes, garbanzo beans, chipotle chiles, and other seasonings is placed on the rocks, and a grate is put over the top. The meat, wrapped in maguey leaves, is placed on the grate, so as the meat cooks, the juices drip into the pot and flavor the broth. It's difficult to duplicate the flavor of wrapping meat or poultry in leaves and cooking it in a pit, but we're going to make a noble effort. This dish can be made in an oven or, as we have here, in a clay pot. Use lard for authentic flavor, but if that offends you, use vegetable oil.* Frijoles Indios *(page 335) and* Salsa Borracha *(page 155) are good accompaniments.*

4 dried guajillo chiles, stems and seeds removed; or substitute dried red New Mexican chiles

4 dried puya chiles, stems and seeds removed; or substitute mirasol chiles

1 ancho chile, stem and seeds removed

One 4-inch piece cinnamon stick, crushed

½ teaspoon allspice berries

½ teaspoon whole cloves

½ teaspoon black peppercorns

2 teaspoons dried oregano, preferably Mexican

1 teaspoon dried marjoram

1 chipotle chile *en adobo*

6 cloves garlic, chopped

2 tablespoons red wine vinegar

1 cup beef broth

2 tablespoons lard or vegetable oil

1½ to 2 pounds chuck or rump roast, cut in 4 to 6 pieces

Clay pot

1 large onion, sliced

Chopped onions and cilantro for garnish

8 to 12 corn tortillas, warmed

Note: This recipe requires advance preparation.

Heat a heavy skillet over high heat, add the guajillo, puya, and ancho chiles, and dry-roast until they darken slightly, taking care not to burn them. Put the chiles in a bowl, cover with very hot water, and allow them to steep for 15 minutes to soften. Drain the chiles and discard the water.

Reheat the skillet, add the cinnamon, allspice, cloves, and black peppercorns, and roast for 1 minute. Add the oregano and marjoram, and continue to dry-roast until the spices become fragrant, being careful not to burn them. Allow the spices to cool completely, then place them in a spice mill or coffee grinder, and process to a fine powder.

Put the ground spices, chiles, including the chipolte, garlic, vinegar, and broth in a blender or food processor and puree until smooth.

Reheat the skillet over medium heat, add the lard or oil, and when hot, add the chile sauce and sauté, stirring occasionally for a few minutes to slightly thicken the sauce. Allow the sauce to cool.

Place the meat in a nonreactive bowl or a heavy, resealable plastic bag, add the sauce, and marinate the beef in the refrigerator for 4 hours or overnight.

Preheat the oven to 350°F.

Soak the clay pot and the lid in water for at least 30 minutes.

Put the onion slices in the bottom of the pot and place the meat on top. Pour the marinade over the meat, cover with the lid, and cook for 2 hours, or until the meat is tender and can be shredded with a couple of forks, adding more broth if necessary.

Remove the beef and, using a couple of forks, shred the meat. Pour any remaining sauce over the meat, garnish with chopped onions and cilantro, and serve with warmed corn tortillas.

Yield: 4 to 6 servings

Gaucho Grilled Beef with Molho Campanha (Beef with Brazilian Barbecue Sauce)

Gauchos are the cowboys of Brazil's pampas of Rio Grande do Sul, in the southern part of the country. Gaucho churrascos, as barbecues are called in Portuguese, consist of large pieces of meat, usually beef and sausages but sometimes lamb, threaded on large swordlike skewers, and grilled over wood fires. They are served in restaurants called churrascarias *throughout Brazil and are gaining popularity in this country as well. In these restaurants, a variety of marinated meats are served "rodzio style," meaning the waiters circulate with swords of meat through the dining room, cutting pieces of meat to order at the table. This recipe is loosely based on the churrascos Nancy enjoyed in Rio de Janeiro, as well as in the tiny* churrascarias *in the back-country on the way to Igauzu Falls. A typical salsa called* molho campanha *accompanies them. Serve with black beans, white rice, and Hearts of Palm Salad with Caribbean Kuchela Vinaigrette (page 217).*

4 tenderloin or T-bone steaks, about 1 inch thick, or substitute beef cubes

Molho Campanha (recipe opposite)

Marinade

½ cup dry white wine

⅓ cup olive oil

⅓ cup chopped fresh cilantro

3 tablespoons chopped fresh flat-leaf parsley

1 medium onion, coarsely chopped

4 cloves garlic

2 tablespoons lime juice, preferably fresh

2 habanero chiles, stems and seeds removed

2 teaspoons dried oregano

1 bay leaf

1 teaspoon coarsely ground black pepper

1 teaspoon salt

Molho Campanha

2 medium tomatoes, chopped

½ cup finely chopped onions

¼ cup finely chopped green bell pepper

3 malagueta chiles, stems and seeds removed, chopped; or substitute tabasco or piquin chiles

3 tablespoons red wine vinegar

1 tablespoon chopped fresh cilantro

Note: This recipe requires advance preparation.

Place all the ingredients for the barbecue marinade in a blender or food processor and puree until smooth.

Put the steaks in a nonreactive bowl or heavy resealable plastic bag, add the marinade, and marinate the meat in the refrigerator for 12 hours or overnight, the longer the better.

To prepare the meat, remove from the marinade and reserve the marinade for basting.

Heat the grill to medium-hot and grill the steaks, basting frequently with the marinade and turning often, to desired doneness, about 10 to 12 minutes for medium-rare. Remove the meat from the grill and let it sit for 5 minutes for the juices to be re-absorbed. Either slice the beef into thin strips or leave whole.

Arrange the meat on a large serving platter to pass around along with the salsa.

Yield: 4 servings

Variation: Substitute lamb chops or pork cubes for the beef.

Molho Campanha

This is a very easy-to-prepare salsa that accompanies Brazilian barbecues and is similar to the Mexican/southwestern pico de gallo. *Serve this salsa at room temperature for maximum flavor.*

Combine all the ingredients in a bowl and stir to mix. Allow the salsa to sit at room temperature for an hour to blend the flavors.

Yield: 1 to 1½ cups

Pork Loin with Mole Coloradito

Coloradito is one of the seven moles of Oaxaca, and is especially popular during the Day of the Dead festival. It's traditionally placed in bowls on the altars during that time, so the aroma can stimulate the deceased's appetites and lure them to the altar. This dish may appear to be difficult, but as it can all be prepared ahead of time, it's really quite simple. Moles have a long list of ingredients, but the sauce is basically just pureed and heated. This is a great party dish. Serve with beans, white rice, and, of course, warmed corn tortillas. We can't vouch for this dish raising the dead, but the aroma will lure your family and guests to the dining room table. Serve any leftover meat in corn tortillas as a tasty soft taco.

One 3-pound pork loin roast
1 cup orange juice
2 tablespoons olive oil
5 cloves garlic, slightly crushed
1 teaspoon freshly ground black pepper

2 cups *mole coloradito* (page 156)
Sliced white onion rings, chopped
   radishes, and sliced avocado
   for garnish

Place the pork roast in a roasting pan, pour the orange juice over the top, and allow it to sit at room temperature for an hour.

Preheat the oven to 300°F.

To prepare the meat, pour the oil over the roast and sprinkle with the garlic and pepper. Lightly score the meat, and rub some of the mole into the slits. Pour the remaining mole into the pan, add a cup and a half of water, and stir to mix.

Cover the roast and bake for about 1½ hours, basting frequently with the sauce. The internal temperature should register 150°F. Remove the roast, loosely cover with aluminum foil, and let rest for 10 minutes. The juices will be reabsorbed into the meat, and the temperature will rise another 10 degrees.

Skim the fat from the pan juices, simmer the sauce for 10 minutes, and serve on the side.

To serve, cut the meat in thin slices, arrange on a large platter, and garnish with the onion rings, radishes, and avocado.

Yield: 6 servings

Southwestern Spicy Hot Chorizo

Chorizo is another one of those dishes that traveled with the Spanish around the world, so now there are hundreds of variations of chorizo throughout Spain, Portugal, Mexico, and the American Southwest. There are fresh, dried, and smoked versions, and some containing wine, almonds, tomatillos, or fresh chiles. The type of chiles used varies also. In Spain chorizo is seasoned with hot pimentón *powder, in Mexico with ancho, guajillo, and pasilla chiles, and in the Southwest the chiles of choice are the dried New Mexican and chipotle chiles, which impart a smoky taste. Whatever chile combinations you use, it's the paprika that gives chorizo its familiar orange color. Traditionally chorizo is stuffed in casings, air dried, and then stored in a cool room, but since we don't have a sausage grinder and stuffer, we mix our chorizo by hand, form into patties, and freeze to preserve them. And since we are breaking from tradition, we are using a combination of beef and pork, instead of pork alone, to reduce the fat content. A word of caution: cook any chorizo carefully over a low heat—with all the chile, it's easy to scorch, and the taste of the sausage will be very bitter!*

25 black peppercorns

One 4-inch piece cinnamon stick

10 whole cloves

1 teaspoon cumin seeds

½ pound finely ground pork, butt or shoulder

½ pound finely ground beef chuck

3 tablespoons ground Chimayo chile; or substitute other pure ground New Mexican chile

2 tablespoons ground paprika

1 tablespoon ground chipotle chile

¼ cup red wine vinegar

5 cloves garlic, crushed

2 teaspoons brown sugar

2 teaspoons dried oregano, preferably Mexican

1 teaspoon salt

Heat a heavy skillet over high heat; add the peppercorns, cinnamon, cloves, and cumin and dry-roast until the spices become fragrant, being careful not to burn them. Allow the mixture to cool completely, then place in a spice mill or coffee grinder and process to a fine powder.

Combine all the ingredients in a large bowl and, using your hands, mix well.

Heat a small skillet over medium-low heat and sauté a small amount of the chorizo to taste and adjust the seasonings.

Form the chorizo into 2-ounce patties; chill for at least 1 day to cure, and either use or freeze.

Yield: Eight 2-ounce patties

Note: This recipe requires advance preparation.

Korean Chap Chee (Mixed Vegetables with Beef and Vermicelli Noodles)

Whether you call it chap chee, chap chae, *or* jap chae *(a combination of Japan and China), this is a very popular dish that combines a variety of textures, colors, flavors, and simple seasonings along with a Korean staple, noodles. Koreans love beef and serve it more often than pork and chicken, and they never eat lamb or goat. Garlic, ginger, and sesame are common to most Korean beef dishes, and this one is no exception. Traditionally,* chap chee *is spiced up with a bowl of kimchi, a fiery condiment available in Asian markets that contains fermented vegetables such as cabbage and turnips. An acquired taste! The meat will be easier to slice thinly if you put it in the freezer for about 30 minutes and have all the ingredients assembled before stir-frying.*

¾ pound flank or sirloin steak, trimmed and thinly sliced against the grain in strips 2 inches wide

¼ cup dried wood ear mushrooms (available in Asian markets)

4 ounces vermicelli noodles

3 tablespoons vegetable oil

4 cloves garlic, sliced

1 tablespoon grated ginger

4 green onions, finely chopped, including some of the greens

4 Thai chiles, stems removed, minced; or substitute serrano or jalapeño chiles

1 small carrot, julienne-cut in 3-inch-long pieces

1 small red bell pepper, julienne-cut in 3-inch-long pieces

1½ cups chopped fresh spinach

½ cup straw mushrooms

½ cup bean sprouts

Chopped fresh cilantro, toasted sesame seeds, and kimchi for garnish

Sauce

¼ cup soy sauce

2 tablespoons sugar

1 tablespoon sesame seed oil

½ teaspoon freshly ground black pepper

Marinade

1 tablespoon soy sauce

1 tablespoon sugar

1 green onion, chopped

1 teaspoon minced garlic

1 teaspoon sesame seed oil

Combine all the ingredients for the marinade in a bowl and add the beef. Toss to coat and marinate at room temperature for 30 minutes.

Place the wood ears in a bowl and cover with warm water. Allow the mushrooms to steep for 30 minutes to soften. Drain the mushrooms and discard the water.

Cook the noodles according to the directions on the package, drain, and keep warm.

Combine all the sauce ingredients in a bowl and stir to mix.

Heat a wok or heavy skillet over medium-high heat, add the oil and when hot, add the meat and quickly stir-fry until browned, about 2 minutes. Remove and keep warm.

Add the garlic and ginger to the wok and stir-fry until fragrant. Add the onions and chiles, and stir-fry for an additional 2 minutes. Next add the carrots, bell peppers, spinach, mushrooms, and sprouts, and stir-fry for 2 more minutes.

Stir the sauce into the wok and add the noodles. Continue to stir-fry until the noodles absorb the sauce. Return the beef and cook until all the ingredients are hot.

To serve, place the *chap chee* on a large serving platter, garnish with the cilantro and sesame seeds, and serve with the kimchi on the side.

Yield: 4 to 6 servings

Seasoned Meatballs in Spicy Yogurt Sauce

Variations on this dish are found in a number of Middle Eastern countries such as Syria, Lebanon, and Iraq and are a popular addition to a feast to break the fast during Ramadan. Yogurt is considered "cool to a thirsty stomach" and is included in many of the dishes served during this holy time. Using a French seasoning may seem odd, but quatre épices *is popular in the Middle East, especially where the French had a presence. These spicy meatballs are served in a bowl over couscous or bulgur; if you don't have any, rice will do fine. Be sure to serve them with lavash or pita bread for mopping up the spicy sauce.*

1 pound lean ground lamb

½ cup finely chopped onion

3 cloves garlic, minced

2 teaspoons *quatre épices*, store-bought or homemade (page 118)

2 teaspoons ground coriander

1 teaspoon ground cardamom

½ teaspoon ground cumin

½ teaspoon crushed red pepper

Freshly ground black pepper

2 tablespoons vegetable oil

2 cups cooked couscous, or rice for serving

Chopped fresh mint or parsley for garnish

Sauce

1 tablespoon grated fresh ginger

¼ cup chopped onions

1 clove garlic, minced

½ teaspoon ground cinnamon

¼ teaspoon ground cayenne

Pinch saffron

2 medium tomatoes, peeled, seeds removed, chopped

1 cup plain yogurt

2 teaspoons cornstarch

¼ cup raisins

Note: This recipe requires advance preparation.

Preheat the oven to 350°F.

Combine all the ingredients for the meatballs in a bowl and, using your hands, knead until well mixed. Allow to sit at room temperature for 30 minutes to blend the flavors. Form into small meatballs.

Heat a heavy skillet over medium-high heat, add the oil, and when hot, add the meatballs and fry until they are crisp and browned. Remove, drain, and keep warm.

Reheat the skillet, add the ginger, onions, and garlic, and sauté for a couple of minutes until the onions are soft. Add the cinnamon, cayenne, and saffron and cook for few seconds. Stir in the tomatoes and 1 cup of water, raise the heat, and bring to a boil. When the mixture reaches a boil, reduce the heat and leave the skillet partially covered for 15 minutes, then reduce the heat to low.

Combine the yogurt and cornstarch in a bowl and slowly add it to the sauce. Gently simmer for a few minutes to thicken slightly, being careful that it doesn't boil and curdle. Taste and adjust the seasonings.

Pour the sauce into an ovenproof casserole dish and stir in the meatballs. Place in the oven and heat for 15 minutes to further thicken the sauce and heat the meatballs.

To serve, place hot couscous in a serving bowl, top with the meatball sauce, garnish with the mint, and serve with wedges of lavash or pita.

Yield: 4 servings

Glazed Gammon (South African Baked Ham)

Ham is popular in South Africa, and no Christmas table would be complete without some sort of ham dish. Gammon is a Chinese type of ham that is uncooked and very salty. It's not available in the United States; probably Smithfield and Virginia hams are the closest we can come to a true gammon. If an uncooked ham is unavailable, you can alter the cooking time in this recipe and still have an elegant entrée to grace any holiday table.

One 5- to 6-pound ham, rump or shank

2 cups vegetable broth, preferably homemade

3 tablespoons ground ginger

2 tablespoons dry mustard

2 bay leaves

1 tablespoon black peppercorns

6 canned apricot halves

½ cup canned pitted cherries

10 to 15 whole cloves

Glaze

1 cup apricot nectar

⅔ cup honey

⅓ cup Dijon-style mustard, store-bought or homemade (page 117)

¼ cup red wine (optional)

1 tablespoon lemon juice

¼ teaspoon ground cloves

Preheat the oven to 325°F and liberally oil a large baking pan.

Place the ham, fat side up, in the baking pan, and pour the broth over the top. Dust the ham with the ginger and mustard, add the bay leaves and peppercorns, and cover the roast with a lid or aluminum foil.

Bake the ham for 3 to 4 hours, or until an internal thermometer reads 125°F. Remove the meat from the oven and raise the heat to 400°F.

Remove the meat from the pan and pour off the liquid. Peel the outer layer of the skin off the fat of the ham, leaving a good layer of fat. Score the fat with a sharp knife to form a crisscross diamond pattern.

Combine all the ingredients for the glaze in a bowl and stir to mix. Spoon the glaze over the ham and bake, uncovered, for 30 minutes or to an internal temperature of 140°F, basting often with the glaze.

Remove the ham and place on a large serving platter. Garnish with the apricot halves and cherries, using the cloves to anchor them in place, and serve.

Yield: 6 to 8 servings

Fajitas Bulgogii (Fajitas Korean-style)

What is this, fajitas from Korea? Well, not really. We were preparing to marinate meat for fajitas and wanted to do something different from the usual southwestern-style marinade. It started with our recipe for a pepper steak, and from there evolved into a marinade that reminded us of a Korean-style barbecue, and Fajitas Bulgogii *was born. Since its creation, we've used it on other cuts of beef, such as sirloin, T-bone, and rib steaks, with great results. The brown sugar in the marinade will give a nice brown crust to the meat; just be careful not to let the grill flame up and burn it.*

2 teaspoons green peppercorns, packed in water, drained

3 teaspoons black peppercorns

3 teaspoons white peppercorns

2 pounds skirt steak

8 Mexican bulb onions; or substitute large green onions

Vegetable oil

8 flour tortillas

Condiments: Pickled ginger, sour cream, and salsa, such as *salsa borracha* (page 155), or *salsa de chile de arbol* (page 154)

Marinade

2 tablespoons Worcestershire sauce

2 tablespoons soy sauce

2 tablespoons rice vinegar

1 tablespoon habanero hot sauce

1 tablespoon brown sugar

1 teaspoon dark sesame seed oil

2 cloves garlic, pressed

Place all the peppercorns in a clean towel, wrap the towel around them, and pound them with a hammer to coarsely crush. Gently press the mixture into both sides of the skirt steak.

Combine all the ingredients for the marinade in a bowl and stir to mix. Place the steak in a nonreactive dish or heavy, resealable plastic bag and pour the marinade over it. Cover and marinate in the refrigerator overnight.

Heat the grill to hot, brush the onions with vegetable oil, and grill until soft.

Grill the steak over a hot fire until medium-rare, about 10 to 15 minutes. Remove the steak from the grill and slice thinly against the grain.

Quickly heat each tortilla on the grill.

Serve the steak wrapped in a tortilla and topped with a grilled onion, with bowls of the condiments on the side.

Yield: 4 to 6 servings

Note: This recipe requires advance preparation.

Harissa and Seven-Vegetable Couscous

This dish is based on a recipe that Nancy collected during her travels in Morocco; a classic dish, it's traditionally served on Fridays and special holidays, such as the Berber wedding she attended. The recipe has a long list of ingredients, but it's easy to prepare and can be made ahead of time. Like most stews, it tastes even better on the second day.

3 tablespoon vegetable oil

1 pound lamb or beef, cut in 1½-inch cubes

1 large onion, chopped

4 cloves garlic, chopped

½ cup *harissa*, store-bought or homemade (page 120)

3 dried piquin chiles

1½ teaspoons ground cumin

1 teaspoon ground ginger

1 teaspoon ground cinnamon

½ teaspoon allspice

1 quart beef broth

½ teaspoon saffron

1 large potato, peeled and diced

1 small turnip, peeled and diced

4 medium canned tomatoes, chopped

2 medium carrots, peeled and julienne-cut

1 cup canned chickpeas, drained and rinsed

2 small zucchini, julienne-cut

1 small eggplant, peeled and cubed

1 cup frozen peas

4 cups couscous

Salt and freshly ground black pepper to taste

Chopped flat leaf parsley for garnish

Heat a stockpot over high heat and add the oil; when hot, reduce the heat, add the lamb, and sauté until browned. Add the onion and garlic and continue to sauté until they are soft. Add the *harissa*, chiles, cumin, ginger, cinnamon, and allspice and continue to cook for 5 minutes.

Add the broth, saffron, potato, and turnip and bring to a boil. Reduce the heat, cover, and simmer the stew for an hour, adding water if necessary to thin if it becomes too thick.

Add the tomatoes, carrots, and chickpeas and simmer for 20 minutes. Add the zucchini, eggplant, and peas, and simmer until the vegetables are done. Taste and adjust the seasonings.

Put the couscous in a bowl and add an equal amount of boiling water; cover and let stand for 5 minutes.

To serve: Mound the couscous on a platter, top with the stew, and serve with additional *harissa* sauce on the side.

Yield: 6 to 8 servings

Green Chile Stew

A popular dish in New Mexico, green chile stew has been around for hundreds of years—ever since the Spanish introduced domesticated pigs to the area. As with any stew, there are any number of variations. Serve it with or without potatoes or tomatoes, add some beans, or just serve it with pork, onions, and green chile (fresh green New Mexico chiles are best). In the late summer and early fall, when the chile ripens and everyone starts roasting them and putting them up for the coming year, we keep a pot of this stew simmering on the stove to freeze in containers and enjoy during the cold winter months. It's a simple dish, but needs slow simmering to blend the flavors—and always plan to have some left to make wonderful huevos rancheros! For a meatless alternative, substitute pinto beans and vegetable broth for the pork.

1½ pounds lean pork, cut into 1½-inch cubes

1 tablespoon vegetable oil

1 large onion, diced

2 garlic cloves, minced

1 quart chicken or pork broth

6 to 8 green New Mexican chiles, roasted, peeled, stems removed, cut in thin strips

2 small tomatoes, peeled and chopped

1 large potato, peeled and diced

½ teaspoon dried oregano, preferably Mexican

Salt to taste

8 flour tortillas, warmed

Heat a heavy skillet over medium-high heat, add the pork, and brown, adding a little oil if needed. When browned, transfer the pork to a large saucepan or stockpot. Add the onions to the skillet, with additional oil, and sauté the onions until they turn golden brown, about 5 to 10 minutes. Add the garlic and cook for an additional minute. Transfer the mixture to the pot with the pork.

Add 2 cups of broth to the pan, raise the heat, and deglaze the pan, being sure to scrape all the bits and pieces from the sides and bottom. Pour the broth over the pork and onions.

Add the remaining ingredients to the saucepan, bring to just below boiling, reduce the heat, and simmer for 1 to 1½ hours, or until the meat is very tender and starts to fall apart.

Serve the stew in individual bowls accompanied by warmed flour tortillas.

Yield: 4 servings

Bucatini all'Amatriciana (Pasta with Pancetta, Tomatoes, and Chile)

This pasta, cooked in the style of Amatricia, originated in a small town with the same name located approximately 100 miles outside of Rome. Bucatini is a long, thick, smooth, dried pasta tube rather like hollow spaghetti. If you can't find bucatini, look for perciatelli or substitute spaghetti or vermicelli. Bucatini takes longer to cook than most other pastas so be sure to check the package for cooking times.

1 pound bucatini or substitute vermicelli or spaghetti

2 pounds fresh tomatoes or substitute 2½ cups canned Italian plum tomatoes, drained

8 ounces pancetta, cut in pieces ½-inch wide and 1-inch long

2 tablespoons extra-virgin oil

½ cup finely chopped red onion

3 cloves garlic, minced

1 cup dry white wine (optional)

1 teaspoon crushed red chile, such as piquin or cayenne

2 tablespoons chopped fresh basil leaves

½ teaspoon freshly ground black pepper

Salt to taste

½ cup freshly grated pecorino Romano or Parmesan cheese

In a large saucepan or stockpot, bring 4 quarts of salted water to a boil.

If using fresh tomatoes, coarsely chop them, place in a food mill and process to remove the seeds and skins. Transfer the solids to a bowl and discard the liquid.

Heat a heavy skillet over medium heat, add the oil and when hot, add the pancetta and sauté until the pork is crisp. Remove the pancetta and drain on a paper towel.

Add the onions to the skillet and sauté until the onions are soft, then add the garlic. Sauté for an additional 2 minutes. Add the wine, if using, and simmer until the wine is reduced by two thirds.

Add the tomatoes, chile, black pepper, and salt to the skillet, reduce the heat and simmer for 15 minutes, stirring occasionally. Taste and adjust the seasonings.

Add the bucatini and cook the pasta until *al dente*. Drain the pasta but don't rinse.

Add the drained pasta to the tomato sauce along with the basil and pancetta. Increase the heat to high and toss the pasta in the sauce to coat, about 1 minute.

Transfer the pasta to a warmed serving bowl, top with the cheese and serve immediately.

Yield: 4 servings

10 Poultry

Mandarin Orange Chicken Salad with Sesame Ginger Dressing in a Crispy Noodle Bowl

 This entrée salad combines a number of different flavors and textures. Shrimp or even grilled halibut or salmon can be substituted for the chicken or, omitted for a tasty vegetarian alternative.

1 pound Chinese wheat noodles

Sesame oil

Vegetable oil for frying, preferably peanut

3 cups chopped cabbage

1 cup mixed baby greens

1 bunch chopped fresh cilantro

1 small can mandarin orange segments, drained

2 boneless, skinless chicken breasts, grilled and cut in strips

¼ cup sliced radishes

¼ cup toasted, sliced almonds

Sesame Ginger Dressing

3 tablespoons vegetable oil, preferably peanut

2 to 3 teaspoons sesame oil

3 tablespoons rice vinegar

3 Thai chiles, stems removed, minced

1 tablespoon grated ginger

2 teaspoons orange zest

1 teaspoon sugar

1 teaspoon soy sauce

¼ teaspoon dry mustard

Combine all the dressing ingredients in a bowl and whisk to combine. This will make ¼ to ⅓ of a cup. Allow the dressing to sit for 20 minutes to blend the flavors.

To make the noodle bowl, bring about 4 quarts of water in a stockpot to a boil. Boil the noodles until done, 4 to 5 minutes. Drain thoroughly, rinse with cold water, sprinkle with a little of the sesame oil, and toss to coat. Divide into 4 equal portions.

Heat a wok until hot, add the vegetable oil to a depth of 3 inches, and heat to 360°F. Add one of the noodle bunches and use a round, heatproof bowl to press the noodles along the sides to form a bowl. Fry until the noodles are browned and the bowl holds its shape. Drain on paper towels. Repeat with the remaining noodles.

Combine the cabbage, baby greens, cilantro, and dressing in a large bowl and toss.

To assemble the salads, place a noodle bowl on each of 4 individual plates. Divide the cabbage mixture between the bowls. Garnish the plate with some of the orange segments. Arrange the chicken strips on top of the cabbage, and garnish with the radishes, remaining oranges, and almonds. Serve with additional dressing on the side.

Yield: 4 servings

Pan-Roasted Chicken with French Dijon Sauce

This is our take on the French classic lapin à la moutarde, *or rabbit with mustard, here using chicken. We like to use crème fraîche or Mexican* crema *because they add creaminess without being overly sweet. This is a quick and easy recipe to prepare. You can brown the chicken, put it in the oven, and make the rest of the meal while it cooks.*

1 teaspoon vegetable oil

4 chicken pieces, such as legs and thighs or breasts

2 teaspoons chopped shallot

½ cup chicken broth

½ cup dry white wine, such as chardonnay

¼ teaspoon dried thyme

⅛ teaspoon ground marjoram

3 tablespoons Dijon-style mustard, store-bought or homemade (page 117)

3 tablespoons crème fraîche

Grated Parmesan cheese for garnish

Preheat the oven to 400°F.

Heat a heavy skillet with an ovenproof handle over medium heat, add the oil, and when hot, place the chicken pieces in it skin side down and fry for 5 minutes, or until browned and the chicken easily releases from the pan. Turn the pieces over and brown on the other side.

Put the skillet in the oven and roast the chicken until the juices run clear and the internal temperature is 160°F, about 40 minutes. Place the chicken on a plate and keep warm.

Pour off the excess fat from the skillet and put on top of the stove over medium heat. Add the shallots and sauté until they are soft. Add the broth and wine, raise the heat, and deglaze the pan, scraping up all the browned bits and pieces from the bottom. Reduce the heat, add the thyme and marjoram, and simmer to reduce and thicken.

Stir in the mustard and simmer for 2 to 3 minutes. Remove the pan from the heat and stir in the crème fraîche.

Place the chicken on individual plates, pour the sauce over the top, garnish with cheese, and serve.

Yield: 4 servings

Kung Pao Chicken

This classic Sichuan stir-fry dish can be made with shrimp, pork, beef, or even tofu as well as chicken. It was developed during the Qing dynasty (A.D. 1644 to 1911) for the Mandarin nobleman Ting Kung-pao. During that period of time, Beijing's finest households were staffed with chefs from all over the country, so even though kung pao was developed in Beijing, it was created by a Sichuan chef. This is a simple stir-fry with just a few ingredients—chicken, chiles, minimal vegetables, and crunchy peanuts for texture. The complex flavors come from the marinating and seasoning sauces, which contain half of the "eight immortal flavors" in Chinese cooking—salt, sweet, hot, and fragrant.

2 boneless, skinless chicken breasts, cut in bite-size pieces

2 to 3 tablespoons vegetable oil, preferably peanut

4 to 6 whole dried red chiles, such as piquin or cayenne

1 tablespoon chopped garlic

2 teaspoons grated ginger

1 small onion, cubed

½ green bell pepper, cubed

½ cup roasted peanuts

2 teaspoons sesame oil

1 green onion, chopped, including some of the greens for garnish

2 cups cooked white rice for serving

Marinating Sauce

1 tablespoon rice wine or dry sherry

1 tablespoon light soy sauce

1 teaspoon sugar

Seasoning Sauce

¼ cup chicken broth

2 tablespoons Asian chile sauce with garlic (available in Asian markets)

2 tablespoons hoisin sauce (available in Asian markets)

1 tablespoon plus 1 teaspoon hot bean sauce (available in Asian markets)

2 teaspoons light soy sauce

2 teaspoons rice vinegar

2 teaspoons ground Sichuan pepper (*fagara* is available by mail order; you can also substitute equal portions of anise and allspice)

2 teaspoons sugar

1 teaspoon distilled white vinegar

Combine all the ingredients for the marinating sauce, along with 1 tablespoon of water, in a large bowl and stir to mix. Toss the chicken in the sauce to coat and marinate for 30 minutes at room temperature.

In another bowl, combine all the ingredients for the seasoning sauce, stir to mix, and set aside.

Heat a wok or heavy skillet over medium-high heat until hot and add the oil. Add the chiles and stir-fry for 2 minutes, or until they start to blacken. Push them to the side of the wok, add the garlic and ginger, and stir-fry until fragrant.

Drain the chicken and add to the wok. Stir-fry the chicken for 2 to 3 minutes, until the chicken changes color. Remove, drain, and keep warm. Add the onion and bell pepper and stir-fry just until they soften.

Add the seasoning sauce to the wok and cook until the sauce thickens. Return the chicken and toss to coat. Heat until the sauce forms a glaze over the chicken. Add the peanuts and toss to coat. Sprinkle with the sesame oil.

To serve, mound the chicken on a serving platter and garnish with the chopped green onions. Serve with plain white rice.

Yield: 4 servings

Ras el Hanout-Spiced Berber Lemon Chicken Tagine with Almond-Stuffed Green Olives

 Tagine is the word for a Moroccan stew, as well as for the clay pot that it is cooked in. Preserved lemons are traditionally used in this recipe, but since most cooks don't stock these delicacies, we have substituted lemon juice and lemon zest. Couscous is, however, readily available, so we recommend serving this stew over it for an authentic taste.

4 chicken thighs, skin attached, or substitute chicken breasts

1 tablespoon extra-virgin olive oil

1 small onion, sliced thin

1 tablespoon grated ginger

2 cloves garlic, chopped

2 tablespoons *ras el hanout*, store-bought or homemade (page 122)

2 teaspoons finely grated lemon zest

1 tablespoon all-purpose flour

2 cups chicken broth

⅓ cup lemon juice

1 tablespoon honey

1 cup cooked chickpeas

⅓ cup green olives stuffed with almonds

2 cups cooked couscous or rice

Sliced lemon peel and chopped fresh parsley for garnish

Rinse off the chicken, pat dry, and season with salt and pepper.

Heat a heavy saucepan over moderately high heat, add the oil and when hot, place the chicken pieces, skin side down, in the skillet and fry for 5 minutes or until browned. Turn the pieces and brown on the other side. Remove the chicken and keep warm. Pour off all but 1 tablespoon of the fat from the skillet.

Add the onion to the pan and sauté until it is softened. Add the ginger and garlic and cook for an additional couple of minutes. Stir in the *ras el hanout*, lemon zest, and flour. Cook for 1 to 2 minutes, stirring constantly to cook the flour. Whisk in the broth, raise the heat, and scrape all the bits and pieces from the bottom of the pan into the sauce. Add the lemon juice and honey.

Reduce the heat, return the chicken pieces to the pan, and simmer, uncovered, stirring occasionally, for 30 to 40 minutes or until the chicken is just done. Add the chickpeas and olives and simmer for 5 minutes. Taste and adjust the seasonings.

To serve, create a bed of couscous or rice on a large platter, place the chicken pieces on top, and pour the sauce over the chicken. Garnish with the parsley and lemon peel.

Yield: 4 servings

Almond Chicken Oaxacan Style

The Oaxaca marketplace is famous for its incredible selection of chiles and other locally grown produce as well as its moles. This recipe, which Dave collected in Oaxaca, features the ancho chile, the dried version of the poblano, which is available in grocery stores as well as through mail-order sources. This is a relatively simple mole compared with some of the ones Oaxaca is famous for, but it still has the complex blend of flavors typical of their dishes. Serve this rich mole dish over a bed of plain white rice.

One 3½-pound chicken, cut into serving pieces

1 tablespoon vegetable oil

2 large or 4 small ancho chiles, stems and seeds removed

½ cup chopped almonds

4 tomatoes, roasted, peeled, and seeds removed

2 cloves garlic, chopped

1⅓ cups chopped onion

12 black peppercorns

4 cloves

One 2-inch piece cinnamon stick

½ *bolillo*, or small French roll, torn into small pieces

1 tablespoon sugar

3 to 4 cups chicken broth

Salt and freshly ground pepper to taste

Rinse the chicken, pat dry, and season with salt and pepper.

Heat a large heavy skillet over medium-high heat and add the oil. When hot, add the chicken, skin side down, and fry for 5 minutes, or until the chicken is browned and easily releases from the pan. Turn the pieces and brown on the other side. Remove the chicken and keep warm. Drain off all but 1 tablespoon of the fat.

In the same skillet, fry the chiles, all but 2 tablespoons of the almonds, and the tomatoes, garlic, onion, peppercorns, cloves, and cinnamon for 3 to 4 minutes. Put the mixture, along with the bread, into a blender or food processor and puree until smooth, thinning with some of the broth if needed. Return the mixture to the skillet and simmer the paste for a couple of minutes.

Stir the sugar and broth into the sauce, return the chicken to the skillet, and cover. Simmer the mole over low heat until the chicken is tender, about 30 to 40 minutes.

To serve, place the chicken pieces on a large platter or in a large bowl, pour the mole sauce over the top, and garnish with the remaining almonds.

Yield: 4 to 6 servings

Tandoori Murg
(Chicken Cooked Tandoori Style)

Tandoori chicken is one of the most famous Indian dishes and also one of the tastiest. The word tandoori *refers to any food cooked in a* tandoor, *a giant unglazed clay oven. The chicken in this recipe is marinated twice, first with the lemon juice, then with the yogurt mixture. You can approximate a tandoor by using a charcoal grill or gas broiler, but you won't achieve the exact flavor. The taste is hard to duplicate, since the* tandoor *reaches such high temperatures, up to 800°F, but even if the chicken is not strictly traditional, it's still tasty. Those who are watching their fat intake will like cooking in the tandoori style, and using a low-fat yogurt in the marinade will reduce the fat content even further. This chicken is traditionally served with a cooling Mint* Raita *(page 373).*

4 chicken breasts, skin removed

2 to 3 teaspoons ground cayenne

1 tablespoon ground paprika

½ teaspoon freshly ground black pepper

½ cup lemon juice

3 tablespoons melted butter

Lemon slices for garnish

Marinade

1 cup plain yogurt

¼ teaspoon crushed saffron threads, dissolved in ¼ cup hot water

1 tablespoon grated ginger

1 tablespoon chopped garlic

1 tablespoon ground red chile, such as New Mexican

2 teaspoons garam masala, store-bought or homemade (page 135)

1 teaspoon ground coriander

½ teaspoon ground turmeric

½ teaspoon freshly ground black pepper

½ teaspoon ground nutmeg

½ teaspoon ground cinnamon

¼ teaspoon ground cumin

¼ teaspoon ground cloves

½ teaspoon salt

Note: This recipe requires advance preparation.

Line a strainer with dampened cheesecloth, add the yogurt, and place over a bowl. Put in the refrigerator and let the yogurt drain for 4 hours to thicken.

Score the chicken about 2 inches deep, making diagonal cuts. Combine the cayenne, paprika, and black pepper in a bowl and stir to mix. Rub the mixture into the cuts, add the lemon juice, and marinate the chicken for 30 minutes at room temperature, then drain.

Put all the ingredients for the marinade in a blender or food processor and puree until smooth.

Place the chicken in a nonreactive bowl and pour the marinade over the chicken. Using your fingers, rub the marinade into the meat. Cover and refrigerate 24 hours, turning occasionally.

Start a charcoal or hardwood fire in your barbecue. Place the grill 2 inches over the hot coals and grill the chicken for 10 minutes, turning once. Use the marinade to baste the chicken as it cooks. Raise the grill to 5 inches and continue cooking 5 minutes, turning once.

Remove the chicken and brush with the melted butter. Return to the grill and continue to cook for an additional 5 minutes, turning once, until the chicken is done and the juices run clear.

Serve the chicken garnished with lemon slices and serve the mint *raita* on the side.

Yield: 4 servings

Mayan Achiote-Marinated Chicken Cooked in Banana Leaves with Pickled Red Onions

Cooking meats in the pibil—*a pit lined with stones called a* pibil—*dates back to pre-Columbian times, and variations of these dishes can be found in just every restaurant that features local cuisine throughout the Yucatán Peninsula in Mexico. These pits were the center of the Mayan community. This is an easier variation that can be done on the grill or in a smoker, and doesn't require digging a pit in your backyard. Achiote is the same thing as annatto, which is both a spice and an orange coloring agent. Nancy, who collected this recipe during her travels in the Yucatán, prefers to use the paste rather than the seeds, which she says are as easy to grind as steel ball bearings. Guero chiles are substituted for the usual xcatic chiles, which are impossible to find outside of the area. Banana leaves can be found in Asian markets, but you can also use aluminum foil.* Pibils *are traditionally served with pickled red onions (recipe follows).*

4 boneless, skinless chicken breasts

3 fresh banana or guero chiles, stems and seeds removed, cut in strips; or substitute hot yellow wax chiles

1 small red onion, sliced and separated into rings

4 sprigs fresh epazote; or substitute 1 tablespoon dried (available at Latin markets; optional)

4 tablespoons margarine

Banana leaves (available at Asian and Latin markets)

Achiote Marinade

10 whole black peppercorns

¼ teaspoon cumin seeds

3 cloves garlic

2 habanero chiles, stems and seeds removed

2 tablespoons achiote paste

1 teaspoon dried oregano, preferably Mexican

½ teaspoon ground cinnamon

¼ teaspoon ground allspice

2 bay leaves

2 tablespoons lime juice, preferably fresh

2 teaspoons distilled white vinegar

Cebollas Encuridas (Pickled Red Onions)

1 small red onion, thinly sliced

5 black peppercorns

3 allspice berries

¼ teaspoon cumin seeds

¼ teaspoon dried oregano, preferably Mexican

2 cloves garlic, minced

⅓ cup white vinegar

½ teaspoon salt

For the marinade, place the peppercorns and cumin seeds in a spice or coffee grinder and process to a fine powder. Combine the powder with the garlic and habanero chile, place the mixture in a blender or food processor, and puree to form a paste, adding a little water if necessary.

Combine the spice mixture, achiote, oregano, cinnamon, allspice, bay leaves, and lime juice in a bowl and stir to mix. Place the chicken pieces in a nonreactive pan and prick the flesh with a fork. Pour the marinade over the chicken and marinate overnight or for 24 hours in the refrigerator.

To make 4 packets, cut 8 pieces of string about 6 inches long. Place a banana leaf down on a flat surface. Place a piece of chicken on each of the leaves, along with the marinade, and top with the chiles and onions. Place a little epazote on each breast, along with a tablespoon of margarine. Fold the banana leaves over chicken, then fold over the ends. Securely tie the packet both crosswise and lengthwise with two pieces of string. Repeat with the remaining leaves.

Place on the grill over indirect heat and cook for 1 hour. Or, if you are using a smoker, place on the grill with a pan of water between the coals and the wrapped chicken to keep the chicken juicy.

Serve the chicken with warm corn tortillas, pickled onions, and black beans.

Yield: 4 servings

Note: This recipe requires advance preparation.

Cebollas Encuridas (Pickled Red Onions)
These colorful onions are a traditional accompaniment to pibil *dishes. Found on virtually every table throughout the Yucatán, they will keep for a month in the refrigerator.*

Place the onions in a bowl and pour boiling water over them. Let them sit for 1 minute and then drain. Discard the water.

Coarsely grind the peppercorns, allspice, and cumin in a spice or coffee grinder. Add to the onions.

Add the remaining ingredients, and enough water to barely cover. Allow the mixture to marinate for a couple of hours to blend the flavors.

Yield: 1 cup

Caribbean Chicken with Black Pepper Rum Raisin Sauce

 The dominant seasoning in this sauce is black pepper, which also turns the sauce black, but the sweet hint of raisins and pickled ginger balances the heat. This is a strong, richly flavored dish, so serve it with plain side dishes such as white rice and a colorful vegetable.

¼ cup raisins

¼ cup rum

1 tablespoon coriander seeds

2 teaspoons black peppercorns

2 star anise seeds

1 tablespoon vegetable oil

4 chicken breasts

½ cup chopped onions

2 shallots, chopped

1 teaspoon minced garlic

1 teaspoon grated ginger

2 to 3 cups chicken broth

2 teaspoons cornstarch mixed with 2 tablespoons water

1 tablespoon pickled ginger (available at Asian markets)

Orange zest for garnish

Cover the raisins with very hot water, and steep for 15 minutes to plump. Drain the raisins and discard the water. Add the rum to the raisins and steep for an hour.

Preheat the oven to 350°F. Heat a heavy skillet over high heat, add the coriander, peppercorns, and star anise, and dry-roast until the seeds darken and become fragrant, being careful that they don't burn. Allow the mixture to cool completely and then process to a fine powder in a spice mill or coffee grinder.

Reheat the skillet over medium-high heat, add the oil, and when hot, add the chicken, skin side down, and fry for 5 minutes, or until it is browned. Turn and brown on the other side. Remove the chicken, place in an ovenproof casserole, and put in the oven.

Pour off all but 1 tablespoon of the accumulated fat from the skillet, add the onions, shallots, garlic, and ginger, and sauté until soft. Add the spice mixture and cook for a minute. Stir in the chicken broth and bring to a boil, scraping up the bits and pieces from the skillet. Reduce the heat and simmer for 5 minutes until the sauce is slightly thickened. Pour the sauce over the chicken and continue to bake, turning the pieces a few times, for 45 minutes to an hour, or until the chicken is done. Remove the chicken from the sauce and keep warm.

Put the sauce in a saucepan and bring to a boil over high heat; while stirring constantly, slowly add the cornstarch. Reduce the heat and simmer until the sauce thickens. Remove from the heat, add the pickled ginger, raisins, and rum, and stir to mix. To serve, plate a piece of chicken, top with sauce, and garnish with the orange zest.

Yield: 4 servings

Mole Poblano Turkey Stacked Enchilada Pie

Turkey with mole poblano is considered the national dish of Mexico, and turkey smothered in chocolate chile sauce is quite possibly Mexico's finest and most unusual entrée. We've found this to be an excellent way to make an "after the holiday" meal with leftover roast turkey. Enchiladas are not difficult to prepare; in fact, they are quite easy. The trick is to have everything organized and ready to go before assembling. We have stacked the tortillas to make a pie in this recipe, but you can also roll them around the filling to form a more common enchilada.

Vegetable oil for frying

12 corn tortillas

½ cup finely chopped onion

2 cups shredded turkey

1½ cups shredded Mexican Chihuahua, *asadero*, or Monterey Jack cheese

2 cups *mole poblano*, store-bought or homemade (page 157)

1 to 1½ cups Mexican *crema*; or substitute thin sour cream

Chopped fresh cilantro, chopped onions, sliced radishes, sliced avocados, grated *cotija* cheese, or any of the above cheeses, for garnish

Preheat the oven to 350°F, and oil an 8-by-8 baking dish or ovenproof casserole.

Heat a small heavy skillet over medium heat, add the oil to a depth of ½ inch, and when hot, quickly fry each tortilla, one at a time, to soften, about 5 or 10 seconds on each side. Do not fry until crisp. Drain on paper towels. Pour off all but a teaspoon of oil.

In the same skillet, add the onions and sauté until soft. Combine the onion, turkey, and shredded cheese in a bowl and toss to coat.

To assemble, spoon a couple of tablespoons of the mole in the bottom of the casserole, and top with 4 of the tortillas. Spread some of the turkey mixture on the tortillas and top with the sour cream, add another layer of tortillas, then turkey and sour cream, and end with a layer of tortillas.

Pour the remaining mole over the casserole and bake, uncovered, for 20 minutes.

Remove from the oven and let stand for 10 minutes to set. Garnish with cilantro, onions, radishes, avocados, and a sprinkle of grated cheese, and serve.

Yield: 4 servings

Maghreb Chicken Stuffed with Qalat Dagga-Spiced Rice, Apricots, and Walnuts

 The four major nations that make up the Maghreb of North Africa are Morocco, Algeria, Tunisia, and Libya, and variations of this stuffing made with fruits and nuts can be found in all these countries. The stuffing for this bird can be made up to two days in advance; just don't add the nuts to the stuffing until you're just about to put it into the chicken, so that they remain crunchy.

2 tablespoons *qalat dagga* seasoning, store-bought or homemade (page 124), divided

One 3- to 4-pound chicken

Extra-virgin olive oil

Stuffing

1½ cups chicken broth

¼ teaspoon saffron

¾ cup long-grain rice

1 cup coarsely chopped onions

4 cloves garlic, chopped

1 tablespoon extra-virgin olive oil

½ cup dried apricots, cut in large chunks

½ cup chopped walnuts

2 tablespoons chopped fresh flat-leaf parsley

1 tablespoon lemon juice, preferably fresh

Salt to taste

To make the stuffing, combine the broth and saffron in a saucepan and stir to dissolve. Bring the mixture to a boil over high heat. Add the rice, stir once, cover, and simmer until the rice is done, about 20 to 30 minutes. Allow the rice to cool.

Preheat the oven to 400°F.

Combine the rice and the remaining stuffing ingredients and 1 tablespoon *qalat dagga* in a bowl, and stir to mix. Lightly pack the stuffing into the body cavity and neck of the chicken, close the cavity, and secure with skewers. Rub the chicken with oil and sprinkle with the remaining *qalat dagga* and salt. Place the chicken breast side up in a roasting pan.

Roast the chicken until juices come out clear and the internal temperature is 160 degrees, about an hour. Remove the chicken from the oven, loosely cover with aluminum foil, and let sit for 10 minutes so the chicken can reabsorb its juices and finish cooking. To serve, remove the stuffing from the chicken and mound on a platter. Carve the chicken into serving-size pieces, place around the stuffing, and serve.

Yield: 4 to 6 servings

Chicken Basquaise with Espelette Piperade

Piperade is a colorful pepper sauce that is only spicy when made in the Basque region. This simple but delicious dish is often served at the Celebration of the Peppers in the town of Espelette, France. Since Espelette powder may be hard to locate, substitute hot paprika or red New Mexican chile powder. Serve this dish as the French would, with roast potatoes, a green vegetable, a loaf of crusty bread, and a bottle of dry red wine.

⅓ cup extra-virgin olive oil

2 cups chopped onions

3 cloves garlic, minced

2 cups chopped green bell pepper

1 cup chopped red bell pepper

2 large tomatoes, peeled and chopped

3 tablespoons Espelette powder; or substitute hot paprika or red New Mexican chile powder

½ teaspoon dried thyme

One 3-pound chicken, cut in serving-size pieces

Salt and freshly ground black pepper to taste

Heat a large saucepan over medium heat, add ¼ cup of the oil, and when hot, add the onion and garlic and sauté for 5 minutes, stirring occasionally. Add the bell peppers and sauté for an additional 10 minutes. Add the tomatoes and Espelette powder and cook for 20 minutes, stirring occasionally. Stir in the thyme, and season with salt and pepper. Remove the pan from the heat and transfer the mixture to a bowl.

Wipe out the pan and reheat over medium-high heat. Add the remaining oil, and when hot, add the chicken, skin side down, and fry for 5 minutes, or until the chicken is browned and easily releases from the pan. Turn the pieces and brown on the other side. Pour off the excess fat from the pan.

Pour the reserved sauce over the chicken, reduce the heat, cover, and simmer until the chicken is done, about 30 to 40 minutes. Taste and adjust the seasonings.

Place the chicken along with the sauce in a large serving bowl, and serve with crusty French bread.

Yield: 4 to 6 servings

Chicken Biryani

This Pakistani and Indian rice dish has been described as a "dish fit for Shah Jehan, the creator of life." It's reserved for very special occasions, such as weddings, parties, holidays, religious holidays, and important dinners, so it's not an everyday dish. At large celebrations, men prepare biryani in large clay pots over charcoal fires, much as men here barbecue on backyard grills. This dish is of Moghul origin and can be made with lamb or, as in this recipe, chicken. It takes a while to prepare this dish in the traditional manner, but we've simplified it, so you don't need a special occasion.

1 pound chicken, cut in 1½-inch cubes; or substitute 4 boneless, skinless chicken breasts

3 tablespoons milk

1 teaspoon saffron

One 14-ounce can whole, peeled tomatoes, drained and chopped

½ teaspoon ground turmeric

3 green New Mexico chiles, roasted, peeled, stems and seeds removed, and chopped

2 bay leaves

2 to 3 cups chicken broth

1 cup long-grain rice, preferably basmati

1 tablespoon vegetable oil

½ cup sliced onions, separated into rings

¼ cup raisins

¼ cup blanched almonds

Salt to taste

Chopped hard-boiled eggs and chopped fresh mint for garnish

Marinade

12 whole cloves

20 black peppercorns

1½ teaspoons cumin seeds

One 2-inch piece cinnamon stick

2 teaspoons ground cardamom

1 teaspoon ground coriander

½ teaspoon ground mace

½ teaspoon ground turmeric

1 tablespoon chopped ginger

4 cloves garlic, chopped

1 onion, chopped

3 green chiles, such as serrano or jalapeno, stems and seeds removed, chopped

3 tablespoons lemon juice, preferably fresh

2 tablespoons chopped fresh mint leaves

1 cup low-fat plain yogurt

Note: This recipe requires advance preparation.

To make the marinade, heat a heavy skillet over high heat, add the cloves, peppercorns, cumin, and cinnamon, and dry-roast until the seeds darken and become fragrant, being careful that they don't burn. Allow the mixture to cool completely and then place in a spice mill or coffee grinder and process to a fine powder. Place all the marinade ingredients except the yogurt in a blender or food processor and process, using just enough water to form a paste.

Combine the spice paste and the yogurt in a nonreactive bowl and stir to mix. Add the chicken, toss to coat, and marinate overnight in the refrigerator.

Preheat the oven to 325°F.

Heat a small saucepan over low heat, add the milk, remove from the heat, and crumble the saffron over the top. Set aside to soak.

Remove the chicken pieces from the marinade.

Add the tomatoes, turmeric, New Mexican chiles, bay leaves, and 2 cups of the broth to the marinade and stir to mix.

Heat a saucepan over medium heat, add the marinade mix, and slowly bring to a simmer. Simmer the marinade for 5 minutes to blend the flavors. Stir in the rice.

Place the rice in the bottom of an ovenproof casserole dish and add the chicken, pushing the pieces down under the liquid. Pour the saffron milk over top of the casserole.

Cover the chicken and bake for 15 minutes. Remove the lid, stir the rice, and, adding more liquid to keep the dish from drying out, return the pan to the oven. Continue to bake for an additional 15 to 20 minutes. Test the chicken for doneness, and check that the rice is done. Let the casserole stand for 10 minutes.

Heat a small skillet over medium-high heat, add the oil, and when hot, add the onions, and fry until browned and crisp. Remove and drain. Add the raisins and fry until plump; remove and drain.

Ladle the rice and chicken onto a serving platter. Top with the fried onions, raisins, and almonds, garnish with the chopped eggs and mint, and serve.

Yield: 6 to 8 servings

Sanjay's Jeera Chicken

A high heat source is essential for preparing this dish; however, we have been able to closely re-create it on a stovetop. It was cooked for us outdoors at the Shikarbadi Hunting Lodge by guest chef Sanjay Anand over a large gas flame, and consequently took only a few minutes to prepare; at home it takes longer. Jeera is the Indian word for cumin, and because this dish is so highly spiced with cumin and black pepper, it's usually served over plain white rice. Sanjay says this chicken tastes better if the bones are left in, and he also mentioned that chile-heads are permitted to add red chile powder to this dish.

½ cup (1 stick) butter

1 to 2 cups chicken broth

One 2 to 3-pound chicken, skin removed, chopped into 3-inch cubes, bones and all

2 teaspoons salt

1½ teaspoons ground cumin

1 teaspoon whole cumin

1½ tablespoons freshly ground black pepper

2 cups cooked white rice

Heat a large saucepan over high heat. Add the butter, and when it's melted, whisk in 1 cup of the broth. Add the chicken and salt and cook for 2 to 3 minutes.

Add the cumin and black pepper, reduce the heat, and continue to cook for 20 to 25 minutes, stirring often. The sauce needs to be almost a paste, but add more broth if it gets too thick. The chicken is usually done when the butter returns to the top of the paste, but cut into a piece of the chicken to check.

To serve, mound the rice on a serving platter and top with the chicken and sauce.

Yield: 4 to 6 servings

Djeji Mechoui Tangiers
(Grilled Split Chicken Tangiers)

This is our take on how a chicken would be prepared in the port city of Tangiers, Morocco. We used la kama *seasoning, which originated here, to give Tangiers flavor. This dish can also be prepared with Cornish game hens, or the chicken can be left whole and cooked using a rotisserie. The skewers can be metal or wooden; they help to keep the chicken flat for even cooking.*

One 2 to 3-pound chicken

2 to 4 skewers

Chopped green olives for garnish

Seasoning Paste

½ cup (1 stick) butter, softened

2 tablespoons minced
fresh parsley

2 tablespoons minced fresh
cilantro

1 tablespoon *la kama* seasoning,
store-bought or homemade
(page 123)

1 tablespoon minced green onions

2 teaspoons minced garlic

1 teaspoon ground paprika

½ teaspoon ground cayenne

¼ teaspoon ground cumin

¼ teaspoon freshly ground
black pepper

Combine all the ingredients for the seasoning paste in a bowl and stir to mix.

To prepare the chicken, use poultry shears or a heavy knife to cut down both sides of the backbone and cut the hen in half. Remove the backbone and place the chicken on a cutting board, skin side up. Press hard on the breastbone to break it and flatten the bird.

Loosen the skin and rub the paste on the whole hen, over and under the skin.

Take the skewers and force one through the thigh perpendicular to the bone, just above the drumstick, into the breast, and out through the middle joint of the wing. Repeat for the other side of the hen.

Let the chicken marinate for 30 minutes at room temperature, or longer in the refrigerator, covered.

Heat a grill to medium-hot, place the skewered chicken on the grill, and grill slowly, turning as needed to brown evenly, for about 30 minutes, until the chicken is done and the internal temperature reaches 160°F.

To serve, cut the chicken into serving-size pieces, arrange on a platter, and garnish with the olives.

Yield: 4 servings

Southwest Shredded Chicken Tamales with Chile Verde

Preparing tamales for the Christmas holidays is a tradition in the Southwest. Shredded pork and red chile are the most common fillings for tamales, but since they can be filled with almost anything including poultry, seafood, fruits, and vegetables, we always include a batch of chicken tamales for variety. Tamales are surprisingly easy to make, and they become easier the more you make. They freeze well, so while you are making some, make a lot, and enjoy them all year long. Reheat by steaming or in the microwave oven; do not defrost before reheating, or they will become soggy. The name tamale *comes from the Nahuatl Indian word* tamalli, *and they are one of the oldest Mexican foods. These wrapped dishes have migrated north, and are as popular in New Mexico as they are in Old Mexico. Traditionally, lard is used as the fat in making tamales, but for the health-conscious, vegetable shortening can be substituted.*

Filling

2 to 3 cups cooked and shredded chicken

3 to 4 serrano chiles, stems removed, minced; or substitute 2 jalapeño chiles

½ cup minced onion

2 tablespoons chopped fresh cilantro

1 teaspoon minced garlic

1 teaspoon chopped fresh marjoram, or ½ teaspoon dried

½ cup grated *asadero* or Monterey Jack cheese

1½ to 2 cups *salsa verde* (page 164); or substitute a commercial tomatillo sauce

½ to ¾ cup Mexican *crema*; or substitute thin sour cream

Salt and freshly ground black pepper to taste

Tamales

24 dried corn husks (available in Latin markets)

4 cups dried masa

1 teaspoon baking powder

1 teaspoon salt

2½ cups vegetable broth or water

⅔ cup shortening

To prepare the filling, combine the chicken, chiles, onion, cilantro, garlic, marjoram, and cheese in a large bowl, and toss to combine. Add just enough of the salsa to hold the mixture together, lightly mix, and season with salt and pepper.

Place the corn husks in a shallow pan, cover with water, and soak to soften.

To prepare the masa, combine the masa, baking powder, and salt in a bowl and stir to mix. Slowly add the broth or water until the mixture holds together.

Whip or beat the shortening until fluffy. Add the masa to the shortening and continue to beat until fluffy. Drop a teaspoonful of the dough into a glass of cold water; if it floats, it is ready. If it sinks, continue to beat and test until it floats.

To assemble: Place a couple of tablespoons of the masa in the center of a large husk, or 2 smaller husks that are overlapped, and spread thinly. Place a couple of tablespoons of the filling down the center of the masa and top with a dollop of *crema*. Fold the husks around the masa and the filling. Use two strips of leftover corn husk, or two pieces of string, to tie the tamales at both ends.

Place a rack in the bottom of a steamer or large pot, and add water to cover the bottom. Arrange the tamales in the steamer, either standing up or in layers, but do not pack them tightly, as they will expand as they cook. Cover the tamales with a towel or additional corn husks. Steam until the masa has cooked, about 30 to 40 minutes. To test for doneness, open the end of one tamale; if the masa pulls away from the wrapper, it is done.

Allow to cool slightly, pile on a platter, and serve with a bowl of *salsa verde* on the side.

Yield: 24 tamales

African Groundnut Stew (Chicken and Peanut Stew)

Groundnuts, or peanuts, are one of the most popular and essential ingredients in West African cuisine. Dishes containing them are found in many countries and range from the simple, familiar "butter" made of pounded nuts to more complex recipes, such as the following peanut chile stew. Don't skip mixing the peanut butter with a little of the soup before adding to the pot, or the mixture may curdle.

1 small chicken, cut into pieces; or substitute 8 chicken thighs

Salt and freshly ground black pepper to taste

3 to 4 tablespoons vegetable oil, preferably peanut

2 carrots, peeled and diced

1 medium onion, diced

1 tablespoon grated ginger

2 teaspoons crushed red chile, such as piquin

½ teaspoon ground cumin

½ teaspoon ground white pepper

One 15-ounce can whole or diced tomatoes

3 tablespoons tomato paste

3 cups chicken broth

1 yam, peeled and cut in cubes

1 cup creamy peanut butter

Salt to taste

2 cups cooked rice

Chopped peanuts and a chopped hard-boiled egg for garnish

Season the chicken with salt and pepper. Heat a heavy stockpot or saucepan over medium-high heat, add the oil, and when hot, place the chicken in it, skin side down. Brown the chicken about 4 minutes, or until it releases from the pan. Don't crowd the pan; cook in batches if necessary. Turn the chicken and brown on the other side. Remove the chicken, put on a plate, and keep warm.

Pour off all but a couple of tablespoons of oil from the pan, add the carrots, onions, and ginger, and sauté until softened, about 5 minutes, scraping up the brown pieces from the bottom of the pan. Add the chile, cumin, and white pepper and sauté for another minute. Add the tomatoes, tomato paste, broth, and the reserved chicken and any juices that have accumulated on the plate. Bring the mixture to a boil, reduce the heat, and simmer for 15 minutes. Add the yams and continue to simmer until the chicken and yams are done, another 20 to 30 minutes. Skim off any fat that accumulates on the surface.

Combine the peanut butter with ½ cup of the soup in a bowl and stir until smooth. Stir this mixture into the stew and simmer for an additional 5 minutes, or until hot.

Place the rice in individual bowls, top with the stew, garnish with the peanuts and egg, and serve.

Yield: 4 to 6 servings

Gaeng Kheow Wan Gai (Green Curry Chicken)

Don't let the light, sweet aroma of basil and the creamy appearance of the sauce fool you. Of all the wonderful Thai chiles, this dish is always the hottest, which means it can be nearly nuclear. This is a curry that gets better with age, so if you can, prepare it a day ahead up to the point of adding the basil and chiles and refrigerate until ready for service. Commercial curry pastes are acceptable in this recipe, but it does taste best when prepared with a fresh paste. Since curry pastes can be frozen, keep some in the freezer to use in dishes like this. If using canned coconut cream, don't shake or mix the can before measuring—use the thicker cream on top for boiling with the paste.

½ cup coconut cream

¼ to ⅓ cup Thai green curry paste, store-bought or homemade (page 139)

2 chicken breasts, skin removed, cut in bite-size pieces

One 14-ounce can unsweetened coconut milk

1½ cups diced eggplant

1 tablespoon brown sugar

2 to 3 teaspoons Thai fish sauce (available in Asian markets)

6 fresh kaffir lime leaves, or substitute 4 dried (available in Asian markets; optional)

Salt to taste

⅓ cup fresh basil leaves, preferably Thai

4 red Thai chiles, stems and seeds removed, cut in strips; or substitute cayenne chiles

Fresh Thai basil leaves for garnish

Heat a heavy saucepan over medium heat, add the cream, and simmer gently until boiling. Boil for 6 to 8 minutes, or until the cream forms a sheen on top. Add the curry paste and, using the back of a spoon, mash the paste until it becomes smooth. Continue to fry until the mixture darkens and becomes very fragrant, about 2 to 3 minutes. Add the chicken and stir to coat the pieces.

Stir in enough of the coconut milk to reach the desired consistency. Add the eggplant, sugar, fish sauce, lime leaves, if using, and salt to taste. Gently simmer the sauce for 8 to 10 minutes, or until the chicken and eggplant are done. Taste and adjust the seasonings.

Add the basil and chile and continue to cook for an additional 2 minutes.

To serve, remove the kaffir lime leaves, place the curry in a serving bowl, and garnish with the fresh basil leaves.

Yield: 4 to 6 servings

11
Fishes
& Seafood

Bayou Shrimp and Wilted Spinach Salad with Triple Mustard Dressing

In this recipe, three different types of mustard are used. If you want to increase the spice level, add more of the dry mustard, as it will increase the pungency without altering the taste. Any type of loose-leaf lettuce may be used in place of the spinach. Heating the dressing brings out the tangy flavor of the mustard. This is a great summer entrée salad; prepare the salad and dressing, grill the shrimp, and assemble the salad at the table.

1 to 1½ pounds medium shrimp, shelled and deveined

2 to 2½ tablespoons Creole seasoning, store-bought or homemade (page 169)

2 teaspoons vegetable oil

One 10-ounce package baby spinach, or 1 bunch spinach, rinsed and torn in pieces

1 small red onion, sliced thinly in rings and separated, for garnish

Dressing

6 tablespoons extra-virgin olive oil

3 tablespoons red wine vinegar

2 tablespoons Creole mustard, store-bought or homemade (page 168)

2 teaspoons Dijon-style mustard, store-bought or homemade (page 117)

1 teaspoon dry mustard, mixed with 2 teaspoons cold water

¼ teaspoon dried thyme

Salt and freshly ground black pepper

Put the shrimp in a large bowl, and toss with the Creole seasoning to coat well. Marinate the shrimp for 30 minutes at room temperature.

Heat a heavy skillet over medium-high heat, add the oil and when hot, add the shrimp and sauté for about 3 minutes, or until just done. Be careful not to overcook the shrimp or it will toughen. Let the shrimp cool.

Combine the spinach with the onion in a large salad bowl. Top with the cooled shrimp and chill.

To make the dressing, whisk the olive oil, vinegar, three mustards, and thyme together in a saucepan. Season with salt and pepper. Bring the mixture to a boil over medium heat, stirring constantly until all the ingredients are combined and the dressing is hot.

Pour the hot dressing over the salad, and toss to coat well. Garnish with the onion rings, and serve.

Yield: 4 servings

Note: This recipe requires advance preparation.

Tamarind Mint Shrimp Curry

This recipe has its culinary roots in southwest India, where many of the curries are both fragrant as well as colorful. The flavor of this one is enhanced by freshly roasting and grinding the spices for the dry masala. Tamarind, known also as Indian date, is a popular ingredient in curries, where it acts as a souring agent in much the same way as vinegar or lemon juice. In this dish, the explosion of the mint offsets the heat of the chile.

⅓ cup tamarind pulp (available in Asian markets)

2 teaspoons whole black peppercorns

1 teaspoon fenugreek seeds

1 teaspoon coriander seeds

1 teaspoon cardamom seeds

3 medium tomatoes

1 teaspoon vegetable oil

1 teaspoon brown mustard seeds

½ cup chopped onion

4 cloves garlic, minced

1 teaspoon grated ginger

1 cup coconut milk

¼ teaspoon ground cayenne

½ teaspoon ground turmeric

2 green chiles, such as serranos, stems and seeds removed, minced

2 pounds large shrimp, shelled and deveined

¼ cup fresh mint leaves

Salt to taste

Combine the tamarind pulp and 1 cup very warm water in a bowl and let steep for 20 minutes. Squeeze the pulp to extract the juice and then discard, reserving the liquid.

Heat a small, heavy skillet over high heat, add the peppercorns, fenugreek, coriander, and cardamom seeds, and dry-roast until the spices darken and become fragrant, but not burned. Allow the mixture to cool completely.

Place the toasted mixture in a spice mill or coffee grinder and process to a fine powder.

Place the tomatoes and the spice mixture in a blender or food processor and puree until smooth.

Heat a large, heavy skillet over medium heat, add the oil, and when hot, add the mustard seeds. As soon as the mustard seeds begin to pop, add the onion, garlic, and ginger, and fry until the mixture is lightly browned. Add the coconut milk, reserved tamarind liquid, cayenne, turmeric, chiles, and spice paste. Bring the mixture to a boil, stirring constantly, reduce the heat and simmer the sauce for 5 minutes or until thickened.

Add the shrimp and mint to the curry, and simmer over low heat until the shrimp is done, about 5 minutes. Season with salt to taste and serve hot.

Yield: 4 servings

Horseradish Potato-Crusted Salmon

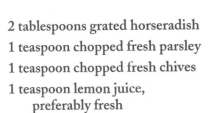

This is an easy-to-make entrée that can be prepared with other strong-flavored fish, such as grouper or mahi mahi, as the pungency of the horseradish will complement the taste. A mild fish will be overwhelmed—and any fish will be overpowered if you use too much topping. Don't, however, skimp on the fat, as it is needed to give a crisp, toasted texture to the topping.

2 tablespoons grated horseradish

1 teaspoon chopped fresh parsley

1 teaspoon chopped fresh chives

1 teaspoon lemon juice, preferably fresh

½ teaspoon dried thyme leaves

½ teaspoon minced garlic

1 small potato, boiled until just tender, chilled, and then peeled

Salt and coarsely ground black pepper

3 tablespoons melted butter

Two 6-ounce salmon steaks

Preheat the oven to 400°F.

Combine the horseradish, parsley, chives, lemon juice, thyme, and garlic in a bowl, and mix to form a paste. Set aside.

In another bowl, grate the potato, using the large holes on grater. Don't apply too much pressure, since you'll want fairly thin shavings. Season with salt and pepper, and toss with 2 tablespoons of the butter.

Place the steaks on a baking sheet and brush with the remaining butter. Top with an even coating of the horseradish mixture. Gently pat the potato on top of the coating so that it sticks to the fish.

Bake for 15 to 18 minutes, or until the fish is done and the crust has browned. If the fish is almost done and the crust hasn't browned, place it under the broiler for a few minutes.

Yield: 2 servings

Variation: Mashed potatoes can be used in place of the grated potatoes.

Thai Pineapple Prawn Curry

Thai curries, unlike their Indian counterparts, are quite quick to prepare, usually taking only a few minutes on the stove once all the ingredients have been assembled. They are also thinner in texture. The kaffir lime leaves in this dish give a sharp citrus flavor as well as a wonderful aroma to the curry. Used like bay leaves, they are removed before the dish is served. This is a delicate, yet hot, curry with a sweet and sour flavor. Substitute smoked salmon for the prawns for a tasty variation.

½ cup coconut cream

2 to 3 tablespoons Thai red curry paste, store-bought or homemade (page 138)

1 stalk lemongrass

1 cup coconut milk

1 tablespoon minced ginger

1 tablespoon tamarind paste

3 fresh kaffir lime leaves; or substitute dried (if unavailable, use ½ teaspoon lime zest)

2 teaspoons sugar

2 to 3 teaspoons Thai fish sauce

1 teaspoon grated galangal (optional)

1 cup chopped fresh pineapple, including any juice

1½ pounds prawns or large shrimp, peeled and deveined

2 cups cooked rice

Chopped fresh cilantro for garnish

Heat a heavy saucepan over medium heat, add the cream, and heat until gently boiling. Boil for 6 to 8 minutes or until the cream forms a sheen on top. Add the curry paste and, using the back of a spoon, mash the paste until it becomes smooth. Continue to fry until the mixture darkens and becomes very fragrant.

Trim the stalk of lemongrass to about 3 inches in length. Trim away any hard portions and discard the outer leaves. Cut into 1-inch pieces.

Stir the coconut milk into the curry paste mixture, add the lemongrass, ginger, tamarind, kaffir lime leaves, sugar, fish sauce, and galangal, if using. Simmer the sauce for 5 minutes to blend the flavors.

Add the pineapple and prawns, and continue to simmer until the prawns turn pink and opaque. Be careful not to overcook the prawns, or they will toughen. Taste and adjust the seasonings.

Remove the kaffir lime leaves, place the curry in a serving bowl, garnish with the cilantro, and serve.

Yield: 4 servings

Wasabi-Flavored Asian Fish Fillets in Rice-Paper Wrapping

Wrapping fish in rice paper before cooking not only seals in the flavor, but keeps the fish moist, while providing a nice crunchy taste. It also enables you to cook the fish with a minimal amount of oil. Easily found in Asian markets and grocery stores, rice-paper wrappings need to be moistened with water first to make them pliable. In this recipe, you can use either wasabi powder or paste. If using a powder, reconstitute it with a tablespoon of the vinegar, and let sit for a couple of minutes to develop the flavor of the wasabi. Ahi tuna fillets also work well in this dish. Lemon-spiced rice, stir-fried green beans, and Sambal Oelek *(page 141) are nice accompaniments to the fish bundles.*

1 tablespoon wasabi powder or paste

3 tablespoons rice vinegar

1 teaspoon sugar

1 teaspoon powdered ginger

¼ teaspoon sesame oil

Four 1-inch thick cod or haddock fillets

2 green onions, finely sliced, including some of the greens

Four 8½-inch round rice-paper wrappings

1 tablespoon vegetable oil

If using powdered wasabi, combine it with 1 tablespoon vinegar, and stir to form a paste. Allow it to sit for 5 minutes for the flavor to develop.

Combine the wasabi, vinegar, sugar, ginger, and sesame oil in a bowl to make the sauce.

Using a pastry brush, lightly moisten the rice paper with water on both sides. Place 1 piece of fish in the center of each wrapper. Spoon some of the sauce over the fish, and top with the green onions. Fold the wrappers around the pieces of fish and close securely. Reserve the remaining sauce.

Heat a large, heavy skillet over medium-high heat, add the oil, and when hot, set the fish in the pan, seam side down, and cook until lightly browned, about 3 minutes. Turn, cover, and cook the fish for an additional 3 minutes. Remove from the heat, cover, and set aside to steam for 4 minutes.

Transfer the fish bundles to individual plates, open, spoon some of the reserved sauce over the top, and serve.

Yield: 4 servings

Marinated Grilled Fish with Malaysian Spice Paste

The heat in this fish dish comes from the inside out. It should be spicy, so increase the chiles to suit your taste. The paste can also be thinned to make a marinade, used as a rub for any meat, poultry, or fish, or used as a base for a sauce. Serve a bowl of Sambal Tomat *(page 142) on the side for additional heat if desired.*

Fish

One 2- to 3-pound whole snapper or pompano, cleaned and dressed

2 tablespoons lime juice, preferably fresh

Salt

Vegetable oil, preferably peanut

2 cups cooked rice

Spice Paste

2 tablespoons vegetable oil, preferably peanut

1 cup chopped onions

4 cloves garlic, chopped

1½ tablespoons chopped ginger

6 dried cayenne chiles, stems and seeds removed

2 teaspoons cardamom seeds

2 teaspoons poppy seeds

½ teaspoon ground nutmeg

1 teaspoon ground cloves

½ teaspoon ground turmeric

2 anchovy fillets, optional

Zest of 1 lime

10 macadamia nuts

½ cup coconut milk

To make the paste, heat a heavy skillet over medium heat, add the oil and when hot, add the onion and sauté until softened. Add the garlic and ginger, and continue to sauté for an additional 2 minutes.

Place all the ingredients for the spice paste, except the coconut milk, in a blender or food processor, and with the machine running, slowly pour in enough coconut milk to make a paste.

Score the fish on both sides, rub with the lime juice, and sprinkle with salt. Rub some of the paste on the outside of the fish, making sure to get it into the slits, and fill the cavity with the remaining paste. Marinate for an hour at room temperature.

Liberally oil the grill, or put the fish in a grilling basket. Place the fish on the grill indirectly over a medium fire, baste with oil, and cook for about 20 minutes, turning twice. To test for doneness, run a sharp knife along the backbone and gently lift. If it pulls away from the bone, it's done. If you grill the fish until it flakes, it will be too dry.

Place the fish on a serving platter, and spoon white rice around it. Carve the fish at the table, and serve it on the rice with a *sambal* on the side.

Yield: 4 to 6 servings

Togarashi Ginger-Glazed Swordfish

This dish has a sweet, hot flavor that needs a strongly flavored fish, or the taste of the fish will be lost. Beware, the heat builds, so don't add more seasoning after the first taste. The cucumber slaw is a cool complement to the "hot" fish. Quick and easy to prepare, it makes a great summer grill entrée, especially when served with Cucumber Slaw (page 374).

4 swordfish steaks

Shichimi togarashi, store-bought or homemade (page 146)

2 cups cooked rice

Glaze

⅓ cup rice wine

2 tablespoons orange juice, preferably fresh

1 tablespoon Dijon-style mustard, store-bought or homemade (page 117)

1 tablespoon brown sugar

1 teaspoon grated ginger

½ teaspoon *shichimi togarashi*, store-bought or homemade (page 146)

½ teaspoon soy sauce

¼ teaspoon freshly ground black pepper

Lime slices for garnish

Liberally sprinkle both sides of the swordfish with the *shichimi togarashi* and let the fish sit at room temperature for 30 minutes.

Heat a small saucepan over high heat, add all the glaze ingredients, and heat to just boiling. Reduce the heat and simmer until the glaze is reduced by half. Allow the mixture to cool.

Liberally oil the grill and heat to medium hot. Brush the glaze on the fish, and grill until done, about 5 minutes per side. Turn the fish a couple of times, brushing frequently with the glaze.

Mound the rice in the center of a serving platter, and arrange the swordfish and garnish with the lime slices. Serve with Cucumber Slaw on the side.

Yield: 4 servings

Panko-Encrusted Triggerfish with Wasabi and Caper Cream Sauce

🔥 Panko *are Japanese-style bread crumbs made from wheat, but lighter than traditional bread crumbs, so they are able to provide a crispy coating without overpowering a delicate fish. If you can't find* panko, *just grill the fish and serve the sauce. The creamy sauce gives a good hit of wasabi without being harsh and overpowering; a mellow mixture of flavors is blended so that the wasabi is rather surprising. This is a quick, simple, and easy-to-prepare dish with an elegant presentation.*

4 triggerfish fillets; or substitute ocean perch or snapper

1 egg

2 to 3 cups *panko* (available in Asian markets)

Vegetable oil

Sauce

1 tablespoon wasabi powder

1 teaspoon vegetable oil

1 teaspoon chopped green onion

1 teaspoon chopped shallots

2 tablespoons rice vinegar

2 to 3 drops dark sesame oil

½ to ¾ cup heavy cream

Salt to taste

1 tablespoons capers

To make the sauce, combine the wasabi powder along with 1 tablespoon hot water and stir to form a paste. Let sit for 5 minutes for the flavor to develop.

Heat a small, heavy saucepan over medium to medium-high heat, add the oil, and when hot, add the onion and shallots. Sauté until they have softened. Add the vinegar and sesame oil, and simmer for a couple of minutes. Stir in the cream, and season with salt. Raise the heat, and cook to reduce the sauce and thicken. Remove from the heat, and stir in the wasabi and capers.

To prepare the fish, whisk the egg in a shallow dish or bowl. In another bowl, pour in the *panko* crumbs.

Heat a heavy skillet over medium-high heat, add the oil to the depth of an inch, and heat.

Dip the fish in the egg and then the *panko* crumbs until coated. Add the fish to the skillet, and fry until browned and done.

Serve the fish with the sauce over the top or in a bowl on the side.

Yield: 4 servings

Grilled Tuna Melt
with Wasabi Mayonnaise

The tuna salad used in this recipe is a "kitchen sink" combination. It was concocted from ingredients that we had on hand, and even though it may seem like an odd combination, the flavors seem to meld together. You can prepare it as a usual tuna melt and put it under the broiler or grill the sandwich. If you have the equipment, it makes a great panini. The higher the quality of tuna the better the sandwich, and if you're feeling decadent, using any leftover ahi tuna will turn this into a truly gourmet sandwich.

Two 6-ounce cans tuna, drained

¼ cup chopped green onions

2 tablespoons coarsely chopped capers

2 tablespoons chopped fresh cilantro or parsley

1 tablespoon lemon juice, preferably fresh

2 to 3 drops sesame oil

¼ cup wasabi mayonnaise, store-bought or homemade

Salt and freshly ground pepper to taste

Grated Monterey Jack cheese

2 *ciabatta* rolls, or other crusty rolls with a soft, chewy crumb

Wasabi Mayonnaise

¼ cup mayonnaise

1 tablespoon wasabi paste; or substitute wasabi powder

1 teaspoon lemon juice

1 teaspoon sherry, optional

Combine all the ingredients for the wasabi mayonnaise in a bowl and mix well.

Combine the tuna, onions, capers, cilantro, lemon juice, and sesame oil in a bowl, and stir to mix. Add just enough of the mayonnaise to hold the mixture together. Season to taste with salt and pepper.

Split each roll horizontally, and remove some inner crumb from the bottom half of the roll. Spread with the tuna mixture, and top with the cheese.

Place the sandwiches open-faced under the broiler, 4 inches from the flame, and heat until the cheese melts, about 2 minutes.

Serve the tuna melts open-faced, or as a sandwich with the top in place.

Yield: 4 servings

Grilled Ponzu-Marinated Sea Scallop Brochettes

 This is one of those entrées that can be served as an appetizer or prepared with other seafood such as fish cubes or shrimp. Ponzu *sauce is a sake-, soy-, and citrus-based sauce that is traditionally used in Japanese cuisine as a dipping sauce. Here we have used it in a marinade, a baste for the scallops while grilling, and a sauce to serve with the brochettes. The salty, tangy, and sweet flavors of the* ponzu *sauce combine with ginger and red pepper for a light and spicy basting sauce that enhances the scallops without overpowering them.*

12 cremini mushrooms, stems removed

1½ pounds scallops

1 small onion, cut into wedges

¼ cup vegetable oil

2 teaspoons cornstarch mixed with 2 teaspoons water

4 skewers

Basting Sauce

⅔ cup *ponzu* sauce, store-bought or homemade (recipe below)

2 tablespoons vegetable oil

2 teaspoons grated ginger

1 teaspoon crushed red pepper, such as piquin

2 green onions, chopped, including some of the greens

Freshly ground black pepper to taste

Ponzu Sauce

1 cup orange juice, preferably fresh

½ cup sake

¼ cup sugar

¼ cup soy sauce

2 tablespoons lime juice, preferably fresh

¼ teaspoon crushed red pepper, such as piquin

1½ teaspoons cornstarch mixed with 2 teaspoons water

Combine all the ingredients for the basting sauce in a bowl, and stir to mix. Add the mushrooms, and allow the mixture to sit at room temperature for the flavors to blend and the mushrooms to marinate.

Blanch the scallops in boiling water for 2½ minutes. Drain, cool, and pat dry. Combine the scallops, onions, and vegetable oil in a bowl, and toss to coat.

Thread the scallops, onions, and mushrooms on skewers, beginning and ending with the scallops.

Heat the grill to medium-hot and grill the scallops until they are golden brown on the outside and opaque throughout, 5 to 6 minutes, turning occasionally and basting continually with the sauce.

Heat a small saucepan over high heat, add the remaining sauce, and bring to a boil. Simmer the sauce for a couple of minutes, stir in the cornstarch mixture, and simmer to thicken.

Serve the kebabs with the basting sauce on the side.

Yield: 4 servings

Ponzu Sauce

Heat a small saucepan over high heat, add all the ingredients, bring to a boil, and cook until the sugar dissolves and the sauce is reduced to 1¼ cups, about 5 minutes. Stir in the cornstarch mixture and cook, stirring constantly, until the sauce thickens and turns clear, about 1 minute.

Yield: 1 cup

Charmoula Salmon en Papillote with North African Salsa

Although this method of cooking fish is not traditional in North Africa, the charmoula *seasoning is traditionally used for fish in Morocco. We've also added a typical salsa to the packets; although not authentic, it's reminiscent of a fish dish that Nancy enjoyed in Marrakech.*

4 salmon fillets; or substitute pompano, snapper, cod, or halibut

½ cup *charmoula* seasoning, store-bought or homemade (page 121)

8 lemon slices

Parchment paper; or substitute aluminum foil

1 egg white

North African Salsa

2 tomatoes, diced

¼ cup diced onions

8 to 10 green olives, chopped

1 to 2 tablespoons capers

1 tablespoon lemon juice, preferably fresh

2 teaspoons extra-virgin olive oil

Salt and freshly ground black pepper to taste

Note: This recipe requires advance preparation.

Preheat the oven to 475°F. Place the fish on a platter and, using a sharp knife, score it deeply. Spoon the *charmoula* seasoning over the fillets, making sure the seasoning gets down into the cuts. Marinate the fish for 2 to 4 hours in the refrigerator.

Combine all the ingredients for the salsa in a bowl, and stir to mix. Allow the salsa to sit for an hour to blend the flavors, then drain off any accumulated liquid.

To assemble the packets, cut a 12-inch square, either from parchment paper or foil. Place the fish in the center of the square. Spoon the salsa on the fillets, and top with the lemon wedges.

If using parchment paper, brush the edges of the paper with the egg white, fold the square over, and make small folds to seal the packet. Do not tightly enclose the fish; there needs to be space for the steam to puff up the bag. If using foil, don't brush with the egg, as the foil will seal tightly without it.

Place the packets on a baking sheet, and bake in the middle of the oven, 10 minutes for each inch thickness of the fillets.

To serve, place the puffed bags on individual plates, and pass around a pair of scissors so guests can cut open their individual packets.

Yield: 4 servings

Grilled Cedar-Planked Pacific Northwest Salmon, Oriental Style

Planking produces a fish that is moist and flavorful, as well as low in fat. The technique is fairly easy to execute on a grill or in an oven, but you do need a plank. Prepared planks are available online or in specialty barbecue shops, but you can easily make one yourself. Buy a piece of cedar 14 x 7 x 2 inches. Be sure to buy untreated lumber, since the chemicals in treated lumber are poisonous. Lightly sand the cooking side, and season with olive or vegetable oil.

1 untreated cedar plank

One 2-pound salmon fillet, 1 inch thick

Toasted sesame seeds and chopped fresh cilantro or parsley for garnish

Asian Sauce

2 tablespoons minced ginger

3 green onions, minced

2 tablespoons black rice vinegar; or substitute balsamic vinegar

Juice of 2 limes

1 tablespoon soy sauce

1 tablespoon brown sugar

Salt and freshly ground black pepper

⅓ cup vegetable oil, preferably peanut

1 tablespoon sesame oil

Sink the plank in a pan of water and weigh it down with something like a brick to ensure that it stays submerged. Soak at least 4 hours, or overnight.

To make the sauce, combine the ginger, green onions, vinegar, lime juice, soy sauce, and brown sugar in a bowl, and whisk to mix. Slowly add the oils to the mix, whisking until the sauce emulsifies and becomes thick. Let sit at room temperature for 30 minutes to blend the flavors. Remove about 2 tablespoons and set aside.

Preheat the grill to medium.

Brush the top, or smooth side, of the plank with vegetable oil, and place the fish, skin side down, on it. Brush the sauce over the fish, place the plank on the center of the grill, and close the lid.

Grill for 10 minutes, brush again with the sauce, close the lid, and cook until the fish is done and easily flakes, about another 10 minutes.

Remove the plank from the grill and, with a clean brush, coat the fish with the reserved sauce. Garnish with the sesame seeds and cilantro, and serve the fish on the plank.

Yield: 6 to 8 servings

Note: This recipe requires advance preparation.

Grilled Tuna Steaks with Salsa Pimentón

 In this seafood specialty from Spain, the pimentón *is used in the marinade and in the sauce that seasons it at serving. Salmon steaks, or the steaks of any large fish, may be substituted. Serve with a Caesar salad and saffron rice.*

2 tablespoons extra-virgin olive oil

3 tablespoons hot *pimentón*; or substitute New Mexican chile powder and chipotle chile powder in equal proportions

2 tablespoons chopped fresh flat-leaf parsley

Salt and freshly ground black pepper to taste

Four 1-inch-thick tuna steaks

1 cup chopped red onion

6 cloves garlic, minced

2 medium tomatoes, chopped

2 red bell peppers, roasted, peeled, stems and seeds removed, and chopped

½ cup minced green olives

Fresh flat-leaf parsley for garnish

Note: This recipe requires advance preparation.

Combine 1 tablespoon of the oil, 1 tablespoon of the *pimentón*, and the parsley in a bowl, and stir to mix. Season to taste with salt and pepper. Rub the mixture over both sides of the tuna steaks, cover, and marinate for 1 hour at room temperature.

Heat a saucepan over medium heat, add the remaining oil, and when hot, add the onion, garlic, and another tablespoon of *pimentón*, and sauté for about 2 minutes. Add the tomatoes and bell peppers, and cook until the mixture thickens, about 5 to 10 minutes.

Place the onion mixture in a blender or food processor, add the remaining *pimentón* and the olives, and puree to a smooth sauce.

Return the sauce to the saucepan and gently simmer.

Grill the fish over a medium fire to the desired doneness, or cook under the broiler.

To serve, place the fish on individual plates, pour the sauce over the top, and garnish with the parsley.

Yield: 4 servings

Fried Flying Fish
with Bajan Seasoning

Dave collected a great number of variations on this popular Bajan specialty in Barbados, but this is probably our favorite version. Flying fish is sometimes available frozen in Florida markets; if it's not available, substitute any mild white fish. This dish is always served with a Bajan hot sauce, such as Windmill or Lottie's, which are readily available from online suppliers.

8 small flying fish fillets, or substitute flounder

Bajan seasoning as needed, store-bought or homemade (page 149)

½ cup bread crumbs

½ cup all-purpose flour

1 tablespoon minced parsley

1 tablespoon minced fresh thyme, or 1 teaspoon dried

Salt and freshly ground black pepper

2 eggs

½ cup butter or margarine

Lime slices and chopped fresh parsley for garnish

Rub the fish with the Bajan seasoning, and place on a plate. Marinate the fillets for 30 minutes at room temperature.

Combine the bread crumbs, flour, parsley, thyme, salt, and pepper in a shallow bowl, and stir to mix.

In another shallow bowl, beat the eggs. Dip the fish in the eggs, let them drain slightly, then dip in the bread crumb mixture.

Heat a heavy skillet over medium heat, add the butter and when hot, add the fish. Fry the fillets until lightly browned, turning once.

To serve, place the fish on a serving platter, garnish with the lime slices and parsley, and serve with the hot sauce on the side.

Yield: 4 servings

Note: This recipe requires advance preparation.

Fish Tacos, Baja Style

Recently Nancy went on a quest to find the perfect legendary Baja fish taco. After traveling almost the length of the peninsula, tasting tacos along the way, she found what she was looking for at a small taco stand called Leonelly's. The batter used to coat the fish varied with the cook, but a wok-shaped disc seemed to be the pan of choice for frying the fish. Leonelly shared this very easy recipe with Nancy; it makes fish that is crisp and tasty, in a coating that doesn't overpower the flavor of the fish. She also noted that some cooks swear that you must use shark fillets, but any firm white fish works well. Serve these tacos as they do in the Baja, with a table full of condiments to use as toppings.

1 large lime
4 white fish fillets, cut in strips about 1 inch wide
2 eggs
1 cup all-purpose flour
Salt

Vegetable oil for frying
8 corn tortillas

Condiments
Salsa verde (page 164)
Salsa de chile de arbol (page 154)

Mexican *crema* or sour cream
Shredded cabbage
Chopped radishes
Chopped tomatoes
Chopped fresh cilantro

Cut the lime in half and squeeze the juice over the fish. Allow the fish to marinate while preparing the batter.

To make the batter, break the eggs in a bowl and whisk. While mixing with a fork, gradually add only enough flour to form a thin batter. Season the batter with salt.

Heat a heavy skillet or wok over medium-high heat, pour in the oil to a depth of 1 to 2-inches, depending on the thickness of the fish, and heat to 365°F.

Dip the fish in the batter and let the excess drip off. Carefully slide the fish in the oil, and fry until the fish is done and the batter is golden brown, about 3 minutes, turning once. Remove and drain on paper towels.

Wrap the tortillas in a towel and microwave on high for 30 seconds.

Place the fish in the tortillas and serve. Serve the condiments in small bowls and allow guests to top the tacos as they desire.

Yield: 4 servings

Zhua Chao Yu (Fried Ginger Prawns)

Deep-fried Chinese food is not heavy, since the Chinese use cornstarch, rather than flour, as a coating. Cornstarch not only produces a light crust that allows the shrimp flavor to come through, it also protects the shrimp from overcooking. Although this is a simple dish, the flavors are complex; the spice of the ginger tempers the tartness of the lemon, and both complement the flavor of the shrimp. An easy dish to prepare, it can be served as an entrée, appetizer, or just one of a number of dishes on a Chinese banquet table.

¾ cup cornstarch

12 ounces prawns or jumbo shrimp, peeled and deveined

Vegetable oil for frying, preferably peanut

2 tablespoons chopped green onion

3 tablespoons grated ginger

2 cups cooked white rice

Lemon slices for garnish

Sauce

2 teaspoons light soy sauce

1 tablespoon Chinese black vinegar

1 tablespoon rice wine or dry sherry

1 teaspoon sugar

½ teaspoon dark sesame oil

Salt and freshly ground white pepper

Combine all the ingredients for the sauce in a small bowl, and stir to mix.

In another bowl, combine the cornstarch with enough water to make a thin paste. Add the prawns, and turn to coat.

Heat a wok or heavy skillet over medium-high heat, pour in the oil to a depth of a couple of inches, and when hot, add the prawns, and stir-fry until they are just golden, about 1½ minutes. Remove and drain on paper towels. Pour off all but 1 tablespoon of the oil from the wok.

Add the onions and ginger to the wok, and stir-fry for 45 seconds. Add the sauce, and bring to a boil. Return the prawns to the wok, and turn carefully in the sauce until the sauce has been completely absorbed into the fish, about 1 minute.

Place the prawns on a serving platter, accompanied by the rice.

Yield: 4 servings

Mustard-Glazed Halibut Fillets

Talk about quick and easy—this dish goes from the refrigerator to the table in less than 30 minutes. And it's healthy too. This recipe can also be prepared on the grill; since the glaze goes on last, the sugar in the glaze won't burn. The balsamic vinegar, brown sugar, and ginger do give it a slightly sweet taste, but the mustard and wasabi keep the sweetness from being overpowering. A crisp garden salad or steamed vegetable will round out the meal.

4 halibut fillets, about 1 inch thick; or substitute salmon or cod

2 tablespoons vegetable oil, preferably peanut

Salt and freshly ground black pepper

Glaze

¼ cup balsamic vinegar

2 teaspoons brown sugar

2 teaspoons Dijon-style mustard, store-bought or homemade (page 117)

1 teaspoon wasabi paste

½ teaspoon grated ginger

2 teaspoons chopped green onion, including some of the greens

Combine all the ingredients for the glaze in a bowl, and set aside.

Brush some of the oil on the fish, and season with salt and pepper.

Heat a heavy skillet over medium-high heat, add the remaining oil, and when hot, add the fish, and cook until browned on one side, about 4 minutes. Turn the fillets, and top each piece with the glaze. Lower the heat, and cook until the fish is opaque but still moist, an additional 4 to 5 minutes.

Place on individual plates and serve.

Yield: 4 servings

Louisiana Barbecue Shrimp

In New Orleans, this dish is called a barbecue, but it really is shrimp cooked in a sauce, rather than on a conventional grill. Traditionally it's served with the shells on the shrimp to be peeled at the table, with a finger bowl to clean hands after the feast. An interesting blend of unusual ingredients, such as rosemary and Worcestershire, somehow work in the sauce. This recipe uses a chef's trick of adding butter to a sauce at the end of the cooking to round out and bind it. Be sure to serve the shrimp on plain, white rice with a crusty French bread to sop up the sauce—and, of course, a cold beer and a bottle of Louisana-style hot sauce!

1½ to 2 pounds shrimp, shelled and deveined

2 tablespoons Creole seasoning, store-bought or homemade (page 169)

2 to 3 tablespoons virgin olive oil

2 tablespoons chopped fresh rosemary

2 teaspoons chopped garlic

½ cup beer

3 tablespoons lemon juice, preferably fresh

3 tablespoons Worcestershire sauce

2 tablespoons brown sugar

1½ teaspoons dried thyme

1 teaspoon dried oregano

¼ teaspoon ground cayenne

Salt and freshly ground black pepper

1 tablespoon butter

Chopped fresh parsley for garnish

2 cups cooked rice

Combine the shrimp and 1 tablespoon of the Creole seasoning in a bowl, and toss to coat. Allow the shrimp to marinate at room temperature for 30 minutes.

Heat a heavy skillet over medium heat, add the oil, and when hot, add the rosemary and garlic, and sauté until the garlic is lightly browned, being careful not to let it burn. Add the shrimp and stir carefully, cooking until just done. Remove and keep warm.

Add the beer to the skillet, raise the heat, and deglaze the pan, being sure to scrape up any bits and pieces from the pan. Add the lemon juice, Worcestershire sauce, sugar, thyme, oregano, cayenne, salt, and pepper. Reduce the heat, and simmer the sauce to reduce and thicken.

Return the shrimp to the sauce, and stir in the butter.

To serve, mound the rice in the bottom of individual bowls, top with the shrimp, garnish with the parsley, and serve with a slice of bread.

Yield: 4 servings

Note: This recipe requires advance preparation.

Pan-Seared Swordfish Steaks with Christophene Ratatouille Laced with Curry Essence

This recipe was shared with us by our friends at Peter Island, in the British Virgin Islands, who also prepare it with tuna or other thick fish steaks, such as striped bass or salmon.

Christophene is another name for chayote, cho-cho, or mirliton, a gnarled, pear-shaped member of the squash or gourd family. First cultivated by the Aztecs and the Maya, it appears in recipes in many tropical areas, including Florida and Louisiana. We've included a recipe for a large amount of the curry essence, as it can be used to add a curry flavor to many dishes. Stored in a jar in a cool dark place or the refrigerator, it will keep for 6 months.

2 tablespoons minced fresh parsley

2 teaspoons coarsely ground black pepper

1 teaspoon coarsely ground white pepper

1 teaspoon ground coriander

Four 1-inch-thick swordfish steaks

2 shallots, minced

1 red bell pepper, stem and seeds removed, cut in small dice

1 christophene, cut in cubes; or substitute yellow squash

1 green zucchini, cut in cubes

1 small eggplant, cut in cubes

Salt and freshly ground black pepper

Chopped fresh parsley for garnish

Curry Essence

2 cups vegetable oil

4 shallots, chopped

2 tablespoons grated ginger

1 tablespoon coriander seeds

1 tablespoon black peppercorns

½ cup chopped fresh cilantro

½ cup West Indian masala, store-bought or homemade (page 151)

To prepare the essence, heat a heavy skillet over medium heat, add 3 tablespoons of the oil and when hot, add the shallots, ginger, coriander, and peppercorns, and sauté until the shallots are soft. Reduce the heat to low, add the cilantro and masala, and continue to cook for 1 minute, then add the remaining oil, and simmer for 10 minutes. Remove, and steep the mixture for 30 minutes. Pass the mixture through a fine sieve, pressing on it slightly. You'll want the essence to be clear.

Combine the minced parsley, black and white pepper, and coriander on a plate, and stir to mix. Brush the ends of the steaks with the curry essence, and roll the ends of the fish then in the parsley mixture, and set aside.

Heat a heavy skillet over medium heat, add 2 tablespoons of the essence, and when hot, add the shallots and bell pepper, and sauté until softened. Add the squashes and eggplant, and continue to sauté until they are just softened. Season to taste with salt and pepper.

Heat a large nonstick sauté pan over medium-high heat, add 2 tablespoons of the essence, and when hot but not smoking, add the fish and cook for 2 minutes. Turn the fish and cook the other side 3 to 4 minutes, or until the fish is opaque all the way though.

To serve, place the ratatouille on individual plates and top with the fish. Drizzle some of the curry essence all around the vegetables, garnish with the parsley, and serve.

Yield: 4 servings

Chiles Rellenos de Jaiba (Crab-Stuffed Chiles)

 Chiles rellenos come in a variety of forms, and are very popular throughout Mexico and the Southwest. They can be included in casseroles that are bound together with a custard-type sauce, or, as here, stuffed and baked. Meat from freshly cooked crab provides the tastiest filling, but any good-quality canned crabmeat will be fine.

1 teaspoon vegetable oil

¼ cup minced onion

1 clove garlic, minced

4 poblano chiles, roasted, peeled, seeds removed

2 cups shredded cooked crab

1 small tomato, finely chopped

1 tablespoon chopped flat-leaf parsley

1 teaspoon dried oregano, preferably Mexican

½ teaspoon dried epazote (available at Latin markets; optional)

2 tablespoons Mexican *crema*; or substitute thin sour cream

Chopped flat-leaf parsley and grated Mexican *cotija* or *añejo* cheese; or substitute Parmesan, for garnish

Sauce

1 tablespoon vegetable oil

½ medium onion, chopped

1 clove garlic, chopped

4 tomatoes, roasted, peeled, chopped

2 chipotle chiles *en adobo*, chopped

1 cup chicken broth

1 tablespoon distilled white vinegar

Salt and freshly ground black pepper to taste

To make the sauce, heat a heavy skillet over medium heat, add the oil and when hot, add the onion and garlic, and sauté until the onion is soft. Add the remaining ingredients and bring to a boil. Reduce the heat and simmer the sauce for 20 minutes. Place the sauce in a blender or food processor and puree until smooth. Pour the sauce into a saucepan, taste, and adjust the seasonings, then keep warm.

Preheat the oven to 350°F, and lightly oil a baking sheet. Heat a small skillet over medium heat, add the oil and when hot, add the onion and garlic, and sauté until the onion is soft. Remove from the heat, and place in a bowl. Add all the remaining filling ingredients to the bowl, and toss to gently mix.

Make a long slit down the side of each chile. Spoon the crab mixture into the chiles and place them on the baking sheet. Bake for about 15 minutes or until thoroughly heated.

Place some of the sauce on individual plates, top with a chile, garnish with chopped parsley and cheese, and serve.

Yield: 4 servings

Smoked Salmon and Pasta Salad with Horseradish Dressing

Using a commercial smoked salmon and prepared tortellini in this recipe makes for an easy-to-prepare entrée. Of course, a piece of smoked fish, such as trout, or even shrimp or scallops, would be a wonderful alternative to the salmon. The horseradish in the vinaigrette is a good complement to the smoky flavor of the fish, and the sun-dried tomato adds a hint of sweetness. Farfalle or spiral pasta are good substitutes for the tortellini, or serve the salad on a mixture of baby green lettuce for yet another variation. Make the dressing well ahead of time, as the flavors improve the longer it sits.

1 pound cracked pepper smoked salmon

8 ounces cheese tortellini

Chopped fresh parsley and grated Parmesan or Asiago cheese

Dressing

1 medium tomato, diced

2 tablespoons tomato paste

3 cloves garlic, minced

2 teaspoons horseradish

1 teaspoon green peppercorn mustard, store-bought or homemade (page 166)

1 teaspoon ground chipotle chile

½ teaspoon anchovy paste

¼ cup red wine vinegar

2 tablespoons olive oil

¼ cup sun-dried tomatoes, chopped

1 teaspoon chopped fresh parsley

Salt and freshly ground black pepper to taste

To make the dressing, place the tomato, tomato paste, garlic, horseradish, mustard, chile, and anchovy paste in a blender or food processor, and puree until smooth. Add the vinegar and, while the machine is running, slowly add the oil until combined. Place the mixture into a bowl and whisk in the sun-dried tomatoes and parsley. Season to taste with salt and pepper, and allow the dressing to sit for an hour at room temperature to blend the flavors. This should make about ½ cup of dressing.

Bring 3 quarts of water to a boil in a stockpot, add a teaspoon of salt to the water, then add the pasta. Bring the water back to a boil, and cook the pasta until al dente. Remove, drain, and rinse the pasta.

To serve, place the room-temperature pasta in a large serving bowl, and toss with the dressing to coat. Flake the salmon over the top, and garnish with chopped parsley and grated cheese.

Yield: 4 servings

12
Meatless Main Courses

Yucatecán Papadzul (Enchiladas Stuffed with Hard-Boiled Eggs)

This dish is unique to the Mayan cuisine of the Yucatán. These enchiladas are filled with hard-boiled eggs and are topped with a subtly flavored green sauce made from pumpkin seeds. Traditionally they would be garnished with a green oil that is squeezed from the toasted seeds, but we've omitted that from the recipe, as they taste just as good without that complicated step. Usually served as an appetizer, they make a wonderful lunch or dinner entrée, smooth in texture and rich in flavor. If your tortillas have become stiff, heat some vegetable oil in a hot skillet and dip the tortillas in the oil for a couple of seconds to soften. Remove and drain on paper towels.

2 large tomatoes, peeled and chopped

3 serrano chiles, stems removed, chopped

2 sprigs fresh epazote; or substitute 2 teaspoons dried (available in Latin markets; optional)

2 cups vegetable broth

2 tablespoons vegetable oil, divided

½ cup chopped white onion

2 cloves garlic, chopped

1 cup toasted pumpkin seeds, finely ground

8 corn tortillas

6 hard-boiled eggs, peeled and chopped

Combine the tomatoes, chiles, epazote, and broth in a saucepan. Bring to a boil and cook for 5 minutes. Remove the pan from the heat and strain, saving both the tomatoes and the broth.

Heat a skillet over medium-high heat, add 1 tablespoon of the oil; when hot, add the onion and garlic and sauté until soft. Add the onions and tomato mixture to a blender or food processor and puree until smooth. Add the remaining oil to the saucepan and heat. Add the sauce and sauté for 5 minutes.

Heat a saucepan over medium heat, add the tomato broth, and slowly stir in the seeds. Reduce the heat and simmer until the mixture thickens to the consistency of thick cream, stirring constantly. Be careful the sauce does not boil, or it may curdle.

Dip the tortillas in the warm pumpkin-seed sauce to coat and soften. Place some of the chopped eggs in the center, roll up, and place on a platter. Pour the remaining pumpkin-seed sauce over the top, then the tomato sauce, and serve with a dish of *cebollas encuridas* (pickled red onions; page 266–267) on the side.

Yield: 4 servings

Avocado Herb Omelet with Hot Chutney

This recipe is based on a wonderful omelet Nancy was served at the Hotel Jaguar in Cahuita, Costa Rica. This chutney doesn't use sugar; instead, the flavor of fresh fruit is used to sweeten naturally. We've not seen Costa Rica's red-skinned avocado outside of that country, so use whatever type is available and ripe.

1 large avocado, peeled and pitted

¼ cup finely minced onion

4 eggs

2 tablespoons chopped fresh cilantro

2 fresh cayenne-type chiles, stems and seeds removed, minced

2 tablespoons butter or olive oil

Cilantro leaves and avocado slices for garnish

Chutney

2 tomatoes, peeled and chopped

3 cups diced papaya

2 tablespoons raisins

1 habanero chile, stem and seeds removed, minced

Combine the ingredients for the chutney in a saucepan and bring to a gentle simmer over a low heat for 20 to 30 minutes, or until the tomatoes have broken down and the sauce has thickened.

Place the avocado in a small bowl and mash with a fork. Add the onion and stir to mix, and set aside. In another bowl, whisk together 2 of the eggs with half of the cilantro and chiles until well combined.

Heat an omelet pan over high heat, add 1 tablespoon of the butter, and tilt the pan so that the butter covers the entire pan. Pour the eggs into the pan and continue to stir, while gently moving the pan, until the mixture starts to thicken. Add the avocado mixture and allow the omelet to finish cooking.

Run a spatula or knife around the edges of the omelet to make sure it doesn't stick to the pan. Slide the eggs to the front of the pan and fold over the top.

Turn the omelet onto a plate; garnish with avocado slices and a few cilantro leaves, and serve with the chutney on the side. Repeat with the remaining ingredients.

Yield: 2 servings

Dal Curry

Dal is the Hindu word for several legumes that resemble lentils and/or split peas. In India they can be found both fresh and dried, but here we almost always find them dried. The bean used in this curry, channa dal, resembles a yellow split pea. Pulses, or dried lentils, are sometimes hard to digest, so cooks in India, where they are staples, prepare them with ginger or turmeric to make them go down easier. This recipe contains both. Don't forget the coconut garnish, which gives this curry a tasty, sweet, crunch.

½ cup yellow split peas (*channa dal*), cleaned and rinsed

3 cups vegetable broth

1 medium potato, peeled and diced

½ teaspoon ground cayenne

¼ teaspoon ground turmeric

1 tablespoon vegetable oil

1 tablespoon minced fresh ginger

½ cup chopped onions

1 clove garlic, chopped

3 serrano chiles, stems removed, chopped

1 teaspoon ground coriander

½ teaspoon ground cumin

1 medium tomato, peeled and chopped

2 cups cooked white rice

Flaked coconut and chopped fresh cilantro for garnish

Combine the split peas, broth, potato, cayenne, and turmeric in a large saucepan over medium-hot heat and bring the mixture to a boil. Reduce the heat and simmer, partially covered, for 45 minutes or until the peas are tender and the mixture is the consistency of a thick soup, adding more broth if necessary.

Heat a heavy skillet over medium heat, add the oil and when hot, add the ginger, onions, garlic, and chiles and sauté until they are soft. Add the coriander, cumin, and tomato and continue to cook for 5 more minutes.

Add the tomato mixture to the dal and simmer until heated through.

To serve, place some rice in the bottom of a bowl and ladle the dal over the top. Garnish with the coconut and cilantro.

Yield: 4 to 6 servings

Habanero-Spiced Black Beans and Rice with Cuban Sofrito

This is a variation of the popular Cuban classic "Moors and Christians," which gets its name from the black of the beans and the white of the rice. Sofritos, a mixture of sautéed vegetables and seasonings, are used to flavor soups, sauces, and dishes in Spanish and Italian cooking. In the following recipe, the beans are cooked from scratch, but if you are pressed for time, substitute canned black beans. Epazote is an herb that is always used when cooking black beans in Mexico and throughout the Caribbean.

1 pound black beans, rinsed and picked over

1 teaspoon dried epazote (available in Latin markets; optional)

1 habanero chile, stem and seeds removed

1 tomato, peeled and chopped

2 tablespoons cider vinegar

2 tablespoons dry sherry (optional)

Salt to taste

2 cups cooked long-grain rice

Sofrito

2 tablespoons olive oil

1 small green bell pepper, stem and seeds removed, sliced

1 small onion, sliced

4 large cloves garlic, minced

2 habanero chiles, stems and seeds removed, chopped

1 teaspoon dried oregano

½ teaspoon ground cumin

1 bay leaf

¼ teaspoon freshly ground black pepper

Place the beans in a stockpot and add cold water to cover. Bring the mixture to a boil over high heat, and boil the beans uncovered for 2 minutes. Remove the pot from the heat, cover, and allow the beans to sit for 1 hour. Drain and rinse the beans.

Return the beans to the pot; add the epazote, if using, habanero, and 2 quarts of water, and bring the mixture to a boil. Reduce the heat slightly and cook for 1 to 2 hours, or until the beans are tender. Add the tomato, vinegar, and sherry, if using, and season to taste with salt. Simmer for an additional 10 minutes to blend the flavors.

To make the *sofrito*, heat a heavy skillet over medium heat and add the olive oil; when hot, add the green pepper, onions, garlic, and chiles. Sauté the vegetables for a couple of minutes until softened. Add the oregano, cumin, bay leaf, and black pepper and continue to sauté for an additional minute. Cover and simmer for an additional 15 to 20 minutes.

To serve, place the rice on a large serving platter, ladle the beans along with some of the sauce on the rice, and top with the *sofrito*.

Yield: 4 to 6 servings

Mottai Kolambu
(Egg Curry in Coconut Gravy)

Egg curries are popular all over India, where they are served for lunch, as an afternoon snack, for brunch, and as a quick and easy dish to serve unexpected dinner guests. In a country that doesn't have an abundance of protein sources, eggs are invaluable. This version is from Madras, which is known for its spicy cuisine; in fact, it's one of the biggest exporters of Indian spices. In this dish, the sweetness of the coconut milk complements the pungency of the chiles. Serve mottai kolambu *with rice and a salad for a quick, easy, light supper.*

6 hard-boiled eggs, peeled

2 tablespoons vegetable oil

1 cup finely chopped onion

2 teaspoons grated ginger

1 tomato, peeled, seeded and chopped

1½ teaspoons ground cayenne

2 teaspoons ground coriander

1 teaspoon ground cumin

½ teaspoon ground turmeric

½ teaspoon ground cinnamon

⅛ teaspoon freshly grated nutmeg

¾ to 1 cup unsweetened coconut milk

1 tablespoon lime juice, preferably fresh

1 cup roasted cashew nuts

½ cup chopped fresh cilantro or mint leaves

Salt to taste

Cut the eggs in half and arrange them in a serving dish.

Heat a heavy saucepan over medium heat, add the oil, and when hot, add the onions and sauté until they are soft. Add the ginger and sauté for a couple of minutes, or until the onions start to brown. Stir in the tomatoes, cayenne, coriander, cumin, turmeric, cinnamon, and nutmeg. Reduce the heat and simmer, stirring occasionally, until the tomatoes break down and the mixture thickens.

Stir in the coconut milk and lime juice, and continue to simmer to thicken the sauce. Taste and adjust the seasonings.

Add the cashews and fresh cilantro or mint, reserving some of the latter for a garnish. Simmer the sauce for an additional 2 minutes.

To serve, pour the curry sauce over the eggs and garnish with the reserved herbs.

Yield: 4 to 6 servings

Caribbean Roti with Potato Curry

Rotis are traditional fare throughout the Caribbean and have been called the West Indian version of the burrito. The griddle-bread wrapper is East Indian in origin and can be served whole, torn into pieces for dipping into sauces, or wrapped around a filling. This recipe is based on rotis that Nancy was served at Foxy's Tamarind Bar in Jost, Van Dyke Island in the British Virgin Islands.

1 to 2 tablespoons vegetable oil

1 tablespoon minced ginger

1 Scotch bonnet chile, stem and seeds removed, minced; or substitute habanero chile

¼ cup diced onion

2 cloves garlic, minced

3 tablespoons store-bought curry powder, or homemade *bafat* (page 136)

1 teaspoon dried thyme

½ teaspoon ground cloves

½ teaspoon freshly ground black pepper

¼ teaspoon salt

1½ cups cooked, peeled, diced potato

2 tablespoons tamarind paste, dissolved in ¼ cup water

½ cup cooked garbanzo beans, either dried or canned

Vegetable oil for frying

Roti

4 cups all-purpose flour

2 teaspoons baking powder

1 teaspoon salt

¼ cup vegetable oil

1 cup water

To make the rotis, sift all the dry ingredients together in a bowl. Gradually stir in the oil and enough water to form a ball. Knead the dough for 5 minutes or until soft. Gather into a ball, cover, and let rise for 15 minutes.

Meanwhile, heat a heavy saucepan over medium heat and add the oil; when hot, add the ginger and chile and sauté for a couple of minutes. Add the onion, garlic, and seasonings and sauté until the onions are soft. Add the potatoes, tamarind, garbanzo beans, and 2 cups of water. Simmer for 15 minutes, or until very soft but not mushy.

On a lightly floured surface, divide the dough into 4 equal balls. Flatten each and roll out into a circle, 8 to 9 inches in diameter. Heat 2 tablespoons of oil in a skillet until very hot. Place the rotis in the pan one at a time, and cook for 2 to 3 minutes, or until browned. Turn and brown the other side. Remove and cover with a towel until ready to serve.

To serve, place about a cup of the filling in the center of a roti. Fold over the sides and fold up the ends, as you would with a burrito. Serve accompanied with a chutney and/or your favorite hot sauce.

Yield: 4 servings

Tortilla Española with Salsa Romesco (Spanish Omelet)

This is probably the most widely eaten dish in Spain, and it's not anything like a Mexican tortilla. There are countless variations on this large, thick, omelet-like cake made with potatoes, eggs, and other ingredients, which is commonly served at room temperature.

3 pounds (approximately 10) medium-size potatoes, peeled and sliced into ⅛-inch slices

⅓ cup extra-virgin olive oil, preferably Spanish

1 medium-size onion, thinly sliced

6 eggs, beaten

¼ teaspoon salt

Romesco sauce, store-bought or homemade (page 115)

Preheat the oven to 350°F.

In a roasting pan, toss the potatoes with the oil, cover with aluminum foil, and bake for 20 minutes. Uncover the pan and spread the onion slices evenly over the potatoes. Cover and bake for an additional 10 minutes, or until the potatoes are just done. Remove the pan and pour off the oil, reserving it. Cool the potatoes to room temperature.

Beat the eggs in a large bowl and season with the salt. Gently fold the potato and onion mixture into the eggs, and mix carefully.

Heat a nonstick sauté pan over high heat with a few tablespoons of the reserved oil. When it's hot, carefully add the egg mixture. Allow the eggs to set on high heat for 1 minute while gently shaking the pan so they don't stick. Reduce the heat to the lowest temperature and cook for 15 to 20 minutes, or until the mixture is firm.

Place a plate on top (upside down as you look at it) of the sauté pan and flip the tortilla onto the plate. (Do this over your sink.) Reheat the skillet over high heat and carefully slide the tortilla back into the pan. Reduce the heat to low and cook the other side until the tortilla feels firm to the touch, about 8 minutes.

Cool the tortilla to room temperature, and slice it into wedges. When you are ready to serve the tortilla, spoon some of the Romesco sauce onto a plate and place a wedge on top.

Yield: 6 wedges, or 16 bite-size pieces

Torta de Huevos
(Egg Fritters in Chile Sauce)

These light chile fritters are a popular meatless egg dish served on Fridays during Lent in the homes of the descendants of Spanish colonial settlers of northern New Mexico, as well as in some restaurants. Torrejas, *as they are sometimes called, are made from the recipe that we use to coat chiles for* chiles rellenos. *They are light and airy, so their flavor is sometimes overwhelmed by the red chile sauce in which they are traditionally served. We've taken some liberties, adding some nontraditional ingredients to the fritters and serving them with a lighter* pipian verde *sauce. Don't wait for Lent to make these, as they are a great brunch dish.*

2 cups *pipian verde*, store-bought or homemade (page 158)

4 eggs, separated

3 tablespoons all-purpose flour

½ teaspoon baking powder

½ teaspoon salt

½ cup crumbled Mexican *cotija*, *queso fresco*, or feta cheese

¼ cup finely chopped onion

1 tablespoon chopped fresh cilantro

½ teaspoon dried thyme

Vegetable for oil frying

Pour the *pipian* sauce in a small saucepan and heat.

Place the egg whites in a bowl and, using a mixer or a whisk, beat until stiff but not dry.

Combine the egg yolks, flour, baking powder, and salt in a bowl and stir to combine. Add the cheese, onion, cilantro, and thyme and stir to combine.

Add the egg yolk mixture to the egg whites and gently fold just to combine; you don't want to deflate the whites by mixing too vigorously.

Heat a large, heavy skillet over medium-high heat, pour in the oil to a depth of 1½ inches, and heat to 375°F. Add the mixture a spoonful at a time to the oil and fry until golden brown.

To serve, pour some of the *pipian* sauce on individual dishes. Top with the tortas and serve.

Yield: 4 servings

Spaghetti a Cacio e Pepe (Spaghetti with Black Pepper and Pecorino)

Simple, rustic, and popular, spaghetti with black pepper is one of the tastiest dishes found in the Roman trattorias offering traditional foods. The dish originated in the province of Romano Lazio, where pecorino Romano cheese is made from the flocks of sheep that graze the hills around Rome. Pecorino Romano is a sharp, hard cheese that is used both in sauces and as a cheese to eat at the end of a meal. This ultra-rich pasta is so quick to prepare, you'll be amazed that a dish so easy tastes so good. There are a couple of tricks to making the perfect spaghetti a cacio e pepe. First, use the ragged-edged holes of a box grater, not the small holes, for cheese that will melt easily and not clump. And the second tip is to use a technique called mantecare, *"to mix and meld," diluting the cheese and pepper with some of the starchy cooking water before tossing it with the spaghetti.*

½ pound dried spaghetti

2 tablespoons extra-virgin olive oil

2 cloves garlic, sliced

2 tablespoons butter

1 tablespoon freshly ground
    black pepper

1 to 2 cups grated pecorino
    Romano cheese, divided

Salt to taste

In a large saucepan or stockpot, bring 4 quarts salted water to a boil, add the spaghetti, and cook the pasta until *al dente*. Reserve at least 1 cup of the cooking liquid, then drain the pasta, but do not rinse it.

Heat a small skillet over medium heat, add the olive oil, and when hot, add the garlic and sauté until golden, but not brown. Remove the garlic, as it will continue to cook and burn. Add the butter and pepper to the pan.

Return ½ to 1 cup of the cooking water to the saucepan, add the olive oil mixture and 1 cup of the cheese, stir, and heat over medium heat. Add the pasta, and toss for about 3 minutes, until the cheese melts and the sauce coats the pasta, adding more reserved cooking liquid if dry. Taste and season with salt.

Place the pasta in a large bowl, top with the reserved garlic, and serve with the cheese on the side.

Yield: 2 servings as an entrée, 4 as a first course

Vegetable Pad Thai
(Stir-Fried Rice Noodles Thai Style)

Pad thai *is a popular, healthy, noodle dish served in restaurants, by street vendors, and in homes in Thailand. There are many variations of this one-meal dish; it can use seafood, chicken, meat, or just vegetables, as this one does, or any combination. Thailand was settled in the twelfth century by refugees from southern China, and the Chinese influence is reflected in this dish, the name of which means "Thai stir-fry." The cuisine of Thailand reflects a number of influences—not just Chinese, but those of its other neighbors, Burma, India, Vietnam, and Laos, as well. Their food is known for its freshness and the way it balances a variety of flavors, as in this dish.* Nam pla, *fermented fish sauce, which is thin, salty, and not terribly fishy, is used here instead of soy sauce.*

8 ounces firm tofu

2 to 3 tablespoons vegetable oil, preferably peanut

2 eggs, lightly beaten

4 to 6 Thai chiles, stems removed, chopped

3 to 4 cloves garlic, minced

3 shallots, thinly sliced

1 tablespoon distilled vinegar

2 teaspoons sugar

½ pound dried rice stick noodles (*ban pho* noodles), available in Asian markets

1 tablespoon Thai fish sauce

¼ cup chopped fresh Thai basil (optional)

1 cup bean sprouts

¼ cup chopped peanuts

4 green onions, thinly sliced

Chopped cilantro and lime wedges for garnish

Place 3 to 4 paper towels on a plate, add the tofu, top with additional towels, place another plate on top, and weight down with a heavy skillet to extract the excess moisture, for about 15 minutes. Rinse with cold water and drain. Cut the tofu into strips about 1½ inches long, and ½ inch wide and thick.

Heat a wok over high heat, add 1 tablespoon of oil, swirl to coat the pan, and when hot, add the tofu and stir-fry until golden, about 20 seconds. Remove and drain on paper towels.

Add a little more oil, to the wok if necessary, heat, and add the eggs. Allow the eggs to set, turning over as needed until cooked—don't scramble. Remove and cut into chunks.

Add additional oil, if necessary, and add the chiles, garlic, and shallots, then stir for 15 to 20 seconds, or until fragrant. Stir in the vinegar and sugar.

Add another tablespoon of the oil, and when it's very hot, add the noodles and toss to stir-fry, adding a little water if the mixture starts to dry. To stir-fry, spread and pull the noodles into a thin layer, scrape, and gently turn them over. Repeat this process several times until the stiff, white noodles soften and curl.

Season the noodles with the fish sauce and turn them until coated. Add the basil (if using), bean sprouts, peanuts, and onions and toss. Return the tofu and eggs, and toss to mix. Taste and adjust the seasonings.

To serve: place the *pad thai* on a serving platter and garnish with the cilantro. Arrange the limes around the platter; guests can squeeze the lime over the top before eating.

Yield: 2 to 4 servings

Pasta alle Melanzane (Roasted Eggplant and Garlic Pasta)

There are many variations on a combination of tomatoes and eggplant all over the Mediterranean, but we like this one from Abulia in southern Italy, where they prefer their food spicy. The residents of Abulia air-dry cherry tomatoes, like chiles, and then use the half-dried tomatoes in dishes such as this, but we have substituted canned tomatoes so you can prepare this pasta year-round. We like to roast the eggplant rather than sauté it, which retains more of its texture and flavor, giving the dish an almost meaty flavor.

1 medium eggplant, ends trimmed,
cut into 1-inch chunks

4 cloves garlic, minced

2 to 3 tablespoons extra-virgin olive oil

Salt and freshly ground black pepper

1½ cups chopped onion

Two 14-ounce cans chopped tomatoes, including the liquid

2 tablespoons chopped flat-leaf parsley

3 tablespoon coarsely chopped cured black olives

1 tablespoon dry red wine (optional)

1 tablespoon chopped fresh basil

2 teaspoons dried oregano

1 anchovy, mashed (optional)

2 to 4 dried peperoncinos, crushed; or substitute 1 to 2 teaspoons crushed red chile, such as piquin

8 ounces penne pasta

Grated Parmesan cheese

Preheat the oven to 350°F. Place the eggplant and garlic in a bowl, add 2 tablespoons of the olive oil, season with salt and pepper, and toss to coat. Put on a sheet pan in a single layer.

Place the pan on the center rack of the oven, and roast for 10 minutes. Stir and turn the eggplant, and roast for an additional 10 to 15 minutes or until the eggplant is browned.

Pour the remaining tablespoon of oil into a saucepan, heat, and add the onion. Sauté the onion until soft and golden, about 5 minutes; do not brown. Add the tomatoes, parsley, olives, wine (if using), basil, oregano, anchovy (if using), and chiles. Bring to a boil, reduce the heat, and simmer, stirring occasionally, until the mixture has thickened, about 20 to 30 minutes. Add the eggplant and heat through.

Bring a large stockpot of cold water to a boil, add salt, then add the pasta. Cook the pasta until *al dente*. Drain the pasta, but don't rinse, and transfer to a warmed, large bowl. Toss the pasta with the sauce and serve with the cheese on the side.

Yield: 4 servings

Missayeko Dal Haru
(Nepalese Mixed Lentils)

Pat Chapman, the "Curry King of England," collected this recipe on one of his many trips to the subcontinent, where they grow more than sixty types of lentils, or dals. According to Pat, "In Nepal, these lentils are either eaten freshly picked, when they are lovely and soft, or in the more familiar dried form." Since it is impossible to obtain these legumes fresh outside the subcontinent, he uses dried lentils. There is a difference, of course, but who is to say which is better?

2 ounces whole black *urad dal*, a black-skinned white lentil (available in Asian markets)

2 ounces whole red *masoor dal*, an orange-red lentil with green skin (available in Asian markets)

2 ounces whole green *moong dal*, used to make bean sprouts (available in Asian markets)

2 ounces split yellow *chana dal*, yellow split peas (available in Asian markets)

3 to 4 tablespoons *ghee* (page 238); or substitute vegetable oil

½ cup finely chopped onion

4 cloves garlic, finely chopped

1 tablespoon grated ginger

1 teaspoon ground cumin

1 teaspoon ground coriander

1 teaspoon garam masala, store-bought or homemade (page 135)

1 teaspoon ground turmeric

1 teaspoon ground red chile, such as New Mexican

Salt to taste

Chopped fresh cilantro for garnish

Pick through the lentils to remove any grit or impurities. Combine them in a bowl, cover with water, and soak for at least 4 hours, adding more water if necessary. Drain, rinse several times, then drain again.

Measure twice the lentils' volume of water into a large saucepan and bring to a boil over high heat. Add the lentils, reduce the heat, and simmer for 30 minutes, stirring as the water is absorbed.

Heat a wok over medium-high heat, add the ghee or oil, and when hot, add the onions, garlic, and ginger. Stir-fry the mixture until fragrant, about 2 minutes. Add the spices and continue to stir-fry for about 5 more minutes, adding a little water to prevent sticking.

Add the stir-fry mixture to the lentils and stir to mix well. Taste and adjust the seasonings.

To serve, place the lentils in a large bowl and garnish with the cilantro.

Yield: 4 servings

Note: This recipe requires advance preparation.

Chilaquiles en Salsa Chipotle (Chilaquiles in Chipotle Sauce)

Chilaquiles, *pronounced "chee-lay-key-lays," means "broken-up sombrero." This is a simple dish that "recycles" day-old corn tortillas that have become dry by "breaking the sombrero (tortilla)" in pieces and smothering them in a chile sauce.* Chilaquiles *are a great breakfast dish, but are also good for brunch or a light supper.*

Vegetable oil for frying

1 dozen corn tortillas, cut in triangles

½ cup chopped white onion

1 cup crumbled *queso fresco*; or substitute grated Monterey Jack cheese

Chopped fresh cilantro and Mexican *crema*; or substitute thin sour cream for garnish

Sauce

2 dried red New Mexican chiles, stems and seeds removed

2 tablespoons vegetable oil

1 ancho chile, stems and seeds removed

½ cup chopped onion

2 cloves garlic, minced

3 chipotle chiles *en adobo*

3 medium tomatoes, roasted, peeled, seeds removed, and chopped

1 teaspoon dried oregano, preferably Mexican

Salt to taste

To make the sauce, place the dried chiles in a bowl and cover with very hot water. Allow the chiles to steep for 15 minutes to soften. Drain the chiles and discard the water.

Heat a heavy skillet over medium-high heat, add 1 tablespoon of the oil, and when hot, add the onion and garlic and sauté until soft. Place all the chiles, the cooked onions, tomatoes, and oregano in a blender or food processor and puree to a smooth sauce. Strain the sauce to remove any small pieces of chile.

Add the remaining tablespoon of oil to the skillet and, when it's hot, carefully add the sauce. Reduce the heat and simmer until the sauce thickens, about 15 minutes. Season to taste with salt.

Pour the oil to a depth of 1 inch in a heavy skillet and heat over medium-high heat until the temperature reads 350°F. Fry the tortillas, a few at a time, until they are golden, about 1 minute. Remove and drain on paper towels. Place the chopped white onion in a strainer and run under cold water for a minute to remove any bitterness. Add the tortillas to the sauce and quickly stir to coat; you do not want them to soften. Immediately spoon them onto individual plates, and top with onions, cheese, and cilantro. Pour a little of the *crema* over the top and serve.

Yield: 4 servings

Dijon-Sauced Portobello Mushrooms with Blue Cheese

There isn't any reason why those of you who are either giving up or trying to cut back on red meat can't enjoy a dish with a "meaty" beef flavor. Portobello mushrooms have a steaklike texture and flavor, so why not serve them with a sauce that goes equally well with meat? This simple, creamy sauce doesn't overpower the flavor of the mushroom. We suggest you serve these mushrooms with a wild rice pilaf and Stir-fry Walnut Asparagus (page 322).

2 large portobello mushrooms

Extra-virgin olive oil

Crumbled blue cheese for garnish

Sauce

2 tablespoons butter

3 tablespoons chopped shallots

½ cup dry white wine

1 cup heavy cream

3 to 4 tablespoons Dijon-style mustard, store-bought or homemade (page 117)

1 teaspoon minced fresh thyme

Salt and freshly ground black pepper

To make the sauce, heat a saucepan over medium heat, add the butter, and when hot, add the shallots and sauté until soft. Add the wine and simmer until the liquid has reduced by half. Stir in the cream, mustard, and thyme and continue to simmer until the sauce has thickened. Season to taste with salt and pepper.

Adjust the broiler pan to its lowest setting from the heat source and preheat. Lightly oil a sheet pan, place the mushrooms on it, gill side up, and brush with olive oil. Place under the broiler for 5 minutes. Turn the mushrooms, and brush with more oil.

Set the oven to 425°F. Place the sheet pan in the middle of the oven and bake for 15 minutes, or until the mushrooms are done.

To serve, slice the mushrooms at an angle. Spoon some of the mustard sauce on individual plates, top with the mushroom slices, garnish with blue cheese, and serve.

Yield: 4 servings

13
Sizzling Sides

Bayou Ratatouille (Louisiana Roasted Eggplant)

This is the Louisiana variation on a classic French dish. We like to prepare it during the summertime, when we can take advantage of fresh summer vegetables and alter the mixture depending on what is fresh and in season. Ratatouille can be served either hot or cold, so when we make it, we make a big batch to enjoy at many meals. Remember, the eggplant must be soaked before using to remove the bitterness.

1 medium eggplant, peeled and cubed

1 medium zucchini, peeled and cubed

1 red bell pepper, stem and seeds removed, cut in strips

2 medium tomatoes, chopped

2 tablespoons olive oil

2 serrano chiles, stems removed and chopped

3 cloves garlic, minced

1 tablespoon chopped fresh basil

2 teaspoons chopped fresh thyme

2 teaspoons Creole seasoning, store-bought or homemade (page 169)

1 teaspoon ground paprika

1 bay leaf

Salt and freshly ground black pepper

Place the eggplant in a bowl, cover with salted water, and let sit for 30 minutes. Rinse, drain, and dry.

Preheat the oven to 400°F.

Combine all the vegetables in a bowl. Add the oil and remaining ingredients, and gently toss to coat.

Spread the mixture on a roasting pan and bake for 1 hour, then gently stir, and bake 30 minutes more, or until the vegetables are very soft.

Place the ratatouille in a bowl, remove the bay leaf, and serve.

Yield: 4 to 6 servings

Note: This recipe requires advance preparation.

Stir-Fry Walnut Asparagus

This elegant vegetable dish is a great accompaniment to just about any meal, so don't limit yourself to Asian or Chinese foods. The dish must be prepared with fresh asparagus, never frozen. If asparagus is out of season, substitute other fresh vegetables, such as green beans or broccoli.

1 pound fresh asparagus,
    cut in 1½- to 2-inch pieces

2 teaspoons vegetable oil,
    preferably peanut

1 clove garlic, minced

1 teaspoon crushed red chiles

1 heaping tablespoon hoisin sauce
    (available in Asian markets)

¼ cup rice wine

½ teaspoon sugar

½ teaspoon vinegar

2 teaspoons cornstarch mixed
    with 2 teaspoons water

¼ cup chopped walnuts

In a large kettle or saucepan, heat a quart of water over high heat until boiling. Add the asparagus and blanch it for 10 to 20 seconds. Remove the asparagus, and immediately immerse in ice water to stop the cooking process.

In a wok or heavy skillet over medium-high heat, add the oil; when hot, add the asparagus and garlic and stir-fry for 1 minute. Add the chile, hoisin sauce, wine, sugar, and vinegar. Stir-fry for another 2 minutes, or until the asparagus is tender but still crisp.

Raise the heat, slowly stir in the cornstarch mixture, and simmer until the sauce thickens.

To serve, place the asparagus in a serving bowl or on a platter and garnish with the walnuts.

Yield: 4 servings

Palak Pachadi (Spinach in Yogurt)

Spinach goes by many names in India—palak, saag, *and* saag palak. *The* pachadi *in the title refers to yogurt. Popular all over the subcontinent and Afghanistan, it's prepared in many ways, such as with* paneer, *a very distinctive Indian cheese, or with a ricotta-type cheese, or in curries called* thorens. *This version of the creamed spinach dish uses yogurt for the "cream" base, so it is low in fat. Yogurt has a tendency to curdle, so be sure to add it at the end of cooking.*

10 to 12 ounces fresh spinach, stems removed; or substitute one 10-ounce package frozen leaf spinach

½ cup chopped onion

1 tablespoon grated ginger

1 clove garlic, chopped

2 tablespoon vegetable oil

2 teaspoons brown mustard seeds

½ teaspoon ground cayenne

¼ teaspoon ground cumin

½ cup plain yogurt

1 tablespoon garam masala, store-bought or homemade (page 135)

Salt to taste

If using fresh spinach, steam until done and drain well. For frozen, defrost the spinach and squeeze out the excess water. Put the spinach in a bowl and mash with a fork until well broken up.

Place the onion, ginger, and garlic in a blender or food processor and puree to a paste, adding 1 tablespoon of the oil if necessary.

Heat a heavy skillet over medium-high heat, add the remaining oil, and when hot, add the onion paste and the mustard seeds and sauté for 2 to 3 minutes, until fragrant.

Add the spinach, cayenne, and cumin to the skillet, cover, and simmer for 5 minutes, until all the liquid has evaporated, stirring occasionally.

Stir in the yogurt, season with the masala and salt, and serve.

Yield: 4 servings

Gobi aur Matar Ki Bhaji (Curried Cauliflower with Peas)

Millions of Indians are vegetarians, so it's no wonder that they have such a dazzling number of tasty vegetable recipes in their varied cuisine. Cauliflower and peas are very popular vegetables, both on their own and as ingredients in other dishes. Most vegetable curries are cooked until they are dry and the flavors infuse the vegetables. Serve this colorful dish with a bread such as chapati *or* poori.

1 tablespoon coarsely chopped ginger

2 to 3 tablespoons vegetable oil

¼ teaspoon ground turmeric

1 teaspoon cumin seeds

¼ teaspoon yellow mustard seeds

1 small head cauliflower, separated into small florets

3 green New Mexican chiles, roasted, peeled, stems and seeds removed, and diced

1 cup green peas, preferably fresh

1 tomato, peeled and chopped

1 teaspoon ground coriander

2 teaspoons lemon juice, preferably fresh

2 to 3 tablespoons chopped fresh cilantro

Salt to taste

Put the ginger in a blender or food processor, add ¼ cup water, and puree until smooth.

Heat a wok or heavy skillet over medium heat, add the oil, and when hot, add the ginger puree and turmeric and stir-fry for 2 minutes, stirring constantly. Add the cumin and mustard seeds and roast until the seeds start to pop.

Add the cauliflower and chiles and stir-fry for 5 minutes, adding more oil to the pan if necessary.

Stir in the peas, tomato, coriander, and lemon juice, season with salt, and toss to combine. Add ¼ cup of water, reduce the heat, and cook until the cauliflower is just tender but still crisp, about 15 minutes, the liquid has been absorbed, and the curry is dry.

To serve, put the curry in a serving bowl, sprinkle the cilantro over the top, and toss to mix.

Yield: 4 to 6 servings

Spicy Ginger Garlic Green Beans

This recipe is best prepared with Asian green or long beans, but any thin, fresh green bean will do. It's a sweet, hot, and crunchy dish with lots of flavor that almost begs to be served with plain white rice. Although it's not essential to use the black vinegar, it does add another layer of complex flavors that can't be replicated with another vinegar. These beans can be steamed ahead of time and kept cool. Go ahead and prepare the rest of the meal and then finish off the stir-fry before serving, or prepare the beans and cool, let stand at room temperature, and serve. They are good either hot from the wok or at room temperature.

1 pound thin green beans or Asian long beans, cut diagonally into 2- to 3-inch pieces

1 tablespoon vegetable oil, preferably peanut

1 tablespoon minced garlic

1 tablespoon chopped fresh ginger

Toasted sesame seeds for garnish

Sauce

2 tablespoons black vinegar (available in Asian markets); or substitute rice vinegar

2 teaspoons sugar

½ teaspoon crushed red chile, such as piquin

½ teaspoon black sesame oil (available in Asian markets)

¼ teaspoon ground white pepper

Combine all the sauce ingredients in a small bowl, stir to mix, and set aside.

Put the green beans in a steamer in a wok or heavy saucepan, along with ½ cup water; cover and heat over high heat. Steam the beans until bright green and almost done, but still crunchy. Remove and drain off the water. If finishing off later, run the beans under cold water to stop the cooking process.

Heat the wok over high heat, and when hot, add the vegetable oil and heat. Add the garlic and ginger and stir-fry for a minute or two, until fragrant. Return the green beans to the pan and stir-fry until almost done.

Add the sauce ingredients to the pan and continue to stir-fry until the sauce has thickened and coats the beans.

Place the beans in a serving bowl or platter, garnish with sesame seeds, and serve.

Yield: 4 servings

Roasted Potatoes
with Dijon-Style Mustard

These creamy, easy-to-prepare potatoes go well with plain grilled poultry or meats. The first bite brings a strong taste of mustard, then all the flavor of the other ingredients come through. It's a side dish with a bold flavor that needs plain meats or strongly flavored fish such as tuna or salmon to complement it.

12 small red-skinned potatoes, quartered

3 to 4 cloves garlic, chopped

½ teaspoon dried thyme

¼ teaspoon ground cayenne

Extra-virgin olive oil

2 tablespoons butter, melted

3 tablespoons Dijon-style mustard, store-bought or homemade (page 117)

2 tablespoons chopped fresh parsley

Salt and freshly ground black pepper

Chopped fresh parsley for garnish

Preheat the oven to 350°F.

Combine the potatoes, garlic, thyme, and cayenne in a bowl. Sprinkle some olive oil over the top and toss to coat the potatoes with the mixture.

Place the potatoes in one layer in a roasting pan, cover the pan tightly with aluminum foil, and bake for 45 to 60 minutes, or until the potatoes are just done.

In a large bowl, whisk together the butter, mustard, and parsley. Season with the salt and pepper. Add the hot potatoes and toss to coat with the sauce. Return the potatoes to the pan and bake, uncovered, for an additional 10 minutes.

Place the potatoes in a serving bowl, garnish with the parsley, and serve.

Yield: 4 to 6 servings

Mango Rice

This quick and easy rice dish provides a colorful, bright accent to any plate. In India it would be made with green mangoes, and do use them if you can find them. We have had good results using canned mangoes, which can be easier to find. Asafetida, which can be found in Indian markets, is derived from the resin of a large fennel-like plant grown in India and Iran. Rather odoriferous, it's used in small quantities for its flavor but mostly for its digestive properties. There is no substitute, so omit it if you can't find it.

5 tablespoons flaked coconut

4 teaspoons brown mustard seeds

½ teaspoon asafetida powder (optional)

½ teaspoon ground turmeric

4 to 6 small dried red chiles, such as piquins

One 15-ounce can mangoes, drained

3 tablespoons vegetable oil

1 tablespoon *sambhar* powder, store-bought or homemade (page 133)

¼ cup raw peanuts

2 cups cooked rice

Salt to taste

Put the coconut, 2 teaspoons mustard seeds, asafetida, turmeric, chiles, and half of the mangoes in a blender or food processor and puree into a smooth paste, adding a little water if necessary.

Heat a heavy skillet over medium-high heat, add the oil, and when hot, add the remaining mustard seeds and heat until the seeds start to pop. Add the sambhar powder and peanuts and continue to fry, stirring constantly, until the peanuts brown, a minute or two.

Stir in the coconut mixture a little at a time until well blended. Add the rice to the pan and stir to coat and heat.

Chop the remaining mango.

To serve, mound the rice on a serving platter and garnish with the chopped mango.

Yield: 4 to 6 servings

Sesame Dan Dan Noodles

 Dan dan noodles are the most famous street food of the Sichuan province in China. They get their name from the sound of the vendors hitting two sticks together as they walk the streets, announcing their arrival. Traditionally they are served with everything on the side, so the customer can buy what he or she wants. We toss the ingredients in with the noodles for a side dish. These noodles can be served hot or cold and with any number of toppings, so they are very versatile. We use the ramen noodles in those three-minute soup packages, as they are so quick and easy and work well in this dish.

1 package dried ramen noodle soup

1 cup grated carrots

¼ cup thinly sliced mushrooms

¼ cup chopped fresh cilantro

2 tablespoons toasted sesame seeds

Sauce

2 tablespoons peanut oil

1 to 2 teaspoons crushed red chile, such as piquin

2 teaspoons grated ginger

1 large clove garlic, minced

2 tablespoons sesame oil

2 tablespoons rice vinegar

2 teaspoons sugar

½ teaspoon salt

Note: This recipe requires advance preparation.

To make the sauce, heat a small skillet over medium-high heat, add the peanut oil, and when hot, add the chiles and stir-fry until the oil turns red, taking care the chiles don't burn. Add the ginger and garlic and cook for 1 minute. Remove from the heat and cool.

Combine all the ingredients for the sauce in a bowl and whisk to combine. Allow the dressing to sit for 30 minutes at room temperature to blend the flavors.

Open the soup package and discard the flavor packet, or save for another use. Cook the noodles, following the directions on the package, until done. Drain the noodles.

Combine the noodles and the dressing in a large bowl and toss to coat. Add the carrots, mushrooms, cilantro, and sesame seeds and toss to distribute all the vegetables.

Place the noodles in a large bowl or mound on a platter and serve.

Yield: 4 servings

Peppercorn Pilao
with Toasted Cumin Seeds

Pilao (also called pilaf) refers to a dish that always has you brown the rice before cooking. A simple dish to prepare, this is a wonderful accompaniment to meat, poultry, and fish, not just curries. The vermicelli and nuts give a nice flavor, and the mellow heat from the pepper complements other spicy dishes. We recommend using basmati rice in this recipe. Basmati is Sanskrit for "queen of fragrance," and this rice has a nutlike aroma and flavor that further enhance the taste of this pilao.

2 tablespoons vegetable oil

1 medium onion, ½ chopped and ½ thinly sliced

2 teaspoons coarsely crushed black peppercorns

1 teaspoon coarsely crushed cumin seeds

¼ teaspoon ground turmeric

½ cup vermicelli, broken into 1-inch pieces

¾ cup basmati rice

2 cups chicken or vegetable broth

1 teaspoon salt

¾ cup frozen peas

1 tablespoon butter

⅓ cup cashew nuts

Heat a heavy skillet over medium-high heat, add 1 tablespoon of the oil, and when hot, add the chopped onion and sauté until softened but not browned. Add the pepper, cumin, and turmeric and sauté, stirring continuously, until fragrant, about 1 minute. Remove and place the mixture into a bowl.

Add the vermicelli to the skillet and sauté until golden. Add the rice and continue to sauté until the vermicelli is lightly browned. Add to the spice mixture.

Pour the broth into a large saucepan and bring to a boil. Add the rice mixture and salt, and stir to mix. When the broth returns to a boil, reduce the heat, cover, and simmer until the rice is done, about 20 to 30 minutes. Stir in the peas and cover until the peas have cooked, about 5 minutes.

Heat a small skillet over medium heat, add the butter and remaining oil, and when hot, add the sliced onions and sauté until they start to brown, about 8 minutes. Add the nuts and cook, stirring constantly, until golden brown, 4 to 5 minutes. Remove and drain on paper towels.

Mound the rice on a platter or in a bowl, garnish with the toasted onions and cashews, and serve.

Yield: 4 servings

Nasi Kunyit (Yellow Festive Rice)

We thank Devagi Shanmugan, who runs the Thomson Cooking School in Singapore, for this rice recipe. Colorful and fragrant, it goes well with meat dishes. If you ever get to Singapore, be sure to take some of her classes. Remember to use coconut milk in this recipe, not canned coconut cream, which is too sweet. To make the garnish, simply slice the white part of a green onion into rings and fry them in a little vegetable oil.

4 stalks lemongrass

4 teaspoons ground coriander

2 teaspoons ground cumin

1 teaspoon ground turmeric

½ teaspoon cayenne powder

One 5-inch piece of fresh ginger, peeled

3 cloves garlic

20 shallots

6 tablespoons vegetable oil

6 cups coconut milk

3 cups rice, washed and drained

Salt to taste

Fried green onion rings for garnish

Trim the stalks of lemongrass to about 3 inches in length. Trim away any hard portions, discard the outer leaves, and coarsely chop.

Place the coriander, cumin, turmeric, cayenne, ginger, garlic, shallots, and 1 cup of water in a blender or food processor and puree until smooth.

Heat a heavy skillet over high heat, add the oil, and when very hot, add the spice blend. Sauté in the oil until fragrant, about 1 minute.

Add the coconut milk and bring to a slow boil. Reduce the heat to a simmer. Add the rice and lemongrass, cover, and cook until the rice is done—about 40 minutes. Taste and adjust the seasonings.

Heat a small skillet over medium-high heat, add a tablespoon of oil, and when hot, add the rings of a sliced green onion and fry until crispy. Remove and drain on paper towels.

Mound the rice on a platter, garnish with the onion rings, and serve.

Yield: 6 servings

Steamed Artichokes with Dipping Sauces

We love artichokes, and we keep finding new ways to serve them. They are versatile in that they can be served hot, cold, or at room temperature, stuffed or not stuffed; and by changing the dipping sauces, you change the dish. This year we came up with two very diverse sauces; one with an Eastern flair containing wasabi, and one with the European flavor of horseradish. Always serve artichokes with an empty bowl for the discarded leaves.

4 small artichokes

Horseradish Sauce

2 tablespoons mayonnaise

1 tablespoon sour cream

2 teaspoons prepared horseradish, store-bought or homemade (page 112)

¼ teaspoon dry dill weed

¼ teaspoon garlic salt

Pinch ground mace

Wasabi-Jalapeño Butter Sauce

2 tablespoons butter

4 teaspoons wasabi paste

2 teaspoons lime juice, preferably fresh

1 teaspoon lime zest

1 teaspoon minced jalapeño chile

1 tablespoon chopped green onions, including some of the greens

In a stockpot or large saucepan, add water to a depth of 2 inches. Place the artichokes bottom side up in a steaming basket, place the basket in the stockpot, cover, and bring the water to a boil over high heat. Steam the artichokes until done, 35 to 40 minutes. Remove and drain.

To make the horseradish sauce, combine all the ingredients in a bowl and stir to mix. Allow to sit at room temperature for 20 minutes to blend the flavors.

To make the wasabi butter, heat a small saucepan over medium heat and add the butter; when it's melted, add the wasabi, lime juice and zest, and jalapeño chile. Simmer the sauce for a couple of minutes and remove from the heat. Add the onions and allow the mixture to sit for 10 minutes to blend the flavors.

To serve, place the artichokes on individual plates. Spoon the sauces into small bowls such as ramekins, place the two sauces on each plate, and serve with another bowl for the leaves.

Yield: 4 servings

Wasabi Potato Pancakes

Pancakes as a side dish for dinner? If made from potatoes, they can be served as a crisp accent to a meal in place of bland mashed potatoes. This is another of those basic recipes that can be altered by changing the ingredients added to the potatoes to vary the taste and to complement the entrée with which they are being served. We've added horseradish, chiles, cheese, and other seasonings.

1½ pounds russet or red-skinned potatoes

¼ cup chopped green onions, including some of the greens

3 tablespoons chopped fresh cilantro

2 tablespoons all-purpose flour

2 tablespoons wasabi paste

2 teaspoons chopped garlic

2 eggs

1 teaspoon salt

Vegetable oil for frying

Peel and grate the potatoes into a bowl and add cold water to cover. Let stand 15 minutes to extract the starch from the potatoes. Using a slotted spoon, remove the potatoes, drain, and let the water they were soaking in sit for a few minutes.

Carefully pour off the water, leaving the sediment in the bowl. This sediment is the starch from the potatoes and will help the pancakes to bind.

Place the potatoes in a clean towel and gently squeeze out any remaining water.

Add the onions, cilantro, flour, wasabi, garlic, eggs, and salt to the bowl with the potato starch and mix to combine. Add the potatoes and stir to mix.

Heat a large, heavy skillet over medium heat, pour in the oil to a depth of ¼ inch, and when it's hot, spoon ¼ to ⅓ cup of the potato mixture into the oil. Flatten the pancakes to about ½-inch thick.

Fry the pancake for 6 minutes, or until browned, turn over, and fry the other side until browned.

Remove and drain the pancakes on a paper towel before serving.

Yield: 4 to 6 servings

Spicy Mustard Greens with Asian Noodles

This dish has a spicy sweet taste offset by the peppery bite of the mustard greens and goes well with many grilled meats, fish, or poultry entrées. It makes a pretty presentation on any plate, with the bright green of the mustard and the white noodles. To change the flavor, add other mushrooms and substitute spinach for the mustard greens, or add beef strips or shrimp and serve as an entrée. It tastes great served hot or at room temperature.

4 ounces soba noodles; or substitute other Asian noodles such as *udon*, *somen*, or ramen (available in Asian markets)

2 teaspoons sesame oil; or substitute peanut oil

1 tablespoon vegetable oil, preferably peanut

1 tablespoon grated fresh ginger

2 teaspoons minced garlic

½ teaspoon crushed red chile, such as piquin

¼ cup chicken or vegetable broth

8 ounces mustard greens, stems removed and coarsely chopped; or substitute Asian baby greens

2 ounces straw mushrooms

1 cup mung bean sprouts

1 tablespoon toasted sesame seeds for garnish

Sauce

1 tablespoon balsamic vinegar

4 teaspoons rice vinegar

1 tablespoon peanut oil

2 teaspoons light soy sauce

1 green onion, chopped

¼ teaspoon dark sesame oil

¼ teaspoon crushed red chile, such as piquin or Santaka

¼ teaspoon sugar

Cook the noodles according to the directions on the package. Drain and rinse the noodles and place in a bowl. Add the sesame oil and toss to coat.

Combine all the sauce ingredients in a bowl and stir to mix.

Heat a heavy skillet or wok over medium-high heat, add the vegetable oil, and when hot, add the ginger, garlic, and chile and stir-fry for a couple of minutes.

Add the broth, and when simmering, add the greens and cook until done. Add the mushrooms and mung beans and cook for a couple of minutes.

Stir the sauce into the vegetable mixture, add the noodles, and toss to coat and reheat.

Put the noodles into a bowl, garnish with toasted sesame seeds, and serve.

Yield: 4 to 6 servings

Tortitas de Papa con Cilantro (Potato Cakes with Cilantro)

Remember those Tater Tots from the school cafeteria? Well, here is our adult version. This recipe is based on one from South America, where these potatoes are a popular appetizer, served with a bowl of salsa. We've added some of our favorite ingredients to the recipe, so serve them as a side dish at dinner or at breakfast or brunch in place of hash browns. The onions are rinsed, as the cakes don't cook long enough to remove their sharpness.

2 medium potatoes, peeled and diced

3 tablespoons finely chopped onions

½ cup coarsely grated *cotija* cheese; or substitute Parmesan

2 tablespoons chopped fresh cilantro

1 large egg, lightly beaten

1 chipotle chile *en adobo*, finely chopped

Salt to taste

Vegetable oil for frying

Put the potatoes in a saucepan, cover with water, and cook until tender. Remove, drain, and place in a bowl. Roughly mash the potatoes, using a fork, so that they still have some texture.

Place the onions in a strainer and hold under cold running water for a minute to remove any bitterness. Drain well and add to the potatoes. Add all the remaining ingredients, except the oil, and lightly toss to mix, using a couple of forks or even your hands to prevent the potatoes from breaking down. They need to retain some of the lumps and texture.

Heat a heavy wide skillet over medium-high heat, add the oil to a depth of ¼ inch, and when hot, drop the potato mixture by the heaping tablespoon into the pan and gently press with a spatula to form little cakes. Fry until brown on one side, turn once, and brown on the other side.

Yield: 4 servings

Frijoles Indios (Indian Pinto Beans with Chorizo and Cheese)

Beans in some form are served with almost every meal in Mexico, including breakfast. And when beans are combined with another staple, steamy hot corn tortillas, you have a healthy, low-fat meal with complete protein. In northern Mexico, the beans of choice are pinto beans. Frijoles are usually cooked in clay pots called ollas, *which impart an earthy taste to the dish, but a saucepan, Crock-Pot, or pressure cooker will produce a tasty product. You must use lard to get an authentic flavor in these beans, but you may substitute vegetable oil. Beans are better if you cook them the day before, and remember to never salt them until they are done, or they will never become tender.*

2 cups dried pinto beans

2 tablespoons lard; or substitute vegetable oil

¼ pound chorizo, store-bought or homemade (page 247)

1 small onion, chopped

2 cloves garlic, crushed

1 to 2 teaspoons crushed de arbol chile; or substitute piquin

Salt to taste

2 cups grated Chihuahua cheese; or substitute Monterey Jack or *queso añejo*

Put the beans in a large saucepan or stockpot, add 2 quarts of water, and remove any beans that float to the top. Bring the mixture slowly to a boil, cover, and reduce the heat. Simmer the beans for 2 hours or until tender, adding more water if necessary. When the beans begin to wrinkle, add the lard, and when they're completely done, add the salt and simmer for an additional 2 minutes. Drain the beans, reserving the liquid.

Return the beans to the saucepan and mash, adding the bean liquid as needed to produce a smooth consistency. Keep adding liquid to keep the beans rather soupy, as they will thicken as they sit.

Heat a skillet over medium heat, add the chorizo, and cook until done, about 10 minutes. Using a slotted spoon, remove the chorizo and add to the beans. Add the onion and garlic to the skillet and sauté until soft. Add the chiles, cook for another minute, and add to the beans.

Stir the cheese into the beans, a little at time, reserving some for the garnish. If the beans are getting too thick, add more of the reserved bean water.

Ladle the beans into a bowl, garnish with the reserved cheese, and serve.

Yield: 4 to 6 servings

Peas 'n' Rice

A dish commonly associated with the Bahamas, peas 'n' rice is believed to have originated with the African slaves that were brought to the islands. Since pigeon peas are grown in just about every backyard in all the islands, it's no wonder they make an appearance at almost every meal. They are dried before using, and the water they are boiled in becomes dark brown and is used to both color and flavor the rice. We were served this dish almost everywhere we ate dinner, from the small establishments to the fanciest of restaurants, throughout the islands.

¼ pound salt pork, chopped

1 onion, chopped

½ cup chopped green bell pepper

1 stalk celery, chopped

2 fresh tomatoes, chopped

2 tablespoons tomato paste

2 teaspoons dried thyme

2 fresh cayenne chiles, stems and
 seeds removed, chopped;
 or substitute jalapeños

2 cups rice

½ cup dried pigeon peas (available
 in Latin markets)

1 quart chicken broth

Salt and freshly ground black pepper
 to taste

Fresh thyme sprigs for garnish

Heat a heavy skillet over medium heat, add the salt pork, and cook to render the fat. Add the onion, bell pepper, and celery and sauté until soft. Stir in the tomatoes, tomato paste, thyme, and chiles, and simmer for 15 minutes. Transfer the mixture to a saucepan.

Add the rice and peas to the saucepan, stir in the broth, and bring to a boil. Reduce the heat, cover, and simmer until the rice is tender and the liquid is absorbed, about 35 minutes.

To serve, mound the rice on a platter and garnish with fresh thyme.

Yield: 4 to 6 servings

Picante de Aguacates (Spicy Chilean Avocados)

The avocado made its way south from Mexico into Peru, Ecuador, and Chile, and was in Peru at the time the Spanish conquistador Francisco Pizarro arrived. Avocados have been popular ever since throughout the Americas, where they make an appearance in dishes ranging from a simple guacamole salsa to soup, and even to a dessert pudding. This spicy, stuffed avocado is a very rich side dish for grilled meats or some of that fine Chilean fish.

2 hard-boiled egg yolks

2 fresh ají chiles, stems and seeds removed, minced; or substitute hot yellow wax chiles or jalapeños

⅓ cup finely chopped onion

1 clove garlic, minced

2 tablespoons chopped fresh cilantro

2 tablespoons champagne vinegar

½ teaspoon salt

¼ teaspoon freshly ground black pepper

3 large ripe avocados

Place the egg yolks in a bowl and mash, using a fork. Add all the remaining ingredients, except the avocados, and mix thoroughly. Taste and adjust the seasonings.

Peel 1 of the avocados, discard the pit, and coarsely chop. Add the avocado to the egg yolk mixture and gently mix.

To serve, cut the remaining avocados in half and discard the pits. Mound the stuffing into the halves and place on individual plates.

Yield: 4 servings

Note: This dish should be prepared as close to serving time as possible, because avocados will start to blacken when exposed to air.

Kossa Mashiya Bil Kibbeh
(Zucchini Stuffed with Kibbeh)

This recipe is based on one provided by Pat Chapman, who says that zucchini look especially attractive when stuffed. In this Lebanese recipe, he uses a kibbeh or meat mixture, but for a nonmeat alternative, an all-bulgur mixture can be substituted. Kibbeh originated thousands of years ago in the Fertile Crescent and to this day is regarded as the national dish of Lebanon and Syria. Although it is sometimes eaten raw, we recommend you eat it fried, or, as in this dish, as a stuffing for vegetables. The success of the dish, according to Pat, depends on using smallish squash, and on coring them neatly. Special corers called ma'wara *with sharp tips are used on larger zucchinis, but an apple corer works well with the smaller ones. This dish can be served as a side or as an entrée.*

8 small zucchini

4 tablespoons vegetable oil

Kibbeh mixture (see below)

2 tablespoons finely chopped onion

1 teaspoon *baharat* seasoning, store-bought or homemade (page 126)

Chopped fresh flat-leaf parsley for garnish

Kibbeh

2 ounces bulgur or *burghul*

¼ pound ground lamb

1 teaspoon fresh mint; or substitute flat-leaf parsley

½ teaspoon ground cinnamon

2 teaspoons *baharat* seasoning, store-bought or homemade (page 126)

2 tablespoons finely chopped onion

Sauce

1 cup plain yogurt

2 teaspoons cornstarch mixed with 2 teaspoons water

Preheat the oven to 325°F.

Cut the tops and stem ends off the zucchini and carefully hollow out the center of each with an apple corer, removing the core. Leave about ¼ inch of skin and flesh all around, and don't pierce the skin, or it will probably split during cooking.

To make the filling, place the bulgur in a fine sieve and rinse well under cold running water. Drain and squeeze until dry. Combine the bulgur, meat, mint, cinnamon, *baharat* seasoning, and onion in a blender or food processor and pulse to form a paste-like, rather sticky mixture.

Heat a heavy skillet over medium-high heat, add the oil, and stir-fry the kibbeh, onion, and *baharat* seasoning for 7 to 8 minutes. Remove and allow the mixture to cool.

Carefully stuff the zucchini with the kibbeh mixture and line them up, side by side, on an baking dish. Bake for 15 to 20 minutes, or until tender.

To make the sauce, place the yogurt in a small saucepan and slowly bring to a simmer, being careful it doesn't curdle. Slowly add the cornstarch mixture and simmer to thicken.

Place the zucchini on a platter, pour the sauce over the top, garnish with the parsley, and serve.

Yield: 4 servings

South African Green Bean Atjar (Green Bean Pickles)

The word atjar *means "a variety of pickles" and is a South African corruption of the Indian achards. This recipe originated in Java and was brought to Cape Town, South Africa, by the Cape Malay workers, who are reputed to be some of the country's best cooks. It is extremely popular, and every Javanese district had its own type of* atjar. *Served as a side dish on just about every table, this is a dish of vegetables and unripened fruits, preserved in a spiced oil mixture. Traditionally, the oil was fish oil, but today vegetable oils are used. The use of fenugreek, turmeric, and curry reflects the tastes of the subcontinent.*

2 pounds stringless green beans, trimmed and cut in 1½-inch pieces

2 tablespoons salt

1½ cups vegetable oil

2 tablespoon curry powder, store-bought or homemade (page 131)

1 teaspoon ground turmeric

2 tablespoons chopped fresh cayenne chiles; or substitute 1 teaspoon ground cayenne

1 teaspoon minced garlic

1 teaspoon ground fenugreek

Note: This recipe requires advance preparation.

Bring a saucepan of water to a boil, add the beans, and blanch for 2 minutes. Remove and rinse in cold water to stop the cooking, and drain.

Place the beans in a bowl, add the salt, and toss to mix. Allow the beans to sit for 2 or 3 hours to remove the liquid. Rinse, drain, and squeeze gently to remove as much moisture as possible.

Heat a small skillet over low heat, add ¼ cup of the oil, and when warm, add the curry and turmeric and stir. Add the chiles, garlic, and fenugreek and, while stirring constantly and slowly, add the remaining oil and cook for 5 minutes.

Pour the seasoned oil over the beans in the jar and let cool for 1 hour. Cover and refrigerate two days before serving.

Yield: Makes about 3 pints

Papas con Rajas
(Potatoes with Chile Strips)

Rajas *means "strips" in Spanish, and refers to a chile that is roasted, peeled, and cut into strips. Dishes such as this are served as a condiment, as a vegetable side dish, or even as a filling in a taco or tamale. This is a simple side dish with a great flavor that can be made more substantial with the addition of chorizo or* longaniza *sausage, or with scrambled eggs. If fresh poblanos aren't available, substitute a mild variety of green New Mexican or Anaheim chile.*

2 small potatoes, peeled,
    cut in ¼-inch cubes

2 tablespoons vegetable oil

⅓ cup chopped white onion

½ teaspoon dried marjoram

3 poblano chiles, roasted, peeled,
    stems and seeds removed,
    cut in ⅛-inch strips

¾ cup grated *queso fresco*;
    or substitute Monterey Jack

Salt to taste

Place the potatoes in a saucepan, cover with salted water, and bring to a boil. Reduce the heat and simmer until the potatoes are tender but still a little firm. Drain, rinse, and allow the potatoes to dry.

Heat a skillet over medium-high heat, add the oil, and when hot, add the onion, potatoes, and marjoram. Sauté the mixture until the potatoes brown, stirring to keep them from sticking, about 10 to 15 minutes.

Add the chiles to the potatoes and heat. Taste and adjust the seasonings.

Place the potatoes in a bowl, toss with the cheese, and serve.

Yield: 4 servings

14
Beverages, Breads, & Desserts

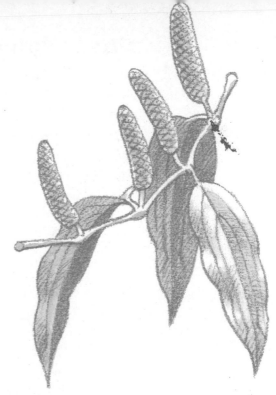

Chai (Spiced Tea)

Chai, which rhymes with pie, *is an Indian word for tea, as well as the name of this beverage. For centuries it's been prepared all over India; the spices used in it vary, but the most common are cardamom, cinnamon, ginger, cloves, and black pepper.* Chai *derives a warming, soothing effect from the cinnamon, cloves, and pepper, while the ginger and cardamom act as natural digestive aids. It's reputed to give one a wonderful sense of well-being, so it's no wonder that drinking* chai *has become a way of life in India. Don't omit the sugar in the recipe, as you need enough to bring out the spice flavor. Somehow* chais *seem to lose their full robustness without it. This tea is sweet and spicy, and is rich enough to be served in place of a dessert. The following is our recipe for* chai, *but feel free to alter it to suit your tastes.*

One 3-inch piece cinnamon stick

1 tablespoon minced ginger

4 whole cloves

6 green cardamom pods, slightly crushed, or substitute ½ teaspoon ground

¼ teaspoon black peppercorns, coarsely crushed

2 allspice berries

½ teaspoon ground nutmeg

2 cups milk

4 to 6 teaspoons sugar, or to taste

2 tablespoons loose tea, preferably black or Darjeeling

Put 2 cups of water and the spices in a saucepan and bring to a boil over high heat. Cover the pot, reduce the heat, and simmer for 10 minutes.

Add the milk and sugar and bring the mixture to a simmer. Add the tea leaves, cover the pot, and turn off the heat. Allow the tea to steep for 2 minutes.

Strain the *chai* into a teapot or individual cups and serve immediately.

Yield: 4 servings

Chile-Flavored Vodka

When we write "flavored," we mean it, as we have chosen the chiles that we think impart the most distinct flavors. The raisiny flavor of the pasilla melds with the apricot overtones of the habanero and the earthiness of the New Mexican chile to create a finely tuned fiery sipping vodka. We recommend using a premium vodka.

1 liter vodka

1 pasilla chile, seeds and stems removed,
    cut into thin strips

½ dried red New Mexican chile pod, seeds
    and stems removed, cut in fourths

¼ habanero chile, seeds and stems
    removed, left whole

Open the bottle of vodka and drink some of it to make room in the bottle. Add the chiles and recap. Let sit for at least 3 days to generate some heat; the vodka will get progressively hotter over the weeks. As you drink the vodka, replace it with more fresh vodka, and the process will go on for some time.

Note: This recipe requires advance preparation.

Yield: About 1 quart

The Great Montezuma

Two of the culinary treasures that Cortez found when he invaded the Aztec empire of Mexico were chocolate and the chile. Chiles and cacao pods were paid as tributes or taxes to the emperor Montezuma, who was quite fond of combining the two. Our friend Richard Sterling developed this recipe, his version of how the Spaniards transformed Montezuma's favorite beverage, with the addition of alcohol. He commented, "Salud! Drink to the Old World and the New."

12 ounces prepared hot chocolate
   (not too sweet)

2 tablespoons honey

½ teaspoon vanilla extract

2 jiggers chile-flavored vodka
   (page 345)

2 tablespoons heavy cream

Ground cayenne and cinnamon
   sticks for garnish

Combine the chocolate, honey, vanilla, and vodka in a small pitcher and stir to mix. Pour into two long-stemmed glasses or Irish coffee glasses.

To serve, float the cream on the tops of the drink, dust with a pinch of cayenne, and garnish with the cinnamon sticks.

Yield: 2 servings

Wasabi Bloody Caesar

This recipe was shared by Larry Greenly, who told us, "In 1969, our Canadian neighbors in Calgary invented the Caesar cocktail to celebrate a new restaurant. The drink now consistently ranks in the top ten favorites. With the addition of wasabi, this recipe takes the Bloody Caesar to where no drink has gone before!"

1 teaspoon wasabi paste
1½ ounces vodka
Celery salt to taste
Salt to taste
Lime wedge

6 ounces Clamato juice
Freshly ground black pepper
Dash hot sauce of choice
Dash Worcestershire sauce
Celery stalk for garnish

Place the wasabi in a small bowl, pour in the vodka, and stir until blended.

Place the celery salt on a small plate. Rub a highball glass rim with the lime wedge, and dip in the celery salt and salt. Add ice to the glass and pour the vodka mixture into the glass.

Add the Clamato juice, pepper, hot sauce, and Worcestershire sauce and stir to mix. Taste and adjust the seasonings.

Squeeze the lime wedge into the glass, stir, and garnish with the celery stalk.

Yield: 1 drink

Hot Lemon-Ginger Tea

This tea is very soothing and refreshing. It's great hot when you have a cold or an upset stomach, but it also can be served over ice to cool and refresh you on a hot summer day. It's simple to prepare—you can even make it when you don't feel well.

⅓ cup thinly sliced pieces peeled ginger
1 tablespoon lemon juice, preferably fresh
Two 3-inch pieces cinnamon stick
1 to 2 tablespoons honey
4 tea bags, preferably black tea

Combine the ginger, lemon juice, cinnamon sticks, and 5 cups of water in a saucepan; bring to a boil. Reduce the heat, and simmer 5 minutes. Remove and discard the ginger and cinnamon sticks. Add enough honey to the mixture to suit your taste.

Place the tea bags in a teapot, and pour the hot ginger mixture over the top. Allow to steep for 3 to 4 minutes, remove the tea bags, and serve.

Yield: 4 servings

Habanero Hot Sauce Bloody Mary

We continue to experiment and alter our recipe in our quest for the perfect Bloody Mary and we believe this may be the one. Two elements in this recipe are of paramount importance: a great vodka and a great habanero hot sauce. Considering all the options available for the latter, imbibers should have no problem selecting a commercial sauce.

2 teaspoons fresh lime juice, preferably Key lime

⅔ cup tomato juice; or substitute V-8
    for a more full-bodied vegetable flavor

⅓ cup chile-flavored vodka (page 345)

2 drops Worcestershire sauce

½ teaspoon store-bought habanero hot sauce,
    your choice

Freshly ground black pepper

1 stalk celery with leaves or 1 green onion for garnish

Fill a large mixing glass with ice cubes, and add the lime juice, tomato juice, vodka, Worcestershire, and habanero hot sauce. Grind some black pepper to taste into the drink.

Place a shaker on top of the mixing glass and, grasping them firmly together with both hands, shake vigorously 17 times.

Remove the shaker, place a strainer on top of the mixing glass, strain the drink into a serving glass, and garnish with the celery or green onion.

Yield: 1 serving

Note: We like our Bloody Marys shaken, not stirred!

Royal Chocolate with Chile

Although this drink was served to royalty in the large Mayan cities, the discovery of chile in conjunction with cacao at the Cerén archaeological site indicates that even commoners knew how to make this concoction. Simple to prepare, it's a spicy drink that will warm you much more quickly than the mundane hot chocolate with marshmallows.

¼ cup cocoa
1 tablespoon honey
¼ teaspoon hot chile powder, such as piquin
1 vanilla bean pod for garnish

In a small saucepan, bring 1½ cups water to a boil over high heat. Add the cocoa, honey, and chile and stir to mix.

Serve immediately with the vanilla bean for garnish in the drink.

Yield: 1 serving

Ginger Ale

There is a long way and a short way to make ginger ale. Since the long one involves boiling and straining, cooling, bottling, and resting, with the possibility of exploding bottles, we are going to go with the short one. The ginger syrup can be prepared ahead of time and refrigerated for a day before use.

¼ cup coarsely grated ginger
1 cup sugar
1 quart seltzer or sparkling mineral water
1 to 2 tablespoons lime juice, preferably fresh
Fresh mint sprigs for garnish

In a saucepan, place the ginger along with 2 cups of water and bring to a boil over moderate heat. Gently boil for 5 minutes, remove from the heat, cover, and steep at room temperature for at least 12 hours.

Note: This recipe requires advance preparation.

Strain the mixture through a sieve lined with a double layer of damp cheesecloth into a bowl. Gather the cheesecloth together and squeeze to extract as much of the liquid as possible from the ginger, and discard the solids.

Return the ginger liquid to the saucepan, add the sugar, stir to dissolve, and bring to a boil over medium heat. Boil until reduced to 1 cup, about 5 minutes. Remove and cool. You may store the syrup in the refrigerator, tightly covered, for a few days.

To serve, pour the seltzer into a large pitcher and add the ginger syrup. Add lime juice to taste. Fill tall glasses with ice, pour the ginger ale over the ice, garnish with the mint, and serve.

Yield: 1 quart

Ginger Beer

There are numerous recipes for making ginger beer. Some contain alcohol, and some don't. We've included one that will produce alcohol but doesn't take as long to ferment as if you were making "regular" beer. The goal here is to produce lots of carbon dioxide in a short period. Once you see a steady fermentation in the liquid, the beer is bottled, stored, and ready to drink in a few days. Just as in making wine or beer, the yeast is multiplying rapidly while consuming sugar, and giving off the byproducts of alcohol and carbon dioxide. No matter how much filtering you do, there will be some sediment at the bottom of your bottles from the yeast and the ginger. You can drink it, or just carefully pour the beer into glasses without disturbing the sediment. If you do have additional questions about making beer, we recommend you consult the many books or Web sites on the subject, or your local beer-making supplier.

1 lemon

1 pound sugar

1½ ounces grated ginger

1 ounce cream of tartar

1 ounce brewer's, wine, or champagne yeast (available at beer-making supply stores)

Note: This recipe requires advance preparation.

Finely peel the zest off the lemon, removing only the outer waxy layer. Reserve the peeled lemon.

Place the sugar, ginger, lemon rind, and cream of tartar into a bucket or large bowl. Heat 2 quarts of water of water to boiling in a large saucepan over high heat. Pour the boiling water over the sugar mixture, add the juice from the reserved lemon, and stir well. Allow the mixture to reach to 70°F, and taste. This will be approximately the taste of the finished product, adjust the taste and, if necessary, add more ginger. Remove a cup of the liquid and stir in the yeast. Add the yeast mixture back into the liquid.

Cover the container with a clean cloth, being sure that the cloth can't come into contact with the top of the liquid. Tie a string around the top of the container to secure the cloth and leave in a warm place, around 70°F, for 24 hours to ferment.

Strain the liquid through a fine cloth, or skim off the froth from the top, and carefully pour out the liquid so as not to disturb the sediment at the bottom.

Pour the beer into sterilized bottles, cap, and store them in a cool dark place. The beer should be ready to drink after 2 to 3 days.

Yield: 2 quarts

Finjan Kirfee (Syrian Spice Drink)

Pronounced "fi-yan-ki-fee," finjan kirfee *is a popular drink in Syria. Composed just of steeped spices, it is considered to be healthful and is traditionally served to visitors who drop by to welcome the birth of a baby.*

2 cinnamon sticks	1 tablespoon anise seeds
2 whole cloves	Sugar to taste
2 tablespoons coarsely chopped ginger	Whole almonds or walnuts for garnish

Combine the spices in a saucepan along with 1 quart of water and bring to a boil over medium-high heat. Boil the mixture until the water turns dark. Strain the mixture into a serving pot. Season to taste with sugar.

To serve, add a nut to each cup, pour the drink into the cups, and serve.

Yield: 4 servings

Michelada (Spicy Beer Cocktail)

Michelada *is a popular cocktail south of the border, but has only recently made its way north—you probably aren't familiar with it unless you've traveled in Mexico or live in the border states. Essentially it's a cocktail prepared with beer and served over ice, and it's very refreshing in the tropical heat. It has been touted as a surefire cure for the "tequila flu."*

1 fresh lime, preferably Key lime
Coarse salt or margarita salt
2 dashes Worcestershire sauce
1 dash soy sauce
1 dash habanero hot sauce

Freshly ground black pepper
One 12-ounce bottle dark Mexican beer, such as Negra Modelo or Bohemia

Cut the lime in half; rub one half around the rim of a large glass, and reserve the other half. Pour the salt onto a plate and dip the rim of the glass in the salt to coat.

Fill the glass with ice and squeeze the juice from the reserved lime half into the glass. Add the Worcestershire, soy, and habanero sauces, along with a few grindings of the pepper.

Pour in the beer, stir, and serve.

Yield: 1 serving

Mustard Dill Bread

This recipe was provided by Nancy's husband, Jeff, who is the bread baker of this bunch. This bread, according to him, "is begging for some ham and cheese." Easy to prepare, it can be made by hand or in a bread machine. If you make it in a machine, follow the directions in the manufacturer's manual.

½ cup plus 2 tablespoons very warm water, 110 to 115°F

1½ teaspoons active dry yeast

3 cups bread flour

2 tablespoons dry milk powder

1 tablespoon sugar

¾ teaspoon salt

1 tablespoon Dijon-style mustard, store-bought or homemade (page 117)

1 tablespoon melted butter

2 teaspoons dry dill weed; or substitute dill seeds

Put the warm water in a small bowl, sprinkle the yeast over the top, and let stand for 5 minutes, or until the yeast dissolves.

Combine all the remaining ingredients and mix to combine, using your hands if necessary. Add the yeast and continue to mix until the dough comes together, adding more flour or water if needed.

Turn the dough onto a floured board and knead until the dough is smooth and elastic.

Place the dough in an oiled mixing bowl, cover loosely with plastic wrap, and let rise in a warm place until doubled, about 1 to 1½ hours.

Oil a 1-pound loaf pan. Punch the dough down, and form into a loaf. Place the dough in the pan and let rise until doubled again.

Preheat the oven to 350°F.

Bake the bread for 35 to 40 minutes or until the top is browned, and the bottom, sounds hollow when tapped. Turn onto a rack to cool.

Yield: 1 pound loaf

Note: This recipe requires advance preparation.

Niter Kebbeh Ambasha (Ethiopian Flat Bread)

The breads of Ethiopia tend to be round, rather flat breads, so they are perfect for baking on a pizza pan, and many, such as ambasha, *are baked with spices. This bread is decorated to look like a round wheel with a ball or knob in the center. If you don't have a batch of* berbere *prepared, just brush the top of the baked bread with butter and sprinkle a mixture of ground cayenne, ground ginger, ground cinnamon, and a pinch of cloves on it.*

¼ cup warm water, 110 to 115°F

1 tablespoon active dry yeast

2 tablespoons ground coriander

1 teaspoon ground cardamom

½ teaspoon ground white pepper

1 teaspoon ground fenugreek

2 teaspoons salt

⅓ cup *niter kebbeh* (page 130); or substitute vegetable oil

1¼ cup lukewarm water

5 cups unbleached bread flour

Berbere, store-bought or homemade (page 129), and *niter kebbeh* (page 130); or substitute butter, for topping

Note: This recipe requires advance preparation.

Pour the warm water in a small bowl, sprinkle the yeast over the top, and stir to dissolve. Allow the mixture to sit for 5 to 10 minutes, or until the yeast starts to bubble.

Combine the yeast, water, coriander, cardamom, pepper, fenugreek, and salt in a large bowl and stir to mix. Add the oil and 1¼ cups water, and stir to blend. Slowly add the flour until it can be gathered into a ball. If the dough becomes too stiff, you may have to use your hands.

Turn the dough onto a floured board and knead for 10 minutes, or until it's smooth and tiny bubbles form. This recipe produces a stickier dough than usual, so don't add a lot of flour. Reserve a 1-inch piece of dough and set aside.

With floured hands, spread the dough out on an ungreased pizza pan no more than 1 inch thick. Using a sharp knife, score the dough in a design similar to the spokes of a bicycle or wagon wheel but do not cut all the way through. Roll the piece of the reserved dough into a ball, place in the center of the scored round of dough, and flatten it slightly to secure. Cover and let the bread rise for 1 hour.

Preheat the oven to 350°F. Bake the bread for 1 hour or until golden brown. Remove the bread and slide it off onto a wire rack to cool. While it's still warm, brush with the oil or butter and then the *berbere*.

Yield: One 12-inch-round bread

Caribbean Curry Crackers

Crackers are great with dips and salsas, but you don't have to limit your selection to what's on the grocer's shelves. Just about any bread dough can be made into a cracker by rolling it out to a thickness of about ⅛ inch thick and cutting into shapes. Some doughs produce a very crisp cracker, while others, such as this one, result in a little more breadlike consistency. These crackers don't store well, so either bake them fresh or store in an airtight tin for a day.

1½ cups milk

½ teaspoon active dry yeast

2¾ cups all-purpose flour

1½ teaspoons salt

¼ cup West Indian masala, store-bought
   or homemade (page 151)

2 teaspoons ground habanero chile

Cornmeal for the pan

Melted butter and poppy seeds
   for topping

Place the milk in a small saucepan and slowly warm over low heat to 100°F. Remove from the heat and pour into a large mixing bowl. Sprinkle the yeast over the top and stir to dissolve. Allow the mixture to sit for 3 to 4 minutes.

Sift all the dry ingredients into a bowl. Add the dry ingredients to the yeast mixture and stir to mix. Turn the dough onto a floured surface and knead until the dough is elastic, about 5 to 8 minutes.

Lightly oil a bowl, add the dough, cover, and let rise until doubled, about 1 hour.

Preheat the oven to 375°F.

Punch down the dough and place on a floured surface. Roll out the dough until it is very thin, ⅛ to ¹⁄₁₆ inch. The thinner the dough, the crisper the cracker. Allow the dough to rest for 15 minutes.

Sprinkle a little cornmeal on a sheet pan. Cut the dough into the desired shapes—triangles, circles, squares—and place on the sheet pan. Brush them with the butter and sprinkle the poppy seeds over the top.

Bake for 20 to 30 minutes, or until brown and crisp. Remove the crackers from the pan and cool on a wire rack.

Yield: 2 to 3 dozen, depending on size

Note: This recipe requires advance preparation.

Egyptian Focaccia

It may sound odd, but when we thought about dipping bread in olive oil and then dukkah, *we thought, Hey, why don't we make it simpler by combining it all in one recipe? From there it wasn't a big stretch to throw in some other Mediterranean ingredients to come up with a Middle Eastern version of this classic Italian bread.*

1½ cups warm water,
100 to 115°F

2¼ teaspoons active dry yeast

2 tablespoons sun-dried
tomatoes packed in oil

3½ cups bread flour

1 teaspoon salt

2 teaspoons sugar

1 to 2 tablespoons chopped
kalamata olives

2 tablespoons olive oil

Topping

3 tablespoons *dukkah,*
store-bought or
homemade (page 127)

Coarse salt

*Note: This recipe
requires advance
preparation.*

Pour the warm water into a bowl and sprinkle the yeast over the top. Let the mixture sit for 15 minutes so the yeast can develop.

Drain the tomatoes, reserving the oil, and chop. Sift 3 cups of the flour, and the salt and sugar into a large bowl. Make a well in the center and add the yeast, water, and olive oil. Using your hands, bring the flour into the center to mix. Add the tomatoes and olives and mix. Turn the dough onto a floured surface and knead, adding more flour if necessary, until smooth and elastic, about 5 to 10 minutes. Oil a bowl with the olive oil, put in the dough, turn over, and cover with a damp towel. Allow the dough to rise until doubled, about 1 hour and 45 minutes.

Lightly oil a 12-by-16-inch sheet pan. Punch down the dough and put on the pan. Using the heel of your hand, press and stretch the dough to fill the pan. Allow the dough to rise one more time.

Preheat the oven to 400°F.

Make indentations over the top of the dough, using your fingers. Brush the reserved oil from the tomatoes, and sprinkle the *dukkah* and salt over the top.

Bake the focaccia for 20 to 25 minutes, or until golden. Remove the pan and cool on a rack. When cool, cut in pieces.

Yield: Serves 12 as an appetizer

Taos Corn-Husk Muffins with Blue Corn, Chipotle, and Cheese

These muffins are a tasty alternative to the usual slices of plain cornbread served at barbecues and make a great presentation in their own corn-husk wrappers. They have a buttery texture, a sweet and nutty cornmeal flavor, and a spicy "kick" from the chipotle chiles. We like to use blue corn in this recipe because of its nutty taste, but if it isn't available, substitute yellow—the muffins will be just as good. Corn husks are available in Latin food markets, but if you can't find them, you can make the muffins in tins, as you normally would.

6 to 8 dry corn husks

1 cup all-purpose flour

¾ cup blue cornmeal

⅓ cup sugar

3 teaspoons baking powder

¾ teaspoon salt

1 cup milk

1 egg, beaten

1 cup grated cheddar cheese, divided

3 tablespoon melted margarine

3 chipotle chiles *en adobo*,
    drained and chopped

Place the corn husks in a bowl, cover with very hot water, and soak until soft and pliable, 20 to 30 minutes. Remove, drain, and pat dry with a paper towel. Tear the husks into lengthwise strips, 1½ to 2 inches wide.

Preheat the oven to 375°F.

Sift all the dry ingredients together in a large mixing bowl.

Combine the milk, egg, ½ cup of cheese, margarine, and the chiles in another bowl. Add the liquid ingredients to the dry and stir to just moisten. Do not overmix!

Lightly oil a muffin tin and line each cup with 2 to 3 strips of the husks, crosswise in the bottom and with the ends extending beyond the cup. Fill each cup three-quarters full and top with the remaining cheese.

Bake the muffins for 20 to 25 minutes, or until a toothpick inserted into the middle of a muffin comes out clean.

Lift the muffins out of the tin and cool on a rack. Serve warm or at room temperature.

Yield: 12 to 15 muffins

Ginger Scones

Scones are a Scottish quick bread whose popularity has spread to the British Isles and across the ocean to the United States. They are similar to biscuits, but richer, with a slightly cakelike texture. Scones usually contain moist additions such as currants, the traditional choice, or more unusually, ham, cheese, sun-dried tomatoes, and often in the Southwest, green chile. These scones combine two forms of ginger, ground and crystallized, and are much moister than the traditional ones.

1 cup plus 2 tablespoons milk

2 tablespoons honey

4 cups unbleached flour

¼ cup sugar

2 tablespoons baking powder

1 teaspoon salt

1 teaspoon ground ginger

1 cup (2 sticks) butter, softened and cut into small pieces

½ cup crystallized ginger, finely chopped and dredged in flour

½ cup raisins, dredged in flour

Preheat the oven to 400°F, and lightly oil a sheet pan.

Combine 2 tablespoons of the milk and the honey in a small saucepan over medium-low heat, and stir until the honey is dissolved. Remove from the heat and keep warm.

Sift all the dry ingredients into a large bowl.

Add the butter and cut it into the dry ingredients using either a pastry blender or two forks, until coarse crumbs are formed.

Add the crystallized ginger, the remaining milk and warm honey mixture to the flour and gently mix just until a soft dough is formed. Do not overmix. Turn the dough onto a lightly floured surface and gently knead 5 times.

Roll out the dough to form a thick 8-inch square. Cut the square into quarters, diagonally. Cut each quarter in half to make triangles.

Place the scones 1 inch apart on the sheet pan.

Bake for 15 minutes, or until they are lightly browned. Place them on a rack to cool and serve warm or at room temperature.

Yield: 8 scones

Spiced Cranberry Pumpkin Loaf

The flavors of cranberries, pumpkin, and habanero chile blend well together, producing a bread that is sweet, tart, and hot. Pumpkins and cranberries are usually associated with fall harvests, but with the availability of frozen cranberries and canned pumpkin, this bread can be a year-round favorite. Serve these at Thanksgiving and enjoy traditional tastes with one the Pilgrims never heard of—chile!

3½ cups all-purpose flour

2 teaspoons baking soda

½ teaspoon baking powder

1 teaspoon salt

1 teaspoon ground habanero chile

1 teaspoon ground cinnamon

½ teaspoon ground cloves

¼ teaspoon ground nutmeg

⅔ cup chopped cranberries

One 8-ounce package cream cheese, softened

8 tablespoons (1 stick) butter, softened

2½ cups sugar

4 eggs

2 cups canned pumpkin puree

2 teaspoons orange zest

Preheat the oven to 350°F, and lightly oil 2 loaf pans.

Sift the dry ingredients, except the sugar, together into a bowl. Add the cranberries and stir to coat.

In another large mixing bowl, cream the cheese, butter, and sugar together until fluffy. This can be done by hand or with a mixer. Add the eggs, one at a time, beating well after each addition. Beat in the pumpkin and orange zest and mix well.

Add the dry ingredients to the pumpkin mix and stir just to mix. Do not overmix, or the bread will be tough. Divide the batter between the two loaf pans.

Bake the bread for 60 to 75 minutes, or until a toothpick inserted into the middle of a loaf comes out clean.

Cool the bread on a wire on a rack for 15 minutes. Remove the bread from the pans and continue to cool. Serve them warm or at room temperature.

Yield: 2 loaves

Gingerbread with Lemon Whipped Cream

Gingerbread dates back to the Middle Ages, when it was given to knights before they went to compete in tournaments. The only baked product older than gingerbread is bread itself. This spicy cake is dark, dense, and moist, and we like to serve it with lemon whipped cream. The tartness of the lemon complements the rich spiciness of the gingerbread.

1¾ cup flour

2 teaspoons ground ginger

1¼ teaspoon ground cardamom

1 teaspoon baking soda

½ teaspoon ground black pepper

¼ teaspoon ground cinnamon

¼ teaspoon ground cloves

¼ teaspoon salt

½ cup butter, at room temperature

½ cup light brown sugar

1 large egg

1 cup unsulfured molasses

2 teaspoons grated orange zest

½ cup boiling water

Lemon Whipped Cream

1 cup chilled heavy cream

2 teaspoons sugar

2 drops lemon extract

½ teaspoon lemon zest

Preheat the oven to 350°F. Grease and flour a 9-inch cake pan with 2-inch-high sides.

Sift the dry ingredients into a bowl.

In a large mixing bowl, cream the butter and brown sugar together until well mixed. Add the egg and continue to beat until fluffy. Slowly mix in the molasses and orange zest. Add the dry ingredients to the butter mixture and mix until just combined. Gradually mix in the boiling water.

Pour the batter into the pan and bake for 40 to 50 minutes, until a toothpick that is inserted into the center of the bread comes out clean and the cake pulls from the sides. Be aware that the cake may sink in the center—this is normal.

Cool on a rack for 10 minutes, then run a knife around the edge and invert the cake on another rack to finish cooling.

Pour the cream in a chilled bowl and, using chilled beaters, beat until thickened. Add the remaining ingredients and continue to beat until whipped and light.

To serve, cut the gingerbread into squares, place on individual serving plates, and garnish with a dollop of lemon whipped cream.

Yield: 6 to 8 servings

Red Chile Amaretto Truffles

Chocolate truffles really did get their name from those famous French fungi. Early chocolate truffles were rather "free-form," and when they had been dusted with cocoa, they did resemble those that are found underground. When we first starting combining chiles and chocolate years ago, people thought we'd lost our minds, but the rest of the chocolate lovers have caught up. Now even noted chocolatiers in Europe like Leysieffer of Osnabruck and Adolph Andersen of Hamburg are including chile in their creations. These rich, hot candies are well worth the extra effort it takes to make them. Because the filling needs to be refrigerated overnight, they do require advance preparation. Chile takes a back seat, with a fairly mild presence.

1 pound semisweet baking chocolate, preferably Lindt or Valrhona

2 tablespoons unsalted butter

1 tablespoon light cornstarch

½ cup whipping cream

2 tablespoons amaretto

2 to 3 teaspoons Chimayó or other New Mexican chile powder

To make the filling, chop or break 9 ounces of the chocolate into small pieces and place in a heat-resistant bowl, along with the butter and cornstarch.

Pour the cream into a heavy saucepan and bring to a rolling boil over medium-high heat. Pour the cream over the chocolate and stir until all the chocolate has melted. Allow the mixture to cool, stir in the amaretto and chile, and mix well. Cover the bowl and place in the refrigerator overnight to set. The filling should be firm, like frosting.

Line a cookie sheet with wax paper, drop the filling onto the pan by the tablespoon, and roll to form a ball. This is more easily done if your hands are cold; if you find that the filling is becoming sticky and hard to work with, put it back in the refrigerator to chill again and wash your hands with cold water before continuing. When done making the balls, cool the filling in the refrigerator until firm.

Place the remaining chocolate in the top of a double boiler or small saucepan over simmering water. Stir the chocolate continuously until melted, being careful that absolutely no water gets into the chocolate! Dip the chilled filling balls in the chocolate to cover and place back on the cookie sheet. Place the pan in the refrigerator to firm again.

Yield: Approximately 2 dozen

Note: This recipe requires advance preparation.

Ginger Gelato

A number of toppings go well with this dish. We've added a topping of crystallized ginger for a double ginger hit, but chocolate sauce and sliced fresh strawberries are also good. Be sure to add all the sugar called for, as freezing dulls the flavor—what may taste too sweet in the sauce may be just right when frozen. Since ginger aids digestion, this rich and tasty gelato is the perfect way to end a meal.

1 cup heavy cream

1 cup whole milk

¼ cup plus 2 tablespoons sugar

3 to 4 tablespoons coarsely grated ginger

1 teaspoon vanilla extract

2 egg yolks

Topping: ⅓ cup crystallized ginger, finely chopped, store-bought or homemade (page 111)

Combine the cream, milk, sugar, and ginger in a heavy saucepan and heat over medium heat, stirring occasionally, until the sugar is dissolved and the mixture is hot.

Pour the custard through a sieve into a bowl, pressing down on the ginger to release every drop of extract. Stir in the vanilla.

Place the egg yolks in a bowl and whisk briefly. While whisking, slowly add in about 1 cup of the hot liquid to the eggs.

When the mixture is smooth, slowly pour it into the liquid in the saucepan, whisking constantly.

Cook the mixture over medium heat, stirring constantly, until it thickens slightly and coats the back of a spoon, about 6 minutes. Be sure not to let the mixture boil at any time, or it will curdle.

Strain the mixture into a clean bowl. Cool and then cover.

Freeze the gelato in a commercial ice cream maker, according to the manufacturer's directions.

Yield: About 1 pint

Green Chile Piñon Ice Cream

Don't let appearances fool you; this is not a sweet pistachio ice cream. You can control the heat by the chile you use; a Big Jim will give you a mild ice cream; a Sandia or Barker, a hot one. Both hot and cool, this is a wonderful dessert to finish a summer barbecue. Galliano is an Italian liqueur with a bright yellow color and a unique flavor derived from a combination of 35 herbs and spices. Piñon nuts, or pinoli in Italian, are pine nuts.

2 cups heavy cream

1 cup milk

⅔ cup sugar

¼ teaspoon salt

3 egg yolks

1 cup mashed avocado

1 tablespoon lemon juice

¼ cup Galliano (optional)

⅓ cup chopped green
New Mexican chile

3 tablespoons piñon nuts

Combine the cream, milk, sugar, and salt in the top of a double boiler and mix well. Bring to a boil while stirring constantly. Remove from the heat.

In a bowl, whisk together the egg yolks. While whisking the egg yolks, slowly add one-third of the hot cream mixture. Reheat the remaining cream mixture and add the egg mixture. Cook the mixture, stirring constantly, until moderately thickened. Remove and chill.

Put the avocados, lemon juice, and Galliano, if using, in the blender or food processor and process until smooth. Slowly add the avocados to the chilled cream mixture, and stir to mix. Add the green chile and piñons, and mix. Chill the mixture.

Freeze the ice cream in a commercial ice cream maker according to the manufacturer's directions.

Yield: 3 to 4 cups

Tangerine and Cracked Black Pepper Sorbet

Here's a sweet and spicy sorbet that will surprise and delight guests. The combination of fruit and black pepper may seem strange, but the pepper actually enhances the fresh flavor of the tangerine. If you don't have an ice cream maker, make a granita, a frozen dish that is intentionally made to have a grainy texture similar to shaved ice. Just follow the recipe but pour the mixture into a shallow metal dish and place in the freezer. Every hour, stir to cause ice crystals to form, until the mixture resembles shaved ice.

1 cup sugar

½ teaspoon lemon juice

4 cups tangerine juice (about 15 tangerines)

1 tablespoon finely grated tangerine zest

1½ teaspoons freshly coarse-ground black pepper

Fresh mint sprigs for garnish

Combine the sugar, 1 cup water, and lemon juice in a saucepan and bring to a boil over medium heat. Reduce the heat and simmer over low heat until all the sugar is dissolved and the mixture is clear. Skim off any foam that forms. Cool the syrup in the refrigerator.

When the syrup is cold, combine it with the tangerine juice, tangerine zest, and black pepper. Freeze the sorbet in an ice cream maker according to the manufacturer's directions.

Serve the sorbet in chilled martini glasses with a sprig of mint.

Yield: 6 to 8 servings

Crostada del Diavolo (Devil's Tart)

Harald Zoschke collected this recipe for us in Calabria. He comments, "Sweet heat is popular in southern Italy, as evidenced by this tart, which is a specialty of the Sabbia d'Oro restaurant in the Calabrian province of Cosenza." Chile jam is readily available from mail-order sources and specialty shops.

8 tablespoons (1 stick) unsalted butter, softened

⅔ cup sugar

1 large egg, plus 2 egg yolks

½ teaspoon grated lemon peel

2 cups flour

1 tablespoon baking powder

⅓ cup orange marmalade

⅓ cup store-bought *marmellata di peperoncino* (red chile jam)

½ cup almonds, peeled and chopped

2 tablespoons confectioner's sugar

Preheat the oven to 350°F.

In a large bowl, cream the butter and sugar together, add the egg, egg yolks, and lemon peel, and continue to beat until fluffy.

In another bowl, sift together the flour and baking powder. Slowly add the dry ingredients to the butter mixture. Stir to just combine.

Divide the dough in half; roll out one half and spread it over the bottom of a tart or pie pan.

Spread the orange jam evenly on the dough in the pie dish, then spread the chile jam evenly on top of the orange jam.

Work the almonds into the remaining dough. Roll out the dough to the size of the tart pan.

Tightly cover the tart in the dish with the rolled-out dough sheet.

Bake the tart for 25 to 30 minutes, or until golden brown. Remove from the oven and cool on a rack.

Dust the tart with the confectioner's sugar before serving.

Yield: 4 to 6 servings

Fresh Peach Shortcake
with Ginger Crème Anglaise

This dessert sauce is made from the same ingredients as crème brûlée, but is cooked on top of the stove and stirred so that it doesn't gel. The trick to making this sauce is to heat slowly and stir constantly to prevent the mixture from curdling. Crème anglaise transforms a simple dessert into one that is elegant. We like to serve it over fruit shortcakes in place of the usual whipped cream; the touch of ginger complements the fruit. The sauce can be made up to 2 days ahead and refrigerated.

3 cups sliced fresh peaches
Sugar
4 biscuits or shortcakes
Fresh mint leaves for garnish

Crème Anglaise

1 cup whole milk
½ cup heavy cream
1 tablespoon grated ginger
⅓ cup sugar
5 egg yolks
1 teaspoon vanilla extract

To make the sauce, combine the milk, cream, and ginger in a heavy saucepan and slowly heat until hot. Remove from the heat and let steep for 15 minutes. Return the saucepan to the stove and reheat until small bubbles form around the edges of the liquid.

Combine the sugar and the egg yolks in a bowl and whisk until slightly thickened. Slowly strain the hot milk into the eggs while whisking. It's important to do this slowly so that the eggs temper rather than cook. Discard the solids from the sieve.

Transfer the mixture to a small saucepan and cook over moderately low heat, stirring constantly, until the sauce thickens and coats the back of a spoon or reaches a temperature of 170°F, about 5 minutes. Do not let the mixture boil.

Again strain the sauce through a clean sieve into a bowl, stir in the vanilla, and cover the surface with plastic wrap to prevent a "skin" from forming. Cool and chill.

Place the peaches in a bowl, sprinkle with sugar and set aside.

To serve, place a biscuit or cake on individual plates and top with the peaches. Ladle the crème anglaise over the peaches, garnish with the mint leaves, and serve.

Yield: 4 servings

Fresh Margarita Strawberries with Tequila and Cracked Black Peppercorns

This is a margarita that you eat with a spoon, not drink! If you don't like to use alcohol, you can simply leave the tequila out of the recipe; the flavor will be different, but still tasty. This quick and easy dessert has a sweet and sour taste, and the peppercorns leave your mouth warm after eating a bowl of strawberries. Denice Skrepcinski shared this recipe; since she is a food stylist, she knows how to turn a simple bowl of fruit into a very special dessert.

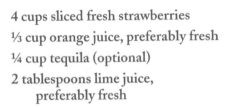

4 cups sliced fresh strawberries

⅓ cup orange juice, preferably fresh

¼ cup tequila (optional)

2 tablespoons lime juice, preferably fresh

1 to 1½ teaspoons balsamic vinegar

1½ teaspoons freshly ground coarse black pepper

Sugar to taste

Lime slices for garnish

Combine the strawberries, orange juice, tequila, if using, lime juice, and vinegar and toss to coat. Add the pepper and toss again.

For a dramatic presentation, rub the rims of margarita glasses with lime juice and dip them into the sugar. Divide the strawberries between the glasses, sprinkle a little sugar over the berries, garnish with lime slices, and serve.

Yield: 4 servings

Pfeffernusse (Peppernut Cookies)

Whether you call them pfeffernusse *in Germany,* pebernodder *in Denmark, or* pepparnotter *in Sweden, these spicy drop cookies have been traditional Christmas fare since the Middle Ages. Over the years many variations have evolved, in both ingredients and methods. Now these cookies can be glazed with a frosting, or just rolled in or dusted with powdered sugar. The original German recipe contained black pepper, but over the years some recipes have eliminated it. According to Nancy's grandmother, whose family recipe this is, the black pepper is absolutely necessary, as it enhances the spice flavor. Besides the pepper, the earliest pfeffernusse recipes used cinnamon, allspice, and cloves, which were called spice nails in the Middle Ages. These cookies do tend to become hard rather quickly; to soften them again, just place an apple slice in an open plastic bag in the container, throwing it away after a few days. They can be stored in an airtight container for 2 months or frozen indefinitely.*

1¼ to 1½ cups all-purpose flour

1 teaspoon ground cinnamon

¾ teaspoon coarsely ground black pepper

½ teaspoon ground cardamom

½ teaspoon ground ginger

½ teaspoon ground cloves

¼ teaspoon mace

¼ teaspoon ground allspice

¼ teaspoon baking powder

⅛ teaspoon baking soda

⅛ teaspoon salt

4 tablespoons (½ stick) unsalted butter, softened

½ cup sugar

1 large egg yolk

¼ cup slivered blanched almonds, finely chopped

¼ cup finely chopped candied orange peel

¼ cup finely chopped candied citron

1 teaspoon finely grated lemon zest

3 tablespoons molasses

3 tablespoons brandy

½ cup powdered sugar

Note: This recipe requires advance preparation.

Sift all the dry ingredients, except the powdered sugar, into a bowl.

In another bowl, cream the butter and sugar together, add the egg yolk, and beat until fluffy.

In yet another bowl, combine the nuts, fruits, molasses, and brandy.

Stir the flour mixture into the butter mixture in 3 parts, alternating with molasses and brandy. Cover the bowl and refrigerate for a couple of days to blend the flavors.

Position the oven rack in the upper third of the oven and preheat to 350°F. Grease a couple of sheet pans.

Roll the cookie dough in ¾-inch balls and space them about 1 inch apart on the sheet pans.

Bake for 12 to 14 minutes, or until the tops just begin to color. Rotate the pans halfway through for even baking.

Remove the pan and put on a rack to slightly cool. Either roll the cookies in, or lightly dust with the powdered sugar.

Yield: About 5 dozen

15 Soothing Counterpoints: Cool-Downs

Mint Raita

Raitas *are yogurt-based salsas or salads served as cooling counterpoints to hot and spicy Indian foods. The vegetables used can be raw or cooked, and low-fat or whole-milk yogurt can be used. If using whole-fat yogurt, thin with a little water to produce a smooth texture. Because of the coolness of the yogurt,* raitas *are served only during hot weather. This* raita *can also be served with crudités or pieces of Indian bread or naan as an appetizer.*

½ cup plain yogurt

2 tablespoons chopped fresh mint

1 tablespoon minced onion

½ teaspoon garam masala, store-
   bought or homemade (page 135)

½ teaspoon minced serrano chile

Pinch of sugar

Salt to taste

Combine all the ingredients in a bowl, cover, and let sit at room temperature for an hour to blend the flavors. Refrigerate until ready to use.

Yield: ½ cup

Cucumber Slaw

Simple and easy to prepare, this salad is a great accompaniment to any hot grilled fish. It combines the cool, crispy taste of cucumbers with a slightly hot sweet and sour sauce.

1 large cucumber, peeled and julienned

2 green onions, sliced, including
    some of the greens

2 tablespoons chopped fresh cilantro

Dressing

¼ cup rice vinegar

1 teaspoon sugar

½ teaspoon crushed red chile

¼ teaspoon sesame oil

In a bowl, whisk together all the dressing ingredients until well blended.

In another bowl combine the cucumber and green onions. Pour the dressing over the top, toss to coat, and garnish with the cilantro.

Yield: 4 servings

Queso Napolitano (Flan)

Flans, Spanish in origin, are very popular throughout all of Mexico, where they are typically offered at the end of a spicy meal. This flan is served in the Yucatán area; it is firmer than most, almost like a cheesecake rather than the usual delicate baked custard. Because it's firm, you can top it with any number of fresh fruits, or eliminate the caramel and top with a different sauce.

½ cup sugar
One 14-ounce can condensed milk
One 12-ounce can evaporated milk
6 eggs

1 tablespoon vanilla
One 8-ounce package cream cheese, softened

Preheat the oven to 350°F.

Combine the sugar and ¼ cup water in a heavy saucepan over medium-low heat and simmer to dissolve the sugar, stirring a couple of times. Raise the heat and bring to a boil. Reduce the heat to medium, and simmer while swirling the pan until the sugar turns golden and is caramelized. Immediately pour into the flan mold and tilt so that the sugar covers the bottom of the pan.

Combine the remaining ingredients in a bowl, beat until smooth, and pour into the mold. Cover the mold with aluminum foil.

Place the mold in a pan of water that reaches to within an inch of the top. Put in the center of the oven and bake for 40 to 50 minutes, or until a knife inserted in the center comes out clean.

Let cool, then place in refrigerator for 1 hour before unmolding.

Yield: 12 servings

Note: This is best prepared using a flan mold, but you can also use a soufflé dish, or any round ovenproof dish.

Chilled Natillas with Shaved Chocolate

This soft custard pudding, which is also called "Spanish cream," is one of the ways New Mexicans tame the flames of chiles. It's commonly served plain, but we like to add some chocolate shavings for added flavor. To shave chocolate, chill until almost frozen and use a vegetable peeler to peel off long, thin curls. Natillas are an easy dessert to prepare, and the cook has the enjoyable task of selecting the chocolate bar for the garnish.

3 eggs, separated
¾ cup sugar
2 tablespoons all-purpose flour
2 cups whole milk

¼ teaspoon ground cinnamon
⅛ teaspoon ground nutmeg
Shaved chocolate of any type
    for garnish

Beat the egg whites in a bowl, and gradually add 1 tablespoon of the sugar. Beat until they are stiff but not dry.

Combine the egg yolks, flour, and 1 cup of milk in a bowl and beat to form a smooth paste.

Combine the remaining milk and sugar in a saucepan over medium heat, and cook until the milk is just below the boiling point, or scalded. Add the egg mixture and continue to cook, on medium heat, until thickened to a soft custard consistency. Remove from the heat and stir in the cinnamon and nutmeg.

Gently fold the egg whites into the hot custard mixture. Dish the mixture into individual shallow bowls and chill until ready to serve.

Serve the pudding warmed or chilled and garnished with the shaved chocolate curls.

Yield: 6 to 8 servings

Bot Bo Go (Eight Treasures Pudding)

An elaborate Chinese banquet often ends with a serving of this fruit-filled pudding. Through many centuries of Chinese history, the Eight Treasures has served to ward off evil and bring goodness. The Eight Treasures are depicted on clothing and as motifs in porcelain and embroidery, as well as used in this traditional holiday dessert.

4 cups glutinous rice, washed and drained

1 cup sugar

3 tablespoons vegetable oil

1 jar sweet bean paste (available in Asian markets)

Treasures

Raisins

Canned gingko nuts (available at Asian markets)

Chestnuts

Walnuts

Candied red and green cherries

Candied melon

Candied ginger

Candied kumquats

Wash and drain the rice and place in a heavy saucepan. Add 2½ cups cold water, cover, and bring to a boil over high heat, about 20 minutes. Reduce the heat to very low and continue cooking another 30 minutes.

Combine the sugar and the oil in a bowl and mix until the sugar dissolves. Add the cooked rice and stir to completely coat the rice.

Oil the bottom of a large, deep bowl and arrange the fruits and nuts in a decorative design. Add a layer of rice and top with the sweet bean paste. Alternate the rows until you've used up the rice.

Place a trivet in the bottom of a stockpot large enough to hold the bowl with the pudding. Add water to the bottom of the pot and place the bowl on the trivet. Cover and steam the pudding for an hour.

Remove the bowl and place a large round plate over the top of the bowl. Quickly invert the bowl onto the plate and remove the bowl. The pudding should be intact, with the fruit design on top.

Serve this steamed pudding either warm or chilled.

Yield: 6 to 8 servings

N'awlins Creole Bread Pudding with Bourbon Sauce

This is the way southern women traditionally use up stale bread, and it has become one of the South's comfort foods. Travel to New Orleans, and you will find variations of this dessert served everywhere from the most modest establishments to the fanciest of restaurants. The pudding can be prepared ahead of time, but it should be served warm.

½ cup raisins

¼ cup bourbon (optional)

5 cups stale bread, about 12 slices, crusts trimmed, cut into 1-inch cubes

1½ cups whole milk

1 cup sugar

1 cup heavy cream

3 large eggs

1 teaspoon vanilla extract

¾ teaspoon ground cinnamon

¼ teaspoon freshly ground nutmeg

⅓ cup toasted pecan pieces

Whipped cream for garnish

Bourbon Sauce

1 cup heavy cream

½ cup light brown sugar

5 tablespoons unsalted butter

¼ cup bourbon

Note: This recipe requires advance preparation.

Combine the raisins and bourbon, if using, in a small bowl and allow them to steep for 30 minutes to soften. Drain and reserve the raisins. Place the bread in a large bowl. In another bowl, whisk the milk, sugar, cream, eggs, vanilla, cinnamon, and nutmeg to combine and pour over the bread. Add the raisins and pecans and gently mix. Soak the bread for 30 minutes to an hour.

Preheat the oven to 350°F. Butter a 9-by-5-inch or 11-by-7-inch baking dish. Pour the pudding into the baking dish, cover with aluminum foil, and bake for 40 minutes. Remove the foil and continue to bake until the top is golden brown and a tester inserted into the center comes out clean, about 20 to 30 minutes.

To make the sauce, combine the cream and sugar in a heavy saucepan over medium-high heat and bring to a boil, stirring constantly. Boil until the mixture bubbles and thickens, about 5 minutes. Add the butter and bring back to a boil, whisking constantly. Remove from the heat; stir in the bourbon and cool the sauce until it's warm. The sauce can be made ahead of time and warmed before serving.

To serve, cut the pudding into serving-size pieces, place on plates, and top with bourbon sauce and a dollop of whipped cream.

Yield: 6 servings

Lemon Pudding Cake

Somehow the fresh taste of citrus is always a good way to cleanse the palate and end a meal. This dish is a great cool-down, and can be made using lime juice and lime zest as a variation. According to Mary Jane Wilan, who serves this to Dave after one of his spicy meals, "It tastes best when it's cooled slightly."

3 eggs, separated

¼ teaspoon salt

1 cup sugar

3 tablespoons butter, softened

¼ cup flour

2 teaspoons lemon zest

¼ cup lemon juice

1½ cups milk

¼ teaspoon salt

Preheat the oven to 325°F, and butter a 1½-quart baking dish.

Combine the egg whites and salt in a bowl and beat until the whites are stiff. Gradually beat in ½ cup of the sugar. Set aside.

In another bowl, combine the butter, remaining sugar, and flour and stir to mix. Add the egg yolks, lemon zest, lemon juice, milk, and salt and beat thoroughly.

Gently fold the egg yolk mixture into the egg whites.

Pour the mixture into the baking dish. Create a water bath by setting the dish in a larger pan filled with water to a depth of about 1 inch.

Bake the pudding cake for about 1 hour. The mixture will still seem a little shaky because of the pudding mixture on the bottom, but don't overbake it. Chill slightly.

Yield: 6 servings

Country Fruit Cobbler

Fruit or berry cobblers are always a soothing counterpoint to a spicy meal, or actually any meal. They are quick and easy to prepare, and any kind of fresh fruit or berries will work beautifully.

2 cups berries or chopped fruit

¼ to ½ cup sugar, depending on the
    sweetness of the fruit

6 tablespoons butter

¾ cup flour

⅓ cup sugar

2 teaspoons baking powder

½ teaspoon salt

⅓ cup brown sugar

¾ cup milk

½ teaspoon grated lemon zest

Preheat the oven to 350°F.

Combine the fruit and ¼ to ½ cup of sugar in a bowl, toss to mix, and set aside.

Melt the butter in an 8-inch-square glass baking dish.

Sift the flour, sugar, baking powder, and salt together in a large bowl, add the brown sugar and stir to mix. Add the milk and lemon zest and mix.

Pour the batter into the dish of melted butter. Do not mix. Top with the fruit and bake for 40 to 50 minutes. Cool the cobbler on a wire rack.

Yield: 6 servings

Mexican Fruitcake

This is an incredibly easy cake to prepare and is a dessert for those with a serious sweet tooth and who love fruitcake. The pineapple is refreshing, while the nuts add a nice crunch.

One 20-ounce can crushed pineapple
    with juice

2¼ cups flour

1 cup coarsely chopped walnuts
    or pecans

2 teaspoons baking soda

2 cups sugar

2 eggs

One 8-ounce package cream cheese,
    softened

2 cups powdered sugar

4 tablespoons (½ stick) melted butter

1 teaspoon vanilla

Preheat the oven to 350°F.

Combine the pineapple, along with its juice, with the flour, nuts, baking soda, sugar, and eggs in a bowl and beat to thoroughly mix.

Pour the mixture into an ungreased 13-by-9-inch pan and bake for 35 to 45 minutes.

Place the cake on a wire rack to cool slightly.

Make the frosting, working quickly; the cake should be frosted while it is still warm.

Combine the cream cheese, powdered sugar, melted butter, and vanilla in a bowl and beat to mix completely.

Spread the frosting on the hot cake and allow the cake to cool slightly before serving.

Yield: 8 to 10 servings

Margarita Pie

This recipe was provided by Dave's wife Mary Jane, who makes excellent desserts. According to her, "This dessert is refreshing, alcoholic, with a crunchy crust—what more can you ask for in a dessert? The recipe comes together quickly, and can be made ahead of time and chilled. It's just like a margarita, but you use a fork." If you do not want to use raw egg whites, you can substitute ⅓ cup whipping cream. Whip the cream, slowly add the remaining ½ cup of sugar, and fold into the chilled, cooked mixture.

Crust

¾ cup coarsely crushed lightly
   salted pretzels

⅓ cup melted butter

3 tablespoons sugar

Filling

¼ cup fresh lime juice

¼ cup fresh lemon juice

1 envelope plain gelatin

4 eggs, separated

1 cup sugar

¼ teaspoon salt

½ teaspoon lemon zest

½ teaspoon lime zest

⅓ cup white tequila

3 tablespoons triple sec

Combine all the crust ingredients in a bowl and mix. Press the mixture into a 9-inch pie pan and chill.

Pour the lime and lemon juice into a bowl, sprinkle the gelatin over them, and let stand until the gelatin is soft.

Place the egg yolks in the top of a double boiler and, while heating, slowly beat in ½ cup of the sugar, the salt, and the lemon and lime zest. Add the gelatin mixture and cook over gently boiling water, stirring constantly, until the mixture is slightly thickened.

Place the mixture in a bowl, blend in the tequila and triple sec, and chill the filling.

In another bowl, beat the egg whites until foamy. While beating, gradually add the remaining ½ cup of sugar. Continue beating the whites until they form stiff peaks. Gently fold the mixture into the chilled, cooked mixture.

Pour the filling into the crust and chill until firm.

Yield: 6 to 8 servings

Horchata (Ground Rice Drink)

The Spaniards, who had been introduced to drinks made from steeped nuts and grains by the Moors, brought the idea for these drinks to the New World. They were a hit, and remain popular throughout Mexico. Travel anywhere in the country, and you will find street carts selling agua fresca, *or fruit juice, and* horchata. *An interesting way to serve rice, this refreshing, soothing drink not only cools down a spicy meal but is also rumored to cure a hangover. We have found it better to process the rice in a blender rather than a food processor, as the latter makes the rice gummy. You can make a creamier* horchata *by adding milk. Serve this drink during a meal as well as after.*

6 tablespoons long-grain rice
¼ cup blanched almonds, optional
Two 2-inch cinnamon sticks, broken in pieces
1 to 2 cups sugar

Place the rice and nuts in a spice or coffee grinder and process to a fine powder. Combine the powder with 1 quart of water in a bowl and stir to mix. Add the cinnamon sticks, cover, and soak overnight.

Note: This recipe requires advance preparation.

Remove the cinnamon sticks and discard. Process the rice mixture in batches in a blender until it's as smooth as possible.

Pour the rice into a heavy saucepan, add the sugar and another quart of water, and bring to a simmer over medium heat. Simmer the mixture for 20 minutes. Taste and adjust the seasonings.

Strain through a fine sieve or 3 pieces of cheesecloth, pressing or squeezing to remove as much liquid as possible.

Dilute the *horchata* to the desired consistency with water or milk. Chill and serve.

Yield: 1 to 2 quarts

Shrikhand (Indian Yogurt Pudding)

In India, yogurt is used to soothe the mouth after a spicy curry. They use it in the form of raitas, *in drinks, or in desserts such as this one. Although it has few ingredients and is easy to prepare, it does require that it be started the day before serving. Some cooks add ¼ teaspoon saffron soaked in a little warm milk, and ¾ teaspoon ground cardamom to make a more spicy shrikhand.*

2 pints plain yogurt
6 tablespoons sugar
¼ cup chopped pistachio nuts

Note: This recipe requires advance preparation.

Line a strainer with a large piece of cheesecloth and place over a bowl. Pour the yogurt into the cheesecloth, and leave it overnight in the refrigerator to drain.

Combine the yogurt curds with the sugar in a bowl and whisk to mix. Chill the mixture until time to serve.

Ladle the pudding into individual bowls, garnish with pistachio nuts, and serve.

Yield: 4 servings

Mango Lassi

This refreshing yogurt drink originated in India, where it is often served for dessert after a meal of fiery hot curries. Fruits such as strawberries, peaches, or pineapples may be added to or substituted for the mango.

2 cups plain yogurt
2 cups buttermilk, or substitute whole milk
Pulp of two ripe mangoes
Juice of one lemon
1 teaspoon sugar

Place all the ingredients in a blender and process until smooth. Serve the lassi over ice, or freeze until slushy and then serve.

Yield: 4 servings

Sopaipillas (Fried Bread)

If you've ever traveled in New Mexico, you've probably seen those little plastic bears filled with honey that grace the tables of restaurants and diners and wondered what they were for. They are there for the sopaipillas, *the most commonly served bread in New Mexico after tortillas. Sopaipillas, "little pillows," are squares or triangles of bread that puff up when fried. They are served in baskets with traditional meals, accompanied with a dispenser of honey. The combination of the sugar in the honey and the starch of the bread cuts the heat of hot chiles. To eat, tear or bite off a corner of the bread, pour in the honey, and enjoy. For very light sopaipillas, do not handle the dough more than necessary.*

2 cups all-purpose flour
2 teaspoons baking powder
½ teaspoon salt

2 tablespoons shortening
Vegetable oil for deep-frying

Combine the flour, baking powder, and salt in a large bowl and stir to mix. Cut in the shortening using a pastry cutter or two forks until the flour resembles coarse meal.

Add ⅔ cup warm water, a little at a time, until the dough is moist and can be gathered into a ball. Knead a couple of times, cover with a towel, and let sit for 30 minutes.

In a deep fryer or large pot, add the oil and heat to 400°F.

On a lightly floured board, roll the dough until it forms a rectangle ¼ inch thick. Cut into rectangles about 2 by 3 inches.

Place the sopaipillas, 3 or 4 at a time, in the hot oil and spoon a little oil over the top of each to start them puffing. When they have browned on one side, about 20 to 30 seconds, turn them over and brown on the other side. Turn only once. Remove and drain on paper towels.

Serve immediately, with a dispenser of honey.

Yield: Approximately 2 dozen

Pooris (Indian Deep-Fried Bread)

This type of deep-fried unleavened bread is eaten with most every Indian meal and is best when eaten hot. The basic recipe is also used to make chapatis, another popular bread. Pooris are easy to make, but the oil must be hot, or they will not puff up like balloons. They can also be served stuffed with a lentil or meat mixture by cutting the dough into 2-inch circles, placing the filling on half, topping with another piece, and sealing. Keep the bread you are not working with covered with a towel to keep it from drying out.

2 cups whole wheat flour

¼ teaspoon salt

2 tablespoons vegetable oil, plus additional for deep frying

Combine the flour and salt in a bowl and stir to mix. Drizzle the 2 tablespoons of oil over the flour and, using your fingers, work it into the flour until it resembles coarse bread crumbs. Slowly add enough water to make a dough that can be gathered into a ball.

Turn the dough onto a floured surface and knead the dough until elastic, about 5 minutes. Cover the dough with a damp cloth and set aside for 1½ to 2 hours.

Heat the oil in a deep fryer or large wok to 365°F.

Knead the dough again, roll it out until it's very thin, and cut into 4-inch circles.

Add a couple of *pooris* to the oil and press down gently with a pancake turner or slotted spoon so the *poori* puffs up. Turn to the other side and fry until the *poori* is golden brown and puffy on both sides. Remove and drain on paper towels.

Serve immediately while still very hot.

Yield: 4 to 6 servings

part three:
serving spicy foods

16 Balancing the Spice

Most cooks would probably serve a single spicy dish from this book and make the other dishes complementary, but not as hot. If, however, you simply love spicy stuff, or wish to plan a meal around our Spicy Feasts of the World (page 392), remember that in any of our recipes, the spice amounts can be increased or decreased. Plan the spice amounts in the various dishes so that they can be served from mildest to hottest; you wouldn't want to serve an extremely hot appetizer before a milder entree and burn everyone out.

Complements

Some foods are natural accompaniments to spicy dishes. They are not specifically cool-downs, but rather palate cleansers and give the diners a break from the spicy meal at hand. Here are a few suggestions:

* Sliced fruits such as mango, peach, plum, pineapple, and papaya
* Pickled vegetables such as eggplant, cauliflower, carrots, and cucumbers
* Grated coconut
* Cheese wedges
* High-quality olives
* Chutneys and relishes
* Sorbets
* Breads, flavored tortillas, and crackers

Cool Downs

For years people believed that the mouth's sensitivity for capsaicin was controlled by the number of taste buds, and that super-tasters, people with a higher concentration of taste buds, were much more sensitive to the hot stuff than nontasters, with a genetically-linked lesser number of tastebuds. The problem with this theory is that the taste buds can only detect sour, sweet, bitter, salty, and umami flavors. (Umami is the flavor of monosodium glutamate, or MSG.)

As we've discussed earlier (see pages 23–25), a 2003 study by the University of California, San Francisco, concluded that sensitivity to capsaicin is determined by genetics—some people's lipid molecules have a stronger bond with the capsaicin receptors than others. Since biochemical and pharmacological mechanisms can also play a role, however, some people become desensitized to capsaicin and can take more and more heat.

Many substances have been proposed as antidotes to the heat of chiles, including water, milk, sugar, bread, citrus fruits, beer, and other carbonated beverages. The theory is that such substances can either wash away or dilute the capsaicin, or, like the bread, can absorb it. The problem is that the capsaicin is bound to the nerve receptor sites in the mouth, so it is not easily dislodged or diluted. Remember that capsaicin is very miscible with alcohol, fats, and oils, but not very miscible with water, which is by far the largest component of beer and other drinks.

Dairy products have long been reputed to be the best cool-downs for the burning effects of capsaicin in chiles. But why? Scientists now believe that casein in the milk is responsible for its cooling effects. According to Robert Henkin of The Taste and Smell Clinic in Washington, D.C., casein is a phosphoprotein that acts as a detergent, stripping capsaicin from the nerve receptor binding sites in the mouth. Other possible cool-downs containing casein include thicker dairy products like cream, yogurt, sour cream, ice cream, as well as milk chocolate and some beans and nuts.

17

Spicy Feasts of the World

faith-based feasts

A Maharashtrian Hindu Wedding Feast

In Maharashtra, the Indian state where Mumbai (formerly Bombay) is located, weddings are always followed by a lunch feast, since the wedding is usually in the morning. Originally the guests were seated on the floor to dine, but low tables called *paats* are more common these days. The bride sits on a red *paat*, and she is draped in a nine-yard-long *paithani* sari of royal blue silk edged with maroon and gold. A black dot of coal on her cheek keeps evil spirits away. The floor where diners are seated is decorated with curlicues made with red, green, and white colored powders. Large metal plates are set in the center of each pattern while incense is burned.

Traditionally, the food was served on banana leaves with a dollop of rice coated in ghee on the side, but now plates are used. The food is mostly vegetarian, but occasionally chicken or fish is served. The traditional drink is *mattha*, buttermilk seasoned with cilantro and salt.

Here is our version of the feast:

* Chicken Biryani (page 272) with Nasi Kunyit (page 330)
* *Palak Pachadi* (page 323)
* *Pooris* (page 387)
* Mint Raita (page 373)
* Tamatar Chatni (page 137)
* *Shrikhand* (page 384)
* Chai (page 344)

The wedding feast ends with a sweet *paan*, consisting of betel leaves wrapped around betel nuts, spices, and sugar. *Paan* cleanses the palate and starts the digestive process, and also signifies the sealing of the newly formed union between two individuals and two families.

The Muslim Feast of Sacrifice

Eid-ul-Adha (the "Feast of Sacrifice"), the great festival of Islam, concludes the pilgrimage to Mecca known as the Hajj. Usually falling in February, the feast lasts three days and commemorates Ibrahim's willingness to obey God by sacrificing his son. (In the Bible, Ibrahim is referred to as Abraham.) Every Muslim home is supposed to sacrifice an animal on this day, but sacrifices are more common in the Middle East than in American Muslim neighborhoods. Millions of sheep, goats, cows, and camels are slaughtered and distributed to the pilgrims, and at least one-third of the meat, by tradition, is given to the poor. This holiday is now celebrated in American cities with prayer, community gatherings, and the tradition of dressing up in special clothes to visit friends and relatives. People hold Eid-ul-Adha parties and give presents to their children. And, of course, they feast on pan-Muslim dishes like these:

* Tabouleh (page 180)
* *Fattoush* (page 218)
* Kurdish Shish Kebabs (page 230)
* Kossa Mashiya Bil Kibbeh (page 338)
* Finjan Kirfee (page 353)

A South African Christmas

In South Africa, December is summertime, so often Christmas Day activities happen outdoors—at the beach or at the barbecue. Many Christmas traditions are similar to those in the United States and Canada—people decorate Christmas trees, leave stockings out for Santa to fill, exchange gifts, and go to church—but they don't put up Christmas lights on their houses. They celebrate with a family meal, for which most families have a unique menu that remains constant from year to year.

Ham—called "gammon" here—is probably the most commonly cooked meat for Christmas, and it's traditional to serve ginger beer as a nonalcoholic drink. Our take on the South African Christmas:

* Glazed Gammon (page 252)
* Green Bean *Atjar* (page 340)
* *Komkomer Slaai* (page 223)
* Dried Apricot *Blatjang* (page 132)
* *Pooris* (page 387)
* Ginger Beer (page 352)

The Day of the Dead

There are actually two Days of the Dead celebrated in Mexico: November 1, for children, and November 2, for adults. Each day's activities are centered around visits to the graves of close relatives. At the grave sites, family members clean up the monuments, decorate them with flowers such as marigolds and chrysanthemums, and adorn them with religious amulets and with offerings of food, cigarettes, and alcoholic beverages. They enjoy a picnic, and socialize with other family and community members who have gathered at the cemetery. Families recall the departed by telling stories about them and remembering the good things about their lives.

The meals prepared for these picnics are sumptuous, usually featuring meat dishes in spicy sauces (mole is said to entice the spirits of the dead, luring them to the festive altars), a special egg-batter bread, cookies, chocolate, and sugary confections in a variety of animal or skull shapes.

Despite its ominous name, this commemoration of the dead is not morbid at all, given the friendly social situation, the colorful decorations, and the abundance of food, drink, and good company. The interaction of the living and the dead is the Mexican way of recognizing the cycle of life and death that is human existence. Here's how we would picnic:

* Mexican Ceviche (page 188)
* Nopalitos y Espinacas Ensalada (page 221)
* Pork Loin with *Mole Coloradito* (page 246)
* *Salsa de Chile de Arbol* (page 154)
* *Papas con Rajas* (page 341)
* Queso Napolitano (page 375)
* Horchata (page 383)

time of the season feasts

Chinese New Year

The Chinese calendar is based on a repeating twelve-year cycle. To help people remember the cycle, each year is named for an animal: Rat, Ox, Tiger, Rabbit, Dragon, Snake, Horse, Sheep (or Goat), Monkey, Rooster, Dog, and Pig. New Year's Eve and New Year's Day are family affairs, a time of reunion and thanksgiving. Departed relatives are remembered with great respect because they were responsible for laying the foundations of the family. Community activities include parades, fireworks, and festivals.

Ancestors are acknowledged on New Year's Eve with a feast arranged for them at the family table, where the spirits of the ancestors join the living to celebrate the onset of the New Year. This feast, called "surrounding the stove," or *weilu*, symbolizes family unity and honors past and present generations. Here is our suggested feast, in which each dish has a symbolic meaning:

* Hot and Sour Soup (page 202). Since the Chinese word for "sour" sounds like the word for "grandchildren," this dish signifies lots of grandchildren.
* *Zhua Chao Yu* (page 297). This dish of fried prawns with ginger signifies good fortune and happiness.
* Asian Black Pepper Ribs (page 228). Meat symbolizes wealth.
* Sesame *Dan Dan* Noodles (page 328). This dish signifies long life, but be sure not to cut the noodles!
* Kung Pao Chicken (page 260). This dish is thought to bring prosperity.
* Stir-Fry Walnut Asparagus (page 322). This dish has no symbolism, but does add a vegetable.
* *Bot Bo Go* (Eight Treasures Pudding) (page 377). Since the word for "eight" sounds like the word for "prosperity," eight is considered to be a lucky number.

Fourth of July BBQ Feast

As with most major holidays celebrated in the United States, the Fourth of July is a time to be with family and friends, so feasting is the order of the day. This feast usually takes place in the late afternoon or early evening, and is centered around the barbecue. To occupy themselves before the feast, people organize family sporting activities such as baseball, or watch a game at the stadium or on TV. Of course, many people attend specific Fourth of July events like parades, air shows, or political gatherings.

At homes all across the country, grills are fired up for standard fare, like hamburgers, steaks, hot dogs, accompanied by corn on the cob, potato salad, and watermelon. But here in the Southwest, we tend to spice up the Fourth, so join us for:

* Salad Greens with Honey Chipotle Lime Mustard Dressing (page 219)
* Fajitas *Bulgogii* (page 253) and/or Texas "Chili Queen" Chili (page 241)
* *Frijoles Indios* (page 335)
* *Salsa Borracha* (page 155)
* Taos Corn-Husk Muffins with Blue Corn, Chipotle, and Cheese (page 359)
* Fresh Peach Shortcake with Ginger Crème Anglaise (page 368)

Summer Gaucho Barbecue

Brazil's gauchos roam the pampas in the state of Rio Grande do Sul. These cattlemen have perfected the art of the *churrasco*, or gaucho barbecue. Traditionally, the gaucho would grill his meat on skewers over open campfires. We're sure that this still occasionally happens, but these days you're more likely to find *churrascos* at the popular *churrascarias*, or barbecue restaurants, whose servers offer skewers laden with grilled meats such as sirloin steaks, lamb loin, sausages, and chicken kebabs. Such restaurants have become popular all over the Americas; we even have a *churrascaria*—Tucanos—in Albuquerque.

Summer for the gauchos is winter for the Anglos, so on the next moderate day in February, remember it's July in Rio Grande do Sul, and serve the following menu:

* Argentine Empanadas (page 186)
* Ensalada con Quinoa de Bolivia (page 222)
* Gaucho Grilled Beef with *Molho Campanha* (page 244)
* Habanero-spiced Black Beans with Cuban *Sofrito* (page 308)
* *Toritas de Papa con Cilantro* (page 334)
* Picante de Aguacates (page 337)

frantic fiery feasts

New Orleans Mardi Gras

Our friend Jim Fergusson, who lives in New Orleans, says, "So, what is a typical Mardi Gras day? There are very basically two types. One is family oriented; the other is pure debauchery, centered in New Orleans' French Quarter, where tourists and locals lose their inhibitions with a little help from the product of the brewer's art and the mania of the crowd. There you can expect to see, hear, or experience just about anything."

One of the most popular dishes at Mardi Gras is red beans with *tasso* or andouille sausage. The beans are served over steamed long-grain white rice with a green salad and hot crusty French bread slathered with garlic butter. Jim also says that Popeye's or Church's Fried Chicken and biscuits are also a sought-after nibble for parade-goers. "The spicy fried chicken is a favorite with an early-morning Bloody Mary and a big piece of King Cake," he says. "The smell of grilled hamburgers, chicken, and ribs fills the air. Vendors sell hot dogs, pizza, and peanuts on the street." Two other Mardi Gras favorites are jambalaya and gumbo, either of which can be made with seafood, sausage, or chicken. If you can't make it to New Orleans for the next Mardi Gras, at least you can sample the pleasures of the following dishes:

* Crab and Alligator Pear Salad with Remoulade Dressing (page 224)
* Acadiana Deviled Oysters (page 190)
* Chicken and Andouille Gumbo (page 208)
* Louisiana Barbecue Shrimp (page 299) on Rice
* Bayou Ratatouille (page 321)
* N'awlins Creole Bread Pudding with Bourbon Sauce (page 378)

Oktoberfest

Our friend Harald Zoschke, who lives in southern Germany, tells us that Oktoberfest in Munich is the world's largest public festival, with six million visitors flooding into the 100 acres of festival grounds. Other Oktoberfests have sprung up around the world; in addition to Munich, Harald tells us that he's been to celebrations in Las Vegas and Alpine Village, California.

The huge Oktoberfest grounds offer carousels, roller coasters, and food booths, but the main attraction are the giant beer tents (so huge they call them halls) that cater to thousands of beer lovers. Each one is operated by a Bavarian brewery and has its own Oktoberfest brass band. About six million liters of beer are consumed at Oktoberfest (we would have thought more than that).

"The music plus all the people add up to a jetlike noise level," Harald says. "The food includes *Brez'n*, fresh baked giant pretzels, which aren't better anywhere than at this famous festival. Also served are grilled chicken (*Hendl*), mackerel grilled on a stick, *Hax'n* (grilled pig leg) and the famous *Schweinswürstl* (pork bratwursts, always served by the pair)."

Because weather is often unpredictable in October, the two-week-long festival has been moved to the end of September. Despite the date, it is still good old Oktoberfest, celebrated for the 171st time in 2004. Here are our suggestions for your very own Oktoberfest:

* Roasted Red Beet and Endive Salad with Toasted Walnuts and Horseradish Cream (page 215)
* Bratwursts Boiled in Beer with German-Style Mustard (page 119)
* *Gurkensalat mit Senfsauce* (page 220)
* Gingerbread with Lemon Whipped Cream (page 362)

Carnival in Trinidad: The Spiced-Up Festival

"If we could channel half the thought, devotion, and energy that we produce for Carnival into economic production," wrote Andrew Carr in 1975, "Trinidad and Tobago would become one of the most productive countries in the world."

Carr's observation is only slightly exaggerated; Carnival is such a mammoth spectacle that it requires many months to plan and many thousands of people to produce. Of course, many Caribbean countries celebrate Carnival, but none on the scale of Trinidad and Tobago. Many observers believe that T&T's Carnival is the finest such celebration in the world, eclipsing even the Mardi Gras parades and parties in New Orleans and Rio de Janeiro.

The first Carnival day (actually night) is Dimanche Gras, "fat Sunday," the Sunday night before Ash Wednesday. This is the night for private fêtes all over the country—at homes, restaurants, nightclubs, and hotels.

On Mardi Gras, "Fat Tuesday," the entire parade process begins again. And the revelers must drink and eat. Writer Ann Elliot recalled, as a child, sitting outside calypso tents just before Carnival: "We were given delicious morsels of things to eat: pastello (corn wrapped around meat and steamed in a plantain leaf), pelau (a cook-up of rice and meat), crab-back (crabs taken out of the shell, mixed with all kinds of fragrant herbs, sprinkled with breadcrumbs and red salt butter, and baked au gratin)."

Here is our pan-Caribbean Carnival menu:

* Hearts of Palm Salad with Caribbean *Kuchela* Vinaigrette (page 217)
* Jamaican Jerk Pork (page 239)
* Peas 'n' Rice (page 336)
* Habanero-spiced Black Beans with Cuban *Sofrito* (page 308)
* Chilled Fruit and Yogurt Soup

18 Pairing Beverages with Spicy Foods

More and more Americans are consuming hot and spicy dishes from a number of world cuisines, yet most cookbook authors and magazine writers on the subject have avoided matching beverages to hot and spicy foods. Should peppery cocktails, such as those made with chile pepper vodkas, be served with spicy foods, or is such a practice culinary overkill? Which wines to match with the enormous variety of exotic, incendiary dishes? What role does beer play? And isn't it only polite to provide cool-down drinks for guests whose palates have not yet adapted to the heat levels of the fiery food being served?

Peppery Cocktails

Since cocktails always precede the meal, it makes perfect sense that a burning beverage is the best way to prepare guests for the fiery feast to follow. The most basic peppery cocktail is one that has the heat already in it—namely, a liquor treated with some variety of chile pepper.

It is ironic that chile-pepper-flavored liquors originated in a country virtually devoid of fiery foods: Russia. The word *vodka* is the Russian diminutive for "water," which gives a fairly good indication of just how basic and important this liquor is there. In fact, the people love it so much, they cannot leave it alone. They make about forty different flavored vodkas, using herbs and spices ranging from heather and mint to nutmeg, cloves, cinnamon—and, of course, cayenne powder.

A favorite brand of Russian chile pepper vodka is Stolichnaya Pertsovka, the famous "Stoly," which has been infused with white and black pepper combined with cayenne powder and then filtered to remove all solids. Disappointingly, the reddish tint of the vodka comes from added coloring rather than chiles, but it still tastes great and has a nice bite. Other popular brands of hot vodkas are Absolut Peppar from Sweden and America's own Gordon's Pepper Flavored Vodka.

Today, Bloody Marys are often made with chile-infused vodkas; variations on the Bloody Mary include replacing the vodka with tequila—a "Bloody Maria"—or with Japanese sake, a "Bloody Mary Quite Contrary." The cocktail can be made with one of the chile pepper vodkas to supply the pungency, or it can be spiced up with a favorite brand of bottled hot sauce. Since the various chiles used in these sauces all have their own unique flavors, the taste of Bloody Marys can vary significantly. Tabasco is still the most commonly used hot sauce to spice up this drink, but these days people are experimenting with hot sauces based upon the cayenne, habanero, jalapeño, and even chipotle chiles.

For those guests who prefer non-alcoholic beverages, serve a volatile Virgin Mary, which retains the hot sauce but eliminates the vodka.

Matching Wines and Beers with Spicy Entrées

The fiery main courses have been selected, whether at home or in a restaurant. But what beverages should accompany the incendiary dishes in this book? Certainly not the same peppery cocktail you've been drinking before the meal; the pungency of the drink will mask the complex flavors and spiciness of the entrée. Since wines and beers are traditionally served with meals all over the world, the crucial questions are: Will the fiery foods overwhelm the wine? Do wines and beers extinguish the fire of the chiles?

Wine expert Roy Andries de Groot believes that wines do indeed cut the heat of chile dishes. He suggests serving cold white wines with most spicy foods and claims that a Chablis, chenin blanc, or Colombard is "excellent for putting out chile fires." Undoubtedly, he has heard the argument that beer and wine have some efficacy as cooldowns because capsaicin—the chemical that gives chiles their heat—dissolves readily in alcohol but does not mix with water. This theory holds that alcohol dilutes the capsaicin and thus reduces the heat sensation. However, since both beer and wine are more than 80 percent water, the alcohol content actually has little effect on the heat levels.

So do not expect wines and beers to reduce the pungency of the dishes being served. Although the cool temperature at which many beers and wines are served may give the illusion of reducing heat, in reality they do not temper the sting of capsaicin very much, and in some cases may even increase it. Beverage consultant Ronn Wiegand, writing in Marlena Spieler's book *Hot & Spicy*, warns, "The tannin content of most young red wines can actually magnify the heat."

With beer and wine accompaniments, the heat level is not nearly as important as a harmonious blending of flavors and textures. For example, we usually drink beer with the hottest Mexican and Chinese foods because it is a perfect complement, not because of its reputation as a cool-down. With some of the spicy New Southwest meals, a slightly fruity white wine such as a chenin blanc or Riesling seems to be a better pairing.

De Groot has put some thought into what wines to serve with fiery foods and advises, "My theory of the successful marriage of wine with these cuisines is to know (and separate) the gentle dishes, the spicy dishes, and the fiery dishes. The menu is then planned so that each group of dishes is paired with the wine that adds certain essential contrasts and harmonies." For example, he recommends a Bordeaux or a cabernet sauvignon as the best wine to accompany the chocolate-flavored *mole poblano*, calling the combination "one of the more memorable marriages of exotic gastronomy." For curries, de Groot suggests a fumé blanc or a soft semillon; for the entrées that top the heat scale he has surprising advice—an American light wine. Since he believes that white wine cuts the heat, he advises that the wine should be low in alcohol so it can be consumed in great quantities without discomfort.

Ronn Wiegand recommends serving the wine that fits your budget. Fine and rare wines are not perfect beverages with fiery foods, he suggests, because their flavor nuances are overwhelmed by the strong spices, but he admits that sometimes no other drink will do. "At such times," he writes, "simply upgrade the quality of the wine you would normally serve with a given dish, and enjoy the inevitable fireworks."

When deciding which beers to offer guests who are about to assault their senses with chile heat, one logical solution is a regional match: Carta Blanca with Mexican foods, a Tsingtao with Sichuan dishes, Tusker with African entrées, Red Stripe with Jamaican foods, and so on. With American spicy specialties, such as New Mexican or Cajun, we suggest forgetting every American beer advertised on TV—they are all mediocre at best. Instead, serve one of the finer regional specialty beers, such as Capitol or Augsburger from Wisconsin, or Anchor Steam from San Francisco.

Incidentally, some writers insist that dark beers should never be served with spicy foods because they are traditionally served in cool climates rather than tropical ones. Such a judgment makes little culinary sense; one often needs a heavy, dark beer to match a meal measuring eight or more on the heat scale. Besides, the theory is proven false in Mexico, where such fine dark beers as Negra Modelo and Dos Equis are commonly served with the hottest meals.

For hosts still in a quandary about which beers and wine to offer, why not present a number of selections to your guests and have them decide—by tasting them all—which wines and beers go best with the fiery foods being served?

After-Dinner Cool-Downs

Believe it or not, some chile addicts believe that every course of the meal should burn. After peppery cocktails, fiery appetizers, spicy soup, and three different incendiary entrées, they have the nerve to serve jalapeño sorbet for dessert. Fortunately, the vast majority of chile cooks believes that enough is enough and prefer a soothing cool-down as the perfect finish for a fiery feast.

As with beers and wines, a debate rages over precisely which drinks actually tame the heat of chiles. Recommendations range from ice water to hot tea to lemon juice to one of our favorites, Scotch on the rocks. Most of these liquids can be dismissed out of hand. Ice water is totally useless: capsaicin and water don't mix. As soon as the water leaves the mouth, the fire rages on. Hot tea is a legendary Vietnamese remedy, but there is no logical reason for it to work, since it is 99 percent water. Lemon juice seems to help some people, but somehow we can't picture our guests sitting around the table sucking on lemons after a marvelous fiery feast. And as for Scotch on the rocks, well, if you drink enough of it, you soon won't care about cooling down.

Actually, it was East Indian cooks who found the perfect after-dinner cool-down. The most effective antidote for capsaicin, they discovered, is dairy products, particularly yogurt. The Indian yogurt and fruit drink called lassi commonly served after hot curry meals is sweet, refreshing, and effective. No one seems to know precisely why milk, sour cream, yogurt, and ice cream cut the heat, but they do. Some experts suggest that the protein casein in the milk counteracts the capsaicin, but all we know is that it works.

sources

Chile Seeds and Plants

Cross Country Nurseries

This company carries more than 500 varieties of live chile plants in season, as well as fresh pods.

P.O. Box 170
199 Kingwood-Locktown Road
Rosemont, New Jersey 08556
Phone: (908) 996-4646
Fax: (908) 996-4638
www.chileplants.com

Native Seeds/SEARCH

An Arizona organization for preserving southwestern plants, which supplies seeds to consumers.

526 N. 4th Avenue
Tucson, Arizona 85705
Phone: (520) 622-5561
Fax: (520) 622-5591
E-Mail: info@nativeseeds.org
www.nativeseeds.org

Seed Savers Exchange

Collectors and seed savers join this Iowa organization to trade heirloom seeds. You will need to join to receive their complete catalog.

3094 North Winn Road
Decorah, Iowa 52101
Phone: (563) 382-5990
Fax: (563) 382-5872
www.seedsavers.org

Tomato Growers Supply Company

Many varieties of chile pepper seeds

P.O. Box 60015
Fort Myers, Florida 33906
Toll Free: (888) 478-7333
Toll Free Fax: (888) 768-3476
www.tomatogrowers.com

Fresh and Frozen Chiles

Chile Traditions

Fresh New Mexican chile in season

8204 Montgomery NE
Albuquerque, New Mexico 87109
Toll Free: (877) VERY HOT (837-9468)
E-Mail: nmchile111@aol.com
www.chiletraditions.com

Hatch Chile Express

Fresh New Mexican chiles in season, frozen out of season

P.O. Box 350
Hatch, New Mexico 87937
E-Mail: hatchchile@zianet.com
www.hatch-chile.com

Dried and Processed Chiles

Frieda's

A wide variety of fresh and dried chiles

www.friedas.com

Melissa's

Pods, powders, and pickles

Melissa's/World Variety Produce, Inc.

P.O. Box 21127

Los Angeles, California 90021

Toll Free: (800) 588-0151

E-Mail: hotline@melissas.com

www.melissas.com

Fiery Foods and Condiments

Fiery Foods & Barbecue Industry Directory

More than 500 suppliers and sellers

www.fiery-foods.com/directory/default.htm

Recommended Retailers of Fiery Foods

More than 2,000 hot and spicy products

www.fiery-foods.com/dave/retailers.asp

The "Condiments and Sauces" section of the Yahoo Shopping Directory

A valuable resource with hundreds of listings

http://dir.yahoo.com/Business_and_Economy/
Shopping_and_Services/Food_and_Drink/
Condiments_and_Sauces/

Ethnic Foods

Caribbean Island Grocer

P.O. Box 22271

Hialeah, Florida 33002

Phone: (305) 817-9220

Fax: (305) 817-9248

www.caribbeanislandsgrocer.com

El Mercado Grande

South American foods

Mesa, Arizona

Phone: (480) 862-2964

www.elmercadogrande.com

EthnicGrocer.com

An astounding variety of world foods

695 Lunt Avenue

Elk Grove Village, Illinois 60007

Phone: (312) 373-1777

Fax: (312) 373-1777

E-Mail: support@ethnicgrocer.com

www.ethnicgrocer.com

GourmetSpot.com

A portal for ethnic foods

www.gourmetspot.com/ethnicfoods.htm

Hot Headz

The best source for spicy food in the U.K.

Unit C5 Phoenix Trading Estate

London Road, Thrupp,

Stroud, Glos. GL5 2BX England

Phone: (+44 (0) 1453) 731052

Fax: (+44 (0) 1453) 731747

E-Mail: enquiries@hot-headz.com

www.hot-headz.com

Indian Foods Company

8305 Franklin Avenue

Minneapolis, Minnesota 55426

Phone: (952) 593-3000

www.indianfoodsco.com

Kalustyans

Spices, herbs, and foods from around the world; specializing in Middle Eastern and Indian cuisines.
123 Lexington Avenue
New York, New York 10016
Toll Free: (800) 352-3451
Fax: (212) 683-8458
E-Mail: sales@kalustyans.com
www.kalustyans.com

Mahabazaar

Indian foods
7611-A, Rickenbacker Drive
Gaithersburg, Maryland 20879
Phone: (301) 990-7425
Fax: (301) 990-8913
E-Mail: service@mahabazaar.com
www.mahabazaar.com

MexGrocer.com

Every kind of Mexican food product
www.mexgrocer.com

Pacific Rim Gourmet

Exotic ingredients from the Pacific Rim
4905 Morena Boulevard, Suite 1313
San Diego, California 92117
Toll Free: (800) 910-WOKS (9657)
www.i-clipse.com/default.asp

Pepperworld

The best source for spicy food in Germany
Suncoast Peppers GmbH
Postfach 9132
D-88075 Kressbronn
Germany
Phone: (+49 7543) 500 997
Fax: (+49 7543) 500 998
www.pepperworld.com

South African Food Shop

Fullwood Plaza
11229 E. Independence Boulevard
Matthews, North Carolina 28105
Phone: (704) 849-2660
Fax: (704) 849-2660
http://lekker.safeshopper.com/

Thai Supermarket Online

All Thai foods
P.O. Box 2054
Issaquah, Washington 98027
Toll Free: (888) 618-THAI (8424)
Phone: (425) 687-1708
Fax: (425) 687-8413
E-Mail: info@importfood.com
http://importfood.com

General Spices

Herbies

Spices of the world
745 Darling Street
Rozelle, New South Wales
2039 Australia
Phone: (02) 9555 6035
Fax: (02) 9555 6037
www.herbies.com.au

Pendery's, Inc.

Many spices, black pepper, and chile peppers
1221 Manufacturing Street
Dallas, Texas 75207
Toll Free: (800) 533-1870
E-Mail: email@penderys.com
www.penderys.com

Penzeys Spices

Spices of all kinds; black, white, and pink peppercorns. Retail stores throughout the Midwest.

Toll Free: (800) 741-7787

Fax: (262) 785-7678

www.penzeys.com

Australian Mountain Pepper

Diemen Pepper Supplies

Mountain pepper leaf and berries, plus other products.

21 Bay Road

New Town, Tasmania, 7008

E-Mail: diemen.pepper@tassie.net.au

www.diemenpepper.com

Ginger

Aloha Tropicals

Many varieties of ginger plants. Nursery visits by appointment only.

P.O. Box 6042

Oceanside, California 92054

Phone: (760) 631-2880

Fax: (760) 631-2880

E-Mail: alohatrop@aol.com

www.alohatropicals.com

Gingerpeople

A large selection of ginger products

2700 Garden Road, Suite G

Monterey, California 93940

Toll Free: (800) 551-5284

Fax: (831) 645-1094

E-Mail: info@gingerpeople.com

www.gingerpeople.com

Horseradish

Bert's Gourmet Horseradish

Horseradish plants

10 Capri Drive

Sagamore Hills, Ohio 44067

Phone: (216) 544-7757

E-Mail: sales@horseradishplants.com

www.horseradishplants.com

Lakeside Foods Gourmet Horseradish

Horseradish and mustard from Wisconsin

Long Lake Distributing

W7954 Cloverleaf Lake Road

Clintonville, Wisconsin 54929

Toll Free: (877) 893-5522

Fax: (715) 823-3269

E-Mail: info@hotroots.com

www.hotroots.com

Silver Spring Gardens

The world's largest grower and processor of horseradish

www.silverspringgardens.com

Welly's Horseradish

Producing horseradish products for more than fifty years

141 N. Monroe Street

Fremont, Ohio 43420

Phone: (419) 334-3134

Fax: (419) 898-2657

E-Mail: info@wellyshorseradish.com

www.wellyshorseradish.com

Mustard

Greatfoodz

Large selection of domestic and foreign mustards

Toll Free: (877) 755-4920

www.greatfoodz.com

**Mount Horeb Mustard Museum
& Gourmet Foods Emporium**

Eight hundred varieties

P.O. Box 468
100 West Main Street
Mount Horeb, Wisconsin 53572
Toll Free: (800) 438-6878
www.mustardmuseum.com

Peppercorns

The Internet Black Pepper Specialty Store

Peppercorns, peppermills, and recipes

www.blackpepper.com

Life's a Grind

A wide selection of peppermills and pepper grinders

www.lifesagrind.com

Pure Spice

Many varieties of black pepper

Toll Free: (866) 532-1703
www.purespice.com/peppercorns.asp

Seedman.com

Black pepper seeds to plant

Jim Johnson, Seedman
3421 Bream Street
Gautier, Mississippi 39553
Toll Free: (800) 336-2064
Fax: (228) 497-5488
www.seedman.com

Wasabi

Frogfarm Wasabi

Seattle company that sells bare-root plants, with detailed growing instructions, to hobby growers and others.

3408 NE 193rd Street
Seattle, Washington 98155
Phone: (206) 361-1981
Fax: (206) 361-5920
E-Mail: frogfarm@Interserv.com
www.wasabifarm.com

Pacific Coast Wasabi, Ltd.

Firm in Vancouver, British Columbia, that sells fresh wasabi

450-1050 Alberni Street
Vancouver, British Columbia
V6E 1A3 Canada
E-Mail: info@wasabia.ca
www.wasabia.ca

Pacific Farms

Oregon company that grows plants for customers who want to grow wasabi as a hobby. Currently, they also import frozen wasabi roots, which they make into fresh wasabi paste and sell in 1.5 oz tubes.

Pacific Farms USA LP
P.O. Box 51505
Eugene, Oregon 97439
Toll Free: (800) 927-2248 Ext. 313
www.freshwasabi.com

bibliography

Achaya, K. T. *Indian Food: A Historical Companion.* Delhi: Oxford University Press, 1994.

Agovino, Theresa. "Red Gold." *Saveur*, no. 32 (January/February 1999): 35.

American Spice Trade Association. "America Enters the Spice Trade." 2000. www.astaspice.org.

_____. "Spices in the Middle Ages." 2000. www.astaspice.org.

_____. "The Age of Discovery." 2000. www.astaspice.org.

_____. "The Spices of Antiquity." 2000. www.astaspice.org.

_____. "Wars and the New Spice Monopolies." 2000. www.astaspice.org.

Anand, Mulk Raj. *Curries and Other Indian Dishes.* London: Desmond Harmsworth, 1932.

Andersen, Juel. *Juel Andersen's Curry Primer.* Berkeley, Calif.: Creative Arts Communications, 1984.

Anderson, E. N. *The Food of China.* New Haven, Conn.: Yale University Press, 1988.

Andrews, Jean. *Peppers: The Domesticated Capsicums.* Austin: University of Texas Press, 1984.

Antel, Marie Nadine. *The Incredible Secrets of Mustard.* Garden City, N.Y.: Avery, 1999.

"Archaeologists Uncover Ancient Maritime Spice Route between India, Egypt." 2002. www.popular-science.net.

Associated Press. "Curry Ingredient May Fight Cystic Fibrosis." *Globe and Mail*, April 22, 2004. www.theglobeandmail.com.

Asswaprapa, Phawana. "Medicinal/Nutrition Properties and Uses of Pepper in Thailand." International Pepper Community, 2000. www.ipcnet.org.

Atal, C. K., and J. N. Ojha. "Studies on the Genus *Piper*, Part IV: Long Peppers of Indian Commerce." *Economic Botany* 19, no. 2 (1965): 157.

Athenaeus. *The Deipnosophists; or, Banquet of the Learned.* Translated by C. D. Yonge. London: George Bell and Sons, 1909.

Baker, Margaret, Robin Corringham, and Jill Dark. *Native Plants of the Sydney Region.* Winmalee, New South Wales: n.p., 1986.

Berriedale-Johnson, Michelle. *The British Museum Cookbook.* New York: Abbeville Press, 1987.

Billing, Jennifer, and Paul W. Sherman. "Antimicrobial Functions of Spices: Why Some Like It Hot." *Quarterly Review of Biology* 73, no.1 (March 1998).

Boyer, James. "Hot Property." *Out There*, December 1997. www.outthere.co.za/97/1224/destdec.html.

Brennan, Jennifer. *The Cuisines of Asia.* London: Macdonald, 1984.

_____. *Curries and Bugles: A Memoir and Cookbook of the British Raj.* New York: HarperCollins, 1990.

Brierly, Joanna Hall. *Spices: The Story of Indonesia's Spice Trade.* Kuala Lumpur: Oxford University Press, 1994.

Brothwell, Don, and Patricia Brothwell. *Food in Antiquity.* London: Thames & Hudson, 1969.

Brown, Deni. *New Encyclopedia of Herb sand Their Uses.* New York: Dorling Kindersley, 2001.

Bruneateau, Jean-Paul. *Tukka: Real Australian Food.* Sydney: Angus & Robertson, 1996.

Carr, Andrew. "Carnival." In *David Frost Introduces Trinidad and Tobago.* London: Andre Deutsch, 1975.

Castro, Filipe. "Nossa Senhora dos Martires." December 2000. www.abc.se.

Chapman, Pat. *Favourite Middle Eastern Recipes.* London: Piatkus, 1989.

_____. "250 Favourite Curries and Accompaniments." *Curry Club Magazine* (London), no. 31 (summer/autumn 1992): 8.

Chapman, Peter. "The Curry Houses of London." *Bon Appetit*, October 1992.

Christie, Robert H. "Twenty-Two Authentic Banquets from India." In *Banquets of the Nations.* 1911. Reprint, New York: Dover, 1975.

Claiborne, Craig, and Pierre Franey. "Peppers in Every Pot." *New York Times Magazine*, September 23, 1984, 61.

Cobo, Father Bernabe. *History of the Incan Empire.* 1653. Translated by Roland Hamilton. Austin: University of Texas Press, 1979.

Coe, Sophie D. *America's First Cuisine.* Austin: University of Texas Press, 1994.

Coetzee, Renata. *The South African Culinary Tradition.* Cape Town: C. Struik, 1977.

Coleman, Jim, with Candace Hagan. "Pepper: The King of Spices." 2002. www.theepicentre.com.

Colmenares, Ana Maria Guzman de Vasquez. *Tradiciones Gastronómicas Oaxaqueñas*. Oaxaca: Talleres Impresos Pérez, 1982.

Cooke, Jean, and Ann Kramer. *History's Timeline*. New York: Crescent, 1981.

Corn, Charles. *The Scents of Eden: A Narrative of the Spice Trade*. New York: Kodansha America, 1998.

Cost, Bruce. *Bruce Cost's Asian Ingredients*. New York: William Morrow, 1988.

Coyle, L. Patrick. *Cook's Books*. New York: Facts on File, 1985.

Cranwell, John Philips. *The Hellfire Cookbook*. New York: Quadrangle, 1975.

Dalby, Andrew. *Dangerous Tastes: The Story of Spices*. Berkeley: University of California Press, 2000.

Dalby, Andrew, and Sally Grainger. *The Classical Cookbook*. Los Angeles: J. Paul Getty Museum, 1996.

David, Elizabeth. *Spices, Salt, and Aromatics in the English Kitchen*. Middlesex, England: Penguin, 1970.

Davidson, Alan. *The Oxford Companion to Food*. Oxford: Oxford University Press, 1999.

Davies, D. W. *A Primer of Dutch Seventeenth Century Overseas Trade*. The Hague: Martinus Nijhoff, 1961.

Day, Harvey, with Sarojini Mudnani. *Curries of India*. Bombay: Jaico, 1963.

DeGaray, Rodolfo, and Thomas Brown. "Cuban Foods That Bite Back." *Chile Pepper*, January–February 1992: 29.

De la Vega, Garcilaso (El Inca). *Royal Commentaries of the Incas*. 1609. Translated by Harold V. Livermore. Austin: University of Texas Press, 1966.

De Schlippe, Pierre. *Shifting Cultivation in Africa*. London: Routledge & Kegan Paul, 1956.

Det, Paulus Amin, and Wong Ting Hung. "Development of Pepper Industry in Sarawak, Malaysia." International Pepper Community, May 2000. www.ipcnet.org.

DeWitt, Dave. *The Chile Pepper Encyclopedia*. New York: William Morrow & Co., 1999.

_____, ed. The Fiery-Foods SuperSite. Since 1997. www.fiery-foods.com.

DeWitt, Dave, and Paul W. Bosland. *Peppers of the World: An Identification Guide*. Berkeley, Calif.: Ten Speed Press, 1996.

DeWitt, Dave, and Chuck Evans. *The Hot Sauce Bible*. Freedom, Calif.: Crossing Press, 1996.

DeWitt, Dave, and Nancy Gerlach. *The Whole Chile Pepper Book*. Boston: Little, Brown & Co., 1990.

_____. *Barbecue Inferno*. Berkeley, Calif.: Ten Speed Press, 2001.

DeWitt, Dave, and Patrick Holian. *Peppers and People*. Pt. 1 of *Heat Up Your Life!* Video documentary. Las Cruces: Leading Object Media Group, New Mexico State University, 2000.

_____. *From Seed to Salsa*. Pt. 2 of *Heat Up Your Life!* Video documentary. Las Cruces: Leading Object Media Group, New Mexico State University, 2000.

_____. *Hot Plates*. Pt. 3 of *Heat Up Your Life!* Video documentary. Las Cruces: Leading Object Media Group, New Mexico State University, 2000.

DeWitt, Dave, and Arthur Pais. *A World of Curries*. Boston: Little, Brown & Co., 1994.

DeWitt, Dave, and Mary Jane Wilan. *Callaloo, Calypso and Carnival: The Cuisines of Trinidad and Tobago*. Freedom, Calif.: Crossing Press, 1993.

_____. *The Food Lover's Handbook to the Southwest*. Rocklin, Calif.: Prima, 1992.

DeWitt, Dave, Mary Jane Wilan, and Melissa T. Stock. *Hot and Spicy and Meatless*. Rocklin, Calif.: Prima, 1994.

_____. *Hot and Spicy Chili*. Rocklin, Calif.: Prima, 1994.

_____. *Hot and Spicy Latin Dishes*. Rocklin, Calif.: Prima, 1995.

_____. *Hot and Spicy Southeast Asian Dishes*. Rocklin, Calif.: Prima, 1995.

_____. *Flavors of Africa Cookbook*. Rocklin, Calif.: Prima, 1998.

Disney, A. R. *Twilight of the Pepper Empire: Portuguese Trade in Southwest India in the Early Seventeenth Century*. Cambridge, Mass.: Harvard University Press, 1978.

Dove, Michael R. "The 'Banana Tree at the Gate': Perceptions of Production of Piper nigrum (Piperaceae) in a Seventeenth-Century Malay State." *Economic Botany* 51, no. 4 (1997): 347.

Duarte, Maria de Lourdes Reis, and Fernando Carneiro de Albuquerque. "Development of Pepper Industry in Brazil." International Pepper Community, May 2000. www.ipcnet.org.

"The East India Companies." *Economist*, December 23, 1999.

Evans, Edith. "Dining with Martial." *Archaeology Magazine*, October 23, 2001. www.archaeology.org.

Everett, T. H., ed. "Piper–Pepper." In *The New Illustrated Encyclopedia of Gardening*, 2356. New York: Greystone Press, 1964.

Faas, Patrick. *Around the Roman Table: Food and Feasting in Ancient Rome*. New York: Palgrave Macmillan, 2003.

Fallows, James A. "The Pepper Paper." Fortnightly Club, Redlands, Calif., January 30, 1997. www.redlandsfortnightly.org.

Fisher, M. F. K. *With Bold Knife and Fork*. New York: G. P. Putnam's Sons, 1968.

Flandrin, Jean-Louis, and Massimo Montanari, eds. *Food: A Culinary History*. New York: Columbia University Press, 1996.

Fuchs, Leonhard. *De Historia Stiripum Commentarii Insignees*. Basel, 1542.

Gentry, Howard Scott. "Introducing Black Pepper into America." *Economic Botany* 9 (1955): 256.

Gerlach, Nancy, and Jeff Gerlach. *Foods of the Maya: A Taste of the Yucatán*. Freedom, Calif.: Crossing Press, 1994.

Greenly, Larry. "Singing Pepper's Praises." *La Cocinita* (Albuquerque), October 2000: 24.

Greer, Anne Lindsay. "Flavors of the American Southwest." *Gourmet*, November 1984: 62.

Gregg, Josiah. *The Commerce of the Prairies*. London: Holburn, 1958.

Grun, Bernard. *The Timetables of History*. New York: Touchstone, 1975.

Guenin, Patrick. "Vietnam Islanders Spice Life with Pepper." Reuters Online, August 7, 1999.

Halász, Zoltán. *Hungarian Paprika through the Ages*. Budapest: Corvina Press, 1963.

Harris, Jessica B. *Hot Stuff: A Cookbook in Praise of the Piquant*. New York: Ballantine, 1985.

Hatchen, Harva. *Kitchen Safari*. New York: Atheneum, 1970.

Hazen, Janet. *Mustard*. San Francisco: Chronicle, 1993.

Heinerman, John. *The Complete Book of Spices*. New Canaan, Conn.: Keats, 1983.

Heiser, Charles. "Some Like It Hot." *Natural History* 61 (September 1951): 307.

Hemphill, Ian. *Spice Notes*. Sydney: Pan Macmillan Australia, 2000.

Hesser, Amanda. "What Peppercorns Only Dream of Being." *New York Times*, May 3, 2000.

Hillman, Howard. *The Cook's Book*. New York: Avon, 1981.

Hobson, Henry. *Seeds of Change*. New York: Harper and Row, 1985.

Indonesian Heritage. "The Pepper Empires of Sundra and Sumatra." 2002. www.indonesianheritage.com/encyclopedia.

Johnson, Dinah. "Specialty Mustard and Horseradish." *Gourmet Retailer*, April 1991: 58.

Jordan, Michele Anna. *The Good Cook's Book of Mustard*. Reading, Mass.: Addison-Wesley, 1994.

_____. *Salt and Pepper*. New York: Broadway, 1999.

Jordan, Shirley. "Savoring the Isle of Spice." *Chile Pepper*, September/October 1994: 16.

Krishnaswany, Neelam, and Kamala Krishnaswany. "Nutritional Value of Pepper." International Pepper Community, May 2000. www.ipcnet.org.

Krochmal, Connie, and Arnold Krochmal. "Ginger, a Rhizome That's Both Plantable and Edible." *San Juan Star*, February 7, 1988.

Landis, Denise. "Sichuan's Signature Fire Is Going Out. Or Is It?" *Times Digest*, February 4, 2004, 6.

Langer, Richard W. *Where There's Smoke, There's Flavor*. Boston: Little, Brown & Co., 1996.

Lescot, Marie-Pascale. "The Spark of Harissa." *Saveur*, no. 69 (October 2003): 29.

Leyel, Mrs. C. F. *The Magic of Herbs*. London: Jonathan Cape, 1926.

Libin, Tita. "The Voodoo Foods of Bahia." *Chile Pepper*, July/August 1994.

Literature Production Center. *Black Pepper in the Caroline Islands*. Agricultural Bulletin 4. Saipan, Mariana Islands: Literature Production Center, 1967.

Lomelí, Arturo. *El Chile y Otros Picantes*. Mexico City: Asociación Méxicana de Estudios para La Defensa del Comsumidor, 1986.

Low, Tim. *Wild Food Plants of Australia*. North Ryde, Australia: Angus & Robertson, 1988.

Mahindru, S. N. *Spices in Indian Life*. New Delhi: Sultan Chand & Sons, 1982.

Marks, Copeland. *The Exotic Kitchens of Indonesia*. New York: M. Evans & Co., 1989.

Mathew, A. G. "Medicinal Uses of Pepper." International Pepper Community, May 2000. www.ipcnet.org.

McGee, Harold. *On Food and Cooking: The Science and Lore of the Kitchen*. New York: Charles Scribner's Sons, 1984.

Mendel, Janet. *Traditional Spanish Cooking*. London: Garnett, 1996.

Menon, K. P. G. "Global Market Outlook for Pepper and Other Spices." International Pepper Community, August 24, 2002. www.ipcnet.org.

Mesfin, D. J. *Exotic Ethiopian Cooking*. Falls Church, Va.: Ethiopian Cookbook Enterprises, 1990.

Miller, J. Innes. *The Spice Trade of the Roman Empire*. Oxford: Clarendon Press, 1969.

Morgan, Jinx, and Jennifer Morgan. "Guadeloupe: Island with a French Accent." *Bon Appétit*, July 1990: 30.

Morphy, Countess. *Recipes of All Nations*. New York: William H. Wise, 1935.

Natta, Larry. "The Changing Market for Specialty Mustard." *Fancy Food*, May 1989: 25.

"New Strategies for Spice Export." *Hindu*, May 2, 2002. www.hinduonnet.com.

Nightingale, Pamela. *A Medieval Mercantile Community*. New Haven, Conn.: Yale University Press, 1995.

Nybe, E. V., and K. V. Peter. "Harness the Potential for Diversified Uses of Black Pepper." International Pepper Community, May 2000. www.ipcnet.org.

Ortiz, Elisabeth Lambert. *The Encyclopedia of Herbs, Spices, & Flavorings*. New York: Dorling Kindersley, 1992.

Oviedo, Gonzalo Fernándo de. "Della Naturale e Generale Istoria dell'Indie." In *Navigazione e Viaggi*, edited by Giovanni Batista Ramusio, vol. 5. Torino: Einaudi, 1985.

Parry, John W. *The Story of Spices*. New York: Chemical, 1953.

_____. *Spices*. New York: Chemical, 1969.

Passmore, Jacki. *The Letts Companion to Asian Food and Cooking*. London: Charles Letts, 1991.

Payne, Bob. "Martinique: Romance, Rum and Red Peppers in the French Caribbean." Bon Appétit, February 1994.

Pendergrast, Sam. "Requiem for Texas Chili." *Whole Chile Pepper*, winter 1989: 28.

Penzey, Bill, et al. *Penzeys Spices Catalog of Seasonings*. Muskego, Wis.: Penzeys Spices, 2000.

Pepper Marketing Board Malaysia. "Pepper Marketing Board Malaysia." August 20, 2002. http://agrolink.moa.my.

Pepper Marketing Board Malaysia. "Value-Added Pepper Products and New Uses of Pepper." International Pepper Community, May 200. www.ipcnet.org.

Peppertrade Board. "Pepper Prices in New York." August 25, 2002. www.olcom.com.br.

Philpotts, Kaui. "Ginger." *Saveur*, no. 10 (January/February 1996): 63.

Prakash, Om. *The Dutch East India Company and the Economy of Bengal, 1630-1720*. Princeton, N.J.: Princeton University Press, 1985.

Prescott, Elizabeth D., and David Julius. "A Modular PIP2 Binding Site as a Determinant of Capsaicin Receptor Sensitivity." *Science* 300 (May 23, 2003): 1284.

Purser, Jan. "Great Balls of Fire." *Good Taste* (Australia), August 2000, 40.

Quittner, Jeremy. "Keeping the Old Family Mustard Mill from Grinding to a Halt." *Business Week On-Line,* June 2, 1999. www.businessweek.com.

Raichlen, Steven. *The Caribbean Pantry Cookbook*. New York: Artisan, 1995.

Rau, Santha Rama. *The Cooking of India*. New York: Time-Life, 1969.

Raveendran, K. G. "Ayurvedic Medicinal Properties of Pepper." International Pepper Community, May 2000.

www.ipcnet.org.

Ravindram, P. N., ed. *Black Pepper*. Amsterdam: Harwood Academic, 2000.

_____. Introduction to *Black Pepper*. Amsterdam: Harwood Academic, 2000.

Ream, Amanda. "The Secret Life of Horseradish." *Mother Earth News*, no. 150 (June/July 1995): 14.

Riely, Elizabeth. "All about Mustard." *Bon Appetit*, November 1988, 232.

Ritchie, Carson I. A. *Food in Civilization*. Sydney: Methuen Australia, 1981.

Robbins, Maria Polushkin. *A Cook's Alphabet of Quotations*. New York: Dutton, 1991.

Robins, Juleigh. *Wild Lime: Cooking from the Bushfood Garden*. St. Leonards, Australia: Allen & Unwin, 1996.

Robinson, Les. *Field Guide to the Native Plants of Sydney*. East Roseville, Australia: Kangaroo Press, 1991.

Rodriguez, Nancy C. "Turning Up the Heat." *Food Product Design*, May 2001.

Root, Waverly. *Food*. New York: Simon and Schuster, 1980.

Rozin, Elisabeth. *The Primal Cheeseburger*. New York: Penguin, 1994.

Sahagún, Bernardino de. *The General History of the Things of New Spain; Florentine Codex*. Translated by A. J. O. Anderson and C. E. Dibble. Monograph no. 14. Santa Fe, N.M.: School of American Research, 1963.

Sahni, Julie. "An Indian Spice Sampler." *Gourmet*, May 1984: 42.

Saparamdu, Anura. Telephone interview with Dave DeWitt, May 1993.

Schneider, Elizabeth. "Perfect Your Pepper Power." *Food Arts*, October 1992: 38.

Schivelbusch, Wolfgang. *Tastes of Paradise*. New York: Vintage, 1993.

Sertyl, William. "Avez-Vous du Vrai Poupon?" *Saveur*, no. 5 (March/April 1995): 34.

Sheff, David. "Pale Fire," *Saveur*, no. 37 (September/October 1999): 43.

Sherman, Paul W., and Geoffrey A. Hash. "Why Vegetable Recipes Are Not Very Spicy." *Evolution and Human Behavior* 72 (June 2001): 147–63.

Singh, Dharamjit. *Classic Cooking from India*. Boston: Houghton Mifflin, 1956.

_____. *Indian Cookery*. Middlesex, England: Penguin, 1970.

Smith, Keith and Irene. *Grow Your Own Bushfoods*. Sydney, Australia: New Holland, 1999.

Sokolov, Raymond. "Cutting the Mustard." *Natural History* 93 (July 1984): 70.

Spaeth, Anthony. "In Guntur, India, Even at 107 Degrees, It's Always Chili." *Wall Street Journal*, June 30, 1988.

"The Spice Trade: A Taste of Adventure." *Economist*, December 19, 1998.

Stevenel, L. "Red Pepper, a Too Much Forgotten Therapeutic Agent against Anorexia, Liver Congestion, and Vascular Troubles." *Bulletin de la Société de Pathologie Exotique* 49, no. 5 (1956): 841–43.

Stobart, Tom. *The Cook's Encyclopedia*. New York: Harper & Row, 1980.

Stuckey, Maggie. *The Complete Spice Book*. New York: St. Martin's Press, 1997.

Swahn, J. O. *The Lore of Spices*. New York: Crescent, 1991.

Tannahill, Reay. *Food in History*. New York: Crown, 1988.

Thorne, John. *Just Another Bowl of Texas Red*. Boston: Jackdaw Press, 1985.

Toussaint-Samat, Maguelonne. *History of Food*. Cambridge, Mass.: Blackwell, 1992.

Trade Compass. "Vietnam Becomes World's Largest Pepper Exporter." August 26, 2002. www.tiaca.org.

Trager, James. *The Food Chronology*. New York: Henry Holt, 1995.

U.S. Department of Agriculture. *Composition of Foods: Spices and Herbs (Raw, Processed, and Prepared)*. Handbook no. 8-2, January 1977. Washington, D.C.: U.S. Department of Agriculture, 1977.

Vandaveer, Chelsie. "What Was the Pepper Gate?" May 28, 2002. www.killerplants.com.

Van der Post, Laurens. *African Cooking*. New York: Time-Life, 1970.

"Vietnam: Staking a 'King's Share.'" September 1, 2002. www.new-agri.co.uk.

Walden, Hilaire. *North African Cooking*. Edison, N.J.: Chartwell, 1995.

Wasson, Betty. *Cooks, Gluttons & Gourmets*. Garden City, N.Y.: Doubleday, 1962.

West, Richard. "From Mexico with Love." *Texas Monthly*, February 1977: 90.

Wilson, Ellen Gibson. *A West African Cookbook*. New York: M. Evans, 1971.

Additional Web Sites Consulted

http://ceren.colorado.edu/
www.ag.uiuc.edu
www.agrolink.moa.my
www.asiafood.org

www.barfliers.com
www.blackpepper.com
www.blonnet.com
www.botanical.com
www.botgard.ucla.edu
www.chilepepperinstitute.org
www.cityfarmer.org
www.cpinternet.com
www.dominionherbal.com
www.dressings-sauces.com
www.exressindia.com
www.fabulousfoods.com
www.fao.org
www.foodmarketexchange.com
www.foodproductdesign.com
www.foodreference.com
www.freshwasabi.com
www.gettingwell.com
www.globalgourmet.com
www.go-kingston.com
www.greydragon.org
www.gsdunn.com
www.honeydijon.com
www.horseradish.org
www.horseradishplants.com
www.indiaagronet.com
www.jamaicana.com
www.kertnet.hu
www.littleindia.com
www.mustards.com
www.mustardstore.com
www.mustardweb.com
www.mycookbook.net
www.mycustompak.com
www.mustardweb.com
www.oregonstate.edu
www.questia.com
www.radajamaica.com
www.theworldwidegourmet.com
www.viable-herbal.com
www.wasabi.co.nz
www.chem.uwimona.edu.jm

index

Yemenite hot sauce
(zhug), 72, 128
see also Chutneys;
Dressings; Mustard;
Salsa(s); Sauces
Cookies, peppernut
(pfeffernusse), 370–71
Cool-downs, 372–87
after-dinner beverages,
402
bread, deep-fried, Indian
(pooris), 387
bread, fried (sopaipillas),
386
bread pudding with
bourbon sauce,
N'awlins Creole, 378
cucumber slaw, 374
eight treasures pudding
(bot bo go), 377
flan (queso napolitano),
375
fruitcake, Mexican, 381
fruit cobbler, country,
380
ground rice drink
(horchata), 383
lemon pudding cake, 379
mango *lassi*, 385
margarita pie, 382
mint *raita*, 373
natillas, chilled, with
shaved chocolate, 376
serving, 390–91
yogurt pudding, Indian
(shrikhand), 384
Corn:
grilled, and chipotle
soup, 207
posole, and pork, 211
relish garnish, 207
Corn-husk muffins with
blue corn, chipotle, and
cheese, Taos, 359
Couscous, *harissa* and seven-
vegetable, 254
Crab:
and alligator pear salad
with remoulade
dressing, 224

boil spices, 79, 171
-stuffed chiles, 302
Crackers, curry, Caribbean,
357
Cranberry(ies):
dried, red pepper spiced
pecans and, 174
pumpkin loaf, spiced,
361
Crème anglaise, ginger, 368
Creole (cuisine):
mustard, 168
N'awlins bread pudding
with bourbon sauce,
378
seasoning, 169
Crispy Asian garden salad,
216
Crostada del diavolo, 367
Croutons:
peppered, 198–99
pumpernickel, toasted,
212
spicy, 213
Cuban habanero-spiced
black beans and rice with
sofrito, 308
Cubeb peppers, 61, 62
Cucumber(s):
salad, South African, 223
salad with mustard
dressing, 220
slaw, 374
Cumin (seeds), 1, 2
peppercorn pilao with,
329
Sanjay's *jeera* chicken,
274
Curry(ied)(ies), 72, 80–92
beef, coconut (rendang
daging), 231
cauliflower with peas
(gobi aur matar ki
bhaji), 324
chicken, green (gaeng
kheow wan gai), 279
commercial preparations
for, 91–92
cooking and serving, 92

crackers, Caribbean, 357
dal, 307
egg, in coconut gravy
(mottai kolambu), 309
essence, swordfish steaks
with, 300–301
ginger pumpkin bisque
with peppered
croutons, 198–99
history of, 80–91
pork vindaloo, Goan,
236–37
potato, roti with,
Caribbean, 310
prawn, pineapple, Thai,
284
shrimp, tamarind mint,
282
spiced butter, Ethiopian
(niter kebbe), 72, 130
Curry pastes:
green, Thai, 139
mussaman, 140
red, Thai, 138
Trinidad, 150
Curry powders, 91–92
bafat (hurry curry), 136
curry essence, 300–301
freshly ground, making,
88–89
North African *tabil*, 72,
125
sambhar, 73, 133
South African Cape, 131
West Indian masala, 151
Custards:
chilled *natillas* with
shaved chocolate, 376
flan (queso napolitano),
375

D

Dairy products, as cool-
downs, 390–391, 402
Dal curry, 307
Dan dan noodles, sesame,
328
Day of the Dead, 394

Desserts, 343, 363–371,372
devil's tart (crostada del
diavolo), 367
flan (queso napolitano),
375
fruit cobbler, country,
380
ginger gelato, 364
green chile piñon ice
cream, 365
margarita pie, 382
margarita strawberries
with tequila and
cracked black pepper-
corns, 369
natillas, chilled, with
shaved chocolate, 376
peach shortcake with
ginger crème anglaise,
368
peppernut cookies
(pfeffernusse), 370–71
red chile amaretto
truffles, 363
tangerine and cracked
black pepper sorbet,
366
see also Cakes;
Pudding(s)
Devil's tart, 367
Dill mustard bread, 355
Djeji mechoui Tangiers, 275
Dressings:
adobo, 225
Asian, 216
Dijon lemon, 213
herb, 218
honey chipotle lime
mustard, 219
horseradish, 303
horseradish cream, 215
kuchela vinaigrette,
Caribbean, 217
mustard, 220
peppercorn and feta, 214
remoulade, 224
sesame ginger, 258
Thai, 235
triple mustard, 281